28

INDIANA UNIVERSITY
SOUTH BEND
THE LIBRARY

D1255374

AMERICAN
HISTORICAL ASSOCIATION

INVESTIGATION OF THE
SOCIAL STUDIES IN THE SCHOOLS

∴

STAFF

A. C. KREY
Chairman, Director of the Investigation

G. S. COUNTS
Research Director

W. G. KIMMEL
Executive Secretary

T. L. KELLEY
Psychologist, Advisor on Tests

COMMISSION ON DIRECTION

FRANK W. BALLOU, Superintendent of Schools, Washington, D. C.

CHARLES A. BEARD, formerly Professor of Politics, Columbia University; author of many books in the fields of history and politics.

ISAIAH BOWMAN, Director, American Geographical Society of New York; President of the International Geographical Union.

ADA COMSTOCK, President of Radcliffe College.

GEORGE S. COUNTS, Professor of Education, Teachers College, Columbia University.

AVERY O. CRAVEN, Professor of History, University of Chicago.

EDMUND E. DAY, formerly Dean of School of Business Administration, University of Michigan; now Director of Social Sciences, Rockefeller Foundation.

GUY STANTON FORD, Professor of History, Dean of the Graduate School, University of Minnesota.

CARLTON J. H. HAYES, Professor of History, Columbia University.

ERNEST HORN, Professor of Education, University of Iowa.

HENRY JOHNSON, Professor of History, Teachers College, Columbia University.

A. C. KREY, Professor of History, University of Minnesota.

LEON C. MARSHALL, Institute for the Study of Law, Johns Hopkins University.

CHARLES E. MERRIAM, Professor of Political Science, University of Chicago.

JESSE H. NEWLON, Professor of Education, Teachers College, Columbia University; Director of Lincoln Experimental School.

JESSE F. STEINER, Professor of Sociology, University of Washington.

THE SOCIAL SCIENCES AS
SCHOOL SUBJECTS

REPORT OF THE COMMISSION
ON THE SOCIAL STUDIES
PART XI

THE SOCIAL SCIENCES AS
SCHOOL SUBJECTS

BY

ROLLA M. TRYON

*Professor of the Teaching of History in the
University of Chicago*

CHARLES SCRIBNER'S SONS

NEW YORK   CHICAGO   BOSTON   ATLANTA
SAN FRANCISCO   DALLAS

Copyright, 1935, by
CHARLES SCRIBNER'S SONS

——————

Printed in the United States of America

*All rights reserved. No part of this book
may be reproduced in any form without
the permission of Charles Scribner's Sons*

H62
.T7

INDIANA UNIVERSITY
SOUTH BEND
THE LIBRARY

PREFACE

The present work deals directly with the national experience in the organization of the social sciences for school purposes. That experience has largely determined the habits of our schools in making their programs in this field. The Commission recognized the fact that any changes in curriculum which it may suggest must rest upon past practice as a base. A clear and comprehensive statement of that practice was therefore vitally necessary to the work of the Commission. It is this need which the present volume meets.

The author of the work, Rolla M. Tryon, Professor of the Teaching of History, University of Chicago, has been a leader in his field of work for many years. When the Commission appointed its advisory committee on the Organization of Content and Methods of Instruction, Curriculum Committee for short, he was appointed Chairman of that Committee. This committee formulated the plans for the investigation of this area of the problem and the Chairman of the Committee was prevailed upon by the Commission to undertake the study of curricular organization. The achievement of this task would have been impossible in the time available were it not for the systematic collection of material which he had been making in the many years of his professional activity. The first draft of this work was submitted to the members of the Commission in the spring of 1933. Since that time the author has revised the manuscript in light of the suggestions and criticisms received from members of the Commission and others as indicated in his preface.

The work brings together the enormous amount of data which has appeared from time to time in scattered publication. The collection and systematic arrangement of these data is a service which will be appreciated by all teachers and especially by those in charge of the training of teachers. The author has added to it his own interpretation of trends and conditions to which his extended experience lends peculiar value. The Commission is especially happy to present this work to the teachers of social science subjects and to all interested in education.

A. C. KREY, *Chairman.*

AUTHOR'S NOTE

This volume could have been with propriety entitled *An Introduction to the Social Sciences as School Subjects*. To treat adequately each of the five divisions composing it would require many more pages than were available. Divisions Two, Three, Four, and Five could be profitably expanded into a volume equal in size to the present one. Because of the abundance of data, selection and condensation had to be practiced with much vigor throughout each of the divisions. If some important phases of the subject have been omitted—and they have been—such omissions were always dictated by the introductory nature of the treatment.

The discussion throughout holds somewhat tenaciously to its paramount interest, namely, what has been and is in the realm of the social sciences as school subjects. This means, of course, that expressions of approval and disapproval have been made to play a very minor rôle. Such imperatives as "shall," "should," "ought," and "must" have been avoided. Personal likes and dislikes are inappropriate in a work that claims to be bound by the dictates of the scientific method. However, in spite of a sincere attempt to be objective and impartial, personal views on many of the controversial issues discussed no doubt have crept in, for an attitude of complete impartiality seems to be beyond the ability of any one to maintain.

The data on which the discussion is based are of two general types—facts and ideas. In securing the facts, heavy reliance on the work of others was unavoidable. The life of one individual is scarcely long enough to collect single-handed all of the facts in this volume. Due recognition has been accorded all of those whose material has been utilized. Direct quotations have been used in all cases where such seemed best to convey the idea. For permission to use these quotations grateful acknowledgment is hereby made to those who hold the copyright.

A word of explanation of the bibliographical aspects of the volume seems not out of place here. To avoid a large amount of repetition a general bibliography has been omitted. In order to supply complete bibliographical data for each reference, complete data are included the first time that a reference is mentioned in a division. If a reference is cited more than once in a division, the bibliographical details are omitted in the second and subsequent uses. The references and tables are numbered serially by divisions.

The appearance of the volume at this time was made possible by a generous grant from the Commission of the American Historical Association on the Social Studies in the Schools and the release from all teaching duties in the university with which the writer is connected. For each of these very substantial aids grateful appreciation is hereby expressed.

R. M. T.

CONTENTS

xi

DIVISION THREE

DIVISION FOUR

DIVISION FIVE

DIVISION ONE

EFFORTS OF NATIONAL ORGANIZATIONS IN
BEHALF OF THE SOCIAL SCIENCES AS
SCHOOL SUBJECTS

DIVISION ONE

EFFORTS OF NATIONAL ORGANIZATIONS IN BEHALF OF THE SOCIAL SCIENCES AS SCHOOL SUBJECTS

I. NATIONAL EDUCATION ASSOCIATION.—The Committee of Ten (Report of the Conference on History, Civil Government, and Political Economy); the Committee of Fifteen; the Committee of Twelve; the Committee on Social Studies of the Commission on the Reorganization of Secondary Education.

II. AMERICAN HISTORICAL ASSOCIATION.—The Committee of Seven; the Committee of Eight; the Committee of Five; the Committee on History and Education for Citizenship.

III. AMERICAN POLITICAL SCIENCE ASSOCIATION.—The Committee of Five; the Committee of Seven; the Committee on Civics Instruction in High Schools.

IV. THE NATIONAL SOCIETY FOR THE STUDY OF EDUCATION AND THE ASSOCIATION OF COLLEGIATE SCHOOLS OF BUSINESS.— History in the *First Yearbook* of the National Society for the Scientific Study of Education; History in Part I of the *Second Yearbook;* Social Sciences in the *Fourteenth* and Subsequent Yearbooks of the National Society for the Study of Education; Efforts of the Association of Collegiate Schools of Business in Behalf of the Social Sciences.

V. THE AMERICAN BAR ASSOCIATION AND THE NATIONAL SECURITY LEAGUE.—Committee on American Citizenship of the Bar Association; Committee on Constitutional Instruction of the Security League.

VI. THE AMERICAN SCHOOL CITIZENSHIP LEAGUE, THE NATIONAL MUNICIPAL LEAGUE, AND THE AMERICAN SOCIOLOGICAL SOCIETY.—History Committee of the Citizenship League; the Municipal League; Committee of the Sociological Society

on the Teaching of Sociology in the Elementary and High
Schools of America.

The efforts in behalf of the social sciences as school subjects
of certain educational, professional, academic, and welfare
societies, associations, and leagues of national scope have been
both continuous and strenuous for the past forty years. The
results of these efforts have been by no means meager. The
several volumes, of which this is one, comprising the report of
the Commission on the Social Studies are tangible evidence of
the most recent efforts of one of these national organizations,
namely, the American Historical Association. So it seems very
apropos in a volume on the social sciences as school subjects
sponsored by a commission of this association to open the discussion with a considerattion of its efforts, along with those of
other organizations of national scope, in behalf of these subjects. Besides being timely, such a discussion will serve the
useful purpose of furnishing a background, especially since
1890, for the systematic presentations which follow.

Since the early eighteen nineties the following organizations
of national scope have evidenced more than a passing interest
in the social sciences in the schools: National Education Association, American Historical Association, American Political
Science Association, National Society for the Study of Education, Association of Collegiate Schools of Business, American
Economic Association, American Bar Association, National
Security League, American School Citizenship League, National Municipal League, and American Sociological Society.
The interest of these organizations in the social sciences in the
schools has been in the majority of cases objectified in formal
reports of committees—all of which are discussed in some
detail below. The organizations are considered in the order
named above.

I

THE NATIONAL EDUCATION ASSOCIATION

The present National Education Association of the United States was organized in 1857 as the National Teachers' Association. In 1870, the original name was changed to National Educational Association. The present name was adopted in 1907. Almost from its origin, the Association has been interested in the promotion of the social sciences in the schools. At its meeting in 1859, Daniel Read, of Wisconsin, read a paper on "The Importance of Civil Polity as a Branch of Popular Education." A committee of the Association made a report in 1863 on the teaching of the principles of government in the schools. Soon after the close of the Civil War, the Association became active in promoting the history of the United States in the schools. At its meeting in 1869, the following resolution was passed: *"Resolved,* That the National Teachers' Association considers it a part of the duty of all institutions of learning to inculcate the principles of an intelligent citizenship, and to this end they earnestly recommend the more extensive introduction into our public schools the study of United States History, especially with reference to the principles, the structure and the history of our Political Institutions." Interest in United States history was again manifested at the meeting of the Association in Baltimore, in 1876. At this meeting, a Committee made a report on "A Course of Study From Primary School to University." For the common or district schools, this Committee recommended United States history; for the high or preparatory schools, universal history and the constitution of the United States. No formal action was taken on the report of this Committee by the Association.[1]

---

[1] *Addresses and Journal of Proceedings, National Educational Association,* 1876, pp. 58 ff.

THE COMMITTEE OF TEN (REPORT OF THE CONFERENCE ON HISTORY, CIVIL GOVERNMENT, AND POLITICAL ECONOMY), 1893

Prior to 1892, the interest of the Association in the social sciences in the schools never materialized in anything other than mere reports and verbal recommendations. In this year, however, a step toward more concrete results was taken. At its meeting in July, what subsequently became the famous Committee of Ten was appointed. At its first meeting in November, 1892, this committee decided to organize a conference on each of the following subjects and groups of subjects: Latin, Greek; English; other modern languages; mathematics; physics, astronomy, and chemistry; natural history (biology, including botany, zoology, and physiology); history, civil government, and political economy; and geography (physical geography, geology, and meteorology). It was also decided at this meeting that each conference should consist of ten members.[2]

In about a month after its organization the Conference on History, Civil Government, and Political Economy was in session in Madison, Wisconsin. At this first and only session of the Conference, the following specific resolutions relating primarily to the program in history were adopted:

"1. That history and kindred subjects ought to be a sub-

2 The membership of the conference on history, civil government, and political economy and the position each occupied when appointed was as follows: Charles Kendall Adams, President of the University of Wisconsin, Chairman; Edward G. Bourne, Professor of History, Adelbert College; Abram Brown, Principal of the Central High School, Columbus, Ohio; Ray Greene Huling, Principal of the High School, New Bedford, Mass.; Jesse Macy, Professor of Political Science, Iowa College; James Harvey Robinson, Associate Professor of European History, University of Pennsylvania; William A. Scott, Assistant Professor of Political Economy, University of Wisconsin; Henry P. Warren, Head Master of the Albany Academy; Woodrow Wilson, Professor of Jurisprudence and Political Economy, Princeton College; and Albert Bushnell Hart, Assistant Professor of History, Harvard University, Secretary.—*Report of Committee of Ten on Secondary School Studies,* p. 201. New York: American Book Co., 1894.

stantial study in the schools in each of at least eight years.

2. That American history be included in the program.

3. That English history be included in the program.

4. That Greek and Roman history, with their Oriental connections, be included in the program.

5. That French history be included in the program.

6. That one year of the course be devoted to the intensive study of history.

7. That the year of intensive study be devoted to the careful study of some special period, as for example the struggle of France and England for North America, the Renaissance, etc.

8. That a list of suitable topics for the special period be drawn up as a suggestion to teachers.

9. That the eight-year course be consecutive.

10. That the first three years of study be devoted to mythology and biography based on general history and on American history.

11. That the point at which the program should be divided into two groups be fixed at the beginning of the high school course.

12. That the Conference adopt the following as the program for a proper historical course:

1st year. Biography and mythology.

2nd year. Biography and mythology.

3rd year. American history; and elements of civil government.

4th year. Greek and Roman history, with their Oriental connections.

5th year. French history. (To be so taught as to elucidate the general movement of mediæval and modern history.)

6th year. English history. (To be so taught as to elucidate the general movement of mediæval and modern history.)

7th year. American history.

8th year. A special period, studied in an intensive manner; and civil government.

13. That the Conference frame an alternative six-year program.

14. That the following program be recommended for schools which are not able to adopt the longer program.

1st year. Biography and mythology.

2nd year. Biography and mythology.

3rd year. American history and civil government.

4th year. Greek and Roman history, with their Oriental connections.

5th year. English history. (To be so taught as to elucidate the general movement of mediæval and modern history.)

6th year. American history and civil government.

15. That in no year of either course ought the time devoted to these subjects to be less than the equivalent of three forty-minute periods per week throughout the year." [3]

Resolutions applying specifically to civil government and political economy were also adopted. There were three of these:

"1. That civil government in the grammar schools should be taught by oral lessons, with the use of collateral text-books, and in connection with United States history and local geography.

2. That civil government in the high schools should be taught by using a text-book as a basis, with collateral reading and topical work, and observation and instruction in the government of the city, or town, and State in which the pupils live, and with comparisons between American and foreign systems of government.

3. That no formal instruction in political economy be given

[3] *Ibid.*, pp. 162 ff.

in the secondary schools, but that, in connection particularly with United States history, civil government, and commercial geography, instruction be given in those economic topics, a knowledge of which is essential to the understanding of our economic life and development." [4]

The main body of the report of the Conference was devoted to a consideration of the foregoing resolutions. The discussion centered around such topics as (1) objects of historical and kindred studies, (2) arrangement of studies, (3) subjects and programs, (4) college examinations, and (5) methods of historical teaching. With respect to the objects of historical study the Conference was of the opinion that the acquirement of a body of useful facts is the least important outcome of historical study. On this point it spoke as follows:

"The result which is popularly supposed to be gained from history, and which most teachers aim to reach, is the acquirement of a body of useful facts. In our judgment this is in itself the most difficult and the least important outcome of historical study. Facts of themselves are hard to learn, even when supported by artificial systems of memorizing, and the value of detached historical facts is small in proportion to the effort necessary to acquire and retain them. When the facts are chosen with as little discrimination as in many school textbooks, when they are mere lists of lifeless dates, details of military movements, or unexplained genealogies, they are repellant. To know them is hardly better worth while than to remember, as a curious character in Ohio was able to do some years ago, what one has had for dinner every day for the last thirty years. It cannot be too strongly emphasized that facts in history are like digits in arithmetic; they are learned only as a means to an end." [5]

[4] *Ibid.*, p. 165   [5] *Ibid.*, p. 168.

The Conference devoted considerable space to a justification of the fields of history it recommended. Greek, Roman, and English history were justified on the basis of the unity of history. In justifying the other fields the Conference said:

"American history needs no argument; it is already widely introduced; and the danger is not that it will be neglected, but that the schools may think it sufficient in itself. French history also commends itself to the Conference, because from the twelfth to the eighteenth centuries France was the leading nation of Europe, and her history is in a sense the history of civilization. General European history has the advantages of offering subjects capable of detailed and intensive study, and of furnishing a contrast to that development of the Anglo-Saxon race which is the main thought of English and American history." [6]

The year of intensive study of a special period in history recommended by the Conference was defended as follows: "This [intensive study] will offer an opportunity to apply, on a small scale, the kind of training furnished by the best colleges; it will teach careful, painstaking examination and comparison of sources; it will illuminate other broader fields of history; and it will give the pupil a practical power to collect and use historical material, which will serve him and the community throughout all his after life." [7] To illustrate the topics suitable for intensive study the Conference submitted fourteen:

"1. The Struggle between France and England for North America.

2. Spain in the New World.

3. The French Revolution and the Napoleonic Period.

4. Some Phase of the Renaissance.

5. The Puritan Movement in the Seventeenth Century.

[6] *Ibid.*, p. 175.   [7] *Ibid.*, p. 177.

6. The Commerce of the American Colonies during the Seventeenth and Eighteenth Centuries.

7. American Political Leaders from 1783 to 1830.

8. The Territorial Expansion of the United States.

9. American Politics from 1783 to 1830.

10. The Mohammedans in Europe.

11. The Influence of Greece upon Modern Life.

12. Some Phase of the Reorganization of Europe since 1852.

13. Some Phase of the Reformation.

14. Some considerable Phase of Local History."

In considering the report of this Conference the fact must not be overlooked that civil government and political economy were also included in its domain. With respect to the former of these, the Conference spoke in part as follows:

"While recognizing the importance of the study of government as a discipline and as an education for American citizens, we do not feel justified in recommending more time for the subject than is now employed by the best schools. We expect that it will occupy, including the elements of political economy, about one-half the time devoted to the group of historical and kindred studies in each of the two years recommended; and we believe that this distribution is much better than the more common system of giving the subject a considerable number of hours during a few weeks only. But it is expected that good teachers in dealing with history throughout, and especially with American history, will constantly refer to the forms and functions of government with which the children are most familiar." [8]

Political economy as an independent study in high school received no favorable consideration from the Conference in spite of the fact that two of its members had the expression

[8] *Ibid.*, p. 180.

"Political Economy" in their academic titles. The recommendations of the Conference were as indicated above to the effect that no formal instruction in political economy be given in either the grammar or high school, and that the general principles underlying the subject be taught in connection with United States history, civil government, and commercial geography.

There is available a small amount of objective evidence which indicates that the proposals of the Conference were favorably received. In a study[9] of the offerings in history in 1894 in forty high schools throughout the country and the offerings of 160 high schools in 1904, the following facts were revealed: (1) A marked increase in the number of schools offering American history (from 57 per cent to 86 per cent); (2) an increase in the offering in English history from 39 per cent in 1894 to 51 per cent in 1904; (3) an increase in schools offering French history from none in 1894 to 7 per cent in 1904; and (4) an increase in schools offering an intensive study of a special field or topic from none in 1894 to 5 per cent in 1904. While these facts indicate the direct influence of the report, there is evidence in the data for 1904 that many schools had not heeded its prescriptions. The schools offering general history increased from 41 per cent in 1894 to 61 per cent in 1904, even though this subject was not recommended in the report. There was also an increase in the percentage of schools offering Greek history and Roman history.

THE COMMITTEE OF FIFTEEN, 1895

The favorable reception accorded the report of the Committee of Ten stimulated the Board of Directors of the National Educa-

[9] Edwin G. Dexter, "Ten Years' Influence of the Report of the Committee of Ten," *School Review*, XIV (1906), 254 ff.

tion Association to sponsor over a brief period two other committees—one on elementary education in urban communities,
and one on education in rural communities. The former committee, known as the Committee of Fifteen, was created at the
meeting of the Department of Superintendence in Boston, in
February, 1893. It was not, however, until July, 1894, that the
Board agreed to finance the Committee to the extent of $1,000.
In the meantime the Committee of Fifteen had gone along with
the work assigned to it. In order to facilitate this work its
membership was divided into three sub-committees—one on
the training of teachers, one on the correlation of studies in
elementary education, and one on the organization of city
school systems. This discussion is interested only in the report
of the sub-committee on correlation of studies, and especially
that part of the report which dealt with history and civics.

After an extended treatment of correlation of studies, this
sub-committee, of which W. T. Harris, United States Commissioner of Education, was chairman, made some specific
recommendations respecting the teaching of the history and
the Constitution of the United States in the elementary school.
Its tabular exhibit of the time to be devoted to each subject in
the elementary school contained the suggestions: (1) that oral
lessons to the extent of sixty minutes a week for eight years be
given in the field of general history and biography, (2) that
five lessons a week in the seventh year be devoted to United
States history, and (3) that five lessons a week in the second
half of the eighth year be given to the Constitution of the
United States.[10]

To say that the report of the Committee of Fifteen was as
significant for elementary education as the report of the Committee of Ten was for secondary education would probably be

[10] *Report of Committee of Fifteen*, p. 94. New York: American Book Co.,
1895.

a gross exaggeration. In the realm in which this discussion is primarily interested the Committee of Fifteen probably had little influence. Except the recommendation concerning general history, there was nothing in the report of the sub-committee on correlation of studies involving history that went beyond what many schools were doing in 1895. United States history and the federal constitution were more or less generally taught in Grades VII and VIII when the Committee made its report and, furthermore, had been for a number of years previously.

THE COMMITTEE OF TWELVE, 1897

The report of the Committee of Fifteen was made to the Department of Superintendence at its meeting in Cleveland, Ohio, February, 1895. In July of this same year there was created a committee to survey certain aspects of rural education in about the same manner that urban elementary education had been surveyed by the Committee of Fifteen. This committee was given the official title of "Committee of Twelve on Rural Schools." Soon after its appointment the Committee was organized into four sub-committees—one on school maintenance, one on supervision, one on supply of teachers, and one on instruction and discipline. None of these sub-committees was primarily interested in the course of study for the rural schools. In order that specific consideration might be given to this subject, the Committee of Twelve requested one of its members to make some suggestions relative to it. In history it was recommended that children between the ages of five and seven be taught short stories drawn from biography, history, and travel; for children between the ages of seven and nine stories and descriptions relating to current events, lives of eminent historical characters, national manners, customs, and modes of life were proposed. Extension of this work to ages nine to eleven was suggested, with special attention to biography and readings in United States history. To cap the work in history a course in United States history was recommended for the years eleven to thirteen inclusive. For this group selected epochs of general history, with a study of leading historical characters, were also suggested. Morals and civics were to be included in the work of each of the four groups. Emphasis in the last group was to be placed on civics, including the organization and principles of the government of the United States.[11]

COMMITTEE ON SOCIAL STUDIES OF THE COMMISSION ON THE REORGANIZATION OF SECONDARY EDUCATION, 1916

For more than ten years after the report of the Committee of Twelve on Rural Schools, the National Education Association was content to leave to other groups active and constructive work on content and method in elementary and secondary education. In 1913, however, the Association gave evidence through Bulletin No. 41 of the United States Bureau of Education that it had again assumed leadership in the realm of secondary education at least. This bulletin contained the preliminary statements of chairmen of committees which composed what finally came to be known as the Commission of the National Education Association on the Reorganization of Secondary Education, authorized in 1913 by the directors of the National Education Association. It was made up of seventeen committees—fourteen on various high-school subjects, a committee on the articulation of high school and college, a committee on the administration of high schools, and a reviewing

---

[11] *Report of Committee of Twelve on Rural Schools*, pp. 174 ff. Chicago: The University of Chicago Press, 1897.

committee, composed of the chairmen of all of the foregoing committees plus ten members at large.

Of the fourteen committees on the various high-school subjects, the committee which dealt with the social sciences in junior and senior high schools was among the first to make a final report, the official title of which reads:

"The Social Studies in Secondary Education

A Six-year Program Adapted Both to the 6—3—3 and the 8—4 Plans of Organization

Report of the Committee on Social Studies of the Commission on the Reorganization of Secondary Education of the National Education Association."

It should be mentioned in passing that there appeared in 1915 a bulletin entitled *The Teaching of Community Civics*. This bulletin was considered by the Committee as an integral part of its report. In all, then, this Committee on Social Studies issued three small documents: (1) the preliminary reports in 1913, (2) the pamphlet on the teaching of community civics in 1915, and (3) the final report, which appeared as Bulletin, 1916, No. 28, Department of the Interior, Bureau of Education.

It was in this final document that the Committee set forth its revolutionary recommendations with respect to the social sciences in the senior high school. The following is a general outline of the proposals for this level of instruction.

"I. European history to approximately the end of the seventeenth century—1 year.

II. European history (including English history) since approximately the end of the seventeenth century—1 (or ½) year.

III. American history since the seventeenth century—1 (or ½) year.

IV. Problems of American democracy—1 (or ½) year." [12]

The revolutionary aspects of this program were the recommendations relating to problems of American democracy and early European history prior to the end of the seventeenth century. Instead of the then prevailing courses in economics, advanced civics, and sociology, the Committee proposed the new course which it designated Problems of American Democracy. This was a revolutionary proposal. So too, was the proposal to abolish the traditional one-year course in ancient history which was to be replaced by a course in European history down to the end of the seventeenth century.

In discussing the inadequacy of the then existing courses in advanced civics, economics, and sociology the Committee commented as follows: "The traditional courses in civil government are almost as inadequate for the last as for the first year of the high school. Efforts to improve them have usually consisted of only slight modifications of the traditional courses or of an attempted simplification of political science. The results have not met the needs of high-school pupils nor satisfied the demands of economists and sociologists." [13] In defense of its own proposal to meet the existing situation the committee said:

"The only feasible way the committee can see by which to satisfy in reasonable measure the demands of the several social sciences, while maintaining due regard for the requirements of secondary education, is to organize instruction, not on the basis of the formal social sciences, but on the basis of concrete problems of vital importance to society and of immediate interest to the pupil.

"In other words, the suggestion is not to discard one social

---

[12] *The Social Studies in Secondary Education,* Bulletin, 1916, No. 28. Department of the Interior, Bureau of Education, p. 35. Washington, D. C.: Government Printing Office, 1916.
[13] *Ibid.,* p. 52.

science in favor of another, nor attempt to crowd the several social sciences into this year in abridged forms; but to study actual problems, or issues, or conditions, as they occur in life, and in their several aspects, political, economic, and sociological. These problems or issues will naturally vary from year to year, and from class to class, but they should be selected on the ground (1) of their immediate interest to the class and (2) of their vital importance to society." [14]

The proposals relative to history in the senior high school were by no means as revolutionary as those pertaining to the social sciences other than history. As the proposals finally worked out they meant merely (1) a reduction of the time to be spent on ancient history from one to one-half year and (2) an increase in the time to be spent on modern European history from one-half year to one year. In defense of the changes it proposed the Committee maintained that—

"1. In small high schools more than two units of history are impracticable; and in large high schools, where more could be offered, few pupils would (or do) take more than two units, and these often unrelated.

2. The long historical period included in Course I offers a wide range of materials from which to select, and makes possible the development of topics continuously and unhampered by chronological and geographical limitations.

3. The assignment of an equal amount of time (or twice the time if a year is given to each of Courses II and III) to the period since the seventeenth century as to the period prior to that time, expresses the committee's conviction that recent history is richer in suitable materials for secondary education than the more remote periods, and is worthy of more intensive study.

4. The history of any two years that a pupil may elect under

[14] *Ibid.*, p. 53.

this plan will be related; that of Courses II and III is contemporaneous and presents many points of contact, and that of either Course II or III is continuous with that of Course I.

5. Under the present four-unit plan a premium is placed upon ancient and American history, all that goes between being left largely to chance. Under the plan proposed by the committee a much larger proportion of the pupils will secure the benefits of a study of the essentials of European history." [15]

The recommendations of the Committee pertaining to the social sciences in the junior high school were in more or less accord with the prevailing practices of the time. The liberality found in the Committee's proposals is indicated by the alternative plans suggested. The details of these plans follow:

"Seventh year:

    (1) Geography—½ year.

    European history—½ year.

      These two courses may be taught in sequence, or parallel through the year.

    Civics—taught as a phase of the above and of other subjects, or segregated in one or two periods a week, or both.

    Or, (2) European history—1 year.

    Geography—taught incidentally to, and as a factor in, the history.

    Civics—taught as a phase of the above and of other subjects, or segregated in one or two periods a week, or both.

Eighth year:

    American history—½ year.

    Civics—½ year.

      These two courses may be taught in sequence, or parallel through the year.

[15] *Ibid.*, p. 36.

Geography—taught incidentally to, and as a factor in, the above subjects.

Ninth year:

(1) Civics: Continuing the civics of the preceding year, but with more emphasis upon State, national, and world aspects —½ year.

Civics: Economic and vocational aspects—½ year.

History: Much use made of history in relation to the topics of the above courses.

Or, (2) Civics—economic and vocational.

Economic history.

1 year, in sequence or parallel." [16]

No argument was needed in 1916 to convince school people of the value of geography, European history, United States history, and community and vocational civics in the education of youth of junior high-school age. The Committee knew this. Consequently it made no long and wordy defense of these subjects, but devoted its space to a consideration of how they could be made to yield their largest values. While the part of the report dealing with the junior high school was progressive in character, it was not as radical as the part which treated the senior high school.

It would be difficult to overstate the influence of the report of this Committee. Three practices now very common may be traced directly to it. One of these is the practice in a multitude of present-day high schools of offering a course in problems of American democracy. Another relates to the common use of the expression "social studies." While the Committee did not originate this expression, it did give it respectability, thus assuring it a place in the vocabulary of a great many school peo-

[16] *Ibid.*, p. 15.

ple. The third is the one-year course in early European history. Probably one other present-day practice should be attributed to the Committee's influence, the one-year course in American history which has assumed such large proportions recently. It seems certain that this Committee was largely responsible for this course inasmuch as it was the first committee since the Committee of Ten to suggest a full year of American history in the upper grades of the high school.

II

THE AMERICAN HISTORICAL ASSOCIATION

The American Historical Association was founded in 1884 and chartered by Congress in 1889. Since its beginning the membership has been made up primarily of persons engaged in teaching history, writing history, or carrying on research in history. It is the only distinctively national organization in the United States devoted to history in all of its aspects. While the advancement of knowledge in the historical field has always been the paramount aim of the Association, it has not neglected other important aspects of history. One of these aspects to which a very great deal of energy has been devoted by groups of earnest workers is the teaching of history in elementary and secondary schools. Since December, 1898, four committees sponsored by the Association have made reports. Two of these reports—the one by the Committee of Seven, published in June, 1899, and the one by the Committee of Eight, published in 1909—dictated the program in high-school and elementary-grade history for nearly a generation. Reports of the other two committees—the Committee of Five and the Committee on History and Education for Citizenship, the former appearing in 1911 and the latter in 1921—have had some influence but nothing like that of the first two. The proposals of these four committees are discussed below in the order named here.

The Committee of Seven was appointed in the early winter of 1896.[17] After two years of labor which involved a study of the situation with respect to history in the schools of the United States, Germany, France, England, and Canada, the Committee made a report which subsequently came to be looked upon as a document without a parallel in its field. For at least two decades after its appearance, high-school courses in history in the United States were almost 100 per cent dictated by it. In fact even today, more than a generation after the publication of the report, its influence is dominant in probably one-third of the high schools of the country.

The main body of the report was made up of a consideration of (1) the value and continuity of historical study, (2) a four-years' course in high-school history, (3) methods of instruction, (4) the use of sources, (5) intensive study, (6) the need of trained teachers, and (7) college entrance requirements in history. The eight appendixes contained material on the condition of history in the schools of the United States, Germany, France, England, and Canada in 1897; and lists of maps, atlases, and

[17] Those composing the committee and the position that each held at the time the final report was signed were Andrew C. McLaughlin (Chairman), Professor of American History in the University of Michigan; Herbert B. Adams, Professor of American and Institutional History in Johns Hopkins University; George L. Fox, Rector of the Hopkins Grammar School, New Haven, Conn.; Albert Bushnell Hart, Professor of History in Harvard University; Charles H. Haskins, Professor of Institutional History in the University of Wisconsin; Lucy Salmon, Professor of History in Vassar College; and H. Morse Stephens, Professor of Modern European History in Cornell University. —*The Study of History in Schools.* Report to the American Historical Association by the Committee of Seven, p. 136. New York: The Macmillan Co., 1899.

books valuable to both students and teachers of history in the high school.

The presentation of the value of historical study was a very able one. While it lacked the social emphasis found in the report of the Committee on the Social Studies discussed above, it included a masterly treatment of many of the most significant values of history as a school study. The Committee's brief statements of these values follow:

"1. In leading pupils to see the steps in the development of the human race and to gain some perception of his own and his country's place in this development, history has no equal among the subjects of study.

2. History cultivates the judgment by leading the pupil to see relations between cause and effect, as cause and effect appear in human affairs.

3. The study of history gives training in acquiring, arranging, and systematizing facts. This means getting ideas and facts from various sources and putting them together in a new form.

4. History is also helpful in developing what is sometimes called the scientific habit of mind and thought.

5. By the study of history the pupil acquires a knowledge of facts that is to him a source of pleasure and gratification in his after life.

6. History is valuable in the education of youth because of the training it affords in the handling of books and other historical tools which one must use in his everyday life.

7. History is a powerful tool in the hands of a skillful teacher for the quickening, strengthening, and disciplining the imagination.

8. Training in good diction is a valuable by-product of good history teaching. In his speaking and writing the student must

seek apt words of his own with which to describe past conditions inasmuch as there does not exist in history a technical
method of expression and a peculiar terminology as is found in
science and foreign language."

These, then, were the values of historical study so ably presented by the Committee. In stating them here, an attempt was
made to retain the spirit of those who proposed them. Their influence on history in the schools has been tremendous. They
have been accepted by thousands of history teachers as goals of
their endeavors. It would be difficult to overstate the good that
has resulted from them.

No extended treatment of the program of studies recommended by the Committee will be attempted here. Suffice it to
say, however, that this program included the famous four
blocks or periods of ancient history, mediæval and modern history, English history, and American history. In offering these
blocks the Committee said:

"As a thorough and systematic course of study, we recommend four years of work, beginning with ancient history and
ending with American history. For these four years we propose the division of the general field into four blocks or periods, and recommend that they be studied in the order in
which they are here set down, which in large measure accords
with the natural order of events, and shows the sequence of
historical facts:

"(1) Ancient History, with special reference to Greek and
Roman history, but including also a short introductory study
of the more ancient nations. This period should also embrace
the early Middle Ages, and should close with the establishment of the Holy Roman Empire (800), or with the death of
Charlemagne (814), or with the treaty of Verdun (843).

"(2) Mediæval and Modern European History, from the close of the first period to the present time.

"(3) English History.

"(4) American History and Civil Government.

"No one of these fields can be omitted without leaving serious lacunæ in the pupil's knowledge of history. Each department has its special value and teaches its special lesson; above all, the study of the whole field gives a meaning to each portion that it cannot have by itself." [18]

After outlining its program the Committee proceeded to amplify it. Through a number of pages the four fields were defended and suggestions offered for the treatment of each. While these are important pages, space does not admit of a review of them here. Moreover, there is no substitute for the reading of the original report; it is only through a firsthand contact with it that one can imbibe the spirit it contains.

Evidence of the Committee's tremendous influence on history in the high schools may be found in syllabi and textbooks published to conform to its recommendations, and the number of high schools offering and requiring the courses it proposed. Table I contains evidence of the second general type. It requires but a mere glance at it to discover the influence of the Committee of Seven on the offerings in high-school history in 1914–15, sixteen years after its report was published. The presence of ancient history in 6141 high schools of mediæval and modern European in 5745, of English in 4625, and of American in 6201, is ample proof that in their offerings in history high schools throughout the country on the eve of the appearance of the report of the Committee on Social Studies in Secondary Education were closely adhering to the recommendation of the Committee of Seven.

[18] *Ibid.,* pp. 34 f.

There are two other types of evidence evincing the influence of the report of the Committee of Seven on history in the high school. One of these types is textbooks written to conform with the report and the other is syllabi which embodied the ideas of

TABLE I

NUMBER OF 7197 HIGH SCHOOLS IN WHICH CERTAIN FIELDS OF HISTORY WERE REQUIRED AND ELECTIVE IN 1914–15*

FIELD OF HISTORY	First Year		Second Year		Third Year		Fourth Year		Totals		
	REQUIRED	ELECTIVE	REQUIRED	ELECTIVE	REQUIRED	ELECTIVE	REQUIRED	ELECTIVE	REQUIRED	ELECTIVE	GRAND TOTAL
Ancient history	2049	1324	1558	874	158	123	29	26	3794	2347	6141
Medieval and modern European history.............	195	97	1818	1401	1000	1059	70	105	3083	2662	5745
English history	337	191	332	358	1157	1749	133	268	1959	2666	4625
American history...	121	58	114	51	730	360	3376	1391	4341	1860	6201
Industrial history...	22	77	23	103	30	138	38	202	113	520	633
General history	48	9	179	17	45	12	7	9	279	47	326

* U. S. Com. of Educ., *Rep. for 1914–15*, I, 120.

the Committee. Four syllabi were constructed by committees of the New England History Teachers' Association, one for each of the four blocks of history proposed by the Committee—ancient, mediæval and modern European, English, and American. In each of these fields was provided both a general organization with time allotments in percentage for each large aspect of a field and a detailed outline of its contents with an abundance of references. These syllabi were printed in 1901 and subsequently became the dictators of the content of each block of history proposed by the Committee of Seven.

With respect to textbooks, they became as they appeared in rapid succession after 1900 imposing monuments to the Committee's efforts. During the sixteen years following 1900 text after text appeared in each of the fields suggested by the Committee. Occasionally these texts appeared in a series, one for each of the fields. For example, the "Essentials Series" contained volumes entitled *Essentials of Ancient History, Essentials of Mediæval and Modern History, Essentials of English History,* and *Essentials of American History*—four texts each by a different author and in charge of one general editor. The fact of the matter is that a textbook intended for high school use in history published between 1900 and 1915 had hard "sledding" if it failed to claim that it conformed to the report of the Committee of Seven.

THE COMMITTEE OF EIGHT, 1908

The astounding reception accorded the report of the Committee of Seven by persons interested in high-school history led the Association to appoint a committee to undertake in the elementary field what the Committee of Seven had so successfully accomplished in the high-school field. Accordingly, at its meeting during the early winter of 1905 a committee, subsequently known as the Committee of Eight, was appointed.[19] After three years of study and observation of the history situation in the elementary schools of the United States, England, Germany, and France, the Committee made its report. Early in 1909, this report was available for distribution. On the whole it was exceedingly well received. Courses of study in history

[19] The following individuals were named as members of this Committee: James A. James, Northwestern University, Chairman; Henry E. Bourne, Western Reserve University; Eugene C. Brooks, Trinity College, N. C.; Wilbur F. Gordy, Superintendent of Schools, Springfield, Mass.; Mabel Hill, Lowell, Mass., Normal School; Julius Sachs, Teachers College, New York; Henry W. Thurston, Chief Probation Officer, Chicago; and J. H. Van Sickle, Superintendent of Schools, Baltimore.—*The Study of History in the Elementary Schools.* Report to the American Historical Association by the Committee of Eight, p. 122. New York: Charles Scribner's Sons, 1909.

for the elementary school soon began to appear which were almost verbatim duplicates of it.

In some respects the report was revolutionary, but in most respects, mildly progressive. The revolutionary aspects were confined to the proposals for Grade VI, which included a new content to displace the prevailing American history usually found therein. The course suggested subsequently became known as the "European Background of American History" or "Old World Background of American History." Textbooks dealing with this content on the level of sixth grade began to appear soon after 1909. A dozen years after 1909 almost a score of these texts had been published. The school people responded almost unanimously to the efforts of authors and publishers in furnishing material for the new course. After 1912, history in Grade VI very generally became what was between the covers of the available texts on European or Old World background of American history.

The remaining suggestions with respect to the content of the course in history were none beyond what might be termed mildly progressive. For Grades I and II four types of work were proposed—Indian life, historical aspects of Thanksgiving, the story of Washington, and local events. Some attention was to be given to Memorial Day in Grade II. Heroes of other times, Columbus, the Indians, and the historical aspects of July Fourth comprised the basic material recommended for Grade III. Grades IV and V as well as VII and VIII were to be devoted to a study of the history of the United States, using the biographical approach in the former two grades and the chronological in the latter. Much bad and some good material for Grades IV and V appeared soon after 1910. Inasmuch as most of this material was presented in the form of biographies, it is more or less obsolete now in view of the fact that the biographical approach has been generally displaced by other approaches which seem more adequate both for the learner and for the content.

While not exactly in its field, the Committee suggested a program in elementary civics, starting with the special aim of

TABLE II

DISTRIBUTION OF SUBJECT-MATTER IN HISTORY IN GRADES IV–VI
ACCORDING TO GRADE PLACEMENT IN 1910-11*

SUBJECT-MATTER	GRADE IV 244 CASES	GRADE V 251 CASES	GRADE VI 238 CASES
1. Early American history.........	2	...	...
2. Later American history.........	...	3	...
3. Biographical stories of leading Americans....................	0	131	40
4. United States history...........	28	45	54
5. State and local history.........	16	5	5
6. Roman history, biography and mythology....................	125	10	4
7. Greek history, biography and mythology....................	29	9	5
8. English history................	1	9	111
9. Old-World background based on *Ten Boys*, by Jane Andrews.....	5	9	1
10. Course proposed by Committee of Eight......................	...	...	3
11. World history and world heroes.	3	9	2
12. Ancient history...............	3	7	8

* Compiled from R. M. Tryon's *Materials, Methods, and Administration of History in the Elementary Schools of the United States*, Vol. X, No. 9. Indiana University Bulletin, Bloomington, Ind.: Indiana University, 1912.

helping the child to realize himself as a member of each political group that does work for him. In Grades V and VI emphasis was placed on such elements of welfare as protection of life and property, health, education, and communication. In Grades VII and VIII chief consideration was given to the topic "State and National Governments." While there was nothing in these recommendations that went beyond what very many schools were doing in 1909, in making them, the Committee probably went as far as was feasible. It took a firm stand on certain issues which began to loom large after 1917. Reference is here made to the principle of separation which the Commit-

TABLE III

DISTRIBUTION OF THE MAIN ASPECTS OF THE SUBJECT-MATTER IN HISTORY IN GRADES IV–VI ACCORDING TO GRADE PLACEMENT IN FIFTY–SEVEN COURSES OF STUDY, 1928–31*

SUBJECT-MATTER	Frequency of Recommendation					
	GRADE IV B	GRADE IV A	GRADE V B	GRADE V A	GRADE VI B	GRADE VI A
1. Ancient civilization along the Mediterranean..............	..	..	..	3	..	..
2. Biographical stories of leaders and heroes...	9	9	..	..	..	..
3. Biographical stories of leading Americans. .	..	..	2	1	..	..
4. Early American history..............	19	18	36	9	3	3
5. History of the Middle Ages..............	..	..	1	1	..	..
6. History of Rome and Greece..............	..	2	1	..	..	..
7. Later American history..............	..	1	15	38	8	11
8. Old-World background..............	..	..	..	..	34	34
9. State or local history.	15	15	1	1	5	..

* Hannah M. Lindahl, "History in the Intermediate Grades," *Elementary School Journal*, XXXII (1931), 263.

te applied in the treatment of history and civics. While some correlation of these two subjects was suggested by the Committee, in general, each of them was to go its own way and live its own life. The Committee seems never to have heard of the doctrine of unification which was so loudly heralded during the nineteen twenties.

The actual influence of the Committee of Eight is best dis-

covered by examining the offerings in history in the intermediate grades at two different dates—one before the report was
generally known and the other after it was well known. The
data in Tables II and III reveal what happened between these
two dates. The former of these tables indicates that there were
probably not over three schools or school systems in 1910-11
that had adopted the recommendations of the Committee of
Eight as they related to history in the intermediate grades.
This table exhibits the status of history in these grades about
the time the report appeared. In general, Roman history was the
chief subject-matter in Grade IV; biographical stories of leading
Americans in Grade V; and English history in Grade VI.
Table III suggests the situation with respect to history in these
grades in 1931, from which it is evident that the report of the
Committee of Eight was well known at this date. Witness the
frequency of the exact recommendation of this Committee in
Grades IV, V, and VI, especially in Grades V and VI. Tables
II and III furnish excellent proof of the stabilizing influence of
the Committee. There appears no such unanimity of offerings
in the former of these tables as is found in the latter.

THE COMMITTEE OF FIVE, 1910

The Committee of Five need not detain us long. It was appointed in 1907 as a result of a petition from an organization
made up of the headmasters of a few select secondary schools
in the New England and Middle States. These individuals
were dissatisfied with certain aspects of the report of the Committee of Seven. They felt that the field of ancient history was
too extensive chronologically and that there was in the report an
over-emphasis on the cultivation of the reasoning faculty at the
expense of mere memory. The Committee of Five was charged

with the task of looking into the validity of these complaints.[20]

During the three years following its appointment the Committee made a thorough study of the existing situation in high schools and academies with regard to history. On the whole it found that there was general satisfaction with the report of the Committee of Seven and that the two complaints registered by the headmasters mentioned above were not reflected in the answers to the questionnaire used by the Committee to sense the general feeling regarding the complaints. In the course of its investigation the Committee sought information on every complaint that had been registered against the report of the Committee of Seven. Besides the two made by the headmasters others had been made, such as the inadvisability of offering a three-year course covering the field that was formerly included by the one-year course, the impossibility of adequately covering the entire range of history from early Grecian times to the present day in four years, that first year pupils were too immature for ancient history, that modern European history was neglected, and that American government deserved separate treatment from American history were thoroughly considered by the Committe. In the face of these contradictory complaints the Committee of Five stuck to the four-block system originally proposed by the Committee of Seven except in some minor details. Specific recommendations were made respecting the last two of these blocks. On the whole, however, the entire report of the Committee seems to the present-day

[20] Originally the Committee was composed of Andrew C. McLaughlin, Professor of History, University of Chicago, Chairman; Charles H. Haskins, Professor of History, Harvard University; Charles B. Mann, Professor of History, Lewis Institute, Chicago; James Harvey Robinson, Professor of History, Columbia University; James Sullivan, Principal of the Boys' High School, Brooklyn.—*The Study of History in Secondary Schools.* Report to the American Historical Association by a Committee of Five, p. 69. New York: The Macmillan Co., 1911. Professor Mann died in the spring of 1909, two years before the report of the committee was published.

reader an able defense and justification of the report of the Committee of Seven. In some respects the two reports were in reality one. Together they composed a body of the soundest doctrine on the teaching of high-school history propounded in this country before 1910.

Lest the reader infer that the Committee of Five made no specific recommendations respecting the course in history in the high school, the gist of the scheme proposed is hereby presented in the words of the Committee.

"1. Ancient History to 800 A.D. or thereabouts, the events of the last five hundred years to be passed over rapidly. . . .

2. English History, beginning with a brief statement of England's connection with the ancient world. The work should trace the main line of English development to about 1760, include as far as is possible or convenient the chief facts of general European history, especially before the seventeenth century, and give something of the colonial history of America.

3. Modern European History, including such introductory matter concerning later mediæval institutions and the beginnings of the modern age as seems wise or desirable, and giving a suitable treatment of English History from 1760.

4. American History and Government, arranged on such a basis that some time may be secured for the separate study of government." [21]

So far as the writer knows there is no statistical proof that the Committee of Five wielded any significant influence. The report of the Committee of Seven had become too strongly intrenched in the high schools by 1911 to be displaced by a report which was in reality its strongest supporter. Indirectly, however, there is evidence of influence in a certain direction. For example, the attempt to secure greater emphasis on the

[21] *Ibid.*, p. 64.

modern period was by no means in vain. Subsequent events so strengthened the demand for emphasis on this period that by 1924 a course of a year's duration in European history since 1648 was by no means uncommon. In a report made in June, 1924, 1109 out of 2404 high-schools were offering a course in modern history.[22]

THE COMMITTEE ON HISTORY AND EDUCATION FOR CITIZENSHIP, 1920

The origin, membership, and early history of this Committee may best be told in the words of its chairman in his final unofficial report.

"The Great War emphasized, perhaps even exaggerated, the criticisms formerly leveled against the current school programs. There now began to be heard a clamorous demand for recent world history and an equally insistent demand that adequate provision be made for civics or social science. The need of some definite training in American history and in civil government before the close of the sixth grade, where so many children drop out of school, was pressed home also, while new ideals of rigor in training, of time, economy and practicability in instruction gained easy acceptance.

"It was under these circumstances that, acting on a request from the National Education Association, the National Board for Historical Service (an organ of the American Historical Association), in October, 1918, appointed a committee to consider the entire series of problems connected with the teaching of history in the schools, both primary and secondary. Its chairman was Samuel B. Harding and the other members, Daniel C. Knowlton, Frank S. Bogardus, William C. Bagley, and Julian A. C. Chandler. At their meeting in January, 1919, the Council of the American Historical Association adopted the above com-

[22] Edgar Dawson, *The History Inquiry*, p. 19. Philadelphia: McKinley Publishing Co., 1924.

mittee as its own, but added three members—A. C. McLaughlin, Guy Stanton Ford, and Joseph Schafer.

"The first committee, at a meeting in Washington in November, 1918, agreed generally upon the scope of the inquiry to be undertaken and adopted certain rules of procedure. At a meeting of the enlarged committee in Chicago, February 28, 1919, Chairman Harding asked to be relieved of the duties of chairman, whereupon Mr. Schafer was chosen chairman. Mr. Knowlton was elected secretary, and the chairman and secretary devoted several months to the preparation of tentative programs which were considered by the plenary committee at its meeting in Washington, May 30 and 31, 1919." [23]

After two years of strenuous activity on the part of its chairman and secretary, the Committee brought in a report. This report was not formally accepted by the Council of the American Historical Association at its meeting in December, 1920. The Committee was not inclined to pursue its labors further, so asked to be discharged "with leave to print informally such reports as its members might see fit to prepare for the press." This request was granted by the Council. The first installment of the Committee's report was published in March, 1921, in the *Historical Outlook*, Volume XII. Three more installments appeared during the months of April, May, and June of this same year in the same volume of this magazine.

The report as a whole was divided into five parts: Part I, an introductory statement by the chairman; Part II, a discussion of history in the grades; Part III, a syllabus for a ninth-grade study of American industries; Part IV, a syllabus of modern history in the tenth grade; and Part V, a syllabus for eleventh-grade American history. Parts III, IV, and V were syllabi in the narrow meaning of this term. They have long outlived

[23] Joseph Schafer, "Report of Committee on History and Education for Citizenship," *Historical Outlook*, XII (1921), 90.

their value, so need no further treatment here. The aims in history teaching and the general scheme for their accomplishment in Grades I–XII are found in Part I, the preliminary report of the chairman, to which attention is now directed.

Inasmuch as the aims in history teaching adopted by the Committee were in no sense contributions to this aspect of history teaching, they may be passed over without further comment, using the available space for presenting the twelve-year history program proposed by the Committee. This course was organized in terms of the first six elementary grades, the junior high-school, and the senior high-school. The course proposed for the first six grades began in the community and ended in the community, and drew at every stage upon the pupil's experience in the community. It embraced two units or cycles as follows:

"I. The making of the community. From a simple study of changes now visibly in progress the pupil was to be led back to the days of Indian occupation. He was expected to learn what Indians were like, how they lived in pioneer days, and some of the great changes since. The story at no point was to leave the community. This work was designed for the second grade.

II. The making of the United States. A few facts of primary significance in the development of the United States were to be selected and so arranged as to form a simple but connected story. At the end provision was to be made for a study of how we are governed today. This work was designed to begin in the third grade and to continue through the sixth grade, as follows:

1. Third grade: How Europeans found our continent and what they did with it.

2. Fourth grade: How Englishmen became Americans, 1607–1783.

3. Fifth grade: The United States, 1783–1877.

4. Sixth grade: The United States since 1877 (half year). How we are governed today (half year)."

For the junior high school the following proposals were made. The wording is that of the Committee.

"III. American History in its world setting. This will constitute a third unit, or cycle, designed to form a logical and psychological development of the work given in the elementary grades. A few facts of primary significance in the development of human civilization are selected and so arranged as to form a simple but connected story. Our own country is here treated as a part of the world whole, but with special emphasis upon our own contributions and problems. This work is designed for the seventh, eighth and ninth grades, and is divided as follows:

1. Seventh grade: The world before 1607, and the beginnings of American history, including the building of the Spanish Empire in the New World, the basis of the present group of Latin-American Republics.

2. Eighth grade: The world since 1607 viewed in relation to the evolution and expanding world influence of the United States. Treatment is to take account of civic Problems, but to emphasize specially the economic and social features of our history up to recent times.

3. Ninth grade: Community and national activities. This course combines recent economic and social history with commercial geography and civics.

For those pupils of the ninth grade who expect to complete the senior high school, the committee recommends as an alternative to the above course in the progress of civilization from earliest times to about 1650."

The modern world was made the subject of study in the senior high school, the work for each year being—

"1. Tenth grade: Progress toward world democracy, 1650 to the present—a study mainly of European history, but with some attention also to the rest of the non-American world.

2. Eleventh grade: United States history during the national period, with emphasis on a list of topics to be selected for special treatment, and with critical comparisons with institutions and with tendencies in other countries.

3. Twelfth grade: Social, economic, and political principles and problems." [24]

One cannot prove by means of objective evidence that this Committee wielded any significant influence. Its recommendations for Grades VII–XII were so much in harmony with those of the Committee on the Social Studies in Secondary Education which reported in 1916 that it is impossible to assign the changes that have occurred in these grades since 1921 wholly to either of these committees. It should be remarked, however, that the world-emphasis that came into the history courses of junior and senior high schools during the nineteen twenties could have had its beginning in the suggestions of this Committee, for no previous committee used the word "world" in connection with a course in history. The Committee of Seven used the word "general" with a condemnatory emphasis. No committee of national scope representing a learned society or an education association has ever sponsored the course in world history as it is now administered.

III

AMERICAN POLITICAL SCIENCE ASSOCIATION

The American Political Science Association was formed in New Orleans on December 30, 1903, by a group of scholars

[24] *Ibid.*, pp. 90 f.

interested in the scientific study of politics, administration, diplomacy, and public law. Its membership has always been primarily comprised of teachers of political science in colleges and universities. While the interests of its members have been mainly in teaching and research, the Association has since its first meeting in 1904 given considerable attention to political science in the schools below the college. Like the American Historical Association, this Association has made its contributions to the teaching of civics and government in the elementary and high school grades in the form of committee reports—three in all. These appear in the proceedings of the Association under the captions "Committee of Five," "Committee of Seven," and the "Committee on Civics Instruction in the High Schools."

THE COMMITTEE OF FIVE, 1908

Early in its career the Association became interested in civics in the schools below the college level. Two years after its origin, a report[25] on what students know about government, before taking college courses in political science was made to the section on Instruction in Political Science. The facts exhibited in this report were shocking in the extreme. They were revealed through the following test, administered to 238 students in ten universities.

"I. Explain how members of Congress are chosen and state what you know about their terms, qualifications, and compensation.

II. Write a brief account of the federal courts. What does the Constitution provide in regard to the establishment of a system of United States Courts?

[25] W. A. Schaper, "What Do Students Know About American Government, Before Taking College Courses in Political Science?" *Proceedings American Political Science Association*, II (1905), 207 ff.

III. Describe clearly the process by which the Constitution of the United States may be amended. How may it be interpreted?

IV. Outline the government of a county in your state.

V. What is meant by the New England plan of township government?"

When the papers based on these questions were graded on a scale of 100 it was discovered that the 238 students had made an average of 12.4 per cent on Question I, 2.2 per cent on II, 5.6 per cent on III, 9.5 per cent on IV, and 6.5 per cent on V.

These startling results convinced the Association that some effort ought to be made to remedy the deplorable neglect of civics by the lower schools. Accordingly, at its meeting in December, 1906, a committee of three was appointed to make a study of the amount and kind of instruction in civics in the secondary schools. This Committee's official title was "Committee on Instruction in Government." Two additional members were added to the Committee at the annual meeting in December, 1907.[26] Even before these additional members were appointed the original Committee had launched inquiry into the status of instruction in American government in the secondary schools.

This inquiry was pursued along five lines: (1) number of students enrolled and the time given to the subject; (2) the nature of the course and the plan of instruction; (3) the teacher; (4) the textbook; and (5) the school library. When the returns to the questionnaire were tabulated and analyzed it was evident that instruction in American government in the secondary schools was at a very low ebb in 1907. To remedy the situation

[26] As finally made up the personnel of the Committee was: W. A. Schaper, Professor of Political Science, University of Minnesota, chairman; Isidor Loeb, Professor of Political Science, University of Missouri; Paul S. Reinsch, Professor of Political Science, University of Wisconsin; J. A. James, Professor of History, Northwestern University; and James Sullivan, Principal, Marcy Avenue Boys' High School, Brooklyn, New York.

its questionnaire revealed, the Committee made recommendations respecting the teaching of government on both the elementary and secondary school levels. The recommendations for the upper-elementary grades follow.

"The committee recommends that the discussion of the simple and readily observable functions and organs of local government be introduced into all the grades beginning not later than the fifth. The early instruction should take the form of observations by the class under direction of the teacher, talks or readings by the teacher, intended to add to the pupils' common stock of information, accounts of happenings and experiences, etc. In the eighth grade more formal instruction in local, state and national government should be given using an elementary text and some reference books. This work might well occupy the time of a subject for one-half of the eighth year. The emphasis in the grammar grade work on government should be on local and State governments and should deal with actual projects, activities and methods of doing things rather than consist of a mere collection of lists of officers and their salaries or an analysis of the constitution. The eighth grade classes can profitably be taken by the teacher to observe a session of a local court, city council, convention or polling place. Simple rules of parliamentary procedure can be explained and practiced." [27]

Concerning the teaching of American government in the secondary school the Committee said:

"In any system of schools where the subject has been properly treated in the grades, it is a simple task to plan the work for the high school. American Government should follow upon the work in history and should be a required study to occupy

[27] "Report of the Committee of Five of the American Political Science Association on Instruction in American Government in Secondary Schools," *Proceedings American Political Science Association*, V (1908), 251.

at least five recitations per week for one-half of the fourth year, or three recitations per week for that entire year. This is the minimum time which should be given to the subject. Some high schools are now devoting a full year to it with profit.

"In case the subject has not been taught in the grades, and especially in towns where many boys drop out of the high school before reaching the fourth year, it is highly desirable to offer an elementary course in government in the first or second years, so as to place it within reach of the greatest possible number. In the larger city high schools this elementary course can be offered as an additional elective without serious inconvenience." [28]

The specific advice of the Committee as to textbooks took the negative rather than the positive form.

"1. Avoid the book that consists of clauses of the Constitution with comments thereon.

2. Avoid the book that is in large part historical or an attempt to correlate history and government in one course.

3. Avoid the book that gives the larger portion of its space to the national government and relegates the State government with its rural and urban sub-divisions to a few general chapters.

4. Avoid the book that treats of a multitude of scattered subjects in Economics, Sociology, Statistics, Commercial Law, besides American Government."

THE COMMITTEE OF SEVEN, 1916

The final report of the Committee of Five was made in December, 1908, and published during the following year. The direct influence of the report is very problematical. It would seem that the Association itself must have felt that the Committee's influence was nil, inasmuch as another committee on

[28] *Ibid.*, p. 252.

the teaching of government was created in December, 1911. This Committee was launched under the title "Committee of Seven."

The Committee of Five confined its investigation to civics on the secondary level. The resolution under which the Committee of Seven was created provided for a much larger field of inquiry, namely, "the methods of teaching and studying government now pursued in American schools, colleges, and universities," and "means of enlarging and improving such instruction."[29] The Committee took this assignment seriously. Early in 1912 it launched investigations of (1) the political science offered in colleges and universities, and (2) the changes in civic instruction in the elementary and secondary schools since 1908, the date of the report of the Committee of Five.

The Committee completed its work in 1916. The volume entitled *The Teaching of Government,* which appeared during this year, contained a discussion of the progress of teaching government, a report on the teaching of civics in the secondary schools, suggestions for a course of study in civics and a report on the teaching of political science in colleges and universities.

In connection with its study of civics in secondary schools the Committee discovered certain unsatisfactory conditions. To rectify some of these, it suggested (1) that a year of social science exclusive of history be given in the senior high school and that at least half of the time be devoted to the study of

[29] *The Teaching of Government,* Preface, p. v. Report to the American Political Science Association by the Committee on Instruction. New York: The Macmillan Co., 1916. The personnel of the committee was Charles G. Haines, Professor of Government, University of Texas, Chairman; J. Lynn Barnard, Professor of History and Government, School of Pedagogy, Philadelphia; Edgar Dawson, Professor of Political Science, Hunter College, New York City; Walter L. Fleming, Professor of History, Louisiana State University; Mabel Hill, Associate Director Garland School, Boston, Massachusetts; Frank E. Horah, Professor of Political Science, State University of Iowa; and James A. James, Professor of History, Northwestern University.

government, giving four or five periods a week to the subject; (2) that the colleges be requested to accept a full year of a social science for entrance; (3) that better prepared teachers of government be supplied by normal schools, colleges, and universities; (4) that co-operation with local government and local civic bodies be encouraged; (5) that a collection of a civics library with reference works, government reports and pamphlet literature be made; and (6) that civics instruction be put into practice.[30]

The course of study proposed by the Committee was largely what the wide-awake schools were doing in 1915. For this reason its proposals found an appreciative audience. The recommendations for Grades I–III were not too long to quote in full.

"It should be the purpose of the work in the first grades to lay a foundation of good citizenship by developing in the child some of the fundamental civic virtues. Obedience, cleanliness, orderliness, courtesy, helpfulness, punctuality, truthfulness, thoroughness, honesty, courage, perseverance, self-control—all these, and others that might be named, may be taken up with the class, and somewhat in the order named. Both a knowledge of the right, and a desire to act rightly, may be developed in the pupils through stories, poems, memory gems, games, dramatization, and other class exercises. And these should be accompanied by constant care on the part of the teacher that the children shall be exemplifying these virtues in their daily conduct. Thus, it will be seen that the civics work of these early grades can be little less than a continuous lesson in good morals and good manners.

"The object throughout is to impress on the children that they too can take part in the better citizenship movement by

[30] Ibid., pp. 60 f.

co-operating with the group in the schoolroom, on the play-ground or in the home. The smallest boy or girl in the first primary grade can learn to refrain from doing those things which go against the welfare of the group, and—quite as im-portant—to do those things which will help promote com-munity welfare." [31]

Community service was the keynote of the course the Com-mittee proposed for Grades IV–VI. For these grades class dis-cussions and reports on the policeman, fireman, the street-sweeper, the garbage collector, the postman, water, gas, elec-tricity, telephone, and trolley cars were recommended. Prob-lems of city and country life and important industries of the town or country were also suggested as worth-while subject-matter. By way of summarizing, the Committee remarked:

"To sum up—civics teaching in the elementary school divides itself naturally into three periods—that of the first three or four grades in which emphasis is given to some of the fundamental civic virtues as applied to the home, to the school and to the neighborhood; second—that of grades four to six in which more specific instruction may be undertaken as to local affairs, with emphasis upon some of the functions which government performs and which citizens enjoy as members of a community; third—that of grades seven, eight, and nine—junior high school. In these grades instruction may be made more definite. A text-book may be used to advantage, and while the emphasis is still upon functions some attention should be given to the machinery of government—local, state, and national." [32]

Inasmuch as one of the members of this Committee had been chairman of the Committee that prepared the pamphlet en-titled *The Teaching of Community Civics,* published in 1915, one is not surprised in the Committee's taking over almost in

[31] *Ibid.,* pp. 78 f.   [32] *Ibid.,* p. 81.

toto the contents of this volume for its recommendations for the junior high school. This fact explains the almost *verbatim* aspects of the reports of the Committee on the Social Studies in Secondary Education and the Committee under review as they relate to community civics in the junior high school.

Those acquainted with the contents of the pamphlet referred to above will recall that the work in civics was based on the so-called welfare topics, namely, health, protection of life and property, recreation, education, civic beauty, wealth, communication, transportation, migration, charities, and correction. Inasmuch as both of the reports mentioned above appeared during the same year, 1916, it was fortunate that their proposals for at least one level of instruction did not clash. This fact probably goes a long way in explaining the uniformity that existed in junior high-school civics during the fifteen years after 1916.

With respect to civics in the senior high school, the Committee had no well-matured suggestions. An outline prepared primarily by teachers of civics in the high schools of New York City was substituted for suggestions of the Committee's own formulation. This outline was based on state government and federal government. To most readers of 1916 it must have appeared formal and mechanical. In view of subsequent developments, it was ten years out of date when it was printed.

COMMITTEE ON CIVICS INSTRUCTION IN HIGH SCHOOL, 1921

If one may judge from subsequent actions of the Political Science Association, one is led to conclude that the influence of the Committee of Seven was not wholly satisfactory to the members of the Association. As early as 1920, the Association authorized the appointment of another committee and charged it with the definition of the scope and purpose of a high-school course in civics as well as the preparation of an outline of topics to be included therein. This Committee immediately went into action and was ready to report at the annual meeting of the Association in December, 1921. The report made at this time was thoroughly discussed but was not formally adopted. The following excerpt from it indicates the view of the Committee on civics as a subject of study in the high school.

"The American Political Science Association believes that there is urgent need for an authoritative definition of the term Civics. Originally this term, as applied to high school instruction, was understood to include a study of American government and close-related matters; but its scope has been so greatly broadened in recent years that it is now regarded in many quarters as including the whole range of the social sciences, economics, sociology, ethics, and international relations, with the basic subject of American government thrust far into the background. The result is that high school instruction in the subject, by spreading itself in unguided fashion over so broad an area, has tended to become superficial and ill organized. Too often it affords the pupil a mere smattering of many things, not articulated to each other or bound together by any central concept, and none of which is presented with sufficient thoroughness to make any lasting impression upon him. It is not the breadth of the range alone but the lack of co-ordination that impairs the educational value of the subject. The Association believes that this disintegration has been carried too far and that the time has come not only to establish the "outside boundaries" of Civics but to urge a more effective co-ordination of the topics included within these limits." [33]

The Committee did not stop with mere generalizations but presented an outline intended to indicate in a general way at

[33] "The Study of Civics," *Historical Outlook*, XIII (1922), 42.

least the outside limits of the scope of high-school civics. Space can be spared here but for a brief outline of the course proposed.

"PART I. THE AMERICAN ENVIRONMENT.—Man and Society; the United States; the People, Races and Racial Problems of the United States; the American Home and Community; Economic Factors and Organization

PART II. AMERICAN GOVERNMENT.—The Foundations of Government—the nature and forms of government, rights and duties of the citizen, popular control of government; The Electoral Mechanism—suffrage and elections, party organization and machinery; Local and State Government—counties and rural communities, city government, municipal problems of today, state government; National Government—the national constitution, Congress at work, the President and his cabinet, the courts and the law.

PART III. THE CIVIC ACTIVITIES.—Economic—natural resources and conservation and the public domain, the agricultural interests, the encouragement and regulation of commerce, industry and labor, currency and banking and credit, public utilities, public finance; Social—public health, poor relief and correction and other welfare problems, education; International—national defense, foreign relations, the United States as a world power, the League of Nations, world problems and democracy." [34]

To some, the foregoing outline when it appeared seemed to place kindling on the fire that it was expected to quench. To the adverse critics of the Committee's report the sky seemed the limit of the boundaries of civics. In spite of the failure of the Association formally to adopt the report, subsequent development demonstrated that the Committee had sized up the

[34] *Ibid.*, pp. 43 f.

situation very accurately. Textboks in civics based on the outline above soon appeared and quickly gained a wide following.
Hence, through them the influence of the Committee grew to
considerable dimensions. It seems that since 1916 the surest
way for a committee to gather a following is to have the Association sponsoring it fail to adopt its report. It will be recalled
that about the time that the American Political Science Associa-
ion was in a sense refusing to adopt the report of one of its
committees the Council of the American Historical Association
was doing likewise. One does not have to look far afield for the
reason for happenings like these. When a committee of an
association or society spends two or more years working on a
report it is apt to become much more liberal in its views than
the general run of the members of the organization that created
it. So it often happens that when a committee brings in a
forward-looking report, said report fails of adoption because it
must be passed on by a body either of standpatters or of reac-
tionaries with respect to its content.

IV

THE NATIONAL SOCIETY FOR THE STUDY OF EDUCATION AND THE COLLEGIATE SCHOOLS OF BUSINESS

The National Society for the Study of Education has existed
under two other names. It was originally known as the National Herbart Society and was organized in 1895 for the purpose of securing a scientific study and discussion of leading
problems in public education. Early in 1902, the name of the
parent society was changed to the National Society for the

Scientific Study of Education. In a reorganization of the Society in 1909, the word "scientific" was dropped, thus leaving the name as it now stands. Throughout its career the Society has been interested in one or more of the social sciences as school subjects. In three of the six yearbooks of the parent society considerable space was devoted to various aspects of history, economics, and civics. In these volumes appeared articles on civic education, economics in secondary schools,[35] social functions of history,[36] and mediæval and modern history.[37] These articles were but forerunners of what was to come.

The *First Yearbook* of the National Society for the Scientific Study of Education was devoted entirely to history and geography. Fifty-four pages of the volume were devoted to a unified discussion of certain aspects of the teaching of history.[38] In this discussion a suggested history program for the elementary and high schools was briefly outlined. This program follows along with the few lines of introductory comment.

"The following scheme of work, however, is suggested in the

[35] Frank H. Dixon, "The Teaching of Economics in the Secondary Schools"; and Charles A. McMurry, "The Elementary School and Civic Education," *Third Yearbook,* National Herbart Society, pp. 128 ff. and 138 ff. Chicago: The University of Chicago Press, 1897.

[36] John B. McMaster, "The Social Function of United States History"; M. G. Brumbaugh, "Method of the Social Function of History"; and Frank G. Blair, "The Social Function of History," *Fourth Yearbook,* National Herbart Society, pp. 44 ff., 31 ff., and 26 ff. Chicago: The University of Chicago Press, 1898.

[37] James H. Robinson, "Medieval and Modern History in the High School," *Fifth Yearbook,* National Herbart Society, pp. 42 ff. Chicago: The University of Chicago Press, 1899.

[38] Lucy M. Salmon, "Some Principles in the Teaching of History," *First Yearbook,* National Society for the Scientific Study of Education, pp. 7 ff. Chicago: The University of Chicago Press, 1902.

belief that it can be justified not only by appeal to educational experience, but that it can also be defended as practical inasmuch as it is in principle already carried out either wholly or in part in many schools, both in this country and in Europe.

Grades I and II.—Stories from the Iliad, the Odyssey, the Æneid, the Sagas, the Nibelungen Lied, stories of King Arthur, Odin, Hiawatha; Robinson Crusoe, Arabian Nights.

Grades III and IV.—Biographies of characters prominent in the history of Greece, Rome, Germany, France, England, Southern Europe, Northern Europe and America.

Grade V.—Ancient history to 800 A.D.

Grade VI.—Medieval history.

Grade VII.—Modern history to the present time.

Grade VIII.—American history.

Grade IX.—Ancient history to *circa* 800 A.D.

Grade X.—Medieval and Modern history from *circa* 800 A.D. to the present time.

Grade XI.—English history.

Grade XII.—American history, including civil government." [39]

Those familiar with the concentric-circle idea in the arrangement of the subject-matter in history for the grades and the high school will observe that the foregoing scheme embodies it. There are two cycles in the scheme, one for the elementary grades and one for the high school. The reader will recognize in the second cycle the exact set-up proposed by the Committee of Seven of the American Historical Association four years previously. In recommending this set-up Miss Salmon was in no sense merely repeating the suggestions of others, for in reality she had a vested interest in it, having been a member of the Committee originally proposing it.

[39] *Ibid.*, pp. 54 ff.

HISTORY IN PART I OF THE SECOND YEARBOOK OF THE NATIONAL
SOCIETY FOR THE SCIENTIFIC STUDY OF EDUCATION

There is evidence to show that the material in the *First Yearbook* of the National Society for the Scientific Study of Education was favorably received when it appeared. Part I of the *Second Yearbook* of the Society devoted many pages to the discussions of Miss Salmon's monograph. In these discussions there was nothing but commendation of the material found in the monograph. In addition to this material the *Second Yearbook*, Part I contained two courses in history for the grades, one emphasizing occupations and the other a combination of European and American history. The latter was the work of a dyed-in-the-wool Herbartian, and the former the work of a follower of Colonel Francis W. Parker.[40] Inasmuch as the course emphasizing occupations contained so much that subsequently appeared in the schools, it seems advisable to include it here. It follows by grades.

GRADE I

"1. Occupations: Making and furnishing playhouses. In connection with this work, the primary arts connected with food, clothing, and shelter were introduced.

2. Studies: Comparison of methods of work with those of primitive peoples.

GRADE II

1. Occupations: Cooking, making furniture, weaving, and simple needlework.

[40] Emily J. Rice, "History in the Elementary School," and Charles A. McMurry, "Course of Study in History in the Grades," *Second Yearbook*, National Society for the Scientific Study of Education, Part I, pp. 9 ff. and 15 ff. Chicago: The University of Chicago Press, 1903.

2. Studies: Study of primitive people in the hunter and shepherd stages of culture.

Grade III

1. Occupations: Cooking, gardening, and making of pottery.

2. Studies: Study of primitive farming and the beginnings of trade and city life.

Grade IV

1. Occupations: Wood and metal work.

2. Studies: Local history with the evolution of local industries, and means of intercommunication. Stories of famous explorers. Simple problems of public service.

Grade V

1. Occupations: Weaving and sewing.

2. Studies: Colonial history. The textile industry in colonial times.

Grade VI

1. Occupations: Weaving, sewing; work in wood and clay.

2. Studies: Colonial history. Our struggle for independence and similar struggles in previous times, as in Greece, Switzerland, and Holland. Physical culture and games of Greece. Greek architecture and sculpture. Notable buildings in the locality of the school.

Grade VII

1. Occupations: Printing and bookbinding.

2. Studies: The period of discovery and exploration in American history and the settlement of the West. Development of the arts of printing and of inventions connected with navigation.

GRADE VIII

1. Occupations: Wood and metal work.

2. Studies: home economics, including civic regulations in regard to building and sanitation. Roman or English history, with the emphasis upon the evolution of government. Structure of the local government." [41]

SOCIAL SCIENCES IN THE FOURTEENTH AND SUBSEQUENT YEARBOOKS
OF THE SOCIETY FOR THE STUDY OF EDUCATION

After its vigorous early efforts in behalf of history in the schools, the Society became interested in other lines of endeavor and never got back to history until 1915, when it published a yearbook on minimum essentials in elementary-school subjects. Two other yearbooks were devoted to the same subject—one appearing in 1917 and the other in 1918. These yearbooks heralded a new order in curriculum-making. They introduced curriculum-makers to the objective approach to curriculum content. While it is perhaps true that too little use has, even to this day, been made of this approach, yet its injection into the realm of curriculum-content determination has probably caused more thought to be given to the selection of this content than was given prior to 1915. In the *Fourteenth Yearbook* appeared reports on two studies on the determination of minimum essentials in history. One of these studies used the judgments of specialists in history to make a list of important dates in United States history; the other analyzed textbooks in United States history for Grades VII and VIII to determine the

---

[41] The course proposed by McMurry was a condensation of what appeared the same year in his book *Special Method in History*. New York: The Macmillan Co., 1903.

common material therein. From·these feeble beginnings, the use of the objective method of determining minimum essentials in history became more and more general. Ere ten years had passed objective studies were numbered by the hundreds. The small snowball of objectivity, which was started rolling down the curriculum-making future in 1915, became by 1925 a huge mass of incoherent factual material.

The climax of the Society's efforts in behalf of the social sciences in the schools was reached in 1922 in the publication of Part II of the *Twenty-Second Yearbook,* a volume devoted entirely to these subjects.[42] Certainly no previous effort of the Society in behalf of the social sciences yielded dividends greater than the one represented in this yearbook. While the material it contained was somewhat immature and unrelated, it was full of a multitude of suggestions which subsequently were taken seriously by curriculum-makers in the social sciences. For example, at least a half dozen proposed programs for the social sciences appeared in the volume. These offered the curriculum-maker a variety from which to choose. While few took over any one of the programs in toto, leads were undoubtedly obtained from many of them. Inasmuch as there was no fundamental and unified scheme set forth in the volume, further consideration of its contents seems unnecessary here. The influence of the volume was somewhat temporary and local rather than substantially permanent and general. In this respect it hardly belongs in the same class with the volume produced by the Committee of Seven of the American Historical Association.

---

[42] Mention should be made of the fact that Part I of the *Nineteenth* and Part I of the *Twentieth Yearbooks* were to some extent efforts in behalf of the social sciences. These volumes contained new materials of instruction, some of which fall within the field of the social sciences. They appeared in 1920 and 1921.

EFFORTS OF THE ASSOCIATION OF COLLEGIATE SCHOOLS OF BUSINESS
IN BEHALF OF THE SOCIAL SCIENCES

The Association of Collegiate Schools of Business was organized in 1916 for the purposes of promoting and improving business education in the United States. In February, 1920, an article[43] appeared, challenging the Association to attack the problem of the appropriate correlation of collegiate and secondary education. The Association accepted the challenge and created a commission known as "Commission on Correlation of Secondary and Collegiate Education with Particular Reference to Business Education." [44] Shortly after its creation this Commission submitted (April, 1922) a report of progress largely devoted to the correlation of the six-year junior-senior high-school course and collegiate education.

After discussing (1) social sciences in a business curriculum, (2) previous proposals concerning social sciences in secondary schools, (3) the actual position of social sciences in secondary schools and in secondary commercial curricula, (4) what the collegiate schools of business do by way of correlation, and (5) administrative reorganization of our school system, the Commission turned its attention to the program of social sciences for the junior high school. The recommendations

[43] L. C. Marshall, "The Relation of the Collegiate School of Business to the Secondary-School System," *The Journal of Political Economy*, XXVIII (1920), 137 ff.

[44] The following persons were members of the commission: representing secondary schools, H. V. Church, appointed by the Association of Secondary-School Principals; representing labor, Charles B. Stillman, appointed by the American Federation of Labor; representing employers, H. H. Rice, appointed by the National Industrial Conference Board; representing the Association of Collegiate Schools of Business, R. E. Heilman, W. H. Kiekhofer, C. O. Ruggles, I. Leo Sharfman, and L. C. Marshall.—The Commission on Correlation of Secondary and Collegiate Education with Particular Reference to Business Education, *Social Studies in Secondary Schools*, p. vii. Chicago: The University of Chicago Press, 1922.

relative to a three-year junior high-school program were as follows:

Grade VII

"1. Geographic bases of (physical environment with relation to) United States development.

2. Social science survey (types of social organization).

　(a) Simple industry and simple society.

　(b) The transforming effects of scientific knowledge.

3. Other studies, correlated so far as may be practicable with the social-study material.

Grade VIII

1. The opening of the world to the use of man.

2. Vocational survey, the individual's place in our social organization (presented in functional terms so that it may contribute to an understanding of our type of social organization).

3. Other studies, correlated so far as may be practicable with the social-study material.

Grade IX

1. The history of the United States (presented with "citizenship material" occupying the center of attention).

2. Principles of social organization (economic, political, social).

3. Other studies, correlated so far as may be practicable with the social-study material.

4. A general survey of business administration, elective." [45]

Proposals for a program in the social sciences for the junior high school which departed from those usually found in the schools, as did the foregoing, required material in the form of texts to make them practical. In so far as texts subsequently

[45] *Ibid.*, p. 53.

appeared, the new material suggested by this Commission found its way into junior high schools. Exactly to what extent has never been determined. However, the purpose of the social sciences in the junior high school as stated by the Commission subsequently obtained a large following. It read as follows: "that of giving our youth an awareness of what it means to live together in organized society, an appreciation of how we live together, and an understanding of the conditions precedent to living together well, to the end that our youth may develop those ideals, abilities, and tendencies to act which are essential to effective participation in our society." After 1922 this statement began to appear in increasing numbers of courses of study in the social sciences for the junior high school.[46]

V

THE AMERICAN BAR ASSOCIATION AND THE NATIONAL SECURITY LEAGUE

While the American Bar Association and the National Security League are not organizations primarily educational in character as are the organizations considered above, they have in the recent past become interested in a project which has educational aspects. This project is none other than that of

---

[46] Before passing to a consideration of other organizations mention should be made of the efforts of the American Economic Association in behalf of the social sciences in the schools. As early as 1917 this Association had a committee on "Economics in the Secondary School," bring in a report (*American Economic Review* (Supplement), VIII (1918), 308–312). This report was confined entirely to a presentation of some facts relating to the teaching of economics in the secondary schools which the Committee had collected by means of a questionnaire. Another report was brought in at the meeting of the Association in December, 1921. Inasmuch as the same person was chairman of this Committee who was chairman of the Commission discussed above, the reports coincided in so far as the arrangement of the program of the social sciences was concerned. This fact made further work on the part of the Committee of the American Economic Association unnecessary.

securing adequate and effective teaching of the federal and
state constitutions in public and private schools below the
college level. Between 1921 and 1932 these two organizations
were very active in the securing of legislation making obligatory the teaching of the federal constitution in these schools.

THE COMMITTEE ON AMERICAN CITIZENSHIP OF THE
BAR ASSOCIATION

The older of the foregoing organizations is the American
Bar Association, having been organized in 1878 in Saratoga,
New York. As the name suggests, it is an association of
American lawyers and jurists. Its chief purposes since its organization have been to advance the science of jurisprudence,
to promote the administration of justice, and to secure uniformity of legislation and of judicial decisions. About 1921,
another purpose seems to have been added to these three,
namely, that of the securing of adequate and uniform laws in
all of the states making obligatory the teaching of the federal
constitution in all public and private schools. To prosecute
the work necessary to accomplish this purpose, the Association
appointed a committee known as the "Committee on American
Citizenship." In its first report in 1922, this Committee gave
an account of the organization it had set up. This organization
included state and local committees throughout the country.
The chief duty assigned to each local committee was that of
checking the type of instruction concerning the federal constitution given in the schools of its locality. Local committees
were asked to report to the parent Committee the courses of
instruction, the textbooks used, and the qualification of teachers
for the teaching of the federal constitution.[47]

[47] Report of the Committee on American Citizenship," *Reports of American
Bar Association*, XLVII (1922), 422. Chicago: American Bar Association,
1922.

After completing its organization the Committee entered vigorously upon its work. So effective were its labors that it was able to report in 1927 that thirty-three states had passed laws requiring the teaching of the federal constitution. Most of these laws included state constitutions also. With success along this line assured, the parent Committee undertook a program which included (1) the improvement of the instruction in high schools relating to the federal constitution, (2) the securing of more effective instructional material, and (3) the bettering of the training of teachers of the federal and state constitutions. After deliberating on the improvement of instruction relating to the constitution for three or four years, the Committee finally concluded that a separate course on the United States constituion should be introduced into the schools.[48] In response to this demand, authors and publishers began to produce and publish textbooks on the federal constitution. No less than a half dozen of these texts appeared in quick succession. The exact extent of their use has never been determined.

THE NATIONAL SECURITY LEAGUE

The National Security League is a much younger organization than the American Bar Association, having been formed in 1914. Its paramount purposes have been and still are (1) to promote patriotism and good citizenship, and (2) to combat socialism, bolshevism, and all forms of radicalism. After the close of the World War, the League centered its activities on citizenship training in public and private schools. Because of the existing situation relative to the teaching of the national constitution, revealed in a survey made in 1921 by the League's secretary,[49] a committee on constitutional instruction was

[48] *Ibid.*, LII (1927), 236.
[49] "Civic Department," *National Security League Monthly Report to Members,* November, 1921, p. 1.

organized. This Committee consisted of over two hundred persons prominent in education throughout the states.[50] It was the purpose of this large Committee to place in the public and private schools of the United States compulsory courses on the federal constitution. This Committee co-operated with the one of the American Bar Association discussed above in securing state legislation making obligatory the teaching of the federal constitution in public and private schools. By 1928, the work of the Committee along this line was almost finished. As indicated in the following quotation from a report at this date, the work of the Committee was henceforth to be directed along other lines. "Although 40 states have passed a law requiring the teaching of the constitution, that is only the first step; the next step is to see that the law is enforced."[51]

There is an abundance of objective evidence to show that the work of the two organizations under discussion here was successful in one line at least, namely, the actual securing by 1931 of the passage of a law in each of forty-three states requiring the teaching of either the federal or the state constitution or both. Data relating to the passing of these laws appear in Table IV, which shows how rapidly the two organizations under discussion here achieved their objective. Except the Vermont law all of the laws making obligatory the teaching of the federal constitution were enacted during the decade beginning with 1921, almost half of them in one year, 1923. The moral to this remarkable achievement seems to be: The shortest road to the accomplishment of a reform by means of legal action is through the American Bar Association and the National Security League.

There is a body of evidence relating to the matter of uni-

[50] *Ibid.*, February, 1922, p. 1.
[51] "Constitution Teaching," *National Security League Quarterly*, II (1928), 2.

formity in the laws passed in the states included in Table IV.
Fifteen of the forty-three states listed therein had in 1930 among

TABLE IV

DATE OF ENACTING THE LAWS IN OPERATION IN 1930 IN FORTY-
THREE STATES REQUIRING THE TEACHING OF THE FEDERAL AND
STATE CONSTITUTIONS*

STATES	Date of Enactment of Laws		STATES	Date of Enactment of Laws	
	NATIONAL CONSTITU- TION	STATE CONSTITU- TION		NATIONAL CONSTITU- TION	STATE CONSTITU- TION
Alabama......	1923		New Jersey	1923	
Arizona.......	1925	1925	New Mexico....	1923	1923
Arkansas......	1923	1923	New York......	1924	
California.....	1923		North Carolina..	1923	1923
Colorado......	1925		North Dakota ..	1929	
Delaware......	1923	1923	Ohio..........	1923	1923
Florida........	1925		Oklahoma......	1925	
Georgia.......	1923	1923	Oregon........	1923	
Idaho.........	1923		Pennsylvania....	1923	
Illinois........	1921	1921	Rhode Island ...	1922	1922
Indiana........	1925	1925	South Carolina..	1924	
Iowa..........	1921	1921	South Dakota...	1923	1923
Kansas........	1925		Tennessee.......	1923	1923
Kentucky......	1924		Texas..........	1930	1930
Louisiana	1926		Utah..........	1923	
Maine.........	1925		Vermont........	1915	1915
Massachusetts.	1923		Virginia........	1928	1928
Michigan......	1921	1921	Washington	1925	1925
Minnesota.....	1923		West Virginia...	1923	1923
Missouri......	1927	1927	Wyoming.......	1925	1925
Nebraska......	1927	1927			
Nevada........	1923	1923	Total.........	43	24
New Hampshire	1923	1923			

* Clarence E. Swingley, "Teaching of the National Constitution and the State Constitutions in the Elementary and High Schools of the United States," pp. 23 f. Unpublished Master's thesis, University of Chicago, 1931.

their statutes an almost identical law dealing with the teaching
of the federal and state constitutions. The model followed in
these states was enacted in Iowa in 1921. It was dictated by the

Committee of the American Bar Association and read as follows:

"In all public and private schools located within the state of Iowa, commencing with the school year, 1921, there shall be given regular courses of instruction in the constitution of the United States and the constitution of the state of Iowa.

"Such instruction in the constitution of the United States and the constitution of the State of Iowa shall begin not later than the opening of the eighth grade, and shall continue in the high school to an extent to be determined by the superintendent of public instruction." [52]

It should be remarked, in concluding this review of the activities of these two influential organizations in behalf of the teaching of the federal and state constitutions, that other organizations of a national scope did not sit with folded arms and let the two leaders do all the work. While space is lacking to record their activities, much assistance was rendered the two leaders by the following organizations, clubs, and societies:

"American Legion, Constitution Anniversary Association, Daughters of American Revolution, United Spanish War Veterans, Sons of American Revolution, Women's Federated Clubs, American Academy of Political and Social Science, National Association of Constitutional Government, National Institute of Social Science, Masonic Service Association, Knights of Columbus, Rotary, Exchange, Lions, Kiwanis, Better America Foundation, National Popular Government League, Women's Christian Temperance Union, National Women's League, Anti-Saloon League, Legislative Voters League, American Defense Society, American Rights League, National War Mothers, Young Men's Christian Association, Young Women's Christian Association, Council of Jewish Women,

[52] *Acts of the 39th General Assembly of Iowa*, 1921, chap. 91, secs. 1–2.

American Federation of Labor, Advertising Club of America, Boy Scouts, Chamber of Commerce, National Manufactures Association, Federal Council of Churches, National Society of Colonial Dames of America, National Association of Patriotic Instructors, National Civic Federation, and Patriotic Education Society." [53]

VI

THE AMERICAN SCHOOL CITIZENSHIP LEAGUE, THE NATIONAL MUNICIPAL LEAGUE, AND THE AMERICAN SOCIOLOGICAL SOCIETY

The efforts in behalf of the social sciences as school subjects of the organizations of national scope which have been considered above were supplemented from time to time by other national organizations, clubs, and societies. The efforts of three of these seem of sufficient importance to justify brief notice. As was the case with the organizations considered in the foregoing sections of this division, the three organizations named above made their contributions through special committees, the reports of which are discussed below.

THE HISTORY COMMITTEE OF THE CITIZENSHIP LEAGUE

The American School Citizenship League was organized in 1908. Its chief object since the beginning of its career has been the development of an American citizenship interested in the promotion of a responsible world democracy and co-operation among nations. To accomplish this objective the League has in the past outlined schemes for the teaching of citizenship and history according to plans of its own formulation. "An Ameri-

[53] Swingley, *op cit.*, pp. 10 f.

can Citizenship Course in United States History" is an example of one of these outlines. Work on this course was begun in 1913 by the History Committee of the League.[54] At the end of four years of intermittent labor, the Committee was ready to make its report. This was in 1917, the year the United States entered the World War. Because of the unsettled conditions brought about by this event, the Committee decided to withhold the publication of its report. When the war ended the Committee revised its work to meet the educational needs of the time and made it available to the public in five small volumes. One of these volumes was devoted to a general consideration of the course in history for Grades I–VIII; another, to the course for Grades IV and V; and one each to the courses for Grades VI, VII, and VIII. A course for Grades I, II, and III was suggested by the Committee, but no detailed outline of it was provided. The entire set-up was almost a duplication of that of the Committee of Eight of the American Historical Association.

One feature of the work of the Committee of the Citizenship League was, however, different and new. This was the type studies which were made available for all grades above the third. The four volumes devoted to these studies were expected to be placed in the hands of teachers. The extent of their use has not been made known to date. Even though the Committee did furnish these type studies, its report on the whole was more reactionary than forward-looking. The Committee failed to realize that anything had happened in the

[54] The personnel of this Committee was Wilbur F. Gordy, Hartford, Conn., Chairman; Philander P. Claxton, United States Commissioner of Education; Charles E. Chadsey, Superintendent of Schools, Detroit, Mich.; James H. Van Sickle, Superintendent of Schools, Springfield, Mass.; and John W. Hall, Head of Elementary Education Department, University of Cincinnati. (The position in each case is the one held as of February, 1913. Mrs. John W. Hall was subsequently made a member of the Committee.)

field with which it was dealing during the twelve years preceding the date its report was published. However, in fairness
it should be said that due recognition of its debt to the Committee of Eight was not lacking in the volume devoted to the
general set-up of the course. In other words, the Committee
knew that its proposals were not original.

THE COMMITTEE ON INSTRUCTION IN MUNICIPAL GOVERNMENT
OF THE MUNICIPAL LEAGUE

The National Muncipal League was organized in 1894 and
incorporated in 1923. From its inception till now the League
has been primarily interested in the improvement of municipal
government and administration. Its influence in these realms,
no doubt, has been far reaching during the past twenty-five
years. As early as April, 1903, the League became interested in
civics in the schools. At this date a committee was appointed
to investigate the work in civics, particularly municipal citizenship and government, in the elementary school. This committee brought in a report the next year, 1904.[55] This report
consisted of a lengthy discussion of the general aspects of government and civics and a summary of a questionnaire study of
the teaching of civics in the elementary school. This study
assembled facts relating to (1) the need for moral instruction,
(2) the time allotment to instruction in civics, (3) the daily
work of the classroom, (4) incidental teaching of civics, and
(5) systematic teaching of civics.

The foregoing committee was known as "The Committee
on Instruction in Municipal Government in American Educational Institutions." Besides the main committee there were

[55] F. L. Luqueer, "A Tentative Program for the Teaching of Municipal
Government and Civics in the Elementary School," *Proceedings Tenth Annual
Meeting National Municipal League,* 1904, pp. 249 ff.

two sub-committees—one on the elementary-school program in civics and one on the high-school program. All three of these committees reported in the spring of 1905.[56] The report of the main committee was little more than an introduction to the reports of the two sub-committees. A summary of the recommendations of the sub-committees on the elementary-school program appears below.

"To sum up: moral and civic instruction should permeate the entire school life of the child. An effective part of this instruction will spring incidentally from the rich subject-content of the general course of study.

"In the daily opening exercises, the works of good citizens, the holding up of great examples and incentives, the patriotic songs and recitations are all a part of the civic instruction.

"In the early study of nature, geography and biography, civic ideas spring from deep ground.

"In the early and late contact with the best literature suited to the young pupil,—stories, poems, drama,—the heart-throb is felt of civic emotion and of the deepest life of the people.

"In the study of pictures and historic architecture, ideas of civic beauty and order are inbreathed. In the study of science and invention, of geometry and arithmetic, an exact and honest civic conscience may be aroused.

"The local history is the beginning of instructed citizenship. The country's history is the story of state and national association and government. The historic biography has for its keynote civic virtue. The English history contains all this, in another setting, enables by comparison the pupil to comprehend development, and gives a critical standard. It should do away with prejudice, and may stir the first sense of world-citizenship.

[56] *Proceedings Eleventh Annual Meeting National Municipal League*, 1905, pp. 256 ff.

"All this, and how much there is, is involved in the incidental teaching of civics.

"As to the systematic:

"In the sixth year, a simple reading book on the subject will set these civic ideas in order.

"In the seventh year may be a review and a comparative enrichment.

"In the eighth year, follows a sketch of the activities and the mechanism of state and national government, with a short, intense study of the municipality, its departments, officers and ideals.

"Such, made luminous by the teacher, would seem a sufficient presentation of the subject of national, state and municipal civics, of citizenship, for the elementary school." [57]

The sub-committee on the high-school program in municipal government in substance recommended the following outline.

I. THE ORIGIN AND DEVELOPMENT OF MUNICIPAL GOVERNMENT.—The English Municipality—the borough, influence of the guilds, modern developments; the Growth in America— the colonial period, the period before the Civil War, the industrial period

II. THE SYSTEM OF GOVERNMENT.—The Charter; the Legislative Department; the Executive and Elected Officers; Administrative Boards and Commissions

III. PREVAILING CONDITIONS IN THE UNITED STATES.—Rapid Growth; Unsatisfactory Systems of Government; Incompetent and Unfaithful Officials; Influence of Political Machinery; Foreign Population; Large Bonded Debts; Influence of Municipal Corruption on the State and Nation

IV. SOME REFORM MOVEMENTS.—Home Rule; the Merit System; Time and Manner of Holding Elections; Increased Power

[57] *Ibid.*, pp. 266 f.

and Responsibility of the Mayor; Choosing of Administrative Boards; Ownership and Control of Public Utilities; Terms, Salaries and Checks upon Officers; a Model Program

V. SOME REFORM FORCES.—The Recent Awakening; the Reform Leagues; Education

VI. THE NEW PATRIOTISM.—The True Spirit of Civic Loyalty; the Opportunity and Responsibility of the Individual Citizen.[58]

Originally Superintendent Maxwell, of New York City, was chairman of the Municipal League's Committee on "Instruction in Municipal Government in Elementary and High Schools." Subsequently James J. Sheppard, of the same city, became chairman of the Committee. Sheppard made a report for the Committee in November, 1909, much of which dealt with the teaching of municipal government in the city of New York. A lengthy outline of a course, which had been in successful use for several years in the High School of Commerce in that city, was submitted. The Committee in concluding its report spoke optimistically of the outlook for instruction in municipal civics. "The situation at present is full of encouragement, and we may look forward confidently to a time not far distant when instruction in municipal civics will be firmly established as an important feature of all progressive school courses." [59] Those of the Committee who are yet living are still looking forward. There is no indication that their dream will come true even during the next twenty-five years.

[58] *Ibid.*, pp. 277 f. Mention should be made of two other sub-committees of the League, one on student self-government and one on literature of instruction in municipal government. Both of these committees reported in the spring of 1905. See *Proceedings,* National Municipal League, 1905, pp. 280 ff. and 289 ff.

[59] James J. Sheppard, "Municipal Civics in Elementary and High Schools," *Proceedings Fifteenth Annual Meeting of the National Municipal League,* 1909, p. 379.

THE COMMITTEE ON SOCIOLOGY IN THE ELEMENTARY AND HIGH SCHOOLS OF THE SOCIOLOGICAL SOCIETY

The American Sociological Society was established in 1905. From the beginning its chief interest has been in research. Not until 1918 did the Society become sufficiently interested in sociology below the college level to devote any systematic attention to it. In this year a committee on the teaching of sociology in the elementary and high schools of America was appointed.[60] The first report of the Committee was a tentative one. In it attention was called to the status of the teaching of the social sciences in public high schools and to special agencies actively promoting the teaching of these subjects. A program in the social sciences was proposed for the entire twelve grades of the public schools. In its second report, made in December, 1920, the Committee called attention to such items as (1) ninth-grade course in general social science, (2) the tenth-grade course in history, (3) textbooks, and (4) the universality of secondary education. The program proposed for the various grades was:

"Grades I to VI: One full round of elementary general and American history, with emphasis on the economic and social sides.

"Grades VII and VIII: Geography, American history, and government.

"Grade IX: General social science or 'community civics.'

"Grade X: European history.

[60] The personnel of the Committee was Ross L. Finney, University of Minnesota, Chairman; E. S. Bogardus, University of Southern California; C. A. Ellwood, University of Missouri; Cecil C. North, Ohio State University; John Phelan, Massachusetts Agricultural College; Walter R. Smith, University of Kansas; and A. J. Todd, University of Minnesota.—"Tentative Report of the Committee on Teaching of Sociology in the Grade and High Schools of America," *Publications of the American Sociological Society*, XIV (1919), 251. This report was also published in *School Review*, XXVIII (1920), 255 ff.

"Grade XI: American history.

"Grade XII: Sociology, economics, and civics, or 'problems of democracy.'"[61]

Inasmuch as the three foregoing committees did their work during the time when the committees previously considered did theirs it is not possible to point out specifically the influence of each on the social sciences in the schools. Because of the reactionary character of the report of the History Committee of the American School Citizenship League, its influence must have been negligible. The emphasis on the need for the teaching of municipal government by the Committee representing the National Municipal League probably paved the way for the movement for the study of local institutions which got under way about 1907. The reports of the Committee of the American Sociological Society were influential in backing up the report of the Committee on Social Studies in Secondary Education which appeared in 1916.[62]

[61] "Second Annual Report of the Committee on Teaching Sociology in the Grade and High Schools of America," *Publications American Sociological Society*, XV (1920), 225.

[62] Reference should be made here to a co-operative effort in behalf of the social sciences in the schools of the American Historical Association, American Economic Association, Association of Collegiate Schools of Business, American Sociological Society, American Political Science Association, and the National Council of Teachers of Geography. In December, 1921, a commission consisting of two members from each of these associations was formed. After a year of deliberation this Commission made a report to the Association it represented. This report consisted of brief statements setting forth the distinctive contributions of each of the disciplines represented in the Commission to the social sciences as school subjects.—For these statements see "Contributions of the Social Sciences to the Curriculum," *Journal of Political Economy*, XXXI (1923), 737 ff.

DIVISION TWO

HISTORY AS A SUBJECT OF STUDY IN ELE-
MENTARY AND SECONDARY SCHOOLS

HISTORY AS A SUBJECT OF STUDY IN ELEMENTARY AND SECONDARY SCHOOLS

I

VALUES CLAIMED FOR HISTORY AS A SCHOOL SUBJECT

No one to date has ever been able to prove by means of objective data that history has any value in the education of youth. To secure objective data on a problem of such a subjective nature seems beyond the ingenuity of investigators. Before one could demonstrate quantitatively the contributions of history, for example, to the making of good citizens, one would have to secure data on two groups of citizens—one that had never been exposed to history as a school subject and one that had been. Granting that an investigator could secure two such groups, he would still face the problem of determining objectively the qualities of a good citizen. Could these qualities be determined, he would still be confronted with the elusive question of the contributions of history to the good citizen's qualities. There seems to be no limit to the difficulties that one would encounter in his efforts to determine objectively the specific values of history in the education of youth. The fact, however, that no one has ever objectively determined these values has been no deterrent to those who have had values to proclaim. Certainly the protagonists of history as a school subject have not been modest in their claims for it. The number of specific values that have been promulgated in the past is almost legion. A mere tabulation of them would take more space than their significance seems to justify. In lieu of presenting such a tabulation, consideration is given below to the chief values claimed for history as a school subject (1) prior to 1860; (2) during the eighteen seventies, eighties, and nineties; (3) during the early nineteen hundreds; and (4) since about 1920. Viewing the claimed values of history during these four periods affords the opportunity of noting continuity and emphasis. Attention is first directed to the situation prior to 1860.

THE VALUES PRIOR TO 1860

It has been pointed out by a student of the early teaching of history in the secondary schools of the United States[1] that history edged its way into these schools during the generation prior to 1860 under a banner borne by its advocates with the following values thereon: (1) History provides valuable training in morals. (2) History furnishes abundant opportunity for the profitable use of leisure time. (3) History is a great inspirer of patriotism. (4) History trains for a higher order of citizenship. (5) History affords occasions for religious training. (6) History strengthens and disciplines the minds of those who master its content.

While the protagonists of history as a school subject were able to secure a place for it in the program of studies for the youth of their day under the foregoing stated values, it must be said in due recognition of their services that to them one must now apply the saying: "The evil that men do lives after them." The claim for history as a discipliner of the mind carried in its wake implications of a method of teaching that has done more harm than good to the cause of history as a school subject. In order to discipline their minds, pupils were required to memorize text-books and memorize long lists of dates and events—two practices that hung around a long time after their futility had been acknowledged.

The undesirable effects of the patriotic, moral, and religious values claimed for history by the fathers of history as a school

---

[1] W. F. Russell, "Early Teaching of History in Secondary Schools," *History Teacher's Magazine*, V (1914), 203 f.

subject in this country were in the realm of subject-matter rather than of method. To account for the emphasis on the value of history to inculcate patriotism it is necessary to recall the fact that the generation before the Civil War produced George Bancroft, who, as the reader will recall, was the Father of American history and the founder of the patriotic school of historical writing and interpretation in this country. While Bancroft did not write books used as texts in the schools, he must have set the pace for those who did write them. It should not be inferred, however, that it was a bad thing during the eighteen thirties, forties, and fifties to inculcate the spirit of patriotism in the hearts of those enrolled in the schools. The vicious aspect of the whole matter is found in the fact that history was written for the purpose of making patriots rather than for the purpose of portraying the truth. There seems to be no reason why the process could not have been reversed. Certainly patriotism based on truth is more to be desired than patriotism based on half-truth or untruth.

What has been said above applies quite as forcibly to the moral and the religious values which the early advocates of history as a school subject enunciated. Textbooks in history reflected these values. They were written according to the dictates of the ethical school of historical writing and interpretation. Their authors were followers of Thucydides and forerunners of James Anthony Froude, the English historian, who maintained that history is a voice forever sounding across the centuries the laws of right and wrong.

Two of the values claimed for history as a subject of study during the eighteen thirties, forties, and fifties are yet to be considered. They are the citizenship and leisure-time values. As pointed out above, the specific value of history for the making of good citizens has never been objectively determined.

But neither can it be asserted on the basis of objective evidence that history has a contribution to make to a program of citizenship training. As long as this situation remains, those who believe that history plays an important rôle in training in citizenship will not cease to fight for its retention in the program of studies.

Unlike all of the other values claimed for history in the foregoing discussion, the leisure-time value can and has been demonstrated by means of objective data. Studies of withdrawals from public libraries and of what children read when left to their own choosing show conclusively that history forms a large and important part of what may be termed leisure-time reading. If pupils on leaving the schools possessed a genuine and abiding interest in historical literature, the leisure-time value alone would, in the opinion of some, be enough to justify the time that has been and is now spent on history in the schools. The fathers of history as a school subject, in suggesting that the subject furnishes abundant opportunity for the profitable use of leisure time, probably built more wisely than they knew.

THE VALUES DURING THE GENERATION FOLLOWING THE CIVIL WAR

During the two decades following 1860 there seems to have been a relapse in the interest in history as a subject of study in the schools. The people of the United States both North and South were so busy making history that they had little time to devote to its claims as a school subject. Had they known during the eighteen seventies what is now known concerning the subject of desertion during the Civil War they probably would have been more concerned over ways and means of making a higher type of citizen than the deserters demonstrated. Deserting one's country in a time of grave need has always been considered unimpeachable evidence that desirable citizenship qualities were lacking in the deserter. The fact that the number of deserters reached a total of about 200,000 out of 1,556,678 enlistments in the Union army and about 104,000 out of 1,082,118 enlistments in the army of the Confederacy[2] is ample evidence that, judged by this one standard alone, the schools in which the soldiers had received the meager training possessed by most of them must have been weak in their training for citizenship. Even though those in charge of the schools were not conversant during the eighteen seventies with the foregoing facts, they were not wholly unaware of the need for concentration on the fundamental aspects of the history of the nation and began to seek ways and means of making a firmly united country. More emphasis in the schools on the history and government of the country was one of the ways they advocated to produce a generation in which another Civil War would be unlikely.

In making a case for history as a school subject the generation following the Civil War made few, if any, advances over the generation that had fought the war. The two values on which most emphasis was placed between 1870 and 1900 were the disciplinary and moral, both of which had been put forward by those who were instrumental in placing history in the program of studies a generation previous. Of these two values the disciplinary held almost absolute sway during the eighteen seventies and eighties. Between 1870 and 1890 all subjects in the curriculum were under its domination. The new subjects such as music, drawing, gymnastics, language lessons, natural science, and manual training, which knocked at the door of the school for admittance during these decades, were always

[2] Ella Lonn, *Desertion During the Civil War*, p. 226. New York: The Century Co., 1928.

asked the question, What is your disciplinary value? When admitted into the program of studies, these subjects were all too frequently taught as though they had no value other than the disciplinary one. Speaking of the grip that the disciplinary notion had on teachers in the early eighteen nineties a Herbartian said: "The idea of mental discipline, of training the faculties, is so ingrained into all our educational thinking that it crops out in a hundred ways and holds our courses of study in the beaten track of formal training with a steadiness that is astonishing." [3]

Probably no greater calamity could have befallen the subject of history than this falling into the grip of the disciplinary notion. Not that the idea is entirely void of value; but the ways of history are not wholly its ways. In the hands of a teacher who worshipped at the shrine of learning by rote, history became a memory subject pure and simple, even more so than it had been prior to 1860. The tirades that have been invoked against history as a school subject from 1870 down to the present hour have in a large measure been centered on the evils for which the disciplinary notion in the realm of history teaching has been responsible.

The other value of history as a school subject which received attention, especially during the eighteen nineties, was the moral. Its indefatigable protagonists were the American Herbartians, of whom there was a goodly number during these years. History as a school subject owes a great debt to these faithful followers of the great German pedagogue. As hinted in the quotation above, the Herbartians were untiring opponents of the prevalent practices of considering history a disciplinary subject. Furthermore, they placed history at the head of the list of subjects best suited for the accomplishment

[3] Charles A. McMurry, *Elements of General Method*, p. 45. Bloomington, Ill.: Public School Publishing Co., 1892.

of the chief end of all education according to their belief, namely, the formation of moral notions in children. And finally, their acceptance of United States history as a subject *par excellence* for moral educative purposes greatly increased the interest of school people in this field. Thus it will be seen that the influence of the Herbartians was advantageous to history in three ways: (1) in diluting the detrimental influence of the worshippers of formal discipline; (2) in placing history at the head of their list of subjects of study; and (3) in creating a following for United States history in the elementary grades.

While the two foregoing values of history as a school subject held the center of the stage during the decades of the 1880's and 1890's, other values such as the intellectual, the patriotic, the citizenship, and the cultural had their assiduous proponents. Two values among those proposed prior to 1860 were not emphasized during the period under review. These were the religious and the leisure-time. When education became secularized as it did after 1860, the religious element passed out of the content of the public school curriculum. So, it was only in the parochial schools that the religious value of history was held in high regard. With respect to the leisure-time value it may be said that in the midst of recovering from the Civil War, the panics of 1873 and 1893, and the filling up of the Great West, there was little thought given to provisions for leisure-time activities.

Of the values that played minor rôles during the eighteen eighties and nineties, three deserve consideration beyond mere mentioning. The patriotic value of history as a school subject was frequently proclaimed at educational gatherings. Some held that it was mainly at the altar of history that patriotism fed her fires. This contention, when accepted as it was by many well-meaning persons, certainly did a great deal to enhance the cause of history in the schools. When an appeal was made for more time for history in the program of studies on the basis of its patriotic value, few could or wished to resist the appeal, giving little thought to the possibilities inherent in it of exploiting history. Those who wished to use history as a tool to make patriots probably believed that the sun sends forth its heat and light primarily for the benefit of mankind and .that the moon shines, as some one has remarked, "solely for happy lovers." These individuals evidently accepted such a definition as, "History is anything that history is good for" and belonged to the patriotic school of historical writing and interpretation.

The citizenship and the cultural values of history as a school subject were less in evidence during the eighteen eighties and nineties than was the patriotic. The cultural value was proclaimed by those who considered history a branch of polite literature and also by the opponents of the formal subjects which so largely monopolized the time of the pupils in those days. The cultural-value advocates desired to use history to inculcate a broad, intelligent, and human sympathy. They wished to add "and done" to Matthew Arnold's statement to the effect that the great source of culture is the best things that have been thought and said. Parkman and Macaulay were the historians most read and studied by those who believed that history should contribute in a large way to the cultural education of the race.

The citizenship-value of history as a school subject had its staunch supporters in the 1880's and 1890's just as it had had before the Civil War, and has had since 1900. It is easy to believe that this claim for history greatly enhanced its prospects as a school subject at a time when it needed vigorous

support to make substantial headway. While no one seemed
to be able to specify the qualities of a good citizen, it was felt
that in some unexplainable way history had large value in
the making of something of which no one knew the chief
characteristics.

THE VALUES DURING THE FIRST TWO DECADES OF THE PRESENT CENTURY

During the two decades following the year 1900 considerable
attention was given to the values of history as a school subject
both by educators and by specialists in history. The educators
emphasized such values as the disciplinary, the auxiliary, the
moral, the patriotic, the cultural, the leisure-time, and the
citizenship, just as they had done during the two decades before 1900. The Herbartians of the eighteen nineties found an
able exponent of their claims for history as a purveyor of
moral lessons in G. Stanley Hall, whose influence on education during the decades under review was outstanding. As late
as 1911, Hall wrote relative to the value of history: "For school
purposes, as for Carlyle, history should be to teach the infinite
difference between good and bad, to set forth, even if in loud
colors, the law of right and wrong, justice and injustice." [4]
In this antiquated view of the value of history, Hall had
many followers. What he wrote on any topic received a hearing. So when he spoke as he did above on the value of history,
there was sure to be a hearty response from his readers.

While Hall and the Herbartians had their followers in their
advocacy of the moral value of history, there were those who
voiced a protest against using history for moral ends. As
early as 1908 a specialist in history and the teaching of history
wrote: "The importance of ethical standards and the need of

[4] *Educational Problems*, II, 290. New York: D. Appleton & Co., 1911.

ethical stimulus in our modern life can be denied by no one; the expediency of 'whitewashing' history to secure them may well be doubted." [5] That Johnson was moved to make this statement indicates that he as an authority on the teaching of history was conscious at that date of the pressure in favor of the moral value of history. That this pressure remained throughout these two decades is indicated by the following remarks of another specialist in history and the teaching of history: "To justify the teaching of history on the ground that it is valuable in stimulating patriotism or inculcating ethics is pernicious. When either practice is followed, the temptation to wrest the truth so as to point the moral is well 'nigh irresistible.'" [6]

It will be observed that the word "patriotism" is used in the quotation above. Because of the fact that the United States participated in the World War during the second of the decades under review, the pressure to make history serve the cause of patriotism was at its height. Even the history specialists succumbed to it in a measure. They were called upon to justify the entrance of the United States into the war to the enlisted men and to the prospective buyers of Liberty Bonds, as well as to create a friendly feeling for England and a hatred for Germany. The pamphlets now on file furnish documentary evidence of how completely some of them repudiated their historical training and capitulated to the God of War.

Much the same claims were made for the auxiliary, the cultural, the leisure-time, the disciplinary, and the citizenship values of history as a school subject during the two decades after 1900 as had been made during the preceding twenty

5 Henry Johnson, "The Problem of Adapting History to Children in the Elementary School," *Teachers College Record*, IX (1908), 348.
6 H. C. Hill, "History for History's Sake," *Historical Outlook*, XII (1921), 311.

years. History after 1900 was still expected to make large contributions to a better understanding of many topics in literature, geography, and natural science. It was still hoped that
it would make the pupil acquainted with the best that the
past had produced—thus giving him culture. It was also
believed that it would cultivate in him a discriminating taste
for substantial historical reading, thereby supplying a worthwhile leisure-time activity. It was even believed by some that
it would discipline the imagination, reasoning, memory, and
judgment; and that it would develop constructive and interpretive power, teach how to use books, extract substance from
the printed page, and systematize facts. The large emphasis
given to the disciplinary value of history during these two
decades is traceable to the influence of the report of the
Committee of Seven of the American Historical Association.
It will be recalled that this value loomed large in the values
of history proclaimed by this Committee. The citizenship
value, the last one mentioned above, was neglected during
these years, the tendency being to state values in a more specific way. Merely to claim that history is valuable in the making
of a good citizen was stating the matter in terms too general
for those who dealt in such specifics as disciplining the
imagination and gaining power in the systematization of facts.

Certain values of history appeared between 1900 and 1920
that could be termed new—new in the sense that little or no
emphasis had been placed upon them before. These were the
social, the explaining-the-present, and the historical-mindedness values—all the products of the time in which they arose.
The emphasis on the social value of education called forth the
slogan "Education for Social Efficiency." In order to be in
tune with the time those interested in history as a school subject made large claims for it as an instrument in the training

for social efficiency. The current-event mind, a product of the World War, accounts for the explain-the-present value; and the scientific spirit which had been hovering over history for two or more decades prior to 1910 in this country caused its devotees to advocate the historical-mindedness value. Just as in Gilbert and Sullivan's comic opera "The Mikado," the punishment of offenders was made to fit the crime, so it was with the values of history between 1900 and 1920. They were made to *fit* the *time*.

Those who advocated the social value of history said that it was possible through the right kind of instruction in history to help the pupil become socially intelligent, socially sympathetic, and socially active. To be socially intelligent it was necessary for the pupils to have a knowledge of the ideals, standards, traditions, modes of thought, and actions of the social man. This knowledge, as claimed by some, history was capable of furnishing in an amount unequaled by any other subject. It was also maintained by those who advocated the social value of history that historical knowledge makes for social solidarity. The contacts that pupils get through history with the struggles, failures, hardships, and successes of their own group and groups other than their own was supposed in some way or other to make them socially sympathetic. They were to be made socially active through the acquiring of the social spirit. Some named it social insight and power. Whatever designated, it was expected that the one possessing it would recognize and assume his social duties and sacrifice his own individual good to the welfare of his neighborhood, his state, and his country, which, in fact, was another way of saying that one of the values of history is to produce good citizens.

The advocates of the explain-the-present value of history and the historical-mindedness value became so numerous about 1915 that one could almost speak of them as composing schools of values of history as a school subject. Commenting on this matter in 1914 one writer very aptly remarked:

"At the present time there are two groups or schools of history writers and history teachers, and these two schools are radically and sometimes almost unforgivingly opposed to each other. The older school, which may be termed the conservative, reactionary, stand-pat school, says that history should be studied for history's sake. Some of this school say that the primary, others say that the *only*, object at which the teacher of history should aim is to impart as much knowledge of the history of the *past* as possible; that the function of history teaching is not to enable the pupil to understand or appreciate his social environment and the problems of his own time. These say that such a function is wrong because it is making the study of history bear almost wholly upon the present and the future—wrong because it is always drawing attention to what we are to become. . . .

"In very recent years another school of history writers and history teachers has arisen, which may be termed the insurgent, progressive, radical school. The point of view of this school is fundamentally different from the view of the older school. The newer school says study the past, know the facts of the past, study the things that have been, but *what* things and why? Just *because* the things of the past *have been?* Just because we wish to lay claim to being 'cultured,' 'educated' beings? 'No! No!' This newer school says: study the past, but don't stop *right* there. Study the past not simply to know the past *because* it is the past, but study the past so as to know how the present has come to be. Don't stop there even, says this recent school, but go a step further, and study the *present,* so as to understand the life that now *is.* Study the past and the present so that we may intelligently analyze the present and its problems. This school believes that historical facts or events are comparatively of little value unless they have a bearing upon the present world of thought and action. The real function of history teaching according to the new school is to develop *constructive* and *interpretive power* in order that we may rightly judge contemporaneous problems, movements, institutions, and public leaders. We are to study history not for history's sake, but for our sake and for our children's sake." [7]

While the foregoing is a somewhat overdrawn statement of the two conflicting views on the value of history as a school subject, it does admirably set forth the issue between them. As a rule the history specialists belonged to what is termed the "old school" in the quotation. The educators made up the so-called "new school," which had able leadership in the Dean of American Philosophers, Professor John Dewey, whose statement of their case ran as follows:

"The segregation which kills the vitality of history is divorce from present modes and concerns of social life. The past just as past is no longer our affair. If it were wholly gone and done with, there would be only one reasonable attitude toward it. Let the dead bury their dead. But knowledge of the past is the key to understanding the present. History deals with the past, but this past is the history of the present. An intelligent study of the discovery, explorations, colonization of America, of the pioneer movement westward, of immigration, etc.,

[7] J. Madison Gathany, "The Reconstruction of History Teaching," *History Teacher's Magazine,* V (1914), 223.

should be a study of the United States as it is to-day: of the country we now live in. Studying it in process of formation makes much that is too complex to be directly grasped open to comprehension. Genetic method was perhaps the chief scientific achievement of the latter half of the nineteenth century. Its principle is that the way to get insight into any complex product is to trace the process of its making,—to follow it through the successive stages of its growth. To apply this method to history as if it meant only the truism that the present social state cannot be separated from its past, is one-sided. It means equally that past events cannot be separated from the living present and retain meaning. The true starting point of history is always some present situation with its problems."[8]

The last sentence in this quotation struck the keynote of the matter. The philosophy which is implied in it was accepted by a goodly number of the educators of the time, many of whom attempted to put it into practice with results more or less unsatisfactory.

Those who supported the historical-mindedness value of history were the worshippers of history as a science—a view of history which was in no sense new in 1916. It had been prominent in the universities since the late 1870's and early 1880's, being exported from the German universities. Its early practitioners in this country were Henry C. Lea, John Bach MacMaster, and Henry Adams. Historiography has been different in the United States since these men produced their monumental works. The spirit of their writings soon became the pervading one. Subsequent writers were fired by it to produce works of a similar nature. So it thus came about that a new value of history as a school subject arose and those who

[8] *Democracy and Education*, p. 250 f. New York: The Macmillan Co., 1916.

supported it believed (1) that young people could be made historically-minded; (2) that citizens could be produced who would habitually take the long rather than the short view of current happenings; and (3) that it was possible by means of history to make time-thinkers rather than space-thinkers. They fully realized the dangers of the myopic vision of the current-eventist to whom the trials and tribulations of the present loom large, because of his inability to view them in historical perspective.

The question "What is historical-mindedness?" might with propriety be asked at this point of the discussion. In fairness to its advocates, one of them is permitted to give the answer.

"Historical-mindedness is the mental attitude of the historian in search for truth. It is the attitude which recognizes things as becoming, which sees in past and present continuity, growth, evolution. It is the attitude of mind required for weighing historical evidence and determining its value; which insists on knowing whether a document or relic be genuine; which inquires as to who said such-and-such, what opportunities he had for knowing, what ability he had for relating, what motives caused him to record the tale. In short, historical-mindedness is a frame of mind characterized by inquisitiveness, open-mindedness, eagerness to know the truth, no matter what it be."[9]

THE VALUES SINCE 1920

Two tendencies are noticeable in the discussions of the values of history during the period since 1920. The first of

[9] H. C. Hill, *op. cit.*, p. 312.

these is the stating of the values in terms of three of the major objectives of secondary education proposed in 1918 by the Commission of the National Education Association on the Reorganization of Secondary Education. These objectives were (1) worthy use of leisure, (2) citizenship, and (3) ethical character.[10] Of these three, most emphasis was placed on the value of history in character training. While some attention was given to the citizenship and leisure-time values, it cannot be said that they got as much attention during the years since 1920 as they got during the two decades just prior to this date. With respect to the character-forming value of history, it was claimed that the subject "instills in the mind of the student high ideals, teaches morality by stimulating thought and interest in moral behavior of men and races, develops a healthy philosophy of life, and thus aids in the formation and development of character." Similar statements appear more or less frequently after 1920 in the literature on the values of history as a school subject. These statements and the interest shown in the character-development value of history are explained by reference to the general wave of interest in character education that swept over the country after 1925, culminating in February, 1932, in the publication of a yearbook on character education by the Department of Superintendence of the National Education Association. The committee that had charge of this publication gave history and the other social sciences a favored seat in the front row of subjects possessing great value in character training.

The other noticeable tendency in the discussions of the values of history as a school subject during the period since 1920 was that of specificity in the statement of values. For

[10] *Cardinal Principles of Secondary Education.* Department of the Interior, Bureau of Education, Bulletin, 1918, No. 35. Washington, D. C.: Government Printing Office, 1918.

example, specific claims such as the following are frequently
met in the discussions: (1) History is a valuable medium for
demonstrating the futility of war and the blessings of peace.
(2) History is a valuable tool for use in developing a spirit
of altruism and understanding in order to throttle unhappy
provincialism and enhance an ever extending spirit of co-
operation. (3) History is valuable for use in advancing the
cause of world peace by enlisting the good will of the pupils
to all peoples through a rational and sympathetic study of their
history. (4) History is a powerful instrument for the creation
of an internationally-minded citizenry. (5) The supreme
value of history is found in the possibilities inherent in it
of making the existing state of things intelligible.

In fairness to this last value, explaining the present, it should
be said that much more emphasis was placed on it in the discussions than on the other four named above. More specific
ways of stating it are: (1) History aids one in his efforts to
understand and appreciate the present and in solving contemporary problems pertaining to sociology, economics, and
government. (2) History supplies the knowledge of general
movements necessary for estimating the significance of present-day institutions and current happenings. (3) History aids
one in his attempt to understand the nature, purpose, and
organization of our present-day political life.

This heavy emphasis on the present caused some alarm
among the historians. They were afraid that the background
necessary for effective work in history would be neglected.
If one keeps in mind the emphasis on the teaching of current
topics and the enthusiasm for courses in modern history, which
was running riot during the early 1920's, one can account for
the alarm among the historians. Occasionally one meets a
protest against so heavy an emphasis on the present on the

part of these specialists. For example, in a general discussion of the value of knowing the past one of this group said:

"The very practical man may say that the study of the past has no vital bearing on the present unless it happens to be the very recent past, that it is much more important to be acquainted with the affairs of the world at the present day. But I would put forward [the following] reason why this acquaintance with present-day affairs, without a historical background, is inadequate. . . . Human life is essentially growth and progress in time, and if you only take a view of the world as it is at the present moment it is like taking a photograph of a scene in a play and taking that to represent the whole drama. Drama lies essentially in action, and therefore a photograph of a single scene cannot give the essence of a drama. In the same way the study of history is the study of progress, of continuous life and growth in time; actually that growth is continuous and the present cannot be separated from it. Although particular problems and conditions change from one period to another, every period grows out of the period before it, and the actual continuity of events in history is proved most of all by those movements in history which have been most deliberately an attempt to repudiate the past."[11]

The foregoing list of values of history does not exhaust the categories. For purposes of discussion the remaining ones are classified under three general headings: (1) guidance values, (2) conceptual values, and (3) habits-skills-abilities-attitudes-understandings-appreciations developing values. This last long and cumbersomely named value is the offspring of the

[11] G. F. Hudson, "World History," *The Mid-Pacific*, XXXIX (1930), 163.

traditional disciplinary value. Instead of talking about training the memory, developing the imagination, the reasoning,
and the judgment as was the custom prior to 1915, writers
without special training in history had much to say during
the 1920's about developing desirable habits, skills, abilities,
attitudes, and understandings. An explanation of this about
face in stating certain values of history is found in the acceptance by many persons in the field of education of the
specific-habit psychology. This particular type of psychology
drew its strength largely from experiments relating to the
transfer of training that were carried on between 1890 and
1928. While these experiments were enhancing the cause of
the specific-habit psychology, they were also discrediting in
the minds of some the doctrine of formal discipline. In
spite of evidence to the contrary, statements to the effect that
the transfer experiments had "completely demolished" the
doctrine of formal discipline appeared in more than one textbook in education. The contrary evidence referred to above was
revealed in a study of ninety-nine experiments in the transfer
of training made between 1890 and 1928.[12] Out of this number nearly one-third showed considerable transfer; one-half
appreciable and apparently significant transfer; 8 per cent,
very little; and less than 5 per cent, no transfer. In spite of
findings of this nature, education accepted the dictum of the
less than 5 per cent. Why education accepted this dictum was
admirably explained by one who did not accept it when he
said:

"It was essential at the time that the doctrine of formal discipline should be discredited, for it stood in the way of a very

12 Pedro Orata, *The Theory of Identical Elements*, p. 41. Columbus, Ohio:
Ohio State University Press, 1928.

definite type of progress—namely, the upward expansion of
mass education. To open the high schools and colleges to
large, unselected groups, the monopoly of the older curriculum
had to be broken down. The best defense of the older curriculum was the doctrine of formal discipline as founded upon
the faculty psychology, and education grasped at every straw
that promised to help in breaking down this defense. It
found in the interpretation given to the transfer experiments,
not a feeble straw, but a veritable battering ram. The line of
defense was completely levelled; or, to change the figure, the
doctrine of formal discipline soon had the appearance of being as extinct as the dodo." [13]

When values of history were stated in terms of specific-
habit psychology they ran as follows: (1) History helps
pupils form the habit of weighing evidence and of considering all sides of a question before coming to an historical
judgment and (2) History aids pupils to establish the habit
of correct thinking and sound methods of study as well as the
habit of acting as worthy and useful group members and as
intelligent citizens. These, of course, do not exhaust the list
of habits that history was supposed to inculcate. They are
listed merely to illustrate how values of history in one realm
of the specific-habits psychology were stated. The value of
history in helping pupils acquire certain skills was similarly
stated. For example, among the skills which history was supposed to help pupils acquire were the following: How to read
and take notes, to make an outline, to organize and retain
information, to use books of reference, to make a bibliography,
to secure and weigh evidence, to read periodical literature, to

[13] W. C. Bagley, *Education, Crime and Social Progress,* pp. 129 f. New
York: The Macmillan Co., 1931.

interpret maps and graphs, and to present a subject convincingly to a group. Long lists of abilities, attitudes, ideals, and understandings similar to this one appeared during the latter part of the period under review. In the realm of history, the specific-habit psychology was certainly by no means dormant.

The conceptual value of history related to certain fundamental concepts which were supposed to function directly in one's every-day life. Concepts such as "continuity of civilization," "unity of humanity," "uniformity of human motives," "brotherhood of man," "dependence of the present on the past," "responsibility of the present for the future," "relation of the individual to society," and "dynamic and evolutionary character of human activity and social organization" were some of those that the proponents of the conceptual value of history suggested.

There remains for consideration what has been denominated the guidance value of history. Those who defended this value said that history is to the group or social mind what memory is to the individual. Another way of stating the same thought is, "A people unconscious of its history is like a man smitten with the loss of memory, who wanders about aimlessly till he comes to grief." The truth of these statements is fully realized, said one writer,

"If we think for a moment what life would be worth without the memory, we can get some idea of what civilization today would be worth without history and a knowledge of history. What would friendship mean without memory of past struggles in common? What would home mean without recollections of the common family life? What would one's home town mean without a memory of the life one had lived there? It is precisely in this way that history contributes to

make one at home in the world, and a person with a knowledge of history has quite the same advantage in proving
himself to be a useful citizen as the man of experience has in
any community."[14]

Those who advocated the guidance value of history were
fond of quoting the famous saying attributed to Patrick
Henry: "I have but one lamp by which my feet are guided
and that is the lamp of experience." These advocates maintained that history is capable of supplying the experience
needed by the group for its guidance. Some even held that it
is dangerous for a group not to get the experience that a
knowledge of history gives. "It is just as dangerous not to
know about history as it is not to know about electricity,"
said one. In speaking to this same point another remarked:
"No man is fit to be entrusted with the control of the *Present*,
who is ignorant of the *Past*, and no *People* who are indifferent to their *Past* need hope to make their future great."[15]

In closing this historical view of the values claimed for history attention is called to two general aspects of the matter
which have escaped notice thus far. These are (1) the possible harmfulness of history and (2) the need for truth in history. On the harmfulness of history one writer has commented as follows:

"Perhaps my subject is even more generally history itself,
as I take as a starting point the question which is sometimes
asked: 'What is the value of history?' I conceive that as far
as history is concerned, certain individuals find its study in-

[14] C. R. Fish, *Why Study History*, p. 4. Madison, Wis.: Extension Division
of the University of Wisconsin, 1921.
[15] Quoted by Marcus W. Jernegan, *The American Colonies, 1492–1750*, p. v.
New York: Longmans, Green and Co., 1929.

teresting or amusing or a generally satisfying occupation, that
it has a certain value to that extent, but there still remains the
question, 'Is it of any use from the point of view of the world
at large, of practical affairs, and of the general conduct of human life?' The answer to that question is not at first obvious,
because it is quite possible to make out a case against history
to show that it is not merely useless but can be positively
harmful. I think in recent years it has been possible to observe a great deal of harm which has been done by too much
reading of history. It has tended, especially in politics of modern Europe, to accentuate national enmities and to perpetuate
old feuds. History has been commonly taught as national history, for the glorification of one's own country, for the raking
up of ancient grievances and wrongs which would have been
better forgotten, and for the continuation of attitudes of mind
which have no relation to present-day problems."[16]

The only comment that needs to be made on the matters
mentioned in this quotation is that the harm is not inherent
in history, but is found in the twisting of the truth for a
specific purpose. If those who are guilty of using history for
harmful ends would about face and stick to the position presented in the following quotation, they would achieve useful
rather than harmful results.

"Truth is truth, no matter whom it hurts. If a nation has
been less completely right than it should have been, people
ought to know it and avoid such untoward policies in the
future. If the embattled farmers of the American Revolution
were not altogether united against the tyrant, and were less
heroic sometimes than national pride would have them, the

16 G. F. Hudson, *op. cit.*, p. 161.

truth ought to be told so that the real virtue and heroism of some may be better appreciated. In short, if the lessons of history are to be fully appreciated, both sides of every question should be understood; the foibles and follies as well as the heroism or righteousness must be understood and there is no room for that commodity nowadays known as 'bunk.' Undoubtedly a better understanding among nations and improved prospects for international peace would result if this ideal could be attained. Doubtless a better judgment of men and events in our own country can be had if the full truth is told even though it involves a certain amount of debunking of national gods."[17]

II

THE ENTRANCE OF HISTORY INTO THE SCHOOLS

Compared with reading, writing, arithmetic, geography, Latin, algebra, geometry, and English, history was late in entering the elementary and secondary schools as an independent subject of study. Certainly not until after 1830 was history given an autonomous place in the elementary program of studies that deserves much more than a passing notice. It got a fairly early start in the private schools and academies, being found in some of them before the Revolution and was among the subjects offered in the first high school. Its changing status in these schools before 1860 is portrayed below, attention first being directed to its entrance into them through other subjects.

[17] George E. Anderson, "Reality in History," *Commonweal*, VII (1928), 1063.

THE TEACHING OF HISTORY IN CONNECTION WITH OTHER SUBJECTS

Before history was generally accepted as an independent subject of study in the elementary and secondary schools it was taught to some extent in connection with geography, reading, and the classics. As early as 1784 *Elements of Geography,* by Jedidiah Morse appeared. This was a textbook for use in the elementary schools. It devoted some of its space to the history of each country and state treated therein. In the edition of 1788 was incorporated an account of the United States after the Revolution, comprising nearly twenty pages and written by Noah Webster. In later editions of this volume a considerable amount of space was devoted to the historical aspects of its content. Other geographies, especially those published prior to 1820, used material from history as a part of their content. So wherever geography was taught in the elementary schools between 1784 and 1830 there was apt to be some history taught also.

What was true in the case of geography was equally true with respect to reading. After 1785 there were available textbooks in reading for use in the elementary schools which contained many selections of an historical nature. One[18] of the earliest of these books contained a short history of the settlements of the United States and a selection of speeches connected with the struggle of the colonists for independence. Other readers of the period followed the example set by Webster. So in due time the Bible and the catechism were displaced by reading books which contained the stories of deeds and incidents in the early life of the new nation.

18 *An American Selection of Lessons in Reading and Speaking* by Noah Webster, 1785. This was Part III of his *Grammatical Institutes of the English Language,* Parts I and II having appeared in 1783 and 1784.

The practice of presenting historical material through the channel of reading was kept up for almost a generation after the appearance of Webster's *Selections* in 1785. In due time, however, there began to appear protests against the practice. As early as 1827, in connection with a review of Joseph Worcester's *Elements of History, Ancient and Modern,* the reviewer commented as follows on the practice of teaching history as an adjunct to reading.

"It is a pity, we think, to see money expended for English Readers and Columbian Orators, which might be laid out to so much better advantage on a history of Massachusetts or of the United States, or on a judicious compend of general history. If practice in reading, as an exercise, is the object, these books will furnish it, and in a more intelligible and pleasing form. We do hope the time will soon cease when intelligent parents will feel content to let their children leave school, unacquainted with Geography and History; when by a little effort, and a very little expense, such a vast addition might be made to the elements of early and useful knowledge."[19]

While history as an autonomous subject did not appear among the studies pursued by pupils in the Latin Grammar School, historical content was not entirely neglected in these schools. Greek and Roman antiquities, chronology, and the works of Greek and Roman historians were frequently found among the subjects pursued in this type of school—*Græcæ Historiæ Epitome, Viri Romæ, Cæsar's Commentaries,* and *Xenophon's Anabasis* being generally read in the original. So it seems to be a fact that, although history did not universally

[19] Quoted by J. F. McManis, "History as a Study in the American Elementary School," *Educational Bi-Monthly,* VI (1911), 152.

appear in the elementary and secondary schools as a separate
subject until after 1830, a good deal of history was actually
taught in connection with geography, reading, and the classics.

HISTORY IN THE EARLY ACADEMIES, PRIVATE SCHOOLS, AND HIGH SCHOOLS

Although history did not appear as an independent subject
in the colonial grammar schools, the town, or the common
schools of the period, it was early found among the list of
subjects offered in private schools and academies. For example, an academy was organized by the Catholic Church in
1745 at Bohemia, Cecil County, Maryland, the curriculum of
which embraced the subjects of reading, writing, arithmetic,
Latin, algebra, and history.[20] Furthermore, when the Philadelphia Academy opened in January, 1751, history was among
the subjects in its program of studies. Individuals who oper-
ated private schools in Boston, Philadelphia, and New York
City during the colonial period advertised history as one of the
many subjects taught in their schools. It was offered in one of
these schools in Boston as early as 1734, in Philadelphia in
1759 and in 1770, and in New York City in 1772, 1774, and
1779.[21]

History was included in the list of subjects offered in the
evening school, even before the middle of the eighteenth century.[22] In view of these established facts, the following oft-

[20] J. R. Young, "Relation of the Church and Clergy to Education in the
American Colonies," p. 3. Unpublished Doctor's thesis, University of Chicago,
1916.

[21] R. F. Seybolt, *Source Studies in American Colonial Education: The
Private School*, p. 66. University of Illinois Bulletin, Vol. XXIII, No. 28, 1925.
Urbana, Ill.: University of Illinois, 1925.

[22] R. F. Seybolt, *The Evening School in Colonial America*, p. 32. University
of Illinois Bulletin, XXII, No. 31, 1925. Urbana, Ill.: University of Illinois,
1925.

quoted statement of Noah Webster does not seem to portray conditions as they generally existed:

"When I was young, the books used were chiefly or wholly Dilworth's Spelling Books, the Psalter, Testament, and Bible. No geography was studied before the publication of Dr. Morse's small books on that subject, about the year 1786 or 1787. No history was read, as far as my knowledge extends, for there was no abridged history of the United States. Except the books mentioned, no book for reading was used before the publication of the Third Part of my Institute, in 1785. In some of the early editions of that book, I introduced short notices of the geography and history of the United States, and these led to more enlarged descriptions of the country. In 1788, at the request of Dr. Morse, I wrote an account of the transactions in the United States, after the Revolution; which account fills nearly twenty pages in the first volume of his octavo editions."[23]

After the Revolutionary War was over considerable interest in history as a school subject arose. This interest began early to appear in the academies, history being one of the subjects taught in Phillips Academy at Exeter in 1799. In 1818, the English Department of this same academy included history, elements of ancient history appearing on the list of subjects for the second year and elements of modern history, particularly of the United States, on the list for the third year.[24] Pittsfield Academy included history in its program of studies in 1822 and Leicester Academy did the same in 1824. Even the Boston Latin School introduced differentiated history in 1814, using

[23] "Schools as They Were Sixty Years Ago," *Barnard's Journal of Education,* XIII (1863), 123 f.
[24] A. J. Inglis, *Principles of Secondary Education,* pp. 178 f. Boston: Houghton Mifflin Co., 1918.

Valpy's *Chronology of Ancient and English History* as a text.[25] When the English Classical School (later the English High School) opened in Boston in May, 1821, history was among the subjects required, general history and the history of the United States being included in the subjects pursued by boys in the two lowest classes. When the Girls' High School of Boston opened in 1826, United States history was one of the subjects pursued therein. In 1827, Massachusetts passed a law requiring the teaching of United States history in the high schools of towns of 500 families and over. At this same date general history was required by law in the high schools in towns of 4000 inhabitants and over.[26] So it appears from this scattering evidence that history had been given a place in the curriculum of the secondary school before the end of the third decade of the nineteenth century. The elementary school had to wait a few years for this addition to its curriculum except in a few instances.

EVIDENCE OF THE EXISTENCE OF HISTORY IN THE SCHOOLS
1830–1860

The evidence of the existence of history in the elementary and secondary schools of the United States during the years between 1830 and 1860 is much more abundant than for the period prior to 1830. In fact it was during the generation after 1830 that history actually entered the schools as an independent subject. In presenting the evidence to substantiate this statement, attention is first directed to the elementary-school level.

As early as 1832 United States history was reported as one of the subjects pursued in the schools of 52 towns in the

25 W. F. Russell, *loc. cit.,* p. 312.
26 A. J. Inglis, *The Rise of the High School in Massachusetts,* p. 72. New York: Bureau of Publications, Teachers College, Columbia University, 1911.

state of New York. Two years later this number of towns had doubled.[27] For the year 1842 in this same state the reports from 43 of the 59 counties revealed the following situation with respect to the number of pupils pursuing history, arithmetic, and geography. Of the 173,384 pupils in attendance, 6973 were pursuing history, 64,705, arithmetic, and 41,051, geography. The per cents pursuing these subjects in the order named were 4.02, 37.31, and 23.67.[28] In his report for Courtland County the Deputy Superintendent said: "History, I regret to say, is a new study in most of our schools. Its importance, especially the history of our own country, to those who are hereafter to assume the duties of freemen, need not be insisted on. I trust the succeeding winter will find it introduced into all the leading schools of the country."[29] For the years 1844, '45, '46, and '47 the number of pupils in the elementary schools pursuing certain subjects were reported. Table I shows the number and per cent pursuing history, arithmetic, and geography during these years. The differences in the per cent of pupils pursuing history and the other two subjects indicate that history was in the stage of infancy in the common schools of New York in 1847. Generally speaking, about one pupil out of every twenty was introduced to the subject during the years represented in the table. From three to twelve times as many pupils were pursuing arithmetic during these years and from five to eight times as many were pursuing geography.

Because of the fact that state school systems were in the process of formation during the thirty years prior to 1860,

---

[27] Walter J. Gifford, *Historical Development of the New York State High School System*, p. 34. Albany, N. Y.: Lyon Co., 1922.

[28] *Annual Report of the Superintendent of Common Schools*, State of New York, 1843, p. 7.

[29] *Ibid.*, p. 127.

there were few states that had a system of reporting comparable to that in New York. While data on the number of pupils pursuing history on the high-school level at different dates exist for Massachusetts, they seem to be lacking for the

TABLE I

NUMBER AND PER CENT OF PUPILS IN THE ELEMENTARY SCHOOLS OF THE STATE OF NEW YORK PURSUING HISTORY, ARITHMETIC, AND GEOGRAPHY DURING THE YEARS INDICATED*

YEAR AND TERMS	NUMBER OF PUPILS IN AT-TENDANCE	Pursuing History		Pursuing Arithmetic		Pursuing Geography	
		NUMBER	PER CENT	NUMBER	PER CENT	NUMBER	PER CENT
1844							
Winter.....	313,283	13,141	4.19	108,346	34.58	65,983	21.06
Summer....	187,169	8,248	4.40	61,657	32.94	6,637	3.55
1845							
Winter.....	225,540	14,161	6.27	117,075	51.90	74,788	33.15
Summer....	209,802	9,094	4.33	76,991	36.69	69,142	32.95
1846							
Winter.....	227,760	13,953	6.12	137,585	60.40	75,510	33.15
Summer....	211,747	10,767	5.08	90,636	42.80	82,161	38.80
1847							
Winter.....	270,119	16,197	5.99	172,606	63.90	112,682	41.71
Summer....	247,833	11,133	4.49	113,692	45.87	95,228	38.42

* *Annual Report of the Superintendent of Common Schools for the State of New York,* 1845, pp. 36 and 48; *ibid.,* 1846–47, Abstract of Statistical Information, B and C and pp. 63 and 69; *ibid.,* 1848, pp. 75 and 81.

elementary-school level—the probable reason being that history was not required by law in the elementary schools of this state until 1857. At least one other state besides New York required for a few years after 1854 reports on the number of pupils in the public schools pursuing certain subjects. This was Ohio. Even before 1854, the year of the first report of the Commissioner of Common Schools, a report was made by the Secretary of State on the number of pupils pursuing history in the common schools of this state. In 1848, there were but 26 pupils out of 3978 pursuing the subject during the winter term.[30] Beginning with the year 1854 and for a number of years afterwards, systematic reports were made by

TABLE II

NUMBER AND PER CENT OF PUPILS IN THE PUBLIC SCHOOLS OF OHIO PURSUING HISTORY, 1854–69*

YEAR	TOTAL ENROLLMENT	NUMBER OF PUPILS PURSUING HISTORY	PER CENT OF PUPILS PURSUING HISTORY
1854	456,191	4,108	.90
1855	551,939	6,327	1.14
1856	561,315	5,824	1.03
1857	603,347	6,759	1.12
1858	611,720	8,136	1.33
1859	600,034	8,261	1.37
1860	685,177	9,298	1.35
1861	717,726	9,627	1.34
1862	723,669	10,395	1.43
1864	794,920	8,159	1.02
1865	702,552	6,039	.85
1866	728,990	8,134	1.11
1867	704,767	11,086	1.57
1868	731,772	11,086	1.51
1869	740,382	11,754	1.58

* Based on the reports of the State Commissioner of Common Schools and Superintendent of Public Instruction for the years indicated.

those in charge of the schools to the Commissioner of Common Schools. In 1854, there were four types of public schools in Ohio, namely, high schools, German and English schools, colored schools, and common schools. When the reports from these schools were published they were combined, thus giving what was going on in all of the public schools. Table II contains the number and per cent of pupils in the four classes of schools pursuing history during the fourteen years follow-

[30] *Annual Report of the Secretary of State on the Condition of Common Schools of the State of Ohio for the year 1848,* Table between pp. 34 f.

ing 1854. Beginning with 1855, the increase in the per cent of pupils pursuing history during the fourteen years prior to 1870 was miserably small. The generation living in Ohio during the 1880's and 1890's must have known little history, considering the fact that probably less than two in each one hundred persons ever pursued the subject during their school days. There is no reason to believe that the situation in Ohio was not representative of that in most of the states in the Union in 1860.

In presenting the evidence of the existence of history in the secondary schools between 1830 and 1860 attention is first directed to the academies in the state of New York, because the reports on subjects pursued in these schools are more complete than in any other state, due to the early centralizing of the system of education in this state.

During the fifteen years following 1825, one hundred subjects appeared for the first time in the program of studies in the academies of New York. Of the subjects that found a place among those taught during these fifteen years, general history and the history of the United States attained a prevalency of 75 to 100 per cent. Other subjects attaining the same prevalency were algebra, astronomy, botany, chemistry, geometry, surveying, and mental philosophy.[31] According to the findings of one investigator, the date of the first appearance of certain fields of history in these academies was as follows: general history, 1787; chronology, 1826; Roman antiquities, 1827; history of the United States, 1827; Grecian antiquities, 1828; ecclesiastical history, 1830; history of New York, 1831; biography, 1831; history of England, 1841; history of France, 1841.[32]

[31] Walter J. Gifford, op. cit., p. 20.
[32] Charles F. Wheelock, Secondary Education, pp. 186 ff. Albany: University of the State of New York, 1922.

The situation in 1834 with respect to three of the fields listed above was as follows: In the 63 academies reporting for this year, general history was studied in all of them, United States history in 46, and the history of New York State in 2. There was a total of 5309 pupils exposed to general history, 3812 to United States history, and 283 to the history of New York.[33] There are available for certain years between 1825 and 1860 data relating to the number of academies that offered most of the fields of history listed above. These data show that general history was well entrenched in the academies of New York during the twenty-five or thirty years prior to 1860. The same is true of the history of the United States which was offered in over 50 per cent of the academies after 1830. Roman, Greek, and Biblical antiquities, ecclesiastical history, chronology, the history of New York, and the history of England were also offered with varying frequencies.[34]

In connection with the foregoing facts the observation should be made to the effect that the academies in New York and probably elsewhere for that matter admitted pupils of an elementary-grade level. In fact there were found in them pupils whose ages ranged from six to eighteen or over. About two-thirds of the 1490 pupils in nineteen academies were pursuing elementary subjects in the academies of New York in 1807 and in 1819. Until late in the nineteenth century from one half to three fourths of the pupils in the academies of New York were enrolled in elementary subjects. This fact increases the number reported above of pupils on the elementary-grade level who could have been exposed to history prior to 1860.

[33] *Documents of the Senate of the State of New York,* II (1835), 17–21 and 32–36 of Document No. 70.
[34] William F. Russell, *loc. cit.,* p. 314, and *Sixty-Ninth Annual Report of the Regents of the University of the State of New York,* pp. 298 and 304.

Such then was the situation with respect to history in the academies in one state prior to 1860. Inasmuch as state-wide reports on the subjects offered in academies of other states are not available for these years, one cannot say with exactness what was going on in them. There seem to be no valid reasons for believing, however, that what was true of the academies in the state of New York between 1825 and 1860 was not also in a measure at least true of the other 6000 plus academies in the country at large. Be this as it may, there seem to be no available data to prove or disprove it.

The state of Massachusetts got an early start in the high-school field. From one high school in 1821, the number increased to at least eighteen by 1841. The attention given to history in some of these high schools between 1834 and 1840 may be inferred from the following facts. In 1834, 64 towns of 261 reporting claimed that United States history was offered in their schools; in 1837, this number had increased to 209 out of 294 reporting; in 1838, it was 177 out of 298; in 1839, 178 out of 301; and in 1840, 167 out of 304. The towns claiming to offer history other than United States numbered 29 in 1834, 94 in 1837, 78 in 1838, 93 in 1839, and 62 in 1840.[35] According to Inglis, there were never over eighteen high schools in the state of Massachusetts between 1834 and 1841. So when the number of towns offering history prior to 1841 exceeded eighteen, all above this number were teaching the subject in the elementary grades. Granting that there were eighteen high schools in existence at each of the foregoing dates, there would remain a fair sized number of towns offering history in the elementary grades. This fact should be added to the evidence previously presented respecting history in these grades.

For the year ending in 1842 there are available data on the

[35] A. J. Inglis, *The Rise of the High School in Massachusetts*, p. 75.

number of pupils in Massachusetts actually pursuing certain
high-school subjects. According to Mann's sixth report there
were at this date 10,177 pupils studying United States history
and 2571, general history. Mann said that he was reporting on
the number of pupils in the state who were engaged in studies
above the elementary or statutory course prescribed for the

TABLE III

NUMBER AND PER CENT OF PUPILS ELECTING HISTORY IN THE
HIGH SCHOOLS OF EIGHT TOWNS IN MASSACHUSETTS AND
CONNECTICUT, 1837–59 *

TOWN	YEAR	TOTAL ENROLL-MENT	NUMBER ELECTING HISTORY	PER CENT ELECTING HISTORY
Northampton, Mass.........	1837	247	89	36.0
Haverhill, Mass............	1842	72	26	36.1
Worcester, Mass.	1846	213	70	32.9
Lowell, Mass..............	1847	185	50	27.0
Newburyport, Mass.........	1847	207	126	60.9
Hartford, Conn.............	1856	220	55	25.0
New London, Conn.. .... (Young Ladies High School)	1859	85	35	41.1
New London, Conn......... (Boys High School)	1859	91	40	43.9

* W. F. Russell, *loc. cit.*, p. 313, and Silas Hertzler, *The Rise of the Public High
School in Connecticut*, pp. 206 f. Baltimore: Warwick and York, Inc., 1930.

lowest grade of schools.[36] There is no implication here that
all of the 10,177 pupils studying United States history were
attending high schools. Evidently many not in organized high
schools were included. Data similar to the foregoing do not
exist for other years. There are, however, some scattered facts
on specific towns in Massachusetts and Connecticut. In Table
III these facts are assembled for eight of these towns. History
was by no means an unpopular subject in the high schools of

[36] *Sixth Annual Report of the Board of Education Together with the Sixth
Annual Report of the Secretary of the Board*, p. 55.

the towns represented in this table, the per cent of pupils electing the subject ranging from 25 to almost 61. The years in which the subject could be elected in high schools of certain towns in Massachusetts about 1860 varied from the first to the fourth inclusive. While a few schools offered United States, general and ancient history in the last two years most of the offerings were in the first two. The facts show that history had certainly not invaded the last year of the high schools in Massachusetts to any great extent prior to 1860.[37]

There were a few high schools in existence in states other than Massachusetts and Connecticut in 1860. History was included in the offerings of some of these schools. The Central High School of Philadelphia was offering Roman, Greek, United States, and English history in 1845 as well as the history of civilization. In 1857, ancient history was offered in the first year of the high school of Columbus, Ohio, during the first of three terms in the classical, regular and scientific courses. Modern history was offered in each of these courses during the second term of the first year. Chronology was offered in the classical course during the second and third terms of this year. No United States history was offered.[38] The practice of including short courses in history in the program of studies was not wholly confined to this subject, there being at this date one-term courses in geology, mineralogy, physical geography, uranography, botany, moral science, political economy, constitutional law, and mental philosophy. Those who made the high-school courses during the 1850's seem never to have heard of the saying "A little learning is a dangerous thing."

While the foregoing data relative to the existence of history in the elementary and secondary schools prior to 1860 are

[37] A. J. Inglis, *The Rise of the High School in Massachusetts*, p. 95.
[38] State Commissioner of Common Schools of Ohio, *Fourth Annual Report for the Year 1857*, p. 189.

somewhat piece-meal, they do show that history had actually entered these schools before the beginning of the Civil War. Furthermore, there is some evidence not presented above. This relates to the legal aspects of history in the schools, relative to which it may be remarked that five states passed laws before 1860 requiring the teaching of history in their schools. These states were Massachusetts, Vermont, New Hampshire, Rhode Island, and Virginia. The first two of these made the teaching of national history compulsory in 1827. In Massachusetts the law applied to all towns containing 500 families or households; in Vermont, to each organized town. In both of these states the history of the United States was specified. In 1857, Massachusetts legislated United States history into all of her elementary schools and added general history to the required subjects in the high school. New Hampshire and Rhode Island soon fell in line with Massachusetts and Vermont, the former in 1846 prescribing history as a subject of study for all high schools and the latter about ten years later. Virginia, the only southern state to legislate history into her schools prior to 1860, provided in 1849 for teaching the history of the United States and of Virginia in the district school.[39] So one need not hesitate to conclude on the basis of the laws respecting the teaching of history passed by these states that, if the zeal of the reformers had not outrun public interest and demand, the history of the United States at least was well entrenched in the schools of five states ere the outbreak of the Civil War. However, judging from the opinion of a foreign observer about 1850, the ideal of the reformers had not been fully attained at this date. Commenting on the study of history in the schools of the United States the gentleman said:

[39] Bessie Pierce, *Public Opinion and the Teaching of History*, pp. 6–9. New York: Alfred A. Knopf, 1926.

"History cannot, either, be said to be studied with much zeal, and this is easily explained. The Americans are a new people, and as yet their history has but a few great epochs. It is true, on one occasion when I was present in a grammar school in Boston, I heard the pupils examined in the intricate passages of English history relating to the wars of the White and Red Roses, and such other events; but, nevertheless, history does not hold the same rank among the studies in the schools, as does geography, for instance. In connection with the historical studies some instruction is given in the political laws of the country; but this is a subject on which every man in America will soon obtain information without the aid of the school."[40]

THE CONTENT OF SCHOOL HISTORY PRIOR TO 1860

On account of the fact that courses of study had not come into use prior to 1860, the nature of the content of school history must be sought in the textbooks then current. During the time that history was taught in conjunction with reading and geography, its content was intricately bound up with these subjects. After 1783, the authors of reading books very generally began to introduce historical material into their texts. The incidents receiving most attention were those which took place during the Revolutionary War. The first attempt to introduce material of an historical nature into the reading books, as has been pointed out elsewhere, was that of Noah Webster. In 1785, the third part of his *A Grammatical Institute of the English Language* appeared. The main title of this part was *An American Selection of Lessons in Reading and Speaking, Calculated to Improve the Mind and Refine the Taste of Youth, and Also to Interest them in Geog-*

[40] P. A. Siljeström, *Educational Institutions of the United States*, pp. 221 f. London: John Chapman, 1853.

raphy, History, and Politics of the United States. The following extract from the Preface of this little volume reveals Webster's purpose in the inclusion of historical material.

"In America, it will be useful to furnish schools with additional essays, containing the history, geography, and transactions of the United States. Information of these subjects is
necessary for youth, both in forming their habits and improving their minds. A love of our country, and an acquaintance with its true state, are indispensable. They should be
acquired early in life. . . .

"In the choice of pieces, I have been attentive to the
political interests of America. I consider it as a capital fault
in all our schools, that the books generally used, contain subjects wholly uninteresting to our youth; while the writings
that marked the revolution, which are perhaps not inferior
to the orations of Demosthenes and Cicero, and which are calculated to impress interesting truths upon young minds, lie
neglected and forgotten. Several of those masterly addresses
of Congress, written at the commencement of the late revolution, contain such noble sentiments of liberty and patriotism, that I cannot help wishing to transfuse them into the
breasts of the rising generation. . . ."

In an edition of this work, published in 1790, Webster
added a short history of the settlement of the United States
as well as some geographical descriptions. Among the historical selections appearing in the early editions were "Adventures of General Putnam"; "General Washington's Resig-
nation"; "A Singular Instance of Patriotism"; "Story of
Logan, a Mining Chief"; "History of Pocahontas"; "History
of Columbus"; "Narrative of the Captivity of Mrs. Jemina

Howe, taken by the Indians at Hinsdale, New Hampshire, July 27, 1755"; "Dr. Belknap's Address to the Inhabitants of New Hampshire on the Close of his History of that State"; "Orations of Dr. Joseph Warren"; "Dr. Ames' Speech in Congress on the Subject of Executing the Treaty Between the United States and Great Britain"; "Discovery and Settlement of North America"; and "Brief History of the Late War in America." Besides the foregoing, there were in some of the early editions of the work the first petition of the Continental Congress to the King of Great Britain, the declaration concerning the taking up of arms, Governor Livingston's address, and orations on the anniversary of Independence. About half of the material in these editions dealt with the history and geography of the United States and the addresses delivered in connection with the struggle for indepedence. It would be difficult to over-emphasize Noah Webster's influence on history as an independent subject in the schools prior to 1860. Subsequent writers of reading books followed his example of introducing matter pertaining to United States history as a part of the reading matter for youth. So in the course of time stories of deeds and incidents in the life of the United States were substituted for the Bible and the catechism as reading material for use in the schools.

Passing mention should be made of the fact that Noah Webster's influence on the content of history in the schools extended down into the lower levels of instruction. His *The Little Reader's Assistant* was a work intended for beginners in reading. This book was patterned somewhat after his *American Selections,* the first part containing a collection of incidents relating to the early settlers and the Indians. It was in this book that Webster helped to push historical material down into the lower levels of instruction and to create an

interest among young children in the history of their country. The facts should also be recorded here that Webster was
the author of the historical material appearing in the 1788
edition of Moore's geography and the author of a *History of
the United States,* which appeared in 1832.

The practice inaugurated by Noah Webster in 1785 of in-

TABLE IV

THE HISTORICAL CONTENT OF FOURTEEN SETS OF READERS BY
GRADES *

GRADES	NUMBER OF PAGES OF CONTENT MATERIAL	NUMBER OF PAGES OF HISTORICAL MATERIAL	PERCENTAGE OF HISTORICAL MATERIAL
Grade III..................	3932	397.92	10.1
Grade IV..................	4379	769.87	17.6
Grade V..................	5096	987.34	19.4
Grade VI..................	5446	1151.84	21.2

* Ethel May Praeger, "Historical Materials in Readers for the First Six Grades of
the Elementary School," p. 22. Unpublished Master's thesis, University of Chicago,
1929.

troducing historical material into a school reader was still
prevalent in 1929. During this year a study was made of
the historical material in fourteen sets of readers intended
for the first six grades of the elementary school. The results
of this investigation pertaining to Grades III–VI are revealed
in Table IV, which shows that the emphasis on historical material in readers for Grade VI was somewhat heavier than in
the lower grades. In some of the readers for this grade almost one-third of the content was of an historical nature, the
average for the fourteen readers examined being 21.8 per
cent.

The content of history in the lower schools at least prior
to 1820 was also bound up with that of geography, a practice
advocated in some quarters at the present time. The fact has

already been mentioned that Jedidiah Morse's *Elements of Geography* contained considerable historical material—some of which was furnished by Noah Webster. Besides the historical material supplied by Webster, Morse's book, especially in the editions after 1800, contained a good deal of material of an historical nature intermingled with the geographical material, as well as a chronological table at the end. In the 1806 edition this chronological table of remarkable events, discoveries, and inventions covered eighteen closely-printed pages. "The creation of the World and of Adam and Eve, 4004 B.C." was the first event in the table. The last was "1805 Sept. War Commenced between Russia and Austria on the one part and France on the other." [41]

Subsequent texts in the fields of geography followed the pattern set by Morse more or less closely. In his *An Introduction to Ancient and Modern Geography,* published in 1813, J. A. Cummings made considerable use of historical material. Cummings felt that geography should be used as an aid to history, especially ancient geography. In the Preface of his work he said in substance that in reading ancient history, geography was almost indispensable, in that it gave a view of the places recorded and excited additional interest in studying events and facilitated the recollection of them. He held that the history of any country without a knowledge of its geography lost its reality and to youth appeared visionary. Cummings and Morse seem to have been the co-fathers of the integrating idea in the fields of geography and history which some writers of present-day texts are trying to put into practice.[42]

[41] J. F. McManis, *loc. cit.,* p. 153.
[42] See *Our Country Past and Present, a Unified Course in the History and the Geography of the United States for Elementary Schools,* by W. L. Nida and V. L. Webb. Chicago: Scott, Foresman and Co., 1930.

Even though history was taught for a number of years in the early history of this country in conjunction with reading, geography, and the classics, there finally came a time when it was able to maintain an autonomous existence. In working for the establishing of history as an independent subject of study in the schools, the textbook writers and the practical educators of the 1820's and 1830's were, in the opinion of certain present-day reformers, disregarding the Biblical injunction which says, "Hold fast to that which is good." In the judgment of these reformers, to those who were responsible for the securing of an independent existence for history in the elementary school one should apply the famous saying, "Striving to better, oft we mar what's well." Whether marring or improving "What's well," textbooks in history began to find an independent place in the schools soon after 1820, especially those in general and United States history.

It would take this discussion too far afield to include here a list of the textbooks in history published prior to 1860. The exact number of these publications seems never to have been determined. An inkling of the activity along this line may be attained from the data in Table V. Evidently there was no scarcity in textbooks in history during the forty years prior to 1860.

There are some data on the extent of the use of a few of the books represented in Table V. For example, in the state of New York, the number of towns using in the common schools either the *History of the United States,* by Salma Hale, first published in 1826, or *History of the United States,* by C. A. Goodrich, first published in 1822, was as follows: in 1825, 6; in 1828, 38, in 1830, 83; in 1834, 174; in 1836, 220; in 1837, 244; and in 1838, 288. Inasmuch as there were 813 towns reporting in 1838, the number not reporting history is much larger than the number that did.[43] In the common schools of Ohio, four schools of the 157 reporting in 1848 used Salma Hale's *History of the United States;* three, Jesse Olney's

TABLE V

TEXTBOOKS IN HISTORY PUBLISHED OR USED IN THE UNITED STATES PRIOR TO 1860 *

DATE	United States		General		Ancient		English		Miscellaneous		Total	
	TEXTS	EDITIONS	TEXTS	EDITIONS	TEXTS	EDITIONS	TEXTS	EDITIONS	TEXTS	EDITIONS	TEXTS	EDITIONS
Before 1801...	2	3	5	19	1	1	0	0	1	1	9	24
1801–1810..	2	6	7	21	2	3	0	0	0	0	11	30
1811–1820..	3	3	13	30	6	41	3	48	0	0	25	122
1821–1830..	20	111	18	42	13	29	2	2	5	6	58	190
1831–1840..	19	59	15	69	3	3	2	2	2	2	41	135
1841–1850..	23	45	20	31	16	42	4	5	9	11	72	134
1851–1860..	24	26	23	38	19	33	12	14	11	14	89	125
Not dated....	14	14	13	13	18	18	5	5	5	5	55	55
Total........	107	267	114	263	78	170	28	76	33	39	360	815

* William F. Russell, *loc. cit.*, pp. 316 f. The table reads as follows: "Before 1801 there were published two texts in United States history, which ran into three editions before 1861; five texts in general history, which ran into nineteen editions," etc., etc.

History of the United States; two, Emma Willard's *History of the United States;* two, C. A. Goodrich's *History of the United States;* and one, Marcus Willson's *History of the United States.*[44] In 1834, *Elements of General History,* by A. F. Tytler, was used in 27 of the academies of New York and *History of the United States,* by Salma Hale, in the same number. At this same date *History of the United States,* by

43 *Annual Report of the Superintendent of Common Schools,* State of New York, 1840, p. 103.
44 *Annual Report of the Secretary of State on the Condition of Common Schools of the State of Ohio* for the year 1848, p. 33.

C. A. Goodrich, was used in 18 academies in this state; *Compend of History*, by Samuel Whelpley, in 11; *Elements of History, Ancient and Modern*, by J. E. Worcester, in 9; *Peter Parley's Universal History*, by S. G. Goodrich, in 7; *History of the United States*, by Emma Willard, in 5; and *History of the United States*, by William Grimshaw, in 2; Five other texts also had a limited use at this date.[45]

For the school year 1854–55, fifty-five texts in history were reported in use in the academies of New York, 23 in general history, 13 in United States history, 10 in Roman antiquities, and 9 in Grecian antiquities. Some of those used most frequently in general history were: (1) *Universal History in Perspective, by Emma Willard,* in 50 academies; (2) *Outlines of Ancient and Modern History,* by Royal Robbins, in 30 academies; (3) *Outlines of General History,* by Marcius Willson, in 26 academies; (4) *Peter Parley's Universal History,* by S. G. Goodrich, in 24 academies; and (5) *Elements of History, Ancient and Modern,* by J. E. Worcester, in 6 academies. No one of the remaining twenty-three texts in general history was used in more than three academies, so the foregoing ones practically made up the list in use in this field in 1854–55. The texts in United States history most generally used in these academies during this year were: (1) *History of the United States,* by Emma Willard, in 51 academies; (2) *History of the United States,* by C. A. Goodrich, in 35; (3) *History of the United States,* by Marcius Willson, in 32; and (4) *Primary History of the United States,* by J. B. Lossing and *History of the United States,* by Salma Hale, each in 5. Five of the remaining eight texts on the list were used in but one academy each. In the fields of Grecian and Roman antiquities *Man-*

[45] Gedeon Hawley, *Documents of the Senate of the State of New York,* II (1835), 41, 46, and 49 of Document No. 70.

ual of Greek Antiquities and *Manual of Roman Antiquities,* both by C. Anthon were far in the lead of all other texts, the former being used in 22 academies and the latter in 26. *Roman Antiquities,* by A. Adam, was used in 22 academies. The remainder of the nineteen texts reported in these fields was used in 39 academies, the number of academies using any one of them ranging from one to five.[46]

The character of the content of some of the texts in United States history in use in the academies of New York has been determined by one investigation in terms of the emphasis on the political, military, and social and economic material. The percentage of space devoted to each of these three types of material by eight texts published prior to 1860 is shown in Table VI, which indicates that the texts in use prior to this date placed a very heavy emphasis on political and military history, a practice that subsequently became very hard to live down. These books also originated certain practices with respect to organizing the material which have lasted until the present time. In writing a critical review of the texts in United States history that had appeared up to 1845 an author of one of them said:

"Two different plans of arrangement have been adopted by American historians, in treating of our early colonial history. One plan is that of particular or individual history; the other, that of common, or general history. The former, technically speaking, is history ethnographically arranged, or according to nations and tribes; the latter is history chronographically arranged, in which events in different nations are brought together and given in the order of time in which they oc-

[46] *Sixty-Ninth Annual Report of the Regents of the University of the State of New York,* pp. 317 f. and 321 f.

curred. The first of these methods, as applied to our own country, pursues the history of each colony separately down to the period of the French and Indian War, in 1754, after

TABLE VI

EMPHASIS ON POLITICAL, MILITARY AND SOCIAL AND ECONOMIC MATERIAL BY EIGHT TEXTS IN UNITED STATES HISTORY PUBLISHED PRIOR TO 1860.*

TEXTBOOKS	Percentage devoted to		
	POLITICAL	MILITARY	SOCIAL AND ECONOMIC
C. A. Goodrich, *History of the United States*.................	36.7	37.7	25.6
S. G. Goodrich (Peter Parley), *A Pictorial History of the United States*........................	32.8	56.2	11.0
J. Olney, *A History of the United States*........................	46.6	43.8	9.6
William Sullivan, *History of the United States of America*.........	47.7	43.4	8.9
C. B. Taylor, *A Universal History of the United States of America*....	38.5	49.6	11.9
Noah Webster, *History of the United States*.................	41.5	25.5	34.0
Emma Willard, *Abridged History of the United States*..............	44.7	48.3	7.0
Marcius Willson, *History of the United States*.................	50.3	43.6	6.1
Average........................	38.4	44.3	17.2

* Earl Rugg, *Twenty-second Yearbook* of the National Society for the Study of Education. Appendix, p. 320. (No data are given concerning the exact edition used in each case.)

which, the separate and individual history of each colony is abandoned, and all are united in one common history. This arrangement has been adopted by Hale and Olney; and by Frost, with respect to all the colonies except those of New England.

"The other plan of arrangement carries along together the contemporary events which happened in different colonies, and thus as far as possible, blends the whole in one common history. This latter plan has been adopted by Goodrich [C.A.], Grimshaw, Mrs. Willard, and in the Pictorial History of S. G. Goodrich, the author of Peter Parley's Tales.

"It is obvious that the history of a colony may be learned much more readily where the events are narrated in one unbroken series, and in one chapter, than where the series is frequently interrupted, and the events are found dispersed through a dozen chapters. Let any one search for the colonial history of Virginia in the volumes of Bancroft, and he will find a little here, and a little there; and unless he should read the three volumes through, he will be likely to omit some portion of Virginian history. Let it not, however, be supposed that we depreciate the value of Bancroft's History. We regard it as the best, for its purpose, that has yet been written. In our view, it is well adapted to those already familiar with the separate history of each colony, but exceedingly unfit for a schoolbook. Circumstances in the history of one colony are often narrated by Bancroft in connection with those of another colony, for the purpose of elucidating some important principle. They are links taken from the chain of particular history, and, for especial purposes, formed into new series; and unless the reader can restore them to their proper place, the histories to which they belong must appear incomplete and broken. More fully to show the faultiness of this mode of arrangement for a schoolbook, we refer to Mrs. Willard's History, and to Goodrich's Pictorial History, in both of which this plan is adopted.

"Of those histories that have adopted the other plan of arrangement, the well-known and early work of Hale yet stands pre-eminent in this particular, and greatly in advance of any of its competitors."[47]

The foregoing comments relate to the ways the texts were organized. The writer of the excerpt also took occasion to point out certain weaknessess in the textbooks he was reviewing. One of these weaknesses was inaccuracy, which was commented on as follows:

"The result of the examination given to eight of our most prominent school histories, shows a list of more than TWO HUNDRED AND FIFTY ERRORS; allowing for those that are repeated by different writers; and, of these errors, the most important are found in Mrs. Willard's Abridgement. A large number of those enumerated, consist of errors in dates; and when it is considered that comparatively few dates are found in most of our school histories, the number we have presented, of this class of errors, must appear surprisingly large. In numerous instances, erroneous dates might with justice have been inferred from the context, and from the order of narration; but these we have in most cases passed by. In no cases have we enumerated as errors, dates given accurately either in old style or in new. With one exception, that of the Pictorial History of Goodrich, the works reviewed have been before the public from nine and ten to twenty-five years; during which period abundant time has been allowed the authors and publishers for their correction. One of these works has recently made its appearance as 'Revised and enlarged from the one hundredth edition'; in which, however,

47 M. Willson, "A Critical Review of American Common School Histories," as embraced in a Report submitted to the New Jersey Society of Teachers and Friends of Education, at a quarterly meeting held March 7, 1845. A reprint from the *Biblical Repository* of July, 1845.

notwithstanding the revision, the old errors have been stereo-typed anew. If authors will not take the trouble to correct their own works, how much are they indebted to those who will do the labor for them!"[48]

In addition to the fault of inaccuracy the early texts in United States history were subjected to two other adverse criti-cisms, namely, too general in treatment and too dry and un-interesting in style. In order to account for the first of these adverse criticisms it is necessary to recall the fact that fol-lowing 1820 there spread over this country a Pestalozzian sense-training wave. In the field of history this meant empha-sis on local history. While some histories of a local flavor appeared after 1830 most of the texts in United States history that were published prior to 1860 were general in character, thus inviting the adverse criticism of the Pestalozzians. As to the dry and uninteresting style, especially of those texts writ-ten before the appearance in 1832 of S. G. Goodrich's *The First Book of History, Combined with Geography,* containing the history and geography of the Western Hemisphere, one reviewer said:

"They are not the books from which the youth of our coun-try can gain adequate impressions of their high-spirited ances-try. We believe they would deaden the spirit of patriotism rather than excite it. Much less would they deepen and re-fine it. But still they have the merit of corresponding pretty exactly to the demands of the teachers. . . . We feel that some highly gifted individual must seize this department of edu-cation and breathe through it the free and informal spirit which naturally belongs to American history. That individual

[48] *Ibid.* The texts reviewed were those written by Willard, Hale, Goodrich (C. A.), Olney, Webster, Grimshaw, Frost, and Goodrich (S. G.).

would rank in after ages as one of the creators of the American mind; for our political institutions will avail nothing to us, if they are not impregnated always by the same spirit that originated them." [49]

While the general content of history in the schools prior to 1860 was largely what was between the covers of the textbooks in use, the examination questions of the period actually embodied the areas on which emphasis was placed. Space permits but two examples of these questions, one in general and one in United States history.

In 1845 the first written examination was administered in the Boston grammar schools. The following is the set of questions used in history in the highest class. The questions were based on J. E. Worcester's *Elements of General History*.

1. What is history?
2. What are some of the uses of history?
3. Enumerate some of the sources of history.
4. What nations are among the first mentioned in history?
5. For what were the Egyptians distinguished?
6. For what were the Phœnicians distinguished?
7. Who was the founder of Babylon?
8. Who was the founder of the Persian empire?
9. Who were some of the most distinguished orators and poets of Greece?
10. Who was the founder of Rome?
11. What was the character of the early government of Rome?
12. Can you mention the names of the Roman emperors?
13. Can you give an account of the feudal system?

[49] *American Journal of Education*, II (1827), 743.

14. What were the purposes of the Crusades?

15. In what century was the great French Revolution, and who were some of the characters who figured in it?

16. What nation ruled Britain at the commencement of the Christian era?

17. Who were the Saxons, and how came they to invade Britain?

18. What do you understand by the Norman conquest?

19. What was the period of the Commonwealth in England, and who was the most distinguished character in it?

20. About what period did the first colonists come to New England, and what were the supposed motives for their leaving the mother country?

21. How long did they continue subject to the mother country, and what were some of the assigned reasons for throwing off their government?

22. When did the war of the American Revolution commence, and who were the allies of the Americans?

23. When was the present Federal Constitution formed, during or after the war of the revolution, and how many States accepted it at its formation?

24. About what period was the embargo laid by President Jefferson, and non-intercourse substituted for it?

25. About what period did the last war between Great Britain and the United States commence, and what were the causes assigned by the Americans for its declaration?

26. What do you understand by an embargo?

27. How many more members are there now in the Senate of the United States than there were at its first adoption?

28. What was the result of the invasion of Canada by the Americans in the last war?

29. What is chronology?

30. What are the eras most used in chronology?[50]

In 1857, candidates for admission to the Cincinnati, Ohio, high schools were required to pass the following examination in United States history:

1. Give a history of the capture of Louisburg.
2. Give an account of the capture of Quebec.
3. Give an account of the introduction of African Slavery.
4. Give an account of the "Declaration of Rights."
5. Give an account of the Mechlenburg Convention.
6. Give an account of the commencement of our Revolution.
7. By what body was Washington chosen Commander-in-Chief of the American forces? When? Where?
8. Give an account of Burgoyne's Expedition.
9. Give an account of Arnold's conspiracy.
10. When, where and by whom was the battle of the "Cowpens" fought?
11. After the Revolution, what government existed, and what was the state of the nation?
12. Give an account of the formation and adoption of our present Constitution.
13. What was the "Whisky Insurrection"?
14. Give an account of the Nullification in South Carolina.
15. Give an account of the Missouri Compromise.
16. Name the principal battles in which General Washington was engaged.
17. Give a history of the Black Hawk War.
18. Give an account of Burr's Conspiracy.

[50] *Circulars of Information of the Bureau of Education*, No. 1, 1885, pp. 199 f. John D. Philbrick, "City School Systems in the United States."

19. How does our nation at present compare with it at the close of the Revolutionary War, in extent, population, etc.?

20. Give a brief history of Ohio.[51]

The foregoing examinations illustrate the type from which history has been trying to extricate itself for at least three decades. It will be observed that the questions used in Boston slavishly followed the text and that those comprising the examination administered in Cincinnati were based largely on materials dealing with war. It is evident that those who were responsible for the questions in the Cincinnati examination expected a great deal from those seeking admission to the city's high schools. The time for writing this examination was limited to two hours. In this time a pupil was expected to write not less than fourteen historical accounts, besides answer six questions of a factual nature. There probably would be no congestion in our present-day high schools, if all those seeking admission to them were required to pass the Cincinnati examination of 1857 with a grade of not less than 75 per cent.

III

THE ESTABLISHMENT OF HISTORY AS A SUBJECT OF STUDY IN THE SCHOOLS, 1860–1900

During the last third of the nineteenth century history became firmly established in practically all of the secondary schools of the country as well as in the two top grades of the elementary school. During these same years the subject moved down into the intermediate and primary grades in

[51] *Fourth Annual Report of the State Commissioner of Common Schools to the General Assembly of Ohio* for the year 1857, p. 194.

some quarters. It was not, however, until after 1900 that history was generally found in the program of studies for the lower grades. There is an abundance of evidence to substantiate these statements. A select body of it is presented below, first for the secondary schools and then for the elementary grades.

EVIDENCE OF THE EXISTENCE OF HISTORY IN SECONDARY SCHOOLS
1860–1900

Specific evidence pertaining to the extent of the existence of history in the secondary schools of the country for the years between 1860 and 1890 is not available for all of the states. Few states during these years collected data on the number of pupils pursuing the various secondary-school subjects. When these data were collected they were not always tabulated in terms of the various grade levels. For example, the state of Ohio beginning in 1870 collected data for a number of years on the number of pupils in the public schools pursuing certain subjects. Unfortunately there is no way to determine from the reports how many pupils were enrolled in the high school and how many in the elementary school. Table VII contains certain data from the reports during the 1870's and 1880's. Inasmuch as general history was not taught in the elementary grades during these years it is safe to conclude that those pursuing this subject were enrolled in the high schools. Pupils in the elementary grades were included in the number and per cent of those pursuing United States history. This fact explains the large differences in favor of this subject over general history.

It is evident from the data in Table VII that history was not over-emphasized in the state of Ohio during the thirty years following 1870. Throughout these years the attention given to general history was very, very little, less than two pupils in a hundred pursuing it prior to 1898. While the per cent of

TABLE VII

NUMBER AND PER CENT OF PUPILS IN THE COMMON SCHOOLS OF OHIO PURSUING GENERAL AND UNITED STATES HISTORY, 1870–1900.*

YEAR	TOTAL NUMBER OF YOUTHS OF SCHOOL AGE	TOTAL ENROLL-MENT	Number of pupils pursuing History		Per cent of Pupils Pursuing History		Pursuing U. S. and General History	
			UNITED STATES	GEN-ERAL	UNITED STATES	GEN-ERAL	TOTAL	PER CENT
1870..	1,041,680	724,896	14,348	.....	1.97	....	14,348	1.97
1872..	1,073,274	708,800	16,962	.....	2.39	....	16,962	2.39
1873..	991,708	704,018	16,704	449	2.37	.06	17,153	2.43
1874..	985,947	707,943	18,316	1,531	2.58	.21	19,847	2.80
1876..	1,025,635	722,963	21,733	1,953	3.00	.27	23,686	3.27
1878..	1,041,963	740,194	25,817	1,260	3.48	.17	27,077	3.65
1880..	1,046,225	747,138	31,171	2,054	4.17	.27	33,225	4.44
1882..	1,081,321	751,101	36,746	2,561	4.89	.34	29,307	5.23
1884..	1,082,295	762,755	67,985	2,238	8.91	.29	70,223	9.20
1886..	1,101,358	775,149	89,137	6,532	11.80	.86	95,669	12.66
1888..	1,097,242	777,216	97,108	5,318	12.49	.68	102,426	13.17
1890..	1,123,895	797,439	133,689	6,590	17.74	.82	140,279	18.56
1892..	1,136,539	800,356	139,127	8,951	17.38	1.11	148,078	18.49
1894..	1,147,210	809,780	151,485	14,439	18.70	1.78	165,924	20.48
1896..	1,173,119	820,562	167,282	15,225	20.38	1.85	182,507	22.23
1898..	1,198,704	837,152	196,409	17,786	23.46	2.12	214,195	25.58
1900..	1,226,366	829,160	242,676	73,809	29.26	8.90	316,485	38.16

* Based on data from the annual reports of the Commissioner of Common Schools and the Superintendent of Public Instruction for the years indicated.

pupils pursuing United States history was almost fifteen times greater in 1900 than in 1870, the actual number pursuing the subject was never large when compared with the number that could have pursued it had all youths of school age been in school and given the opportunity. Notice the number of pupils of school age in column 1 of the table.

While data similar to those in Table VII for the state of

Ohio are not generally available, there has been collected material relating to the mere existence of history, without any regard to the number of pupils pursuing it, in the following

TABLE VIII

NUMBER AND PER CENT OF CERTAIN HIGH SCHOOLS IN THE
NORTH CENTRAL STATES OFFERING HISTORY, 1860–1900 *

FIELDS OF HISTORY	1860–1865 20 schools in 5 states		1866–1870 20 Schools in 7 States		1871–1875 20 Schools in 7 States		1876–1885 20 Schools in 8 States		1881–1885 25 Schools in 9 States		1886–1890 30 Schools in 9 States		1891–1895 40 Schools in 10 States		1896–1900 40 Schools in 10 States	
	NO.	%	NO.	%	NO.	%	NO.	%	NO.	%	NO.	%	NO.	%	NO.	%
Ancient	8	40	8	40	4	20	6	30	5	20	10	33	13	32½	15	37½
Medieval	3	15	..	..	1	5	1	5	1	4	5	17	..	..	2	5
Modern	6	30	2	10	3	15	3	15	1	4	5	17	1	2½	3	7½
United States	3	15	4	20	5	25	5	25	8	32	16	53	15	37½	18	45
English	3	15	2	10	..	..	5	25	8	32	13	43	14	35	20	50
French	..	..	..	..	..	..	..	..	..	..	1	3	2	5	4	10
General	3	15	9	45	11	55	10	50	18	72	17	58	25	62½	26	65
Universal	2	10	..	..	1	5	1	5	..	..	..	..	..	..	..	..
Outlines of history	..	..	..	..	1	5	2	10	..	..	..	..	1	2½	..	..
History of civilization	1	5	..	..	..	..	..	..	1	4	..	..	..	..	..	..
State	..	..	..	..	..	..	1	5	..	..	..	..	..	..	..	..
Political	..	..	..	..	..	..	..	..	..	..	..	..	5	2½	..	..
Economic	..	..	..	..	..	..	..	..	..	..	..	..	..	..	1	2½

* J. E. Stout, *The Development of High-School Curricula in the North Central States,* pp. 62–68. Chicago: University of Chicago Press, 1921. In 1860–65 there were two cases in which the field was not designated; in 1866–70, there were four such cases; in 1871–75, four; in 1876–80, three; in 1881–85, five; and in 1896–1900, two.

states for the years 1860–1900: Michigan, Iowa, Ohio, Illinois, Wisconsin, Kansas, Missouri, Indiana, Nebraska, North Dakota, Minnesota, and South Dakota. The situation with respect to history in certain high schools in these states between 1860 and 1900 is portrayed in Table VIII, which shows that thirteen fields of history were offered in the schools represented therein, those offered the most frequently being ancient, general, and United States history. The influence of the Sub-committee on History, Civil Government, and Political Economy of the Committee of Ten is probably shown in the attention given to English and French history during the 1890's.

So far the data with respect to the evidence of the existence of history in secondary schools between 1860 and 1900 have been in terms of groups of high schools. In order to get a little closer to the situation, data on the offerings in the field of the social sciences in certain individual high schools at different dates were assembled. Even though data concerning the social sciences other than history do not properly belong here, they are included to avoid repeating the list of cities elsewhere. It will be observed that in the accompanying tabular view are found some data not included heretofore. These concern the year in which the various fields of history were offered.

Counting all the different courses there are thirty-eight cases represented in the foregoing tabulation. Of these thirty-eight cases almost one-half offered history in the first year of the high school course; twenty-one, in the second year; and fourteen, in the third year. Little history was offered in the fourth year. Generally speaking the emphasis was on history during the first two years and social sciences other than history during the last two years. Subjects such as intellectual science, moral science, moral philosophy, and classical antiquities which appear in the tabulation were carry-overs from the period prior to the Civil War.

The foregoing tabular view portrays the history situation between 1865 and 1900 in individual high schools. The number of cases represented therein is too small to make generalizations for the country as a whole possible. There are, however, available for the 1890's data which evidence the

A TABULAR VIEW OF HISTORY AND OTHER SOCIAL SCIENCES IN THE HIGH SCHOOLS OF CERTAIN CITIES, 1859–1900*

CITY AND STATE	Years and Fields of History and Other Social Sciences Offered Therein			
	FIRST	SECOND	THIRD	FOURTH
1. Ann Arbor, Mich., 1859	United States	General	Intellectual and Moral Science	
2. Cincinnati, Ohio, 1862..........		Ancient Medieval	Modern	United States Constitution
3. Madison, Wis., 1863..........	United States		American	Moral science Political economy
4. Springfield, Mass., 1866				
a. English Course..........	English	English	Science of government	Moral science Political economy
b. Classical Course..........	Roman	Roman Greek		....
5. New Haven, Conn., 1866..........	Modern Ancient	Modern American	United States and Connecticut Constitutions	No fourth year

* Data gathered from Stout, *op. cit.*, and *Barnard's Journal of Education*, XIX (1870), 482–576.

A TABULAR VIEW OF HISTORY AND OTHER SOCIAL SCIENCES IN THE HIGH SCHOOLS OF CERTAIN CITIES, 1859–1900—CONTINUED

CITY AND STATE	Years and Fields of History and Other Social Sciences Offered Therein			
	FIRST	SECOND	THIRD	FOURTH
6. Free Academy, Norwich, Conn., 1866 a. College Preparatory Course	English		Roman Greek	
b. General Course	English		Greek	Moral philosophy Science of government
7. St. Louis, Mo., 1866			Ancient Roman Medieval Modern	United States Constitution
8. Louisville, Ky., Male High School, 1866	General	Government		Mental and moral science
9. Cincinnati, Ohio, 1867	General	General		Moral science United States Constitution

A TABULAR VIEW OF HISTORY AND OTHER SOCIAL SCIENCES IN THE HIGH SCHOOLS OF CERTAIN CITIES, 1859–1900—CONTINUED

CITY AND STATE	Years and Fields of History and Other Social Sciences Offered Therein			
	FIRST	SECOND	THIRD	FOURTH
10. Chicago, Ill., 1867 a. General Course		Universal		United States Constitution Political economy
b. Classical Course		Universal	Classical Antiquities	Classical Antiquities
11. Leavenworth, Kans., 1867	General	United States Constitution Political economy		Moral philosophy
12. Jacksonville, Ill., 1869	Ancient	Ancient Science of government	Moral philosophy	No fourth year
13. Waterloo, Iowa, 1870	History†		Moral philosophy	No fourth year
14. Cincinnati, Ohio, 1872	History	History		United States Constitution

† In three instances the field of history was not designated.

A TABULAR VIEW OF HISTORY AND OTHER SOCIAL SCIENCES IN THE HIGH SCHOOLS OF CERTAIN CITIES, 1859-1900—CONTINUED

CITY AND STATE	Years and Fields of History and Other Social Sciences Offered Therein			
	FIRST	SECOND	THIRD	FOURTH
15. Madison, Wis., 1872..........		General	English Civil government	
16. Chicago, Ill., 1872..........		General		Civil government Political economy
17. Oskaloosa, Iowa, 1876..........			General	United States Constitution
18. Columbus, Ohio, 1878..........		Ancient	Civil government	Political economy
19. Springfield, Ill., 1880..........	General		United States Constitution Political economy	
20. St. Louis, Mo., 1881..........			General	

A TABULAR VIEW OF HISTORY AND OTHER SOCIAL SCIENCES IN THE HIGH SCHOOLS OF CERTAIN CITIES, 1859–1900—CONTINUED

CITY AND STATE	Years and Fields of History and Other Social Sciences Offered Therein			
	FIRST	SECOND	THIRD	FOURTH
21. Auburn, Ind., 1882........	History		General	Civil government
22. Milwaukee, Wis., 1884....		General	Political economy English United States Constitution	
23. Morrison, Ill., 1888.......	United States	Medieval Modern	Ancient Civil government	No fourth year
24. Sandusky, Ohio, 1889.....			English	Greek Roman
25. Columbus, Ohio, 1889 a. General Literary Course.....		Ancient Medieval Modern		
b. English Course...........				United States
c. Business Course..........				General

A TABULAR VIEW OF HISTORY AND OTHER SOCIAL SCIENCES IN THE HIGH SCHOOLS OF CERTAIN CITIES, 1859–1900—Continued

CITY AND STATE	Years and Fields of History and Other Social Sciences Offered Therein			
	FIRST	SECOND	THIRD	FOURTH
26. Evanston, Ill., 1894				
a. Classical Course	English	Civics Ancient		
b. Latin-Scientific Course			General	
c. English Course			Political economy	General
27. Chicago, Ill., English High and Manual Training School, 1895		General	Political economy Civil government	
28. Jamestown, Ohio, 1896		General		Civil government United States
29. Columbus, Ohio (English and Commercial Courses), 1898	Civil government	General	General	History and civics
30. Appleton, Wis., 1900	Ancient French	English United States Constitution		Political economy

history situation throughout the country. These data concern the college entrance requirements in history and the per cent of secondary-school pupils pursuing history. Regarding the status of college entrance requirements in history during 1895–96 the United States Commissioner of Education once remarked as follows with respect to history and civil government:

"The requirements in history seem to be more varied than in any other branch of study. History of the United States is required by 306 institutions, civil government by 129, and state or local history by 9 institutions. General history is required by 127 institutions, history of Greece by 112, and history of Rome by 116. As a rule the institutions requiring the history of Greece also require the history of Rome. History of England is required by 57 institutions, and the history of France and of Germany by but 1." [52]

When one considers the fact that 70.85 per cent of 432 universities and colleges in the United States required in 1895–96 United States history for entrance and that of this same number of institutions 29.35 per cent required general history, 25.92 per cent the history of Greece, and 26.85 per cent the history of Rome, one has a basis for saying that by the time the year 1900 had come history as an independent subject of study in the preparatory schools of the land was firmly and almost universally established. This statement is further substantiated by certain data on history in the preparatory school in the country at large for the years between 1889 to 1900 to which attention is now directed.

In 1889 the United States Commissioner of Education began the collection of data concerning the number of pupils in each secondary school of the land pursuing certain subjects.

[52] U. S. Comr. of Educ., *Rep. for 1896–97*, I, 468.

These data were secured from both public and private secondary schools. While they are valuable sources of information hitherto unavailable, they have to be handled with extreme care, especially in the field of history. One difficulty in interpreting them as they relate to this subject is that of always knowing what history they include. Sometimes the blanks called for history only. At other times for history other than United States and United States history. Even when the blanks differentiated between United States and non-United States history, those tabulating the results did not always do so. For this reason one is never sure when reading the per cents of pupils pursuing history whether they include all history or merely non-United States history. On this matter the chief clerk in the Office of Education in 1932 ruled as follows: "The data prior to 1910 may exclude United States history but for 1910 and since they must include it." [53]

There are two other matters that one must keep in mind when pondering the data in Table IX. These are the number of schools included and the basis on which the per cents were calculated. With respect to the number of schools represented in the Commissioner's report for any given year, the fact that returns were never received from 100 per cent of the schools must be kept in mind. Furthermore, up to 1909–10 the basis for calculating the per cent of pupils pursuing a given subject was the total enrollment in all schools reporting. Using total enrollment as a basis was unfair for the reason that in many of the returns the item relating to number of pupils pursuing subjects was omitted. Because of these omissions the per cent of pupils pursuing any given subject in any given year are too low for the simple reason that all the schools failing to report on subjects pursued were counted as not offer-

[53] L. A. Kalbach in a personal letter to the writer under date of May 3, 1932.

ing them—an assumption without foundation. Beginning with and since the year 1909–10 the per cent has been calculated on the basis of the total enrollment in the schools reporting the number of pupils pursuing subjects. On this basis the per cent gives a true picture of the situation in the schools actually reporting on pupils pursuing subjects. The condition in those schools not reporting on the number of pupils pursuing subjects will never be known. If it were in general the same in them as in the schools reporting, the per cents in Table IX hold good for the total enrollment in all of the schools reporting; and, if in those schools making no reports at all, the number of pupils pursuing certain subjects was on the average about the same as in those reporting, the number and per cents in Table IX are true for all of the public high schools and private high schools and academies in the country for each year in question. In contemplating the data in Table IX one must keep all of the foregoing facts in mind.

It is fair to ask with respect to the data in Table IX, "What do the per cents mean?" Among other things they seem to mean that history other than United States was taught in the two lower grades of the high school. If it had been generally taught in the two upper grades where there were fewer pupils enrolled, the per cents could not have been so high. Furthermore, the per cents seem to mean that as a rule more than one year was devoted to the subject and that it must have been either required or very popular. Had but one year been devoted to it, the per cents could certainly not have been over 50, as they were in many states. Furthermore, if the enrollment in each of the four years had been exactly the same and all pupils in any one year had been pursuing history other than United States, the per cent of those pursuing the subject would have been 25.

TABLE IX

NUMBER AND PER CENT OF PUPILS PURSUING HISTORY OTHER
THAN UNITED STATES IN PUBLIC HIGH SCHOOLS AND PRIVATE
HIGH SCHOOLS AND ACADEMIES DURING THE YEARS OF 1889–
90, 1891–92, 1897–98, AND 1899–1900 *

STATE OR TERRITORY	Number pursuing				Per Cent of Total Number of Secondary Pupils Pursuing			
	1889–1890	1891–1892	1897–1898	1899–1900	1889–1890	1891–1892	1897–1898	1899–1900
United States	82,909	106,666	209,034	238,134	27.83	31.35	37.68	37.80
North Atlantic Division.........	30,716	38,898	71,382	81,738	27.45	31.31	39.21	38.89
Maine..........	1,941	2,354	3,658	4,109	26.38	25.80	31.94	36.89
New Hampshire..	1,141	1,122	2,073	2,268	25.64	25.22	38.80	35.98
Vermont........	957	887	1,179	1,537	21.06	19.75	22.53	34.36
Massachusetts ...	7,611	10,307	20,590	21,329	32.11	39.80	52.94	50.96
Rhode Island.....	897	913	2,041	1,792	36.73	36.84	52.19	43.88
Connecticut......	1,434	2,006	4,133	4,913	25.80	33.09	42.98	45.01
New York.......	7,203	10,537	17,356	23,164	18.58	27.82	29.65	31.53
New Jersey.......	2,422	2,806	6,019	6,845	34.81	27.49	45.01	45.16
Pennsylvania.....	6,110	7,966	14,333	15,781	33.71	34.32	40.15	36.89
South Atlantic Division.........	9,787	11,116	19,811	21,615	38.57	38.78	47.98	45.78
Delaware........	83	308	469	485	10.42	26.16	35.18	35.79
Maryland........	1,284	1,357	3,707	3,902	44.36	42.28	63.72	62.23
District of Columbia............	721	1,732	1,828	2,333	26.98	69.47	48.18	55.05
Virginia.........	2,469	1,911	3,541	3,817	51.40	39.61	50.18	48.12
West Virginia....	168	170	1,111	1,190	20.41	23.80	45.66	40.75
North Carolina ..	1,322	1,720	2,476	2,297	35.88	36.40	41.03	30.92
South Carolina...	1,069	1,102	2,530	2,745	49.88	33.88	52.86	47.85
Georgia..........	2,191	2,311	3,739	4,195	34.04	33.87	42.28	43.78
Florida..........	480	505	410	651	42.80	42.72	34.37	37.18
South Central Division.........	8,464	11,814	22,385	24,596	34.88	35.50	41.46	39.86
Kentucky........	1,221	1,758	3,901	4,026	30.38	36.90	46.58	41.93
Tennessee.......	1,160	2,078	3,139	3,307	24.64	28.85	30.61	29.87
Alabama.........	1,159	1,515	2,146	1,988	40.96	47.86	40.20	32.16
Mississippi.......	867	1,169	2,293	2,267	31.74	23.49	38.95	37.60
Louisiana........	970	1,253	1,888	2,171	49.46	55.71	68.85	62.08
Texas............	2,460	3,509	7,684	9,128	40.34	42.12	46.32	46.01
Arkansas........	573	447	1,232	1,394	33.96	19.62	30.85	30.32
Oklahoma.......	.....	.....	36	89	.....	.....	12.37	25.00
Indian Territory..	52	85	66	226	22.51	27.24	12.84	42.01
North Central Division.........	28,869	37,945	79,752	93,191	24.41	27.41	32.26	33.72

STATE OR TERRITORY	Number Pursuing				Per Cent of Total Number of Secondary Pupils Pursuing			
	1889–1890	1891–1892	1897–1898	1899–1900	1889–1890	1891–1892	1897–1898	1899–1900
Ohio..............	5,044	7,419	14,106	14,242	21.49	27.25	32.43	29.46
Indiana...........	2,512	2,887	8,803	11,126	27.91	28.88	35.41	38.86
Illinois...........	5,266	6,709	12,360	13,751	28.44	28.72	31.62	33.56
Michigan.........	2,967	3,798	8,871	11,091	21.46	24.22	30.95	36.99
Wisconsin........	1,899	2,264	4,398	6,750	19.15	22.39	24.44	30.56
Minnesota.......	1,153	1,892	4,302	5,924	16.91	22.90	32.41	41.85
Iowa.............	3,576	4,469	9,421	9,645	26.10	27.38	32.44	30.89
Missouri.........	2,678	3,613	7,879	9,076	26.55	30.33	36.46	36.14
North Dakota....	65	70	373	365	20.89	25.17	39.02	29.60
South Dakota....	165	212	723	959	29.30	27.67	36.42	32.80
Nebraska........	1,461	2,190	4,526	5,878	28.82	34.19	32.52	36.99
Kansas...........	2,088	2,422	3,990	4,384	29.87	30.36	32.29	27.69
Western Division..	5,073	6,894	15,704	16,994	27.43	42.96	51.93	49.18
Montana.........	123	243	340	453	24.35	37.96	33.33	26.63
Wyoming........	84	21	99	136	46.92	21.00	30.00	38.10
Colorado.........	409	1,382	3,380	4,012	34.31	56.54	66.71	65.70
New Mexico.....	47	22	54	108	35.33	38.59	26.73	31.21
Arizona..........	17	13	47	81	40.47	19.40	28.66	37.67
Utah............	102	343	497	857	27.33	32.60	24.07	31.38
Nevada..........	91	138	333	308	36.54	25.13	65.42	71.46
Idaho............	117	82	181	182	68.02	36.28	34.67	27.45
Washington......	215	480	911	1,199	26.70	26.24	29.88	30.06
Oregon..........	621	468	952	1,249	48.06	29.62	38.78	46.05
California........	3,147	3,702	8,910	8,409	40.07	49.36	59.97	54.96

* From data in U. S. Comr. of Educ., *Rep. for 1889–90*, II, 1388, 1391, 1486, and 1491; *ibid.*, 1891–92, II, 703–705; *ibid.*, 1897–98, II, 2092; and *ibid.*, 1899–1900, II, 2168.

Table IX reveals certain facts that are unexplainable on the basis of the data at hand. Why were fewer pupils exposed to history in the South Atlantic States than in any other division? Why were more pupils so exposed in the Western States than in any other division and why were those in the North Central and North Atlantic States so exposed in about equal numbers? Hypothetical answers to these questions readily come to mind. For instance, it is possible that United States history was emphasized in the South Central States at the expense of history other than United States and that history other than United States was more generally required in the Western States than in any other group. These answers, of course, are not based on known facts, hence must be placed in the realm of conjecture.[54]

Other queries that come to mind in scrutinizing the data in Table IX are: (1) Why were the per cents so high in Maryland, District of Columbia, Louisiana, Colorado, Nevada, and California? (2) Why were they so low in Tennessee, Oklahoma, Ohio, North Dakota, Kansas, and Idaho? (3) Why was history other than United States so uniformly pursued during the decade represented in the table? The pleasure of answering these questions is left to the reader.

EVIDENCE OF THE EXISTENCE OF HISTORY IN THE ELEMENTARY GRADES, 1860–1900

Evidence of the existence of history in the elementary grades during the forty years following 1860 is very fragmentary and none too abundant. Individual cases are picked up here and there, but for the country as a whole, no comprehensive statistics concerning the number of pupils in the elementary grades enrolled in history classes from year to year are available. When one considers the enormous amount of labor involved in collecting and tabulating such statistics and the expense of publishing them, one is not surprised to find them generally missing from state and city school reports. While it seems reasonably sure that United States history had been generally accepted as a subject of study in the two upper

---

[54] That the first half of this answer is conjecture is certain from the fact that there were but 10,109 pupils in 146 public high schools in the fifty largest cities of the country pursuing United States history in 1900–1901.—U. S. Comr. of Educ., *Rep. for 1900–1901*, II, 1907.

grades of the elementary school by 1870, the statistical proof of the fact is lacking. However, scattering evidence, such as that tabulated below for ten cities in the country for the year 1866, is available.

HISTORY IN THE ELEMENTARY GRADES OF TEN CITIES
IN 1866

1. Boston—No history reported in any of the six classes below the grammar school.

In Class 2 of the grammar school Swan's *First Lessons in the History of the United States* was used. This was next to the highest class. In Class 1, the highest class, Worcester's *Elements of History, Ancient and Modern,* was used.

2. New Bedford, Mass.—No history mentioned below the grammar grades.

Historical sketches, composed mostly of biographies of leading characters appeared in the eighth class, the second class of the grammar grades.

United States history to the Revolution, 7th class.

United States history to constitution, 6th class.

United States history completed, 5th class.

3. Springfield, Mass.—No history below the 7th year.

History of United States in 7th year, Summer term.

History of United States in 8th year, Fall, Winter, and Summer terms.

4. New Haven, Conn.—No history in the years below the 7th.

History in 7th year; field not stated.

5. New York City—No history below the grammar schools.

History of the United States in the last three grades of

grammar school. There were seven grades in these schools.

Grade III. United States history to 1753.

Grade II. United States history, 1753–1789.

Grade I. United States history completed.

6. Cincinnati, Ohio—No history below the intermediate schools. This means below the seventh year.

United States history in Grades B and A of the intermediate.schools; Goodrich, *Pictorial History of the United States* used.

7. St. Louis, Mo.—No history below the last year of elementary school.

History and constitution in last year of elementary school; field not stated.

8. Louisville, Ky.—No history below the grammar department.

History of the United States in last two years of grammar department. Anderson's *History of the United States* used in both years.

9. Philadelphia—No history below grammar school department.

United States history in last three divisions of grammar school department. Goodrich, *American Youth's History* used in all three divisions.

10. Chicago—No history below the grammar grades.

United States history to the Revolution, Second Grade, Grammar Division.

History of the United States completed and reviewed, First Grade, Grammar Division.[55]

History was not taught below Grade VII in any of the cities

[55] "Subjects and Course of Instruction in City Public Schools," *Barnard's Journal of Education,* XIX (1870), 465–576.

in the foregoing list. This means that the per cent of pupils exposed to history during their school career in the elementary grades was miserably small. Just how small is indicated by some data on elementary school enrollment in the State of Ohio during the 1870's. Table X contains these data for every other year of the seventies plus those for 1880. To say that

TABLE X

NUMBER AND PER CENT OF PUPILS IN THE ELEMENTARY SCHOOLS
OF OHIO PURSUING UNITED STATES HISTORY, 1870–1880 *

YEAR	ELEMENTARY SCHOOL ENROLLMENT	Elementary Pupils Pursuing United States History	
		NUMBER	PER CENT
1870.................	706,068	6,522	.92
1872.................	687,815	8,547	1.24
1874.................	684,571	9,454	1.38
1876.................	698,233	10,948	1.56
1878.................	713,138	13,988	1.96
1880.................	718,281	17,303	2.40

* Calculated from data in the annual reports of the State Commissioner of Common Schools to the General Assembly of the State of Ohio for the years indicated.

a great number of children in the elementary schools of Ohio during this decade was exposed to United States history would certainly be a gross exaggeration. It will be noted from the table that the number of such exposures was always less than two pupils in each one hundred enrolled during the entire decade of the seventies. There seems to be no reason for believing that more elementary-grade children were exposed to United States history during the 1870's in the other states of the union than were so exposed in Ohio. It is evident from the available material that the generation responsible for the "gay nineties" knew very, very little about the "fabulous forties."

One picks up bits of evidence here and there to the effect that a little attention was given to history in the grades below the seventh during the 1870's. For instance, in the city of St. Louis, Missouri, during the school year 1877–78 an oral lesson in history was given each Friday in Grades I–VII.[56] This practice was evidently not common, there being but one of twenty-eight representative cities a decade later that allotted any time to history in Grades I, II, and III. It was, however, at this date the general practice in these twenty-eight cities to give history a substantial allotment of time in Grades VII and VIII, twenty-one of them allotting an average of 106 minutes a week to the subject in Grade VII and eighteen of them an average of 146 minutes a week in Grade VIII. Five of the cities allotted some time to history in Grade IV, twelve in Grade V, and thirteen in Grade VI.[57] Judging from the somewhat generous allotment of time to the subject in Grades VII and VIII in about two-thirds of the twenty-eight cities, it seems within the bounds of truth to say that history had become fairly well established in these grades prior to 1890.

Thus far in presenting the evidence of the existence of history in the elementary schools during the forty years after 1860 three snap-shot views have been given, one in the sixties, one in the seventies and one in the eighties. In harmony with this plan there is now due one for the nineties, which is at hand in a survey of approximately eighty courses of study in use in 1896. In presenting the general findings of this study, the exact words of the one making it seem most appropriate. An excerpt from his comments relating to history and civil government follows:

56 *Twenty Fourth Annual Report,* Board of Directors, St. Louis Public Schools for the Year ending August 1, 1878, p. 191.
57 U. S. Comr. of Educ., *Rep. for the year 1888–89,* I, 404.

"Several of the subjects regularly found in these courses require special consideration. If we are to take in good faith the suggestion recently (1896) made at the conference of the North Central Colleges and Secondary Schools at Chicago, 'to prolong history downward into the elementary schools,' there is ample opportunity to begin; for in the larger number of the courses examined the work in history was not begun until the last, or next to last year. In the remaining cities it is outlined to cover the last half, and the entire course in about an equal number of instances. One city having a population of 30,000 has but 1½ year's work in history, and that consists of reading Eggleston U. S. History as a part of the supplementary reading. There are other cities which do little more. On the whole the amount of time given to history is slightly in excess of three per cent, very seldom indeed over five, and often unsystematic to the extreme. Not only is it meager in amount, but also rather provincial in spirit. Rarely is there any evidence of an attempt to teach the history of any country besides our own, despite the astounding ignorance of the modern history of Europe, which is repeatedly displayed by press and pulpit. Chicago, and Brookline, Mass., are among the few cities which provide for some study of English history below the high school. General history is scarcely considered. The following, from the Jersey City course of study, is close to the maximum:

" 'In all grades some of the matter selected for supplementary reading should have reference to notable persons and great events in history. The study of United States history should lead the pupil to the reading and study of brief histories of other important countries. By the time the pupil leaves the grammar department he should have some knowledge of general history, and should possess a desire to continue his historical reading.' " [58]

In connection with his study, Croswell discovered that in the ungraded schools of Maine in 1895 an average of 5.66 per cent of all recitation-time was devoted to United States history, a subject taught in fifteen of the twenty schools reporting. In a report on conditions in the schools of Connecticut in about 1890 appeared the following: "In the larger graded schools, where a course of study dominates, there is no neglect of *history* and *geography,* though it might be questioned whether *civil government* has its share of attention. In the smaller graded probably, and certainly in the ungraded schools where there is no course of study, civil government is practically unnoticed, history is neglected by an overwhelming majority, and geography, if it be ultimately studied, is not begun as soon as it should be." [59]

Judging from Croswell's findings there seems to have been little advance in elementary-grade history during the early 1890's. History in these grades evidently remained more or less static, in spite of the enormous amount of propaganda for the subject that was circulated during this decade and the fact that history was one of the rather generally prescribed subjects.[60] With respect to the propaganda for history as an elementary school subject, it is sufficient to refer to the work of the Herbartians, the reports of the Committees of Fifteen and Twelve and the existence of state courses of study in at

[58] T. R. Croswell, "Courses of Study in the Elementary Schools of the United States," *Pedagogical Seminary,* IV (1896), 321 f.

[59] Quoted in *ibid.,* p. 313.

[60] In 1896 United States history was required by statutory provisions in all states but Wyoming, New Hampshire, Connecticut, New Jersey, Delaware, Virginia, Georgia, Texas, Nebraska, Wisconsin, and South Dakota. General history was specified in Maryland and West Virginia.—T. R. Croswell, *op. cit.,* p. 295.

least two dozen states. Commenting on state courses of study Croswell said:

"Ten years ago Massachusetts, Washington, Wisconsin, and Minnesota alone published them. Colorado, Nebraska, Illinois and Kentucky had also adopted courses prior to 1890; and since that date sixteen more have been added. The years 1893 and 1895 are especially noteworthy in the history of the State course. During the former several adopted a course for the first time, and there was a noticeable tendency in other States to revise. In the latter year Vermont adopted a course of study for both the elementary and the high school; the State authorities in Montana, Missouri, and Maine, and the Educational Association in Kansas took action toward publishing State courses of study for elementary schools; in New Hampshire a bill authorizing the publication of a State Course of Study passed the legislature, but was vetoed by the Governor; in California much of the educational interest of the years centered around the work of a Committee of the Educational Council of the State, which was appointed to consider the question of a uniform course of study for the elementary schools." [61]

The fruition of the work of the foregoing agencies did not come to pass in the 1890's. Even as late as 1910 not all of the hopes for history in the elementary schools harbored by the reformers of the 1890's had been realized.

THE CONTENT OF SECONDARY-SCHOOL HISTORY, 1860–1900

During the forty years after 1860 the textbook in history for use in both the elementary and the secondary schools was

[61] *Op. cit.*, p. 303.

"King of Kings" and "Lord of Lords." It was the "be all and end all" of the content in history taught in these schools. While the textbook in history probably reached during these years the lowest depths of degradation that it has ever experienced, it, nevertheless, remained the chief source of content in its field. Old texts, of course, were carried over into this period from the pre-Civil War days, especially in the fields of history other than United States. Lack of space precludes including here a list of all the textbooks in history used in the high schools and the academies between 1860 and 1900. In lieu of such a list, information concerning the extent to which certain texts were used, especially in the academies of New York, is presented below, attention first being directed to those in United States history in use from 1865–1878. A list of these together with the frequency of the use of each in the academies of New York for each of eleven school years after 1865 appears in Table XI, from which it is evident that certain texts in United States history were favorites with those who selected textbooks in history for the academies of New York between 1865 and 1879. Five texts were generously used in each year represented in the table. Based on the total number of academies using each of these five throughout the period, the text most frequently used was J. J. Anderson's *A School History of the United States*. The order of the most frequent use of the remaining four was Quackenbos, Lossing, Willson, and Goodrich. The interesting fact about these five texts is that most of them had had their day by 1879. In all cases but one the use was decreasing. The chief texts used in general history during the same period are listed in Table XII.

Two texts led the field in general history during the period under review. These were J. J. Anderson's *Manual of General History* and Marcius Willson's *Outline of General History*.

After it appeared William Swinton's *Outlines of World History* gained a following with considerable rapidity. This

TABLE XI

TEXTBOOKS IN UNITED STATES HISTORY USED IN THE ACADEMIES
OF NEW YORK STATE, 1865-79 *

TEXTS	Number of Academies Using in										
	1865-6	1867-8	1869-70	1871-2	1872-3	1873-4	1874-5	1875-6	1876-7	1877-8	1878-9
1. J. J. Anderson, *A School History of the United States*	2	3	25	42	46	51	60	59	81	63	47
2. A. S. Barnes, *A Brief History of the United States*	..	..	11	19	16	21	34	30	40	46	
3. A. B. Berard, *School History of the United States*	3	7	7	3	1	..	1	..	..	..	1
4. C. A. Goodrich, *Pictorial History of the United States.* Revised by W. H. Seavey	27	22	16	16	11	9	10	5	3	1	2
5. T. W. Higginson, *Young Folks' History of the United States*	..	..	..	..	..	..	2	5	6	5	7
6. B. J. Lossing, *Primary History of the United States*	31	28	21	18	19	17	15	18	12	10	11
7. G. P. Quackenbos, *Illustrated History of the United States of America*	27	34	31	21	18	21	17	9	9	15	19
8. J. C. Ridpath, *A Popular History of the United States of America*	..	..	..	..	..	..	..	1	8	26	32
9. D. B. Scott, *Manual of U. S. History to 1869*	..	..	1	2	5	2	4	5	4	3	3
10. W. Swinton, *Swinton's Condensed United States*	..	..	..	7	9	14	22	17	16	9	12
11. W. H. Venable, *A School History of the United States*	..	..	..	..	1	2	2	4	2	2	1
12. E. Willard, *Abridged History of the United States*	11	7	9	7	4	3	1	2	1	..	..
13. M. Willson, *History of the United States*	54	45	26	19	14	10	5	5	4	3	2

* *Ninety-Third Annual Report* of the Regents of the University of the State of New York, p. 460. Five texts of very limited use are omitted from the table.

volume was probably the first text in world history for use in the schools ever to appear in this country.

Few changes occurred during the decade following 1879 in the lists of texts most frequently used in the academies of

New York. In United States history Barnes's *Brief History of the United States* led the field. Following more or less closely

TABLE XII

TEXTBOOKS IN GENERAL HISTORY MOST FREQUENTLY USED IN THE ACADEMIES OF NEW YORK STATE, 1865–79 *

TEXTS	Number of Academies Using in										
	1865–6	1867–8	1869–70	1871–2	1872–3	1873–4	1874–5	1875–6	1876–7	1877–8	1878–9
1. J. J. Anderson, *Manual of General History*	..	2	13	35	38	46	42	55	50	48	50
2. E. A. Freeman, *General Sketch of History*	..	..	..	..	1	3	6	5	5	5	3
3. S. G. Goodrich, *Peter Parley's Universal History*	4	5	4	4	4	2	1	1	..	..	..
4. Lord, *Points of History for Schools and Colleges*	1	1	2	6	3	3	2	1	2	1	3
5. R. Robbins, *Outlines of Ancient and Modern History*	12	1	3	2	1	4	3	3	..	1	1
6. William Swinton, *Outlines of World History*	..	..	..	..	..	..	16	22	36	43	52
7. W. C. Taylor, *Manual of Ancient and Modern History*	..	..	..	..	..	..	..	..	..	3	1
8. M. E. Thalheimer, *History of the World, Ancient and Modern*	..	..	..	2	3	2	2	..	2	3	2
9. G. Weber, *Outlines of Universal History*	7	3	2	1	2	1	3	1	3	1	2
10. Emma Willard, *Universal History in Perspective*	13	10	4	5	3	1	..	..	2	..	1
11. Marcius Willson, *Outline of General History*	48	39	39	30	23	18	19	13	11	..	9
12. J. E. Worcester, *Elements of History, Ancient and Modern*	7	10	5	5	5	2	3	3	2	..	..
13. G. P. Quackenbos, *Illustrated School History of the World*	..	..	..	..	..	..	..	..	..	4	6	9

* *Ninety-Third Annual Report* of the Regents of the University of the State of New York, pp. 459 f. Four texts of limited use are omitted from the table.

were: J. J. Anderson's *Common School History of the United States*, G. P. Quackenbos' *History of the United States*, J. C. Ridpath's *History of the United States* and William Swinton's *Condensed School History of the United States*. In general history Swinton's *Outlines of World History* and Anderson's *Manual of General History* had about an equal following.

Barnes's *Brief General History* was used in a little over a dozen academies during each of the four years beginning with 1885. In the fields of Greek and Roman history Sir William Smith's *History of Greece* and R. F. Leighton's *History of Rome* led the fields. Anderson's *School History of England* was the leading text in its field.[62]

It would require an analysis of each book listed in the foregoing tables to discover the exact nature of the content of the history to which pupils in high schools and academies were exposed during the forty years prior to 1900. No such analysis has ever been made. Some work, however, has been done along this line. Although not mentioned above an analysis has been made of Peter Fredet's *Ancient History,* a text that was popular between 1857 and 1894, having been revised ten times during these years. The contents of two editions of this text have been analyzed by a student of trends in the teaching of ancient history in American secondary schools. In order to compare the "then" with the "now" an analysis of J. H. Breasted's *Ancient Times* was also made. The results of these analyses are presented in Table XIII, which shows that most of the topics treated in a popular textbook in ancient history during the 1860's and 1880's were also treated in a popular text that first appeared in 1916. One topic "Creation and Dispersion of Peoples" was treated in the early but not in the later text. Four topics were included in Breasted's text not found in Fredet's. Furthermore, the attention given to the Orient and to Greece is greater in the volume by Breasted than in those by Fredet. Not so, however, with the emphasis on Rome in which case the situation is reversed, the same being true with respect to the emphasis on government and war.

---

[62] *One Hundred and Second Annual Report* of the Regents of the University of the State of New York, p. 962.

In order to determine on what aspects of American life the
writers of textbooks in this field have placed most emphasis,

TABLE XIII

PER CENT OF TOTAL PAGES DEVOTED TO CERTAIN TOPICS AND TO
CERTAIN ASPECTS OF LIFE IN TWO EDITIONS OF PETER FRE-
DET'S *ANCIENT HISTORY* AND IN J. H. BREASTED'S *ANCIENT
TIMES* *

TOPICS AND ASPECTS OF LIFE	Editions of Fredet's *Ancient History*		Breasted's *Ancient Times*
	1867, 496 PP.	1883, 492 PP.	1916, 716 PP.
	Per Cent of Total Pages Devoted to		
1. The Orient..................	17.40	17.71	25.98
2. The Greeks................	25.63	32.64	36.73
3. Rome......................	53.06	45.22	16.34
4. The Roman Empire..........	2.44	2.33	12.16
5. Romano-Teutonic Period.....	....	....	2.38
6. The Saracens...............	....	....	1.12
7. The Biblical Account (Creation and Dispersion of Peoples).....................	1.47	2.10	....
8. Pre-Historic Peoples and Ages	....	....	4.76
9. Geographical Influence.......	.35	.41	2.52
10. Government................	16.17	12.49	9.49
11. War.......................	34.64	35.82	6.80
12. Religion...................	.71	1.22	3.96
13. Society....................	2.42	4.92	4.27
14. Education..................	.10	1.12	2.48
15. Culture....................	1.82	.67	5.66
16. Economic Considerations.....	5.05	6.20	9.03
17. Science and Invention........	....	.61	3.59
18. Miscellaneous†.............	29.56	39.93	28.13

* Harry F. Willebrandt, "Trends in the Content and Methods of Instruction in
Ancient History in American Secondary Schools," pp. 125-131 and 134. Unpublished
Master's thesis, University of Southern California, 1926.
† Included here are biography, mythology, philosophy, civilization, migration of
peoples, ethnological development of nations, causes of national decline, superstition
and ignorance, systems of writing, the city-state, early peoples, efforts for peace,
citizenship, evil results of class rule, evil effects of war, and effects of incompetent
leadership in democracies.

an analysis was made a few years ago of eleven of the texts in
United States history published between 1843 and 1899. The

TABLE XIV

PER CENT OF TOTAL PAGES DEVOTED TO CERTAIN ASPECTS OF LIFE
BY ELEVEN AUTHORS OF TEXTBOOKS IN AMERICAN HISTORY
PUBLISHED PRIOR TO 1900 *

TEXTS	Per Cent of Total Pages Devoted to					
	EUROPEAN BACKGROUND	ECONOMICS	GOVERNMENT	WAR	EDUCATION	SOCIETY
Salma Hale, *History of the United States.* New York: Phinney, 1843...........	12.7	.8	29.0	40.1	.4	...
G. P. Quackenbos, *A School History of the United States.* New York: D. Appleton & Co., 1868.......................	19.4	.2	29.3	41.5	.6	3.2
Emma Willard, *School History of the United States.* New York: Woolworth Ainsworth and Co., 1869............	18.3	2.9	30.2	36.4	.4	2.5
W. H. Venable, *A School History of the United States.* New York: Van Antwerp, Bragg and Co., 1872...........	17.0	4.0	20.4	39.8	1.4	2.2
J. J. Anderson, *A Popular School History of the United States.* New York: Clark and Maynard, 1881.................	22.1	5.9	25.6	31.8	.9	1.9
B. J. Lossing, *A School History of the United States.* New York: Sheldon & Co., 1884.........................	10.6	3.9	17.9	24.5	.1	.5
A. S. Barnes, *A Brief History of the United States.* New York: A. S. Barnes & Co., 1885................................	14.8	7.1	23.1	37.5	2.0	3.0
E. E. Childs, *A History of the United States.* New York: Baker and Taylor, 1886...........................	7.2	2.4	42.6	28.1	1.8	2.8
California State Board of Education, *History of the United States.* Sacramento, California: State Printing, 1888...................	11.9	2.4	28.2	21.0	2.7	1.7
D. H. Montgomery, *Students' American History.* Boston: Ginn and Co., 1897..	15.3	4.3	41.3	20.2	1.3	2.2
John Fiske, *History of the United States for Schools.* New York: Houghton Mifflin & Co., 1899...................	12.7	1.1	24.6	17.3	1.9	1.4

* David McDonald, Jr., "Analysis of the Trends in Content of American History Texts Used in Secondary Schools 1840-1930," pp. 72 f. and *passim.* Unpublished Master's thesis, University of Southern California, 1930.

heavy emphasis on war and government is the conspicuous fact revealed in Table XIV, there being no appreciable gain in the emphasis on society, education, and economics throughout the almost sixty-year period.

The amount of activity during the 1890's in behalf of history in the secondary school was tremendous. It will be recalled from Division One that two important committees representing organizations of national scope reported during this decade, one in the early and the other in the late years. Reference is, of course, made here to the Sub-committee on History, Civil Government, and Political Economy of the Committee of Ten of the National Education Association and the Committee of Seven of the American History Association on the study of history in the schools. Inasmuch as the work of these two committees has been treated in detail elsewhere, the discussion may pass at once to other types of activity in behalf of history during the decade under review.

The fact that most of the universities and colleges of the country in the middle 1890's included history in the list of subjects required for admission made discussions of the fields to be accepted by the colleges very apropos. A pronouncement was made on this matter in 1895 by the New England Association of Colleges and Preparatory Schools. In October of this year this association passed the following resolutions by a vote of thirty-five to seven.

Resolved, That the colleges be requested to include in their requirements for admission a choice of subjects out of the following topics:

(1) The History of Greece to the death of Alexander, with especial reference to Greek life, literature, and art

(2) The History of Rome: the Republic and the Empire to the accession of Commodus

(3) German History ⎫ To be so taught as to elucidate the
(4) French History ⎬ general movement of mediæval and
                    ⎭ modern history

(5) English History, with especial reference to social and political development

(6) American History, with the elements of Civil Government

(7) A detailed study of a limited period, pursued in an intensive manner

—Any two of these topics to constitute a required subject for entrance to college. The colleges are earnestly requested to accept any additional topic or topics from the list as additional preparation for entrance or for advanced standing.[63]

The reader will observe in the foregoing resolution the direct influence of the report of the sub-committee on History, Civil Government, and Political Economy of the Committee of Ten. It will be recalled that this committee recommended English and French history as well as an intensive study of a limited period of history. In 1896, a conference representing six of the leading universities of the East, known as the Columbia Conference, because it was held at Columbia University, accepted the general scheme of the New England Association, but made slight changes in the fields. The latter of these reports more than the former tended to dictate the fields of history to be taught in preparatory schools. So it was during these years that the courses in history in the high schools of the country began to be handed down from above, something from which these schools have been trying to escape ever since.

[63] *School Review*, III (1895), 619.

In the discussions during the '90's, the large attention then given to general history and the slight emphasis on United States history in the high school were mentioned again and again. The attack made on general history during these years came from four fronts. These were (1) the Sub-committee on History, Civil Government, and Political Economy of the Committee of Ten; (2) the Committee on College Entrance Requirements in History of the New England Association of Colleges and Preparatory Schools; (3) the Columbia Conference; and (4) the Committee of Seven of the American Historial Association. It would not be unreasonable to believe that the subject did not survive the attacks made by these bodies. Such a belief, however, would be far from what actually happened. Instead of dying immediately as its attackers wanted it to do, general history decided merely to retire from the front of the stage and await its turn to re-enter, which it did two decades later under the caption "world history." In its return in the form of "old wine in a new bottle" its proponents saw the fulfillment of the old maxim which reads, "Truth crushed to earth shall rise again."

The sentiment of those who deplored the neglect during the 1890's of American history in secondary schools was well expressed by a high-school principal in 1898 when he said:

"I have examined courses of study from secondary schools from every part of the republic, and you have no idea what a large number of them consider it not worth while to study American history. The high schools have just begun to awaken to this subject. I believe the gospel of American history should be preached by this association, and its importance urged upon the secondary schools thruout the republic—that they may see that this subject should have its proper place, and is given a proper amount of time, in the course of the study in the secondary schools. If this is done, there will be no trouble in educating patriotic citizens. When the pupil leaves the public school, he should have a broad and adequate conception of the origin, the development, the struggle for supremacy, and the final triumph of the principles of constitutional, political, and social liberty embodied in the constitution of the United States and exemplified in the institutions of this great republic." [64]

Because of the fact that the textbook had such a dominant place in the teaching of history in the secondary schools of the country during the 1890's, it too came in for its share of the adverse criticisms of the day. An excellent example of what was being said about the textbooks in American history is found in the comments of a committee of the New England History Teachers' Association which reported in 1898. An excerpt from these comments follows:

"The limitations of text-books in American history have been made very apparent to the members of the Committee in the course of their inquiry. A large number of manuals still extensively used are, in their judgment, little adapted to the work they profess to do. The older style of text-book was a curious product. Its author was frequently a literary hack, ready to compile a dictionary, annotate a classical text, or write an algebra, as occasion offered. Of special training in history he had none; but he had read a good deal, had a number of apt stories at his command, and made up for his limited knowledge by a vivid and pliable imagination. To such a writer, the preparation of a school book in American history was an easy

[64] W. C. Lansdon, "Neglect of American History in High School in 1898," *Addresses and Proceedings*, N. E. A., 1898, p. 85.

task. Details aside, the general formula was quite unvarying. Say nothing about the physical features of the continent, but extol the virtues of the noble Indian; dwell on the brilliant intellect, the undaunted courage, and the magnificent faith of Columbus, the hardships of the Pilgrims, the grim sternness of the Puritans, the simplicity of the Quakers, and the quaintness of the Dutch; show how the Revolution was due solely to the brutal tyranny of the British, and how Washington and Franklin had, in supreme degree, all the virtues ever exhibited by men in their respective spheres, and not a single fault; characterize the Constitution as "the greatest product of the human mind," but avoid much reference to it after its adoption; cut up the period after 1789 into four-year morsels, and give to the mastication of each about the same amount of space; dwell on the enormities of England after the peace of 1783, and the glorious victories of the War of 1812, not omitting mention of Jackson's cotton bales and Perry's green-timber fleet; show what a lovely thing the era of good feeling was, and how the South went all wrong about nullification, slavery, and the Civil War; add in an appendix the Constitution, the Declaration of Independence, and a list of Presidents; and then enliven the whole by a profusion of fancy pictures, including 'Washington Crossing the Delaware,' 'A Winter at Valley Forge,' 'An Emigrant Train,' and 'Welcome, Englishmen!'—and you had a book admirably adapted to the training of citizens and patriots." [65]

Textbooks in fields of secondary-school history other than American were also subjected to a great deal of adverse criticism during the late 1890's. In a paper read before the

[65] "Text-books in American History," *Educational Review*, XVI (1898), 483 f. Nineteen texts in American history were reviewed by the committee.

National Herbart Society in 1899 an experienced teacher commented as follows on the shortcomings of the current textbooks in European history:

"The list of defects in existing text-books of European history is not exhaustive—a volume would be required for that—but it includes the most fundamental. Such defects are: the cramming with meaningless names and dates, the emphasis on what is extraordinary and passing rather than on what is typical and permanent, the neglect of causal relations, the projection of latter day moral standards into the past, and the evident lack of scholarship on the part of the authors. Such an exposure of these faults cannot fail to make for their removal. This is especially true of the scourging administered to authors who presume to write texts for the schools without use of the sources of knowledge of books in foreign languages. If some one, speaking with equal authority, would only rise up and scourge the teachers who presume to teach history without a mastery of tongues and use of sources, the day of deserved discredit for history would quickly pass." [66]

In closing this brief treatment of the content of history in the secondary schools of the United States during the forty years following the Civil War reference to the situation as revealed by the Committee of Seven in its report, *The Study of History in the Schools,* seems apropos. After studying the condition of history in 216 schools during the school year 1897–98 this Committee reported that English and American history were taught in more than half the schools, general

[66] Edward Van Dyke Robinson, "Medieval and Modern History in the High School," *School Review,* VIII (1900), 269.

history in almost exactly half, Greek and Roman in almost half, and European (mediæval, modern, French) in one-third. With respect to the succession of subjects the Committee found that four different systems were followed. They were (1) chronological, taking up in succession ancient, general, and modern history—usually English or American; (2) general, ancient, and modern; (3) American or English, general, and ancient; and (4) American, ancient, and general.[67] In its report the Committee followed none of these systems, proposing instead ancient, mediæval and modern, English, and American when a four-year course was desired; and ancient, mediæval and modern, and American when a three-year course was offered.

THE CONTENT OF HISTORY IN THE ELEMENTARY GRADES, 1860–1900

Because of the fact that little history other than United States was taught in the elementary grades during the generation prior to 1900, the discussion below is confined to the content of this field alone. Furthermore, inasmuch as little attention was given to history in the grades below the seventh and almost sole dependence for content was placed on a textbook, the canvass is largely limited to the texts in United States history intended primarily for use in the two top grades of the elementary school.[68] That sole dependence was placed in

[67] The Committee of Seven, *The Study of History in Schools,* pp. 139–141. New York: The Macmillan Co., 1899.

[68] These statements are made with knowledge of the fact that exceptions existed here and there. For example, the Board of Education of St. Louis, Missouri, on August 28, 1877, adopted a course of study in history which made elaborate provisions for the subject in each of the eight elementary grades. The impossibilities inherent in this course make the assumption that it was never carried out seem reasonable.—For a copy of this course, see *Twenty-Fifth Annual Report,* Board of Directors of the St. Louis Public Schools, pp. 240–47.

a textbook in these grades at least in some quarters is evidenced from the statements of eye-witnesses. For example, in a report, submitted in 1883, John B. Peaslee, Superintendent of Schools, Cincinnati, Ohio, commented as follows on history in the upper grades of the elementary schools of his city.

"Previous to 1872 written percented examinations for transfer were held in history. The pupils were required to memorize all the dates, names of persons, and be able to give descriptions of all the events recorded within the covers of Anderson's *United States History,* in order to be prepared for the examinations. Five-lessons a week were given to this stultifying work. The pupils were demerited, coaxed, scolded, driven, in order that they might cram their little minds full enough of this distasteful minutia 'to pass.' It required more time of the children to prepare for recitation in history than in any other two subjects in the school course. Many of the teachers, recognizing the absolute worthlessness and cruelty of compelling the children to commit the textbook to memory, endeavored to have their pupils answer in their own language, but it was found impossible to obtain high per cents in the written examination for transfer unless the children committed the text to memory. They were too young; they had neither the judgment nor the knowledge and use of language to do so without memorizing the words of the book. . . . No encyclopædias, gazetteers, or histories other than the textbooks were brought into the classroom. There was no time for consulting these, for the bugbear of per cents was continually staring both teachers and pupils in the face. The pupils, instead of being encouraged by their teachers, as they are now, to consult reference books and to read good books bearing upon history at their homes, were discouraged from it for fear they would not get as high per cents in the examination." [69]

Turning now to the content of United States history in Grades VII and VIII from 1865 to 1900, attention is first called to an elaborate analysis of the textbooks used during these years. This analysis was made during the school year 1912–13 by graduate students at the University of Illinois. Twenty-three textbooks in United States history intended for Grades VII and VIII were analyzed. During the summer of 1915 the material resulting from this analysis was checked with extreme care and made ready for publication. A year later it was available in published form.[70]

In order to show the emphasis placed on certain large divisions of United States history by each book analyzed, those making the analysis proportioned the number of words that each book devoted to each of the several divisions to the total number of words in the book. The results of this proportioning appear in Table XV. A class using, during the 1890's, any one of the books in this table read in the pages devoted to the period of discovery and exploration treatments of America before Columbus, European background, Spanish explorations, English explorations, French explorations, Dutch explorations, and Portuguese explorations. In the periods of Colonial development and Colonial wars the class studied the thirteen colonies separately and usually in a chronological order, giving special attention to Colonial wars such as King William's, Queen Anne's, King George's and French and Indian. In the prerevolutionary period this class read discussions of the policy of England toward the colonies, Stamp Act, Boston Massacre,

[69] U. S. Comr. of Educ., *Rep. for the year 1883–84*, p. xciii.

[70] W. C. Bagley and H. O. Rugg, *Content of American History as Taught in the Seventh and Eighth Grades*. University of Illinois, School of Education, Bulletin, No. 16. Urbana, Ill.: University of Illinois, 1916.

TABLE XV

PER CENT OF TOTAL WORDS IN EACH OF TEN TEXTBOOKS IN UNITED STATES HISTORY DEVOTED TO CERTAIN LARGE DIVISIONS OF THE FIELD *

AUTHORS AND TITLES OF THE TEXTS	Per Cent of Total Number of Words Devoted to								
	EXPLORATION AND DISCOVERY	COLONIAL DEVELOPMENT	COLONIAL WARS	PRE-REVOLUTION	REVOLUTION	1783-1812	1812-1861	CIVIL WAR	1865 TO PUBLICATION
1. A. B. Berard, *School History of the United States.* Copyright date, 1865; pp., 303; words, 81,200.	2.3	29.4	4.6	1.5	20.0	4.28	13.9	14.8	...
2. Marcius Willson, *History of the United States from the Earliest Discoveries to the Close of the Great Rebellion in 1865.* Copyright date of edition used, 1866; pp., 459; words, 121,400.	7.0	28.0	6.5	3.3	17.0	5.05	14.5	14.5	...
3. C. A. Goodrich, *History of the United States of America for Use of Schools* (revised by W. H. Seavey). Copyright date of revised edition, 1867; pp., 320; words, 36,400.	6.0	11.2	4.7	5.2	18.4	6.8	18.4	23.8	2.51
4. J. J. Anderson, *A Grammar School History of the United States.* Copyright date of revised edition, 1880; pp., 320; words, 39,800.	7.5	15.8	6.8	2.4	15.0	9.27	20.9	12.75	15.4
5. M. E. Thalheimer, *The New Eclectic History of the United States.* Copyright date, 1881; pp., 400; words, 69,800.	8.0	14.8	3.6	2.0	21.0	9.4	14.8	10.75	15.3
6. J. D. Steele and Esther B. Steele, *A Brief History of the United States.* Copyright date, 1877; pp., 410; words, 57,700.	10.8	18.5	4.6	1.8	17.0	3.67	18.7	17.6	11.44
7. E. Eggleston, *A History of the United States and Its People.* Copyright date, 1888; pp., 416; words, 58,200.	5.0	26.8	6.3	1.8	14.0	12.07	13.3	14.3	7.29
8. E. S. Ellis, *School History of the United States.* Copyright date, 1892; pp., 369; words, 50,900.	7.8	15.7	3.6	1.6	12.0	6.54	25.8	19.0	9.15
9. J. H. Shinn, *History of the American People.* Copyright date, 1893; pp., 454; words, 82,900.	16.0	18.9	4.4	2.32	18.0	8.0	15.8	11.7	8.5
10. D. H. Montgomery, *The Leading Facts of American History.* Copyright date, 1890; pp., 360; words, 106,400.	13.0	23.8	2.6	2.2	9.3	5.89	16.9	10.1	16.3

* Based on Table I, p. 22, in Bagley and Rugg. *op. cit.*

Boston "Tea Party," Boston Port Bill, First Continental Congress, Writs of Assistance, new taxes, results of England's policy of taxation.

When this class studied the Revolutionary War most of its attention was centered on the military phases of the war. No matter what book in this list the class used, it met the following: Lexington and Concord; Bunker Hill; siege of Boston; Washington, Commander-in-Chief; Ticonderoga; Long Island; retreat through New Jersey; battle of Trenton; battle of Princeton; Valley Forge; Burgoyne's Campaign; Monmouth; Arnold's treason; Camden; Cowpens; Yorktown; and Treaty of Paris.[71] In studying the period extending from 1783 to 1812 the class gave practically no attention to social and political conditions between 1783 and 1789, a little attention to early governmental activities, considerable to Washington's administration, very little to Adams's administration, about half as much to Jefferson's administration as to Washington's, and very little to Madison's first administration. The practice of organizing the material in terms of presidential administrations after 1789 was well nigh universal among textbook writers of the period. Another practice equally common was the heavy emphasis on wars, treated by years.

In the long period between 1812 and 1861 the books gave large topics such as the War of 1812, the War with Mexico, and political affairs, including problems relating to slavery, much attention. Foreign affairs, finance, territorial growth, industry, invention, and commerce received little consideration. While studying the Civil War the class met the following: Fort Sumter, Bull Run, Trent affair, the blockade, Peninsular campaign, Forts Henry and Donelson, Shiloh, New Orleans, Antietam, *Merrimac* and *Monitor,* Fredericksburg,

[71] Bagley and Rugg, *op. cit.,* p. 34.

Emancipation Proclamation, Chancellorsville, Gettysburg, Vicksburg, Chickamauga, battles around Chattanooga, Wilderness Campaign, Atlanta and Sherman's March, Early's raid, Sheridan's Campaign, fall of Richmond, Appomattox, and the assassination of Lincoln.[72]

In most of the books published prior to 1890 there was little left of the story after the Civil War was over. It seems that the authors used up so much of their energy in fighting the war all over again that they were unable to revive sufficiently to carry on the work to the date of copyright. So when the class reached 1865 it was near the end. In some of the books published or revised during the late 1890's, considerable attention was given to the getting of the Southern states back into the Union. Such then was the content of United States history taught in the two top grades of the elementary school during the forty years prior to 1900. It in reality was the content of the entire course of study in history in the elementary school during these years, except in a limited number of large cities.

Even though it did not come to large fruition there was about as much activity in behalf of history in the elementary school during the decade of the 1890's as there was in behalf of history in the secondary school. It will be recalled that the Herbartians were very active during this decade and that they were strong advocates of history on all levels of instruction. For example, one of their number said in 1892 regarding history as a subject of study below the high school:

"History, in the broad sense, should be the chief constituent of a child's education. That subject-matter which contains the essence of moral culture in generative form deserves to constitute the chief mental food of young people. The conviction

[72] *Ibid.*, p. 45.

of the high moral value of historic subjects and of their peculiar adaptability to children at different ages, brings us to a positive judgment as to their relative value among studies. The first question, preliminary to all others in the common school course, 'What is the most important study?' is answered by putting *history* at the head of the list." [73]

In connection with the activity of the Herbartians in behalf of history in the elementary grades during the 1890's, the work of the Committees of Ten, Fifteen, and Twelve of the National Education Association should be recalled here. It will be remembered from the treatment of these committees in Division One that each of them proposed in general terms a course of study in history for the elementary grades. In view of the fact that these proposals are presented elsewhere, they need not be considered here. So the discussion will return to the efforts of the Herbartians in behalf of history in the elementary school, especially United States history in Grades IV, V, and VI. Some members of the Herbartian school of pedagogy went so far as to claim that United States history could be introduced into the intermediate grades without abandoning the belief in the culture epochs theory. One of them was making an appeal for United States history in these grades as early as 1892. The substance of this appeal is embodied in the excerpt below.

"There is little in our history to appeal to children below the fourth grade, that is, below ten years; but from the beginning of the fourth grade on American history is rich in moral-educative materials of the best quality and suited to children.

[73] C. A. McMurry, *Elements of General Method*, pp. 28 f. Bloomington, Ill.: Public School Publishing Co., 1892.

We are able to distinguish four principal epochs: 1. The age of pioneers, the ocean navigators like Columbus, Drake and Magellan, and the explorers of the continent like Smith, Champlain, LaSalle, and Frémont. 2. The period of settlements, of colonial history and of French and Indian wars. 3. The Revolution and life under the Arcticles of Confederation till the adoption of the Constitution. 4. Self-government under the Union and the growth and strengthening of the federal idea. While drawing largely upon general history for a full and detailed treatment of a few important topics in each of these epochs we should make a still more abundant use of the biographical and literary materials furnished by each. The concentration of school studies, with a historical series suggested by the culture epochs as a basis, would utilize our American history, biography and literature in a manner scarcely dreamed of heretofore." [74]

Whether there is any connection between the foregoing statement and the fact that the city of Baltimore was teaching United States history in Grades IV, V, and VI in 1894, using Eggleston's *First Book of American History* in Grades IV and V and *History of the United States* by the same author in Grade VI,[75] it is hard to say. At any rate, there seems to have been in this fact an occasion for rejoicing among the Herbartians.

The mention of history in the intermediate grades in the city of Baltimore in 1894 suggests the question "What about the primary grades?" A partial answer to this query is found in the following suggestion, for improving the work in history

[74] *Ibid.*, pp. 96 f.
[75] Mary S. Braun, "Teaching the Social Sciences Then and Now," *Baltimore Bulletin of Education*, X (1932), 85.

in the high school, made in 1896 by Professor John Dewey, then of the University of Chicago.

"There is one suggestion to be emphasized. That is that the course might be extended downwards. If there is to be any solution of the congestion in the secondary schools it must be in breaking down the rigid barrier between the so-called higher education and primary education. There are primary schools in existence that have eight years of historical work— schools which begin history in the first grade and keep it up. This introduction of history into the primary grades has come almost entirely without help or pressure from the higher grades. It has come because the teachers in those grades felt the need of getting something more adjusted to the needs of the pupils, something more vital than the usual formal three R's. I think it will be found that the interest of the high school and college would be furthered by devoting a part of their energies to seeing what can be done towards introducing history as a part of the regular work of the lower grades and in improving the methods of teaching history in the lower grades. We can't pile everything into the secondary schools; we must find relief farther back." [76]

Evidence of the small fruition of the large amount of activity in behalf of history in the elementary school during the 1890's is found in a summary of the situation by the Committee of Seven of the American Historical Association. It will be recalled that this Committee was speaking of conditions in about 1897 when it said:

[76] *Proceedings of the First Annual Meeting of the North Central Association of Colleges and Secondary Schools*, p. 22. Chicago: University of Chicago Press, 1896.

"Examination therefore seems to show that the present condition of instruction in history in the grades below the high
school is defective in that uniformity is so seldom found, that
there is no definite, well-defined object in teaching history,
that when an object is presented it is generally the factitious
one of patriotism, that as a rule the course is not prescribed
by experts either in history or in education, that only United
States history and state history are taught, that history is not
studied in connection with other subjects in the curriculum,
that a slavish use is too often made of the text-book, that a
mechanical division of the subject matter by pages or by administrations is often adopted, and that all instruction in this
subject is deferred until so late in the course." [77]

IV

THE MATURATION OF HISTORY AS A
SCHOOL SUBJECT, 1900–1920

During the first two decades of the present century history
as a school subject reached a maturity that was not even approached during the last two decades of the nineteenth century. This maturity was achieved under the guidance of
patterns set by the American Historical Association through
two of its committees on history in the schools, namely, the
Committee of Seven and the Committee of Eight. Speaking
generally, history in the high school reached its maturity according to the pattern set by the first one of these committees
in about 1916. It reached its maturity in the elementary grades
according to the pattern set by the Committee of Eight in
about 1920. After these dates there were many signs of a

[77] *Op. cit.*, pp. 166 f.

revolt from the *status quo* on both of these levels of instruction. Leaving these signs of revolt for later consideration, the discussion will pass directly to the objective evidence of maturity both in the extent of the offerings in history and the content taught.

THE EXTENT OF THE OFFERINGS IN HISTORY IN SECONDARY SCHOOLS, 1900–1916

The four-block set-up for history proposed by the Committee of Seven in December, 1898, and published early in 1899 was rapidly accepted by the secondary schools of the country. Those in charge of these schools had so much confidence and faith in the leadership of the American Historical Association that they almost ceased merely *offering* history, but *required* it instead. A survey of the situation with respect to history in 135 high schools in fourteen states in 1908–09 revealed, as Table XVI exemplifies, the faith that the educators had in the leadership of the historians—a faith, it should be remarked, that has in recent years atrophied, because of the assumption of leadership on the part of the educators themselves, especially after 1916.

The high schools represented in Table XVI on the average offered 3.24 years of history and required 2.31 years, including one-half year of civics both in years offered and required. In their offerings the history departments of these schools attempted to swallow the report of the Committee of Seven "hook, line, and sinker." For purposes of administration ancient history was occasionally taught as Greek history and as Roman history. The same was true of mediæval and modern, being taught as mediæval one-half year and modern one-half year. Some schools taught mediæval and did not teach modern, substituting English history for modern. There were a few left-overs from the old régime. A few hold-outs were still offering general history and fewer still adhering to the proposals of the Sub-committee on History, Civil Government,

TABLE XVI

HISTORY IN 135 HIGH SCHOOLS IN FOURTEEN STATES IN 1908-09*

FIELDS OFFERED	FREQUENCY
1. Greek....................................	31
2. Roman....................................	31
3. Ancient....................................	99
4. Mediæval and Modern.....................	92
5. United States.............................	131
6. English....................................	58
7. Mediæval....................................	21
8. Modern....................................	12
9. General....................................	4
10. French....................................	2
11. European..................................	1
12. Industrial..................................	1
13. History of Commerce......................	1
14. History of Illinois.........................	1

* Seventy-six schools in Indiana, 24 in Wisconsin, and 35 in other states scattered throughout the country except in the South.—O. H. Williams, *History Teaching in the High School*, pp. 46-51. Indiana University Bulletin, Vol. VII, No. 8. Bloomington, Ind.: Indiana University, 1909.

and Political Economy of the Committee of Ten. This Committee, it will be recalled, reported in 1894.

While the material collected by the office of the United States Commissioner of Education for the years 1900-01, 1905-06, 1909-10, and 1914-15 does not reveal the fields of history pursued during these years, it does show in a general way at least what was happening to history throughout the country. The data in Table XVII tell in terms of per cent the story of history in the secondary school for a decade and a half after 1900. This table reveals a number of interesting facts with respect to history in secondary schools during these years. One of these facts is the increase in the per cent of pupils pursuing history. In 1900–01 the per cent in the country as a whole of the total enrollments in all secondary schools reporting to the Commissioner pursuing history was 38.41. In 1914–15, it was 44.77. When the per cent is calculated on the basis of schools reporting on subjects pursued, it becomes 55.67 for 1909–10 and 51.46 for 1914–15. When the per cents in the last two columns of the table are compared with those in columns 5 and 6, the inadequacy of the per cents in the first six columns is demonstrated. The per cents in the last two columns portray the situation as it actually existed in all schools reporting subjects pursued.

Another fact revealed in Table XVII is the heavy emphasis on history in the South Atlantic and South Central states in 1909–10 and 1914–15. In the former of these groups of states 72.79 per cent of secondary-school pupils were pursuing history in 1909–10 and 68.36 per cent in 1914–15. The corresponding per cents in the South Central states were 73.05 and 68.27. Generally speaking the per cent of pupils pursuing history in the secondary schools of the other three groups of states in the table was about 20 per cent less than in the two groups mentioned above. Many other interesting facts are revealed by the data in Table XVII. Inasmuch as many of these relate to particular states, it seems advisable to leave to the reader the pleasure of discovering them.

The data from the reports of the United States Commissioner of Education's office leave untold certain parts of the story, namely, the fields of history pursued and the extent that the recommendations of the Committee of Seven were followed. For these parts of the story reliance has to be placed on other data, a considerable body of which is at hand. For

TABLE XVII

PER CENT OF PUPILS PURSUING HISTORY IN PUBLIC HIGH SCHOOLS AND PRIVATE HIGH SCHOOLS AND ACADEMIES DURING CERTAIN YEARS BETWEEN 1900 AND 1915 *

TERRITORY INCLUDED	Per Cent of Total Enrollment in All Schools Reporting						Per Cent of Enrollment in Schools Reporting Subjects Pursued	
	1900–1901	1902–1903	1904–1905	1905–1906	1909–1910	1914–1915	1909–1910	1914–1915
United States	38.41	38.76	40.51	42.16	40.23	44.77	55.67	51.46
North Atlantic Division	40.25	38.44	39.97	40.87	42.42	44.43	52.73	48.64
Maine	34.83	38.81	42.95	40.16	41.20	39.73	55.01	50.85
New Hampshire	41.24	43.45	41.65	44.21	39.55	39.42	55.35	44.17
Vermont	35.24	33.07	37.87	41.36	46.51	51.75	56.82	56.38
Massachusetts	50.02	47.15	44.78	45.39	44.85	44.11	52.27	46.45
Rhode Island	47.83	53.95	46.40	49.17	42.00	51.71	53.59	52.38
Connecticut	44.71	40.47	47.93	48.52	38.50	40.16	49.56	53.76
New York	37.00	32.48	34.69	34.98	34.79	37.35	44.20	40.70
New Jersey	37.37	36.89	45.11	42.46	42.80	41.39	52.85	43.77
Pennsylvania	36.79	38.78	39.61	43.00	54.47	57.23	66.23	62.43
South Atlantic Division	43.92	45.08	49.67	55.22	46.19	56.50	72.79	68.36
Delaware	37.89	37.28	33.05	35.99	23.01	49.94	76.50	53.52
Maryland	56.80	56.49	52.10	57.87	38.72	54.26	51.99	59.82
District of Columbia	51.01	43.97	52.77	52.97	16.64	23.92	30.06	28.29
Virginia	46.78	48.91	44.71	59.14	51.85	57.27	81.23	69.96
West Virginia	41.94	37.66	56.28	50.07	47.62	52.72	68.78	58.20
North Carolina	32.93	31.40	41.70	44.42	52.09	57.88	78.46	76.66
South Carolina	42.77	47.36	58.37	64.84	51.53	74.80	87.10	91.94
Georgia	41.93	47.78	49.51	56.40	52.80	50.99	84.76	78.53
Florida	35.66	45.99	58.10	60.99	42.37	59.68	75.23	78.49
South Central Division	40.21	40.80	43.65	46.43	43.91	52.32	73.05	68.27
Kentucky	39.62	41.06	40.25	38.00	40.98	50.10	59.86	58.83
Tennessee	32.99	36.59	32.77	35.81	30.66	40.23	62.15	51.48
Alabama	34.11	34.79	46.06	46.16	45.62	54.53	72.15	69.67
Mississippi	35.40	42.33	46.64	53.98	40.63	58.95	80.91	81.61
Louisiana	59.38	55.05	52.82	50.57	41.34	49.11	73.39	59.95
Texas	46.26	44.33	49.90	52.76	54.74	66.86	85.32	80.55
Arkansas	36.61	29.11	35.80	39.44	41.31	49.21	74.36	66.85
Oklahoma	23.64	23.38	28.67	45.49	14.20	44.43	60.10	62.84
Indian Territory	23.52	33.48	29.53	48.50	.....	.....	.....	.....
North Central Division	34.27	35.87	38.02	39.63	36.52	41.88	51.46	48.32
Ohio	29.03	32.81	33.73	33.83	33.68	35.88	45.93	40.96

TERRITORY INCLUDED	Per Cent of Total Enrollment in All Schools Reporting						Per Cent of Enrollment in Schools Reporting Subjects Pursued	
	1900–1901	1902–1903	1904–1905	1905–1906	1909–1910	1914–1915	1909–1910	1914–1915
Indiana	41.75	45.06	44.64	45.55	39.56	43.52	59.56	53.14
Illinois	33.25	35.52	34.86	35.11	32.19	37.26	44.80	42.56
Michigan	36.83	38.47	19.23	41.61	39.59	42.73	54.29	50.98
Wisconsin	31.38	27.76	42.25	44.34	41.65	47.76	54.60	54.15
Minnesota	41.01	41.46	43.67	44.92	43.30	39.25	55.27	42.39
Iowa	31.67	31.48	35.27	34.54	31.10	41.09	48.78	49.13
Missouri	40.42	44.08	45.18	52.16	43.38	57.15	59.54	65.31
North Dakota	28.75	31.72	33.61	37.27	27.81	36.30	47.00	40.73
South Dakota	34.08	37.61	40.51	41.70	34.29	50.14	56.52	56.71
Nebraska	35.08	30.92	31.03	35.59	36.80	44.04	50.06	49.28
Kansas	27.80	29.05	33.50	33.67	32.69	39.07	50.07	45.78
Western Division	48.94	50.22	45.45	37.09	39.65	40.86	55.20	45.83
Montana	40.31	67.73	65.76	65.00	47.56	41.44	57.55	48.45
Wyoming	33.49	41.23	40.64	40.03	60.11	40.74	61.94	56.78
Colorado	61.93	59.54	59.30	59.43	40.29	47.65	56.59	53.11
New Mexico	33.49	39.42	38.87	43.27	42.71	49.42	61.37	54.46
Arizona	29.53	24.72	65.10	66.49	36.80	26.67	55.34	68.64
Utah	14.46	18.07	22.93	24.43	24.13	33.23	38.61	38.45
Nevada	73.98	79.50	88.89	65.89	37.79	29.89	79.00	52.08
Idaho	27.85	39.44	28.84	37.21	41.37	43.16	58.99	53.03
Washington	33.45	41.42	33.07	38.09	35.88	41.18	49.75	45.75
Oregon	52.20	52.51	60.36	52.99	46.78	37.16	64.98	48.42
California	55.77	53.11	44.53	44.58	41.12	41.31	56.30	43.48

* Based on data from the reports of the Commissioner of Education for the years indicated.

All of the history taught in the schools represented above is included in the statistics for the years ending 1910 and 1915. The same statement probably holds for 1906 inasmuch as the blanks for this year included both United States and non-United States history. Probably only history other than United States is included in the data for 1900–1901.

example, a study of the offerings in history in the high schools of 236 cities in 41 states as reflected in 242 courses of study in use in 1914–15 revealed that in 156 of these cities the course in history was composed of ancient, mediæval and modern, English, and American history; in 44, of ancient, mediæval and modern, and American; in 31, of ancient, English, and American.[78] Here is to be seen the direct influence of the Committee of Seven. Evidence of the large acceptance by the schools of the North Central Association of Colleges and Secondary Schools of the four-block system proposed by this Committee is found in Table XVIII.

TABLE XVIII

NUMBER OF PUBLIC HIGH SCHOOLS BY STATES IN THE NORTH CENTRAL ASSOCIATION OFFERING CERTAIN FIELDS OF HISTORY DURING THE SCHOOL YEAR 1916–17 *

STATES	Number of Schools Offering				
	NUMBER OF SCHOOLS	ANCIENT HISTORY	MEDIÆVAL AND MODERN HISTORY	ENGLISH HISTORY	AMERICAN HISTORY
Arizona.........	6	6	6	1	6
Colorado........	36	36	34	20	35
Illinois..........	135	121	101	86	96
Indiana.........	79	79	72	27	79
Iowa...........	76	74	68	28	76
Kansas..........	67	65	62	9	66
Michigan.......	112	111	110	54	112
Minnesota.......	67	67	67	22	64
Missouri........	52	52	52	36	52
Montana........	25	25	24	15	25
Nebraska........	57	56	40	23	56
New Mexico....	4	3	4	2	4
North Dakota...	30	30	27	9	30
Ohio...........	165	145	146	65	161
South Dakota...	24	23	24	8	24
Wisconsin.......	92	92	91	36	91
Wyoming.......	5	5	5	3	5
Total.........	1032	990	933	444	982
Percentage.......	....	95.90	90.40	43.02	95.15

* Calvin O. Davis, *The Accredited Secondary Schools of the North Central Association*, pp. 95-97. United States Bureau of Education, Bulletin, 1919, No. 45, Washington, D. C.: Government Printing Office, 1919.

[78] H. H. Gold, "Method and Content of Courses in History in the High Schools of the United States," *School Review*, XXV (1917), 91.

The general acceptance prior to 1916 of the set-up for secondary-school history recommended by the Committee of Seven was not confined to the states composing the North Central Association. The state of New York adopted the set-up in 1910 and followed it for a decade, making only a slight change in the beginning of the mediæval and modern field and naming it modern history. Maryland likewise adopted the set-up almost in toto, as did most of the other states in the Union. Table I in Division One shows how completely the country as a whole had gone over to the four-block system by 1916. Certainly by this date nation-wide uniformity had been achieved in the field of secondary-school history. Never since has such uniformity existed throughout the country.

THE MATURATION OF ELEMENTARY-SCHOOL HISTORY

History matured more slowly in the grades than in the secondary schools during the two decades following 1900. The reader will recall that the report of the Committee of Eight of the American Historical Association on history in the elementary school corresponding to the report of the Committee of Seven on history in the high school did not appear until December, 1908—ten years after the latter committee's report —thus giving a systematic program in secondary-school history a lead of ten years over a smilar program for the grades. In the process of reaching the maturity that it had achieved in the elementary school by 1920, history moved down the grades in increasing amounts from year to year. Whereas the subject rarely enjoyed an independent existence in the first four grades in 1900, it was more or less common in these grades a few years later. For example, almost one-fourth of fifty selected

cities in the country in 1904 included history in their programs
of study for Grade III. The percentage of cities including
history in all grades at four periods between 1900 and 1925
is shown in Table XIX, from which it is evident that history

TABLE XIX

NUMBER AND PER CENT BY GRADES OF CITIES IN THE UNITED
STATES INCLUDING HISTORY IN THEIR PROGRAMS OF STUDY
IN 1904, 1910, 1914, AND 1924 *

NUMBER OF CITIES OR SCHOOL SYSTEMS	Number and Per Cent Including History in Grade															
	I		II		III		IV		V		VI		VII		VIII	
	NO.	%	NO.	%	NO.	%	NO.	%	NO.	%	NO.	%	NO.	%	NO.	%
1. Fifty selected cities in 1904.........	10	20	11	22	12	24	21	42	25	50	31	62	41	82	46	92
2. Two hundred and fifty-nine schools and school systems in 1910†...	116	44	127	45	147	56	163	62	200	77	209	80	222	85	206	79
3. Fifty largest cities in 1910.........	8	16	9	18	11	22	17	34	31	62	39	78	48	96	50	100
4. Fifty selected cities in 1915.........	13	26	15	30	22	44	35	70	42	84	42	84	49	99	50	100
5. Three hundred and three cities in 1924...........	28	9	35	11	62	20	129	42	224	74	223	73	253	83	218	72

* Data secured from (1) George C. Kyte, *A Study of the Time Allotments in the Elementary School Subjects*, pp. 6, 7, 8. California Curriculum Study Bulletin, No. 1. Berkeley, California: University of California Printing Office, 1925; (2) R. M. Tryon, *Materials, Methods, and Administration of History Study in the Elementary Schools of the United States*, p. 41; (3) William H. Elson, *Annual Report of the Superintendent of Schools*, Cleveland Public Schools, 1909-1910, p. 15; (4) and (5) George C. Kyte, *op. cit.*
† Fractional per cents omitted here and in No. 5.

was firmly established in Grades VII and VIII of certain cities
as early as 1904 and that it remained thus established throughout the years represented in the table. Furthermore, there is
evidence in Table XIX to the effect that history had wended
its way into the intermediate grades by 1910, there being at

this date 80 per cent of 209 schools and school systems including it in their programs of study in Grade VI; 77 per cent in
Grade V; and 62 per cent in Grade IV. At this same date
about half of these schools and school systems included the
subject in their programs of study for Grades I, II, and III.
It is interesting to record that this situation had changed by
1924, at which time history was giving way somewhat to a
unified program in the social sciences.

The general situation in 1904 in the fifty cities included in
Item 1 of Table XIX was concretely set forth as follows by
the individual who studied these cities.

History and civics, as such, do not occur in the lower grades.
The kindred topics which might legitimately be classed under
those titles are historical stories. In fact, below the fifth grade
there seems to exist much confusion in the teaching of history.
It is found under the various captions, history and civics, history and literature, historical narratives, historical stories,
myths and fables, oral history, *et cetera, ad infinitum.* Uniformity of terminology does not always indicate uniformity of content, but certainly one is suspicious in reference to the uniformity of content when the terminology is so varied.[79]

The evidence in Table XIX of the prevalence of history in
the elementary grades during the two decades following 1903
is all in terms of the number and per cent of schools that included the subject in their programs of study. More important than facts of this nature are those relating to the total
time devoted to history in each grade, the number of recitations
a week, the length of the recitation period, and the per cent
of the total school time devoted to history. Data on these
items are at hand for the country as a whole and for certain

[79] Bruce R. Payne, *Public Elementary School Curriculum,* pp. 23 f. New
York: Silver, Burdett and Co., 1905.

TABLE XX

NUMBER OF RECITATIONS AND MINUTES A WEEK, LENGTH OF THE
RECITATION PERIOD, AND THE PER CENT OF THE TOTAL RECI-
TATION TIME DEVOTED TO HISTORY IN THE ELEMENTARY
GRADES, 1910–1915 *

	Grades							
	I	II	III	IV	V	VI	VII	VIII
1. The country at large in 1910								
a. Median number of recitations								
{ Number of systems.....	116	127	147	163	200	209	222	206
{ Number of recitations..	3	3.3	3.6	3.9	5	5	5	5
b. Median duration in minutes of recitation period								
{ Number of systems.....	114	125	142	173	200	207	219	216
{ Number of minutes.....	14.8	14.6	20.8	18.6	27.2	23.5	28.0	30.4
c. Median time per week in minutes devoted to history								
{ Number of systems.....	116	125	147	163	210	215	222	216
{ Time per week in minutes.................	33	43	48	75	85	98	113	132
d. Median per cent of school time devoted to history								
{ Number of systems.....	64	62	88	88	121	128	134	135
{ Per cent of time to history................	5	5	6	6.6	9	9.3	10.7	10.9
2. Fifteen cities and towns in Minnesota in 1911–1912								
a. Average time in minutes a week devoted to history	49	56	67	87	110	111	166	187
b. Average number of recitations in history a week.	5	5	3	4	3	4	4	4
3. Fifty cities in the country at large in 1915								
a. Average allotment in minutes to history.........	1620	1860	2100	3420	4020	4260	5460	7072
b. Average per cent of total recitations devoted to history................	3.1	3.4	3.8	5.8	6.9	7.3	9.2	11.6
c. Lowest allotment in minutes to history.........	540	630	1200	900	900	1200	1980	3220
d. Highest allotment in minutes to history.........	3000	3000	3780	5220	9480	7980	10,020	12,960

* (1) R. M. Tryon, *op. cit.*, pp. 46-49; (2) *Eighteenth Annual Report of the Inspector of State Graded Schools*, State of Minnesota, for the school year ending July 31, 1913, pp. 12, 13, 14; and (3) Henry W. Holmes, "Time Distributions by Subjects and Grades in Representative Cities," *The Fourteenth Yearbook of the National Society for the Study of Education*, Part I (1915), p. 26.

selected cities. They are included in Table XX, which contains conclusive evidence to the effect that history had gained a place of considerable importance in the sun of elementary school programs by 1915. Three recitations a week, nearly fifteen minutes in duration, had been achieved in Grades I and II as early as 1910. By 1915 a little over 3 per cent of the total recitation time in fifty cities was devoted to history. The standing of history must have been on a par with many other subjects in the program of studies in 1910, there being five recitations a week, nearly thirty minutes in duration, devoted to it in all grades above the fourth. It is, therefore, merely recording a fact when one says that history was firmly established in the elementary grades as early as 1910. The gains after this date were primarily in the realm of content.

CONTENT OF SECONDARY-SCHOOL HISTORY, 1900–20

It does not take many words to describe the general content of secondary-school history during the first two decades of the present century. So far as the fields taught are concerned they were almost exactly those recommended by the Committee of Seven of the American Historical Association. In fact, in some states the foregoing time division could be moved forward ten years. Writing as late as 1930 on history in the small high schools of Georgia, the superintendent of schools of Waynesboro said:

"Despite the fact that the social sciences offer perhaps the best means of realizing through classroom instruction one of the 'Cardinal Aims' of secondary education, i.e. training for citizenship, the program of these sciences in the small high school usually follows the recommendations of the Committee of Seven in 1899. That is, the chronological arrangement of history is followed, and history is taught to the exclusion of almost all of the other social sciences. There are still in Georgia high schools offering only English history in the first year, ancient and mediæval history in the second year, modern European history the third year, and advanced American history the final year. Other and more progressive schools have substituted for English history a course in community civics covering either one or two semesters of the first year, and have given really adequate attention to some of the problems of democracy in the fourth year. But the place of ancient and mediæval history in the second year seems permanent and even unchallenged." [80]

The Committee of Seven felt that its work was done when the fields of history to be taught in secondary schools were set up and their boundaries and general content indicated. It was left for others to prepare syllabi for each of the proposed fields. Such syllabi were not long lacking. One appeared for each of the four fields recommended by the Committee two years after its report was published. These syllabi were prepared by special committees of the New England History Teachers' Association.[81] Their influence on history in the secondary school would be difficult to overstate. Appearing as they did so soon after the publication of the report of the Committee of Seven they became models for those who wrote textbooks and made courses of study in conformity with the recommendations of this Committee.

[80] W. T. Knox, "Social Science in the Second Year of High School," *High School Quarterly,* XVIII (1930), 192.

[81] *A History Syllabus for Secondary Schools,* Outlining the Four Years' Course in History Recommended by the Committee of Seven of the American Historical Association. New York: D. C. Heath and Co., 1901.

As would be expected, textbooks began to appear in series soon after 1901, for example, the Essentials Series published by the American Book Company and the Nation Series published by D. Appleton and Company. All of the leading companies of the time engaged in the publication and distribution of textbooks rapidly placed books on the market written to conform to the set-up of the Committee of Seven. The tabulation on page 190 indicates that there was no scarcity of textbook material between 1910 and 1920 in the field of secondary-school history. Those who wished to follow the leadership of the American Historical Association were not handicapped in the realm of textbooks.

There were, of course, books in individual fields other than those tabulated below. All told, there was ample opportunity for selection in the field of texts in history written to conform to the four-block system recommended by the Committee of Seven.

The slavish adherence to a textbook in the hands of the pupils, the prevailing practice during most of the two decades prior to 1920, sooner or later became obnoxious to a number of people who had no texts of their own on the market. The general tone of the adverse criticisms of the textbooks in history is well represented by the following remarks made in 1909 by one of their critics.

"The first defect [of current textbooks in history] lies in the kind of content or subject-matter selected and embodied in the texts, and a study of the matter has led me to conclude that the writers have had little or no perception of the comparative value of the material for cause-and-effect purposes. Instead of testing their material by the criterion, What is most determining? and, What are the really greatest episodes? matter has

TABULAR VIEW OF TEXTBOOKS IN SECONDARY-SCHOOL HISTORY AVAILABLE FROM SIX COMPANIES, 1910–1920

BOOK COMPANY	ANCIENT HISTORY	MEDIÆVAL AND MODERN HISTORY	AMERICAN HISTORY	ENGLISH HISTORY
1. Ginn and Company	Meyers, Ancient History / Breasted, Ancient Times	Meyers, Medieval and Modern History / Robinson, An Introduction to Western Europe and Medieval and Modern Times	Muzzey, An American History / Stephenson, An American History / Montgomery, The Student's American History	Montgomery, The Leading Facts of English History / Cheney, A Short History of England
2. American Book Company	Wolfson, Essentials of American History / Morey, Outlines of Ancient History and Ancient Peoples	Harding, Essentials of Medieval and Modern History / Harding, New Medieval and Modern History	Hart, Essentials of American History and New American History	Walker, Essentials of English History
3. Allyn and Bacon	West, Ancient History and Ancient World	West, Modern History and Modern World	West, American History and Government and History of the American People / Latané, History of the United States	Andrews, A Short History of England
4. D. Appleton and Company	Westerman, The Story of the Ancient Nations	Monroe and Whitcomb, Medieval and Modern History	McLaughlin, History of American Nation	Wrong, The British Nation
5. D. C. Heath and Company	Webster, Ancient History	Webster, Medieval and Modern History	Cousin and Hill, American History for Schools	Thomas, A History of England
6. The Macmillan Company	Botsford, A History of the Ancient World	Adams, Medieval and Modern History	Ashley, American History / Channing, A Students' History of the United States	

been placed in the books because it has been the fashion of previous history writers to put such and such topics in. In other words, our history for schools has been on a traditional basis rather than on a rational. It has been chiefly military and political only, until recently, and it has handled these things in a lifeless, merely enumerative manner.

"There is also a great defect in the texts in that they devote too much time to events remote in time and too little to those which are near. Our histories have commonly proceeded after the spirit of the statement the philosopher Hegel made relative to the Chinese: A Chinaman is first good for something when he is dead. So our textbook makers have supposed that only dead history is good history and the deader the history the better. If it was a matter of general history they would spend most of the time on ancient history; and if either modern or ancient were to be omitted it would be the modern. If it was a case of American history the colonial would get the benefit of the greater time as compared with the national; and some books seemed to think that this present end of our national history was hardly worth mentioning.

"The third defect of texts is in the matter of organization. I should say that most of our histories show a momentous lack of organizing principle. They are mere jumbles of things. I have in mind a text written for secondary schools by one of the reputed historians of our country which is a mere epitome of all the incidents which have in any way got connected with our national career. It is about the best illustration of the original chaos of matter that I can think of. It contains over 600 topics. These topics, in their arrangements, have no relation to each other as a general thing. They are strung together as they are just because their events happened in that order.

It is a mere chronology, not history. It has no indications of thought and rationality." [82]

One who believed in 1917 that history as then organized and taught had little or no value in the education of youths twelve to eighteen years of age commented as follows on the characteristics of existing texts in the field:

"If now we turn to the texts in current use, and very literally adhered to by the large majority of history teachers, we find certain characteristics of organization substantially common to all—and these, I take it, must be assumed to constitute the heart or core of history as an approved school subject by history teachers today. We note the comprehensiveness of treatment, the dominance of the chronological order of presentation; the great inclusiveness of detail; the consequent condensation of description and explanation; the absence of any suggestion (as a rule) of cross reference to contemporary conditions or events that might prove illuminating, or interpretative of the historical situation under consideration or that might exhibit some possible contemporary applications of that which is being studied; and the uniform implicit expectation that 'mastery' of the subject will consist chiefly in the kind of memorization that results in ability verbally to reproduce faithful 'copies' of statements given in the books." [83]

There was much complaint during the second decade of the present century against the textbook because of its over-emphasis on the political and military phases of history and un-

---

[82] John M. Gillette, "Reconstruction of History for Teaching Purposes," *School Review*, XVII (1909), 549 f.

[83] David Snedden, "History and Other Social Sciences in the Education of Youths Twelve to Eighteen Years of Age," *School and Society*, V (1917), 272.

der-emphasis on the social and economic aspects The justness of this complaint is reflected in Table XXI, which portrays the emphasis in twenty-two textbooks in three fields of secondary-school history on certain aspects of the subject. It is evident from this table that the content of secondary-school

TABLE XXI

AVERAGE PER CENT OF TOTAL PAGES DEVOTED TO CERTAIN ASPECTS OF HISTORY BY TWENTY–TWO TEXTBOOKS IN THREE FIELDS OF HIGH–SCHOOL HISTORY IN GENERAL USE ABOUT 1920 *

ASPECTS OF HISTORY	Average Per Cent Devoted to, by Texts in		
	ANCIENT HISTORY (SEVEN TEXTS)	MEDIÆVAL AND MODERN HISTORY (SEVEN TEXTS)	AMERICAN HISTORY (EIGHT TEXTS)
1. Economic........	8.6	8.8	12.0
2. Military.........	15.3	10.2	16.0
3. Political.........	46.1	63.1	61.3
4. Social...........	26.2	15.5	7.9
5. Geographical.....	3.8	3.5	2.8
6. Biographical	32.0	47.0	19.0

* Based on data assembled by Julian B. Hubbell in his "A Suggested Plan for the Reorganization of History Material in Secondary Schools." Unpublished Master's thesis, George Peabody College for Teachers, 1922.

history in the early 1920's was largely political history, more so in mediæval and modern and American history than in ancient. Combining the emphasis on military and political history, one secures an average for the three fields of a little over 70 per cent devoted to these two aspects. While the biographical aspect received considerable attention in the texts, the economical, social, and geographical aspects were evidently neglected. So the bill of particulars against these texts issued by their adverse critics seems to have been founded on facts.

CONTENT OF HISTORY IN THE ELEMENTARY GRADES, 1900–1920

It does not take many words to describe the content of history in the primary grades at the beginning of the period under consideration here. There simply was no content of an historical nature taught in these grades except in a small number of schools and school systems. The intermediate grades contained considerable content of an historical nature, especially Grade VI. The two top grades were well supplied with history content, usually in the form of a textbook in United States history. A study made in 1904 of the historical content in the courses of study[84] of ten cities revealed that topics from American history predominated in all grades in which history appeared. In the three upper grades the same topics frequently appeared. Chief among these were Discoveries, Explorations, Settlements, Colonies, Colonial Government, Revolution, Articles of Confederation, Constitution, French and Indian Wars, War of 1812, Mexican War, Civil War, Spanish-American War, Territorial Expansion, Slavery, Era of Good Feeling, Monroe Doctrine, Missouri Compromise, and Nullification.

Another study of history in the elementary grades which was made at about the same time that the foregoing study by Payne was completed discovered three marked tendencies with respect to content. Stated in the words of the one making the study these tendencies were:

"First, there is evident a very general tendency toward the introduction of biographical and historical tales into the lower grades. Second, this material is now being given a place as a definite part of the curriculum. While much of it may be

[84] Bruce R. Payne, *op. cit.*, p. 50.

merely simple reading material, yet there is coming to be a definite organization into the curriculum and a definite recognition of the subject as history. The importance of this point is to be recognized when we remember that the teacher's aims are very different in reading from that in history work, and the results obtained are apt to be, or at least should be, very different. Third, this tendency reveals a very general use of Greek and Roman myth and legend as well as historical and biographical tales, and a growing tendency to select more and more from the Middle Ages. And the question is raised whether the time is not near at hand for the attempt at organization of these subjects into a more definite course of instruction, to divide with the material of United States history the time and the interest of the students." [85]

There is evidence available which indicates that a few individual schools were doing much more in history than was being done in the cities studied by Payne. For example, in the "Dewey" Elementary School, located on the campus of the University of Chicago, large provision was made for history in the primary and intermediate grades as early as 1905. Inasmuch as what was done in this school later became more or less common, it seems important enough to include here.

HISTORY IN THE "DEWEY" ELEMENTARY SCHOOL, 1905

Grade I. Study of a General Farm: making a farm in sand box; study of farm animals; occupations of the farm; outdoor farm-gardening.

Grade II. Primitive Life: life of primitive people; study of

[85] Paul Monroe, "Actual Condition of Instruction in History in the Public Elementary Schools," *Third Annual Convention* of the Association of History Teachers of the Middle States and Maryland, 1905, p. 65.

country; shell people, or people along the sea; improvements
in weapons; discovery of metals; domestication of animals;
agricultural stage.

Grade III. A study of the Phœnicians, the Eskimo and the
explorations of Hansen, Livingston, and Columbus.

Intermediate Grades. French explorers, settlement of Virginia, New England, and the American Revolution.[86]

During the first ten years of the present century specific
content in history increasingly appeared in the lower elementary grades, so much so that by the end of this decade
history had become the rule rather than the exception in
these grades. It is known with considerable exactness what
the content of history in each of the elementary grades was in
1910. Table XXII contains the results of an elaborate study
of history in the elementary schools of the United States at this
date. The reader will not be surprised over the heavy empha-

TABLE XXII

HISTORY IN THE ELEMENTARY GRADES, 1910

FREQUENCY

I. Topics and Fields Included in Grade I of 180 Schools
    and School Systems
    1. Indian life.................................... 96
    2. Pioneer life.................................. 70
    3. Primitive life............................... 19
    4. Stories, biographies, and celebrations connected
       with United States history................. 57

[86] Laura L. Runyon, "The Teaching of Elementary History in the 'Dewey'
School," pp. 23–25 and 27–29. Unpublished Master's thesis, University of
Chicago, 1906.

There was available as early as 1898 two proposals for a program in history
for each of the elementary grades. See E. W. Kemp, *An Outline of Method
in History*. Terre Haute, Indiana: The Inland Publishing Company, 1896; and
Emily J. Rice, *Course of Study in History and Literature*. Chicago: A. Flanagan, 1898. Before the close of 1903 two additional proposals had appeared.
They were by Lucy W. Salmon and Charles A. McMurry, appearing in the
First Yearbook of the National Society for the Scientific Study of Education,
1902 and in *Special Method in History*. New York: The Macmillan Co., 1903.

FREQUENCY

5. Local history and civics (community life, home, and neighborhood, etc.)..................... 15
6. Elementary Old World history.................. 13
7. Miscellaneous and indefinite.................... 42

II. Topics and Fields Included in Grade II of 200 Schools and School Systems
    1. Material relating to primitive, pioneer, and Indian life... 51
    2. Material from some phase of United States history 124
    3. Material relating to Old World history.......... 95
    4. Material not included above (fairy tales, myths, legends, community life, work correlated with geography, etc.)........................... 51

III. Topics and Fields Included in Grade III of 209 Schools and School Systems
    1. Stories of great Americans..................... 24
    2. The Indians.................................... 11
    3. Stories of pioneer life in America.............. 8
    4. Holidays, birthdays, and celebrations........... 8
    5. Stories of Washington, Lincoln, and Columbus.... 16
    6. Hebrew life and heroes......................... 66
    7. Roman and Norse life, myths, and stories........ 5

IV. Topics and Fields Included in Grade IV of 244 Schools and School Systems
    1. Roman history, biography, and myths........... 125
    2. Greek history, biography, and myths............ 29
    3. Hebrew life.................................... 7
    4. Mediæval history stories and biographies........ 4
    5. English and Norse history stories............... 2

V. Topics and Fields Included in Grade V of 254 Schools and School Systems
    1. United States history........................... 216
        a. United States history, text in hands of the pupils................................... 95
        b. United States history from a biographical standpoint............................. 87
        c. Early colonial history and pioneer life in America................................. 29
        d. State and local history..................... 5

FREQUENCY

2. Old World history............................ 31
    a. Greek and Roman history.................. 22
    b. English history........................... 9

VI. Topics and Fields Included in Grade VI of 238
    Schools and School Systems
   1. United States history
    a. United States history with text in hands of
       pupils................................... 82
    b. Early United States history, including explor-
       ers, settlements, Indians, and pioneers.... 12
    c. United States history (nothing said about the
       text)................................... 21
    d. State history (text used).................. 5
   2. Old World history
    a. English history........................... 111
    b. Greek, Roman, and Ancient history......... 21
    c. European history (continental)............. 10

VII. Chief Topics and Fields Included in Grade VII of
    259 Schools and School Systems
   1. United States history to about 1789............. 100
   2. United States history (no limit stated)........... 135
   3. Discovery, exploration, and colonization......... 9
   4. Entire field of United States history............. 3
   5. United States since 1789....................... 7
   6. State history................................. 2
   7. English history............................... 17
   8. Roman history............................... 3
   9. Greek history................................. 2
  10. Ancient history.............................. 2

VIII. Chief Topics and Fields Included in Grade VIII of
    259 Schools and School Systems
   1. United States history completed................. 170
   2. American history (no amount stated)............ 84
   3. Westward expansion, industrial and political his-
    tory of the United States.................... 2
   4. The making of the American nation............. 2
   5. State history................................. 5
   6. Greek history and life......................... 2
   7. English history............................... 2

FREQUENCY

8. Roman life and stories of the Romans............ 3
9. Stories of the Middle Ages [87]................... 1

sis on United States history shown in the table when he re-
calls the fact that there were in 1903 thirty states that required
by law the teaching of this field of history in the elementary
grades. These states were: Alabama, Arizona, Colorado, Cali-
fornia, Connecticut, Florida, Illinois, Indiana, Iowa, Kansas,
Kentucky, Louisiana, Maryland, Massachusetts, Mississippi,
Montana, Nevada, New Mexico, North Carolina, North
Dakota, Ohio, South Carolina, South Dakota, Tennessee,
Texas, Vermont, Virginia, Washington, West Virginia and
Wisconsin.[88]

It will be observed from Table XXII that United States history composed the bulk of the work in Grades VII and VIII.
Inasmuch as a text in the hands of the pupils furnished practically all of the material, an analysis of typical texts of the
period will show the emphasis that was placed on the various
large divisions of the field. Such an analysis is at hand in
terms of the per cent each of eight texts allotted to these divisions. It is presented in Table XXIII, which shows that between 1900 and 1920 eight of the textbooks in United States
history intended for Grades VII and VIII placed heavy emphasis on the Colonial period prior to the beginning of the
Revolution, devoting about one-fifth of their entire pages to
it. The Revolutionary War and the Civil War also received
major emphasis, each being given about 10 per cent of the
total space. A class in following a composite of the eight texts
in Table XXX would have in a school year of 180 days spent

[87] R. M. Tryon, *op. cit.,* pp. 8–21.
[88] Jesse K. Flanders, *Legislative Control of the Elementary Curriculum,* p.
30. New York: Bureau of Publications, Teachers College, Columbia University, 1925.

TABLE XXIII

PER CENT OF TOTAL WORDS IN EACH OF EIGHT TEXTBOOKS IN
UNITED STATES HISTORY DEVOTED TO CERTAIN LARGE DI-
VISIONS OF THE FIELD *

TEXTS	DISCOVERY AND EXPLORATION	COLONIAL DEVELOPMENT	COLONIAL WARS	PRE-REVOLUTION	REVOLUTION	1783-1812	1812-1861	CIVIL WAR	1865 TO PUBLICATION
1. W. H. Davidson, *A History of the United States*. Copyright date, 1902; pp., 548; words, 88,716..............	11.0	15.9	3.5	3.1	10.0	7.2	23.4	12.5	11.3
2. T. B. Lawler, *Essentials of American History*. Copyright date, 1902; pp., 384; words, 69,400....................	14.0	15.7	3.4	2.8	13.0	3.8	23.6	9.7	13.5
3. W. H. Mace, *A School History of the United States*. Copyright date, 1904; pp., 465; words, 108,900........	6.0	20.2	3.4	4.5	9.0	9.4	23.1	10.5	13.8
4. W. E. Chancellor, *A Textbook of American History*. Copyright date, 1903; pp., 653; words, 106,100........	8.0	15.7	2.6	4.1	12.5	5.0	10.9	10.5	38.8
5. W. A. Mowry, *Essentials of United States History*. Copyright date, 1906; pp., 382; words, 87,100..............	6.0	13.7	2.4	4.4	15.0	10.7	19.7	11.5	16.4
6. J. A. Woodburn and T. F. Moran, *American History and Government*. Copyright date, 1906; pp., 502; words, 127,-100......................	7.0	11.0	3.6	4.6	7.4	27.8	23.6	10.0	9.6
7. J. B. McMaster, *A Brief History of the United States*. Copyright date, 1907; pp., 434; words, 76,756..............	4.1	21.3	5.2	2.4	10.0	15.2	23.2	7.0	13.1
8. Edward Channing, *A Short History of the United States*. Copyright date, 1900; pp., 407; words, 73,000........	6.3	10.5	2.3	6.0	7.8	18.3	24.9	11.7	10.2

* W. C. Bagley and H. O. Rugg, *op. cit.*, pp. 10 f. and 22. For the sake of uniformity and brevity the fractional per cents were limited to one decimal place. They were not always thus limited in the study from which they were taken.

approximately 15 days on Discovery and Exploration, 28 days on Colonial Development, about 8 days each on Colonial Wars and Pre-Revolution, 22 on the Revolutionary War, 20 on the period from 1783–1812, 24 on the period from 1812–1861, 19 on the Civil War, and 29 on the period from 1865 to about 1915.

During the second decade of the present century history in the elementary grades was under the almost complete domination of the report of the Committee of Eight of the American Historical Association, published in 1909. Especially was this true in the elementary grades of city school systems. The rural schools could not do all that the Committee proposed for each grade, so they had to be content with an approximation in some grades. Generally speaking, they continued after 1910 to teach in the top two grades what they had been teaching during the previous decade. Those ambitious rural schools that did attempt to teach history in the grades below the seventh, followed the prevailing practices in the city school systems.

There is at hand a body of evidence relative to the content of history both in the city and the rural schools during the last two or three years prior to 1920. Table XXIV contains the results of a study of the content of history in 1918 as outlined in eighty-six courses of study (mostly city) selected at random from the whole United States. The hand of the Committee of Eight is readily recognized in it. It will be ob-

TABLE XXIV

HISTORY IN THE ELEMENTARY GRADES OF EIGHTY–SIX CITIES, 1918

FREQUENCY

I. Chief Topics and Fields Included in Grade I
  1. Stories of primitive peoples other than Indians... 13
  2. Indian life.....................................   9

served, however, by reference to Table XXII that this Committee actually did little more than induce most of the schools
in the country to undertake what a few were doing when it
made its report. Except the recommendations for Grade VI
there was none made by the Committee of Eight that was not
in practice somewhere in the land when it made its report.
With but fourteen courses from 86 cities outlining European
background of United States history in 1918, it would seem
that old ideas were retained more frequently than new ones
were adopted.

Apropos of the schools using state courses of study in the
elementary grades in about 1920, the available material does
not always indicate what was taught in each grade. Of forty-
four state courses of study for rural schools in force at the
beginning of 1920, twenty provided for Grade VI outlines
based on the European background of United States history,
the course suggested for this grade by the Committee of
Eight.[90] Furthermore, twenty-one of these courses outlined
the history of the United States after 1789 by presidential administrations, following the prevailing practice of the text-

[89] W. G. Reeder, "Materials of History Study in the Elementary Schools of
the United States." An unpublished study on file in the Department of Education Library, University of Chicago, 1918.

[90] Charles M. Reinoehl, *Analytic Survey of State Courses of Study for Rural
Elementary Schools*, p. 79. Bureau of Education Bulletin, 1922, No. 42.
Washington, D. C.: Government Printing Office, 1922.

books of the period in this field. Inasmuch as no grade placement of topics is available, as is the case in courses of study
primarily for city systems, the topics in history appearing in
thirty-five of the forty-four state courses for rural schools are
listed below in the order of their frequency of appearance,
beginning with the one at the top of the list.

HISTORY IN THIRTY-FIVE STATE COURSES OF STUDY FOR RURAL ELEMENTARY SCHOOLS IN FORCE IN 1920

I. Topics Appearing in 80 Per Cent or More of the Courses:

Slavery, slaves
Historical pictures
Colonization, settlements
Manners, customs
Discoveries
Education, schools
Explorations
National constitution
History stories
Famous men, leaders
Home life, shelter
Nationalities in America
Colonial governments
Thanksgiving Day
English settlements

Indians, Indian life
National growth
Biographies
Spanish in America
Dutch in America
European history (background)
Government
Trade, transportation
American Revolution
Civil War
French in America
Declaration of Independence
Indian warfare
Louisiana Purchase
War of 1812

II. Topics Appearing in 60 to 80 Per Cent of the Courses:

International relations
Formation of constitution
Territorial expansion
Food, its distribution
Inventions
Modes of travel
Washington's birthday
Pioneer life
Industries, occupations
Wars, conquests

Agriculture, farming
Comparisons, contrasts
Printing, paper, books
Northwest Territory
Bible stories
Patriots, heroes
Religion, churches
Spanish-American War
Immigration, emigration
Roads, road building

Rivalry between nations
National holidays
Clothing, dress
Foreign affairs
Army, Navy
Missouri Compromise
Mexican War
Continental Congresses
Political parties
Money systems
The telegraph
Articles of Confederation
Tariff and free trade
Panama Canal
Railroads

Capital and labor
The Crusades
Acquisition of Texas
Southern Confederacy
Treaties
Admission of states
Financial affairs
Cities and towns
History of home state
Groups of colonies
Social life and affairs
Sports and amusements
Industrial growth
Products

III. Topics Appearing in 40 to 60 Per Cent of the Courses:

Myths, legends
Manufacturing
Historical poems, songs
Memorial day
Primitive life
Lincoln's birthday
Elections, primaries
Dred Scot Decision
Industrial revolution
Compromises
The Greeks
The Romans
Land claims
Secession
Oregon Territory
Reconstruction in the South
Commercial interference
Gold and silver
Western trade routes
The Confederation
The Critical period
Kansas Nebraska Act
Impressment of seamen
Fourth of July

Cotton, cotton gin
Telephone
Constitutional amendments
Emancipation Proclamation
Abolition of slavery
Colonial life
Religious toleration
Taxation
Canals, waterways
Ordinance of 1787
Growth of the West
United States a world power
Fugitive Slave Law
Spoils System
Spanish Armada
Departments of government
Nullification
Monroe Doctrine
Banks, banking
Military achievements
Local history
Fur trading, furs
Expositions, festivals
The Teutons

New England Confederacy
National Congress
Acquisition of Florida
Erie Canal
The Presidents
Compromise of 1850
Civil-service reform
The steamboat
National highways
State rights, sovereignty
Congressional debates
Boundary disputes
Eastern trade routes
Charter governments
Colonization, motives
The Stamp Act

The Germans
French and Indian Wars
Labor unions
Strikes, lockouts
Alaska Territory
Business depressions, panics
The Magna Charta
Battles, campaigns
Religious persecution
Revenues, expenditures
Cost of wars
Natural resources
Farm machinery, implements
Woman suffrage
Peace, peace conferences

IV. Topics Appearing in Fewer than 40 Per Cent of the Courses:

Arbitration
Diplomacy
Authors, men of letters
Buildings
Temples
Chinese, "open door"
Christmas
Child life
Columbus Day
Communication, means of
Conservation of natural resources
Courts
Trial by jury
Cuban relations
Current events
Domestic affairs
Debts, national and state
Fishing, fisheries
Flags, United States flag
Generals, soldiers
Hawaiian Islands

Inventors
Land surveys
Land tenure
Mining, minerals
Philippine Islands
Plantation life
Population
Porto Rico
Postal system
Preamble to the constitution
Rural free delivery
Scientists, science
Seaports
Ship building
State institutions
Statesmen
Trade relations
Transportation, means of
Trusts, corporations
Universities, colleges
Voting, the ballot
Wars, cost of

Internal improvements   Women, famous
Inaugurations   Life: economic, industrial, insti-
Indian reservations   tutional, political, religious,
                                    social[91]

The foregoing lists by no means include all the topics that
the thirty-five courses of study in history contained. In fact
these lists contain less than 37 per cent of the topics, there being
a total of 456 which appeared in at least two of the courses. So
it is evident even from the lists of topics included above that
those responsible for the content of history in the rural elementary schools in 1920 desired that the pupils in these
schools come in contact with a multitude of historical topics.
Furthermore, they were somewhat provincial in their desires,
inasmuch as most of the topics they selected were from the
field of United States history. On contemplating even the
topics listed above one is led to reflect that, if to secure a 100
per cent effective use of courses of study in history made by
state departments of education in 1920 had been as easy as
the work of making these courses, the pupils in the rural
elementary schools of this country would have left them with
at least a smattering knowledge of the social order in which
they were living.

V

THE REVOLT FROM THE STATUS QUO: THE PERIOD OF EXPERIMENTATION, DIVERSITY, AND CONFUSION

Prior to 1920 there were always a few individuals who were
dissatisfied with the four-block set-up of the Committee of

[91] Reinoehl, op. cit., pp. 79 f.

Seven. The report of the Committee of Five in December, 1910, was an attempt to meet the demands of the dissenters. Subsequent events, however, demonstrated that the dissenters were primarily academicians who wanted to formulate a course of study in secondary-school history in terms of their pet hobbies. The educators had accepted the report of the Committee of Seven at least five years before that of the Committee of Five appeared and they did not care to change their minds so frequently. So the dominance of the Committee of Seven went on undisturbed.

A PERIOD OF UNCERTAINTY IN SECONDARY-SCHOOL HISTORY

There came a time, by-and-by, when the educators decided to change their minds. In the midst of a comprehensive re-organization of secondary education undertaken by the National Education Association during the early part of the 1910's, history in the last six of the twelve years composing the elementary and the secondary-school periods was subjected to a terrific overhauling. The details of this overhauling have been related in Division One and need not be repeated here. Suffice it to say, however, that after the year 1916, the chief question among those in charge of history in the secondary schools was, "Shall we join the revolters or stand pat on the four-block system of the Committee of Seven?" Needless to say, some joined the revolters; some stood pat; and a few even dared to do a little thinking of their own, setting up experiments in fields that had never been recommended by a committee representing a learned society—for example, world history.

The first entire state to abandon the Committee of Seven's four-block system was New Jersey. As early as January, 1916, this state published the following program in history for the high schools therein.

"Early European History to 1700.
"Modern European History since 1700.
"United States History since 1760." [92]

The reader will observe that this is substantially the set-up proposed by the Committee on Social Studies in Secondary Education of the National Education Association. The states of Pennsylvania, Maryland, Indiana, Texas, Colorado, Oklahoma, and others soon followed the lead of New Jersey. New York in 1921 adopted an independent set-up unlike that suggested by any other state or committee. Many individual cities and towns either went over to the proposals of the Committee of the National Education Association on the Social Studies in Secondary Education or began to experiment with a course hitherto unknown. A survey in 1924 revealed that about one-third of 2404 high schools throughout the country was following the suggestions of this Committee, the other two-thirds in about equal numbers either experimenting with new courses or following the suggestions of the Committee of Seven of the American Historical Association.[93]

An excellent illustration of what was taking place during the 1920's in the shift of emphasis from certain fields to others is found in the state of Michigan. For example, in this state the percentage of the high schools belonging to the North Central Association offering world history increased between the school years 1924–25 and 1929–30 from 27.8 to 73.1, an

[92] *The Teaching of Social Studies Including History.* Trenton, New Jersey: Department of Public Instruction, 1916.
[93] Edgar Dawson, *The History Inquiry*, p. 19. Reprinted from the *Historical Outlook*, XV (1924). Philadelphia, Pa.: McKinley Publishing Co., 1924.

increase of 162.9 per cent. In American history the increase was but 3.5 per cent, while in ancient, English, and mediæval and modern the decrease was 33.5, 67.9, and 41.3 respectively.[94] During this same five-year period the increase in schools in the entire Association offering world history was 157.4 per cent. The decrease in schools offering ancient and English history during these years was 24 and 22 per cent respectively. Generally speaking, these facts meant a decrease in the time devoted to history, substituting one year for two.

Commenting on the recent changes in the course in history as well as some of the other social sciences in the secondary schools of the Southern Association, one familiar with these schools said in 1928:

"No subject, perhaps, in the whole secondary school program of studies has undergone a more thorough reorganization than the so-called 'history course' of the old days. Time was, and that not many years ago, when the standard history course in practically all the secondary schools of America was merely a chronological study of historical facts. Ancient history in freshman year, mediæval and modern in the sophomore, English in the junior, and United States history in the senior year, was the almost universal procedure.

"But in the last decade or so, especially since the World War, there has been a growing demand for functional training in the social studies. The advocates of this movement say train the high-school youth to participate in a modern social world rather than master a few dissociated, disconnected, and wellnigh useless historical facts about the Egyptians, Babylonians, or nomadic tribes of other lands. Live, dynamic, functional

[94] George E. Carrothers, "High-School Curriculum Revisions and Innovations," *Junior-Senior High School Clearing House*, VI (1932), 268.

social training is what is needed, and not cold-storage historical facts." [95]

For a number of years the report of the Committee of Seven of the American Historical Association was looked upon as an outstanding contribution to history in the secondary school. However, as time passed and conditions changed, some doubting Thomases appeared. They said that the report was a deterrent to progress; that it fixed a pattern from which schools were unable to extricate themselves. In other words, it "froze" the situation to such an extent that no one could thaw it out. There was, of course, some truth in these contentions. A pattern sponsored by an authoritative body such as the American Historical Association was sure to be held in high esteem and in the end it developed into a tradition. In spite of the scathing attacks on the pattern by a group of educators, it dominated the history curriculum of most of the secondary schools of the land during the 1920's. Evidence of this domination is presented in Table XXV.

TABLE XXV

PER CENT OF PUPILS IN PUBLIC HIGH SCHOOLS AND PRIVATE HIGH SCHOOLS AND ACADEMIES PURSUING EACH OF FOUR FIELDS OF HISTORY IN 1921–22 AND 1927–28 *

| TERRITORY INCLUDED | Per cent pursuing in all schools reporting subjects | | | | | | | |
| | Ancient | | Mediæval and Modern | | American | | English | |
	1921–2	1927–8	1921–2	1927–8	1921–2	1927–8	1921–2	1927–8
Continental U. S..	17.69	11.24	11.21	11.42	15.32	20.97	3.18	1.10
Alabama.........	18.90	14.85	20.12	16.22	15.69	19.87	6.03	4.17
Arizona.........	14.67	2.40	8.88	2.93	17.72	18.49	.42	.10
Arkansas........	26.91	7.31	20.78	7.13	16.70	18.86	3.49	.74
California........	14.32	9.05	12.55	7.36	13.99	14.08	1.27	.52
Colorado.........	18.38	6.54	15.18	5.90	12.56	16.26	1.65	3.56
Connecticut......	14.74	14.92	9.65	10.43	13.29	14.52	3.83	1.36

[95] Joseph Roemer, *op. cit.*, pp. 59 f.

TERRITORY INCLUDED	Per cent pursuing in all schools reporting subjects							
	Ancient		Mediæval and Modern		American		English	
	1921-2	1927-8	1921-2	1927-8	1921-2	1927-8	1921-2	1927-8
Delaware........	21.56	9.34	8.58	10.42	7.78	16.56	1.77	.51
District of Columbia.........	16.41	12.31	6.24	13.98	13.32	21.57	1.23	1.02
Florida..........	41.65	12.89	16.71	10.58	15.37	27.76	7.02	1.85
Georgia.........	21.93	17.00	19.43	15.74	15.00	18.22	10.49	2.78
Idaho...........	22.35	15.67	85.33	9.91	15.17	18.61	2.23	.36
Illinois..........	15.23	12.11	12.61	10.47	11.92	17.43	1.61	.71
Indiana..........	18.76	7.45	14.63	9.67	15.48	20.23	1.97	.23
Iowa............	16.84	7.90	20.18	13.68	19.42	22.09	1.16	.41
Kansas..........	13.52	8.14	12.20	5.78	15.53	18.08	.72	.25
Kentucky........	24.17	14.73	17.37	13.37	14.04	14.37	7.19	2.31
Louisiana........	15.56	7.89	13.65	12.27	9.84	14.80	2.23	1.26
Maine...........	20.76	16.09	8.50	10.79	14.33	17.13	4.84	2.04
Maryland........	16.70	12.56	10.83	10.89	27.72	16.69	10.27	3.01
Massachusetts....	14.29	11.14	8.78	8.52	16.96	17.22	2.44	1.52
Michigan........	17.94	8.78	14.65	7.56	13.60	15.47	2.89	1.02
Minnesota.......	19.44	10.20	14.67	14.25	16.23	18.27	.91	.49
Mississippi.......	21.42	20.55	21.17	18.22	18.46	18.42	6.41	.61
Missouri.........	22.64	9.81	23.47	8.69	14.38	14.78	4.71	.64
Montana........	21.39	9.52	8.48	6.92	15.78	18.71	.71	.21
Nebraska........	18.27	4.61	14.17	7.11	16.24	18.27	1.65	3.89
Nevada (Public).	15.72	7.99	15.78	7.47	16.21	22.04	.60	1.77
New Hampshire..	17.34	14.54	10.90	8.94	17.38	29.15	4.98	4.38
New Jersey.......	14.90	13.61	11.79	23.11	10.86	15.11	1.26	.87
New Mexico.....	20.42	19.10	17.39	13.66	13.67	15.75	1.11	.81
New York.......	10.68	8.59	17.18	12.70	14.30	14.80	1.54	.30
North Carolina ..	23.85	6.26	19.38	18.49	14.26	16.18	7.84	1.80
North Dakota ...	26.36	12.69	16.91	16.70	17.07	18.87	1.71	.14
Ohio............	14.72	8.86	14.11	9.21	14.29	15.34	1.34	.61
Oklahoma.......	29.98	18.77	18.45	16.46	15.33	18.70	5.81	5.74
Oregon..........	18.41	5.89	12.63	5.10	21.04	29.50	.93	.36
Pennsylvania.....	18.51	16.17	19.68	18.49	16.60	14.79	4.40	.54
Rhode Island.....	23.44	23.21	9.51	20.21	36.12	16.64	5.08	2.77
South Carolina...	29.51	23.07	21.37	18.27	19.37	19.62	6.02	2.54
South Dakota....	23.12	14.77	16.83	12.45	17.47	20.22	2.91	2.76
Tennessee........	14.70	21.24	8.82	20.91	9.55	20.50	18.58	1.55
Texas............	32.47	24.01	25.73	21.09	16.25	18.20	7.25	3.25
Utah............	9.79	1.47	17.51	3.91	16.43	22.13	.19	....
Vermont.........	19.97	15.06	10.70	8.28	12.32	14.31	3.49	.81
Virginia.........	21.32	13.62	16.04	15.62	16.55	18.71	14.10	4.96
Washington......	13.91	10.08	14.66	8.25	16.73	19.48	1.72	.69
West Virginia....	21.79	4.33	14.40	5.34	16.08	21.30	1.83	.55
Wisconsin.......	15.57	8.72	18.93	15.00	15.13	19.90	5.61	.57
Wyoming........	22.20	9.80	15.29	5.14	11.72	16.57	1.89	.42

* Based on data found in *Biennial Survey of Education*, 1920-1922, and 1926-1928. Washington: Government Printing Office.

It will be a surprise to those who have dared to suggest that the influence of the Committee of Seven ceased soon after the publication in 1916 of the report of the Committee on the Social Studies in Secondary Education to find that its influence was somewhat dominant during the 1920's. While ancient and English history both declined considerably during this decade, mediæval and modern history held their own and American history increased in popularity. What happened to these fields in individual states is illuminating. For example, in Mississippi very little change is noted in the per cents for the first three fields listed in Table XXV while in Michigan a significant drop in the per cent of pupils pursuing ancient and mediæval and modern history is noted. A similar drop is observed in Indiana, Kansas, Colorado, and Missouri.. In fact in all states where the Committee on the Social Studies in Secondary Education became influential after 1920, there is found a decrease in the per cent of pupils pursuing ancient, mediæval and modern, and English history. One could calculate with a fair degree of accuracy the per cent of pupils pursuing early European history in 1927–28 by subtracting in each state the per cent pursuing ancient history at this date from that pursuing the subject in 1921–22. Such a calculation would not, of course, take care of the per cent of pupils pursuing world history and other fields occasionally offered in the early years of the traditional four-year secondary school.

EVIDENCE OF THE EXISTENCE OF HISTORY IN THE FIRST SIX ELEMENTARY GRADES AFTER 1920

Since 1920, a number of things have happened to history as a subject of study in the elementary grades. Between 1909 and 1920 history in these grades was pretty much under the domination of what the Committee of Eight proposed in its report. As long as the eight-year elementary school maintained the *status quo* the proposals of this committee were in tune with current grade organization. It was too much to expect that this committee anticipate in 1909 the rapid rise of the junior high school even though this type of school did originate about this date. Its inability to anticipate this new type of organization caused its report soon to be out of harmony with a rapidly changing elementary school. Thus it becomes necessary in a discussion of this character to treat history during the 1920's as it existed in a six-year elementary school and in a three-year junior high school.

The coming of the junior high school was not the only movement that tended to upset the *status quo* established by the Committee of Eight. The agitation to abolish history as an independent subject of study both in the six-year elementary school and the junior high school threatened the integrity of the subject in these grades. Generally speaking, history was abolished as an independent subject of study in the primary grades during this decade. It was abolished also in the intermediate and junior-high school grades in certain localities. How far this movement for the abolition of history as a subject of study in these groups of grades will go, no one, of course, at this time can tell. There are those who would like to see the movement succeed as well as those who would be unhappy should it succeed. Whether it succeeds or fails as now conceived, the amount of materials from the field of history utilized in these grades will probably increase as time goes on. There seems to be no escape from this increase according to a widely held notion that the social sciences should form the core of the curriculum in all divisions of the school. Should this notion become common practice, the core of the social sciences will undoubtedly be material from the field of history.

There is at hand a considerable body of material on the status of history in the six-year elementary school and in the junior high school during the 1920's. Certain time-allotment studies which appeared between 1924 and 1927 pictured the place that history held in the first six elementary grades during

TABLE XXVI

TIME ALLOTMENTS TO HISTORY IN THE FIRST SIX ELEMENTARY
GRADES, 1924-1926.*

	Grades					
	I	II	III	IV	V	VI
1. Average number of minutes a week allotted to history in 49 large cities in 1924	17	19	30	54	84	97
2. Per cent of 444 cities allotting time to history in first half of.................	21.8	25.7	44.4	66.2	85.8	91.4
3. Per cent of a group of 15 states recommending time allotments to history in 1926....................................	53	53	67	93	100	100
4. Average number of minutes a week allotted to history in 444 cities in 1926....	8	11	26	57	94	113
5. Per cent of time each grade allotted to history in 444 cities in 1926............	0.6	0.8	1.7	3.6	5.8	7.0

* Carleton Hunter Mann, *How Schools Use Their Time*, pp. 23, 36 and 55 f. New York: Bureau of Publications, Teachers College, Columbia University, 1926, and Kyte, *op. cit.*, p. 16.

these years. Some of the facts revealed in two of these studies appear in Table XXVI, which indicates that history got little recognition as an independent subject in the primary grades in the 444 cities represented therein—the average number of minutes a week allotted to it in Grade I being but eight; in Grade II, eleven; and in Grade III, twenty-six. Even in the intermediate grades of these cities the subject was given the meager time allotment of about ten minutes a day in Grade IV and a little over twenty minutes a day in Grade VI, although a high percentage of the 444 cities actually allotted time to history in these grades. The findings of this study of 444 cities are corroborated by another investigation in which it was shown that of 543 school systems in 48 states 80 or 14.7 per cent offered history in Grade I, 95 or 17.5 per cent in Grade II, and 158 or 29 per cent in Grade III.[96] These data are for the school year 1925–26. It would seem from them that as a school subject in the primary grades history got about as little recognition in these 543 schools as it did in the 444 included in Table XXVI.

With respect to the intermediate grades, the report of the Commission on the Length of Elementary Education revealed the fact that of 542 school systems in the 48 states 296 or 54.6 per cent offered history in Grade IV and 459 or 84.7 per cent offered it in Grade V. Four hundred ninety-one or 90.9 per cent of 540 cities offered the subject in Grade VI. History as a subject of study seems from these data to have been more strongly entrenched in the intermediate grades of the cities in this study than it was in the 444 cities represented in Table XXVI.

SENIOR HIGH SCHOOL HISTORY CONTENT AFTER 1920

In reality the revolt from the *status quo* in the realm of high-school history content began with the report of the Committee on the Social Studies in Secondary Education in 1916. While this committee did not propose any new content, it did suggest a rearrangement of the old, changing the emphasis from the history of long ago to that of the near present. The courses it proposed have been presented in Division One and need not be repeated here. While its recommendations did not sweep the country as did those of the Committee of Seven, they

[96] Charles H. Judd, Chairman, *Report of the Commission on Length of Elementary Education*, pp. 55 f. Chicago: University of Chicago, 1927.

were taken seriously by a number of teachers of history in the high school and writers of textbooks for use therein.

Out of the thinking concerning history in the high school, which was somewhat objectified in the Report of the Committee of Five of the American Historical Association in 1911, came at least six signficant changes in the general and specific content of high-school history. Parenthetically it should be stated that the recommendations of the Committee on the Social Studies in Secondary Education and the direction that the World War caused the thinking with respect to history in the high school to take were also important factors in bringing about the changes in the content of high-school history that the 1920's saw.

The six significant changes mentioned above were (1) the reduction of the time that had been allotted to ancient history for two decades from one year to one-half year; (2) the doubling of the amount of time that had previously been devoted to modern history since about 1648; (3) the general introduction of a one-year course in world history; (4) the doubling of the amount of time that had previously been devoted to American history; (5) the inclusion in the content of more social and economic material than had previously been present; and (6) the placing on the market of a new supply of textbooks in the field of high-school history. These books were, of course, necessitated by the first five outstanding changes mentioned above. In reality, the changes were reflected in the new textbooks.

The crop of textbooks that matured soon after 1916 was almost as big as it was varied. For the field of early European history, the number was not less than half a dozen; for modern European history, it was nearly a dozen; for world history, not less than eight; and for American history, not less than ten.

Many of these books were by the same authors who had written the texts to conform to the set-up of the Committee of Seven. This fact gave the appearance of pouring old wine into new bottles. When such a pouring was practiced, neither the wine nor the bottles benefited thereby. In fact one is perhaps justified in applying the old saying, "All that glitters is not gold," to the scramble to meet the new developments in high-school history that came so rapidly after 1916.

Four of the signficant changes that occurred in the content of high-school history during the 1920's are accounted for in the textbooks mentioned above. Generally speaking the texts in early European history gave about half of their space to the traditional ancient history and half to the traditional mediæval history, thus reducing the content of ancient history by half. The texts in modern European history devoted their entire content to affairs in Europe since about 1648, thus doubling the amount that this field got in the traditional mediæval and modern arrangement. The texts in American history were intended to furnish enough material for a full year of work in this field, preferably to be offered in the eleventh year. Texts in world history also appeared along with those in the other fields; they represented the attempt on the part of authors and publishers to meet the demand of the educators for a one-year course in this field.

There remains to be considered the shift from the heavy emphasis on the political and military aspect of the past—characteristic of secondary-school history during the reign of the Committee of Seven—to the social, industrial, and commercial aspects. Fortunately there is available some factual material which indicates this shift. Table XXVII contains data from the field of modern European history which reveal the topics of a social, industrial, and commercial nature included in six

TABLE XXVII

AVERAGE PER CENT OF SPACE DEVOTED TO CERTAIN TOPICS IN
MODERN EUROPEAN HISTORY BY SIX TEXTBOOKS*

TOPICS	AVERAGE PER CENT OF SPACE DEVOTED TO IN THE SIX TEXTS
1. Clues to Modern European History	.63
2. Reign of William III and Queen Anne	.52
3. Social and Economic England during Seventeenth Century	1.17
4. Age of Louis XIV	2.63
5. Rise of Russia to a Power	1.52
6. Growth of Prussia	1.94
7. Partitions of Poland	.69
8. The "Benevolent Despots"	.66
9. Expansion into New Worlds; Struggle between France and England in India and N. A.	2.63
10. American Revolution and Constitution	.81
11. Progress of Geographical Discovery	.41
12. England under the Georges	2.20
13. Established Church and Protestant Sects	.66
14. Life of People in Country, Towns, and Among Nobility	1.92
15. The Spirit of Reform	1.77
16. Causes of and Eve of the French Revolution	2.64
17. French Revolution	7.07
18. Europe and Napoleon	6.88
19. Congress of Vienna: Restoration	1.23
20. Metternich; Holy Alliance; Central Europe to 1820	.95
21. Reaction; Intervention; Revolution of 1820	.85
22. Independence of Greece and Belgium	.41
23. Thought and Culture of the Early Eighteenth Century	.20
24. France: Revolution of 1830	1.22
25. Industrial and Agrarian Revolutions	2.67
26. Social and Economic Effects of Industrial Revolution	2.57
27. Socialism	.58
28. Commercial Organizations and Policies	1.67

* Elwood Murray, "Analysis of Six Modern European History Textbooks," pp. 20-24. Unpublished Master's thesis, State University of Iowa, 1924.

TOPICS	AVERAGE PER CENT OF SPACE DEVOTED TO IN THE SIX TEXTS
64. The Settlement at Paris	1.62
65. The League of Nations	.49
66. Conditions in World Following the World War	2.37
67. March of Democracy	1.41
68. New Nations in Central and Eastern Europe	1.26

textbooks. Even though the textbooks in high-school history had been frequently criticised adversely for their neglect of the social, economic, and commercial aspect of life, the writers of those analyzed in this table did not take much cognizance of these criticisms. Of the sixty-eight topics listed therein not over sixteen can be classified as social, economic, or commercial. The average per cent of space devoted to four of these sixteen topics is less than one. The insignificant amount of space devoted to these topics leaves the ratio fifty-two to twelve in favor of the political and military phases of life. It is evident from these data that the modern European history taught in the high schools during the first half of the 1920's was largely political and military.

The world-history course seems to have been one of the many aftermaths of the World War. It has never been recommended by a committee of national scope on which there were any historians. It seems to be the "Topsy" of the present day high-school history course. It has had its strongest supporters among school administrators, who, in their efforts to "hold fast to that which was good," when so many new subjects were clamoring for a hearing, found a way to keep history other than American in the program of studies by encompassing in one year what had been included in two or even three years. Because of the fact that the historians did not at the beginning of the movement for world history react favorably toward it,

the supply of textbooks was very limited, in fact most of those
that did appear were nothing more than a rehashing of the old
material that had formerly appeared in textbooks in European
history. Furthermore, these texts had the musty odor of the
traditional texts in general history. Speaking to this point in
1927 one well informed on the matter said:

"World history courses, usually one year in length, but sometimes a year and a half or two years, are frequently found
about the tenth grade level. These courses are increasing in
number and textbooks are multiplying impressively. A few
interesting experiments are being worked out. Yet it cannot
be said that the high schools have really caught the idea of the
new world history. Both the courses and the textbooks remain
in nearly all cases overwhelmingly European in content and
point of view, while the reasons for introducing them are in
many cases utterly reactionary. Any one who has the opportunity of visiting schools and making inquiries will soon
learn that very often the new course is introduced simply to
cover as much ground as possible in the one year of history
other than American which is offered, and the exigencies of a
commercial or technical curriculum or the conflicting demands
of other social studies are the real explanation, rather than any
recognition of a World Community or of the need for a new
world history. Such a practice is simply a reversion to the old
'general history' so vigorously attacked a generation ago and
for many years so completely discredited. Such a change is not
progressive, but reactionary, however much it may superficially
seem to conform to a current fashion. When the substance of
two or three years' work under the Committee of Seven program is crammed into a highly condensed epitome for one
year it is no wonder that children gag and the course is some-

times such a failure that it has to be dropped from the curriculum." [97]

In order to show to what extent this statement was true when it was made, material is presented in Table XXVIII

TABLE XXVIII

AVERAGE PER CENT OF SPACE DEVOTED TO CERTAIN FIELDS AND TOPICS IN FIVE TEXTS IN WORLD HISTORY AND ONE IN GENERAL HISTORY.*

FIELDS AND TOPICS	AVERAGE PER CENT IN FIVE TEXTS IN WORLD HISTORY	PER CENT IN ONE TEXT IN GENERAL HISTORY
1. Introductory and Prehistoric	2.92	1.72
2. Oriental history	5.28	7.58
3. Greek history	8.47	16.49
4. Roman history	8.56	18.21
5. Barbarians	1.77	3.50
6. Development of the church	1.72	1.05
7. Mohammedanism	0.79	1.58
8. Charlemagne	0.78	2.10
9. Feudalism	1.24	1.72
10. Crusades	1.83	1.72
11. Conflict of state and church	1.10	1.59
12. Development of nations	4.22	4.78
13. Life in the Middle Ages	3.16	0.40
14. Renaissance	1.41	1.45
15. Reformation	2.90	2.39
16. French Revolution	3.63	4.12
17. Napoleonic Era	2.99	2.79
18. Industrial Revolution	3.05	0.40
19. Absolutism	7.66	9.30
20. Discovery and Expansion	3.57	1.33
21. Progress in democracy	12.90	6.25
22. Scientific and industrial progress	1.50	0.00
23. Imperialism	7.15	4.78
24. World War (1906 edition of the general history used)	4.74	0.00
25. Problems since the World War	5.24	0.00

*Compiled from material in Ethel Taylor's "The Changing Content and Emphasis in World History Textbooks Between 1900 and 1928." Unpublished Master's thesis, University of Southern California, 1928.

[97] J. Montgomery Gambrill, "The New World History," *Historical Outlook*, XVIII (1927), 267.

which makes possible a comparison of the emphasis in five texts in world history published during the 1920's with that in a text in traditional general history which had a large following in the heyday of its long life. It is clear from the data in this table that the foregoing criticism of world history as it existed in the high schools in 1928 was not overdrawn. On the topics, "Feudalism," "Crusades," "Conflict of Church and State," Development of Nations," "Renaissance," "Reformation," "French Revolution," "Napoleonic Era," and "Development of the Church" the difference in emphasis is certainly not significant and on at least half of the remaining topics used as a basis of comparison the difference is not large enough to be noticed in actual practice. There seems to be no hope for world history in the high school unless it becomes more than the old general history that the Committee of Seven hated so bitterly and tried so hard to exterminate.

CONTENT OF HISTORY IN THE ELEMENTARY SCHOOLS DURING THE 1920'S

With respect to the content of history in the elementary grades during the early 1920's, one can speak with considerable exactness about one of its legal aspects, wholesale legal provision being made for United States history. There is much evidence that these laws and regulations concerning the teaching of United States history were obeyed. The fact that there were in 1923 forty-three states—all but Utah, Rhode Island, New Jersey, Minnesota, and Colorado—requiring either by state legislative enactment or by rulings of state boards of education[98] the teaching of United States history in the grades

[98] *Research Bulletin of the National Education Association*, Vol. I, No. 5, pp. 318–19. Washington, D. C.: National Education Association, 1923.

serves to explain the situation that is portrayed in Table XXIX.

As observed from this table the grades in which United States history appeared most frequently were the intermediate and upper two, the highest per cent being in Grade VII.

TABLE XXIX

PER CENT BY GRADES OF 303 SCHOOL SYSTEMS TEACHING UNITED STATES HISTORY IN 1924*

GRADE	PER CENT	GRADE	PER CENT
IB.........	8.9	VB........	73.6
IA.........	9.6	VA........	74.6
IIB.........	11.9	VIB........	72.6
IIA.........	11.6	VIA........	74.6
IIIB.........	19.5	VIIB........	82.8
IIIA.........	21.8	VIIA........	84.2
IVB.........	41.3	VIIIB........	76.2
IVA.........	44.2	VIIIA........	68.0

* G. C. Kyte, *A Study of the Time Allotments in the Elementary School*, p. 8. California Curriculum Study, Bulletin No. 1. Berkeley: University of California Printing Office, 1925.

Out of this situation arose a problem of grading which has never been solved. As long as United States history was largely confined to Grades VII and VIII there was no problem of grading United States history in the elementary school. While a new aspect of the problem was introduced when this field of history entered Grade V, there has long been the need for adjustment on the upper-grade and high-school levels. This need is still unmet and the addition of one more level makes it the more complicated as well as the more urgent.

Fortunately there is at hand a tabulation of the subject-matter of history in the first six elementary grades as revealed in fifty-three courses of study, most of which having been published between 1922 and 1927. Commenting on the place of history as a subject of study in these fifty-three courses from thirty-eight cities, twelve states, and three counties, the author of the study said:

"History as a subject is omitted in some grades in a number of the courses of study. Of the 53 courses, 22 make no provision for the inclusion of history in the first two grades. The subject is omitted through the third grade in 16 of these 22 courses. Eleven of the 16 continue to make no provision for the teaching of history through the fourth grade. Only 4 of the courses of study omit the subject from all grades below the seventh grade. Even in the courses of study making no definite requirements regarding the inclusion of history in certain grades, there is evidence that a smattering of history is introduced into the schools in these same grades. The subject-matter consists of scattered bits that are associated with various anniversaries and holidays commemorating historical events or the birthdays of famous persons. This sporadically appearing matter is not included in the study from the viewpoint that it does not constitute an organized treatment of historical materials." [99]

Table XXX contains the subject-matter included in each grade for the courses making provisions for history therein. It suggests certain outstanding practices in history in the first six elementary grades in 1927. Chief among these were (1) the practice of outlining history from Grades I and II; (2) the practice of permitting American history to usurp all of the history time in Grades IV and V; (3) the practice of following in Grade VI the course proposed by the Committee of Eight of the American Historical Association; and (4) the practice

[99] George C. Kyte, "Variations in the Organization of the Elementary Courses of Study in History," *Educational Administration and Supervision,* XIII (1927), 362 f.

of permitting history to have an independent existence in Grade III. In general it should be remarked that the hand of the Committee of Eight rested heavily on the work in each grade above Grade II. The saying "Once an Englishman always an Englishman" seems apropos here. Applied to the situation portrayed in Table XXX this statement would read "Once in always in."

TABLE XXX

HISTORY IN FIFTY-THREE COURSES OF STUDY, 1920–1922*

Grade I (31 courses)   FREQUENCY
1. Home and community........................... 10
2. Home and community; and primitive life......... 5
3. Home; and primitive life....................... 4
4. Home and school.............................. 3
5. City.. 3
6. Primitive and pioneer life...................... 3
7. Fairy-tales; fables; and legends................. 2
8. School...................................... 1

Grade II (31 courses)
1. Community; and primitive life................. 10
2. Primitive life................................ 8
3. Home and community; and primitive life......... 5
4. Home and community.......................... 4
5. Community; and Bible stories.................. 2
6. State history; and primitive life............... 2

Grade III (37 courses)
1. Primitive life................................ 6
2. Heroes of the past; and local history............ 5
3. City.. 4
4. City; county; and state....................... 4
5. Local history................................ 3
6. Primitive and pioneer life...................... 3
7. Heroes of the past; and primitive life........... 3
8. Community and school......................... 2
9. American heroes; and city..................... 1
10. American heroes; and primitive life............. 1
11. State pioneers............................... 1

* George C. Kyte, *loc. cit.*, pp. 363–68

FREQUENCY

12. City; and Hebrews and Greeks.................. 1
13. Hebrews and Greeks.......................... 1
14. Greeks....................................... 1
15. Community; and primitive life................. 1

Grade IV (42 courses)

  1. American history to 1763...................... 14
  2. American history to 1700; and state history...... 4
  3. American history to 1790; and state history...... 4
  4. State history................................. 5
  5. City... 4
  6. City and community........................... 1
  7. City and county.............................. 1
  8. American history to 1763; and local history...... 1
  9. American history to 1763; and city............. 1
 10. American history to 1763; and state history...... 1
 11. American history from 1765 to 1850............. 1
 12. Biographies; from Columbus to men of the present 1
 13. Oriental peoples and Greeks................... 1
 14. Hebrews, Greeks and Romans.................. 1
 15. Romans...................................... 1
 16. Romans and mediæval period................. 1

Grade V (49 courses)

  1. United States history......................... 13
  2. United States history, 1774 to date............. 6
  3. American history, 1600 to date................. 4
  4. American history to 1790..................... 3
  5. United States history, 1765–1865; ancient history 3
  6. United States history; and state history.......... 2
  7. "European Background" and American history
        to 1700................................. 2
  8. "European Background"...................... 2
  9. United States history, 1790 to date............. 2
 10. American history from 1492 to date............ 1
 11. United States history, 1790 to date; state; city.... 1
 12. American history to 1763; Roman and English
        history................................. 1
 13. American history to 1763; state history.......... 1
 14. American history to 1763..................... 2
 15. American history, 1700 to date; ancient history... 1
 16. The Revolution and the critical period.......... 1

FREQUENCY

17. Greece, Rome and the Middle Ages..............   1
18. Middle Ages...................................   1
19. Roman and Teuton history.....................   1
20. City..   1

Grade VI (49 courses)

1. "European Background" of American history....   24
2. "European Background"; and state..............   4
3. State history...................................   3
4. American history, 1765 to date..................   3
5. World history to date..........................   2
6. United States history; state history..............   2
7. "European Background"; and American history
      to 1783......................................   1
8. War of the Revolution; and "European Back-
      ground"......................................   1
9. Local; "European Background"; American his-
      tory to 1700.................................   1
10. United States, 1865 to date; "European Back-
       ground"; state..............................   1
11. Greek and Roman history......................   1
12. Mediæval history..............................   1
13. American history to 1783; and state history......   1
14. American history to 1832.......................   1
15. American history to 1843.......................   1
16. United States history, 1783 to date.............   1
17. United States history...........................   1

HISTORY IN THE JUNIOR HIGH SCHOOL

History has had an important place in the junior high school from the very beginning of this institution as it is generally known at the present time. Originating about 1909, this division of the present twelve-year elementary and secondary school system has been adopted by city after city. It is now a generally recognized institution with a unique program of studies. Prior to 1916 little progress was made in providing the junior high school with an actually new program in history. At this date the history that was taught in most of the junior high schools in the country was exactly what had formerly been taught in the traditional seventh and eighth grades of the elementary school and the ninth grade of the four-year high school. This means that in Grade VII, United States history prior to 1789 was taught; in Grade VIII, United States history since 1789; and in Grade IX, ancient history. A study in 1916[100] of the offerings in history in thirty-eight junior high schools in twenty states revealed that United States history was taught in Grades VII and VIII in thirty of them, and ancient history in Grade IX in fourteen. Other fields of history offered in very limited numbers were European background of United States history (the course proposed for Grade VI by the Committee of Eight of the American Historical Association in 1908), state history, English history, industrial history, early European history to about 1700, current history, and Pacific Coast history. These courses all had low frequencies. They represented the innovations that some of the schools were introducing.

The situation with respect to history in junior high schools seems to have changed little between 1916 and 1920. In a study of required and elective subjects in thirty-four junior high schools it was revealed in 1921 that in the academic course United States history was required in the seventh grade of twenty-three of these schools and in the eighth grade of thirty of them, ancient history being elective in Grade IX in fourteen.[101] According to this and the foregoing study it would seem that most of the progress made to date in providing junior high schools with a reorganized history program has been made since 1920.

[100] R. M. Tryon, "History in the Junior High School," *Elementary School Journal*, XVI (1916), 149 ff.
[101] J. Harvey Rogers, "Junior High School Curricula and Programs," *School Review*, XXIX (1921), 204.

Early in the 1920's history other than United States began to invade Grades VII–IX. In 1924, ancient history was offered in Grade VII in nine of forty-nine cities over 8000 in population. The subject was offered in three of these cities in Grade VIII and in thirty-eight in Grade IX. Mediæval history was offered in two of eighteen cities in the foregoing class in Grade VII at the same date, two in Grade VIII, and in twelve of fifteen cities as follows: one each in Grades VII and VIII and eleven in Grade IX. One of eight cities offered general history in Grades VII and VIII and four in Grade IX. Of ten cities, two offered English history in Grades VII and VIII and four in Grade IX.[102] While these cases do not show a nation-wide expansion of the field of history offered in junior high schools, they indicate that scattering attempts were being made in 1924 to introduce into the program of these schools a little history other than United States.

The foregoing innovations do not show all that happened to history in junior high schools during the 1920's. It was during this decade that the integrated, fused, and unified programs in history, geography, and civics arose. What occurred in some schools may be illustrated by a tabular view of the courses of study in the social sciences in twenty-six junior high schools in 1930. Such a view is presented in Table XXXI, on page 332.

It will be observed from the foregoing tabulation that in ten of the twenty-six courses unification of two or more subjects was practiced, the remaining sixteen offering the subjects of history, geography, and civics independently. The extent of the so-called unification movement in 1930 is shown in Table XXXII, the study from which the data are taken being one of the most extensive ones that has been made to date. The data

[102] J. R. McGaughy, "Distribution of Grades in Which Elementary School Subjects Are Taught in 375 Cities," *Second Yearbook*, Department of Superintendence, pp. 161 f.

TABLE XXXI

TABULAR VIEW OF TWENTY-SIX JUNIOR HIGH SCHOOL COURSES OF STUDY IN THE SOCIAL SCIENCES IN 1930*

COURSE	GRADE VII	GRADE VIII	GRADE IX
1.	United States History, Civics	United States History, Civics, Geography	European History, Civics
2.	Geography	European History, United States History	Civics
3.	Geography	United States History, Geography	Civics
4.	European History, United States History, Geography	United States History, Civics, Geography	European History, Civics
5.	United States History, Civics, Geography	United States History, Civics	European History, Civics
6.	European History	United States History	Civics
7.	European History, Geography	United States History, Geography	Civics, United States History
8.	Geography	United States History	Civics, Geography
9.	Geography, United States History, Civics	United States History, Civics	Civics
10.	Geography	United States History	Civics, European History
11.	United States History, Civics, Geography	United States History, Civics, Geography	Civics, European History
12.	Geography, European History	United States History	Civics
13.	Geography, European History	United States History	Civics
14.	United States History	United States History	Civics
15.	Geography	United States History	Civics
16.	Geography	United States History, Civics	European History
17.	United States History and Geography unified in Grades VII-VIII		Civics
18.	United States History and Geography unified in Grades VII-VIII		Civics
19.	United States History and Geography unified in Grades VII-VIII		Civics
20.	United States History and Geography unified in Grades VII-VIII		Civics
21.	United States History, Geography and Civics unified in Grades VII-VIII		Civics
22.	United States History, Geography and Civics unified in Grades VII-VIII		Civics, European History
23.	United States History, Geography and Civics unified in Grades VII-VIII-IX		
24.	United States History, Geography and Civics unified in Grades VII-VIII-IX		

COURSE	GRADE VII	GRADE VIII	GRADE IX
25.	United States History, Geography and Civics unified in Grades VII-VIII-IX		
26.	United States History, Geography and Civics unified in Grades VII-VIII-IX		European History

* Jetta F. Henderson, "Curricular Organization of the Social Studies in the Junior High School," p. 16. Unpublished Master's thesis, University of Southern California, June, 1930.

exhibited in this table show that in 1930 there were at least half a dozen outstanding tendencies in history in the 301 junior high schools included therein. These were (1) a tendency to complete American history in Grade VIII, there being 91

TABLE XXXII

THE SOCIAL SCIENCES IN 301 JUNIOR HIGH SCHOOLS IN 1930*

COURSE	Grade VII		Grade VIII		Grade IX	
	RE-QUIRED	ELEC-TIVE	RE-QUIRED	ELEC-TIVE	RE-QUIRED	ELEC-TIVE
1. American history (entire)....	8	0	91	0	1	0
2. Early American history......	121	0	25	0	0	0
3. Later American history......	1	0	100	1	0	0
4. European backgrounds of American history.........	21	1	0	0	2	1
5. Ancient history............	0	0	0	1	27	31
6. World history..............	0	0	0	0	44	11
7. Geography................	151	0	46	2	12	3
8. Civics, community and vocational..................	21	0	49	3	73	23
9. Fusion courses............	77	0	65	0	35	6

* Howard E. Wilson and Bessie P. Erb, "A Survey of Social-Studies Courses in 301 Junior High Schools," *School Review*, XXXIX (1931), 504. For a general discussion of the offerings see Howard E. Wilson, *The Fusion of Social Studies in Junior High Schools*, chapter ii. Cambridge, Mass.: Harvard University Press, 1933.

schools so doing; (2) a tendency to remove history from Grade VII, thus leaving geography as the chief subject in this grade; (3) a tendency to require all of the history offered in Grades VII and VIII; (4) a tendency to offer history other than United States in Grade IX, there being 116 schools offering

European background, ancient, or world history; (5) a tendency to combine history with other social sciences, thus forming a so-called unified course; and (6) the tendency for history to dominate the offerings in the social sciences. Speaking in general terms it is evident that a little over one-third of the schools represented in Table XXXII were following the practice common in 1916, namely, that of confining the history offered in Grades VII and VIII to American, and in Grade IX to ancient history. Furthermore, it seems that a little less than one-third of the schools confined most of the work in history to Grade VIII, offering geography in Grade VII. And finally, that in Grades VII and VIII considerably less than one-third of the schools were attempting to unite history with the other social sciences.

It is clear from the foregoing facts relative to the existence of history in junior high schools that the subject occupies an important place in these schools. While the general nature of the content included in the course in history has been indicated above, no hint has been given relative to the specific content. To attempt to determine with any great degree of precision the specific content of existing courses of study in junior high-school history would practically lead one into the realm of the undeterminable. At best one can but approximate the exact content. In a recent study of the offering in the junior high schools in New York there appears what seems to be a close approximation of the content of the history courses in these schools.[103] To secure the data included in Table XXXIII the teachers of history were asked to list the basal and supplementary texts they used in each course in history. These texts were analyzed and the average number of pages in each group

[103] Warren W. Coxe and others, *Courses of Study and Curriculum Offerings in Junior High Schools in New York State.* Albany, N. Y.: The State Education Department, 1931.

devoted to specific topics was determined. It is the results of
these analyses that are included in Table XXXIII.

TABLE XXXIII

AVERAGE NUMBER OF PAGES GIVEN TO CERTAIN TOPICS IN TEXT-
BOOKS IN HISTORY FOR GRADES VII AND VIII IN 1930.*

TOPICS	BASAL TEXT	SUPPLE-MENTARY TEXTS
Seventh Grade		
Early civilization................................	16.6	30.1
Events leading to discovery of America............	6.9	12.5
Discovery of America............................	5.7	10.4
Nations interested in America....................	13.1	23.9
Conditions affecting colonization.................	23.4	42.5
European background of colonial culture..........	9.5	17.2
Colonial period.................................	56.4	102.6
American Revolution.............................	31.4	57.1
Critical period..................................	7.1	13.0
Making the constitution	13.8	25.1
Starting the new government.....................	7.2	13.0
Eighth Grade		
Starting the new government.....................	7.1	14.8
Struggle for commercial independence.............	11.8	24.5
Territorial growth...............................	11.3	23.5
Industrial and commercial growth prior to the Civil War...	16.5	34.3
Slavery issue....................................	22.1	45.9
Civil War.......................................	27.3	56.7
Period of Reconstruction........................	9.8	20.3
Industrial and commercial progress since the Civil War...	14.7	30.6
Transportation and communication...............	9.9	20.7
Cultural development............................	3.5	7.3
Study of national issues		
Growth of nationalism........................	4.5	9.4
Political issues...............................	12.1	25.1
Civil Service.................................	1.8	3.8
Tariff and taxes..............................	5.9	12.2
Trusts and corporations.......................	4.2	8.7
Labor problems...............................	7.9	16.5
Conservation of resources.....................	2.5	5.2
Prohibition..................................	1.0	2.1
Public land..................................	2.5	5.2
Immigration..................................	4.3	8.9

TOPICS	BASAL TEXT	SUPPLE-MENTARY TEXTS
Public education	7.1	14.8
Democratic control of government	5.1	10.6
Public welfare................................	1.5	3.1
Race problems................................	1.6	3.4
Reconstruction after World War................	4.8	10.0
American life and growth of population.........	4.0	8.3
Banks and national finances....................	6.1	12.8
Miscellaneous national issues..................	3.2	6.6
International relationships		
In general, including Mexican War..............	19.2	40.0
Spanish-American War.........................	5.4	11.3
World War....................................	14.4	30.0
History of modern foreign countries..............	4.6	9.5

* Warren W. Coxe and others, *op. cit.*, pp. 98 f.

Realizing that many teachers of history do not follow any particular text but instead an outline of their own making, those who conducted the foregoing investigation asked history teachers to list the main topics studied in any given course in the order said topics were presented to the class. The following topics were listed by three or more teachers of history in Grade VII; "European Background," "American Indians," "Exploration and Discovery," "Colonization," "Life in the Colonies," "Rivalry between England and France," "The Constitution," "The American Revolution," "Gaining Respect and Trade Relations," and "The Confederation." Five eighth grade teachers listed the following topics: "Review of Revolution and Confederacy," "Constitution," "Expansion," "Industrial Progress," "Civil War and Reconstruction," "Inventions and Discoveries," "Foreign Relations," "Transportation and Communication," "Labor," "Education and Culture," "Social Life," "Tariff," "United States as a World Power," "Finance and Industry," and "World War." [104] It is clear from these two lists

[104] Warren W. Coxe and others, *op. cit.*, pp. 101 and 104.

of topics and the data in Table XXXIII that the adverse critics of history in the schools will have to change the base of their attacks. No longer can they say that United States history as taught in Grades VII and VIII is largely devoted to military and political history arranged in terms of presidential administrations. If these adverse critics succeed in eliminating history as an independent subject from junior high schools they will have to seek reasons other than those which have been handed down from a previous generation. Content in history has changed in recent time and these changes must be taken into account by all adverse critics of history in the schools.

DIVISION THREE

MATERIALS FROM THE FIELD OF POLITICAL
SCIENCE AS SUBJECTS OF STUDY IN THE
SCHOOLS

MATERIALS FROM THE FIELD OF POLITICAL SCIENCE AS SUBJECTS OF STUDY IN THE SCHOOLS

I. VALUES CLAIMED FOR MATERIALS FROM POLITICAL SCIENCE.—
Nature of the Early Values; Values of Civil Government;
Values of Civics Proper.

II. THE ENTRANCE OF MATERIALS FROM THE FIELD OF POLITICAL
SCIENCE INTO THE SCHOOLS: THE CONSTITUTIONAL PERIOD.
—Evidence of the Extent of the Offerings Prior to 1860;
the First Textbooks Containing Materials from Political
Science; the Nature of the Political Science Material in
the Schools Prior to 1860.

III. THE ESTABLISHMENT OF MATERIALS FROM THE FIELD OF PO-
LITICAL SCIENCE IN ELEMENTARY AND SECONDARY SCHOOLS,
1860–97.—The Prevalence of Materials from Political Science in Secondary Schools; Status of Civil Government
in Elementary Schools; the Content of Courses on the
Constitution, Law, and Government as Reflected in the
Textbooks of the Period.

IV. THE AGE OF CIVIL GOVERNMENT IN THE SCHOOLS, 1897–1915.
—Evidence of the Existence of Civil Government in Secondary Schools; Civil Government in Elementary Schools;
the Content of Civil Government in Secondary Schools;
the Content of Civics in the Elementary Grades.

V. COMMUNITY, VOCATIONAL, ECONOMIC, AND ADVANCED CIVICS
IN THE SCHOOLS, 1915–33.—The Prevalence of Civics in
Traditional Four-Year High Schools and Academies; Evi-
dence of the Existence of Civics in Elementary Schools;
Evidence of the Existence of Civics in Junior High
Schools; Community Civics; Government or Advanced
Civics; Vocational, Occupational, and Economic Civics;
the Content of Civics in the Elementary Grades.

I

VALUES CLAIMED FOR MATERIALS FROM POLITICAL SCIENCE

Viewing the values claimed for certain materials from the field of political science in the education of youth historically, it is proper to begin with the claims of those who were responsible for the introduction of these materials into the schools. Prior to 1860, the authors of textbooks seem to have been the chief advocates of the introduction into the schools of the type of political science material included in their texts. Those who wrote books dealing with the federal constitution and government usually made a strong case for the use of this type of material in the schools. Sometimes their pleas appeared as aims and sometimes as values. For the purposes of this discussion they are all considered as values.

NATURE OF THE EARLY VALUES

According to the findings of one investigator[1] those who wrote the first textbooks in the field of political science for use in the schools below the college claimed that the material their books contained was valuable (1) to train young people to perform their political duties when grown up; (2) to acquaint them with the federal constitution; (3) to cause them to form a strong attachment to the Union; (4) to acquaint them with the theory, principles, and operation of the state and national government; and (5) to furnish them with authentic information respecting the rights and duties of citizenship.

[1] Henry F. Kohlmeyer, "The History of the Development of the Aims of Teaching Civics in the Secondary Schools of the United States." Unpublished Master's thesis, Indiana University, 1925.

The reader will observe that the word "patriotism" does not appear in the statements of these values. The writers of the books containing the foregoing statements defended their material mainly on the basis of its intellectual value. They probably felt that information rather than sentiment was needed in their day. It should be pointed out, however, that one of the foregoing statements in reality involves patriotism. One strongly attached to the Union would probably never have his patriotism questioned. Inasmuch as the writers of the books from which the foregoing values were taken were extremely interested in strengthening the Union in a time when impending dangers were all too numerous, they thought and spoke in terms of the Union rather than in terms of patriotism.

VALUES OF CIVIL GOVERNMENT

During the period of the Civil War interest in materials from the field of political science in the schools went into an eclipse. However, after the Union had been saved and those interested in the making of citizens got back to their normal daily routine, the pre-war enthusiasm for the teaching of the federal constitution and government was revived. Even larger possibilities for these materials were discovered, especially after 1885, than had been suggested prior to 1860. Between 1885 and 1910 educational administrators, teachers, and textbook writers were in substantial agreement respecting the values of materials from the field of political science in the making of useful citizens. They said that these materials were valuable (1) to acquaint young people with the theory and practical character of the federal constitution and government and the nature, organization, function, and interrelations of social institutions; (2) to train them to appreciate their opportunities and perform their duties as good citizens and voters; (3) to cause them to have correct civic habits of thought and action; (4) to form intelligent public opinion; (5) to inculcate patriotism; (6) to inform maturing citizens concerning their relations to government; (7) to support the study of history; (8) to create ideals; (9) to discipline the mind; (10) to arouse civic conscience; and (11) to promote social stability and progress.[2] The values in this list most emphasized between 1885 and 1910 were: to acquaint young people with the theory and practical character of the federal constitution and government, to inform them concerning the social institutions and their interrelations, to promote social stability and progress, to train young people to appreciate their opportunities and to perform their duties as good citizens and voters, and to inculcate patriotism.

The attitude of educators during the 1890's toward the introduction of civil government or civics into the elementary school is well expressed in the reports of two State Superintendents for the years 1895-96 and 1896-98. The following statement accompanied a suggested outline of civics for the elementary schools in Ohio. It was made in 1896.

"The following outline of civics has been prepared in the belief that the safety of the Republic is best to be attained through the development in the people of a lofty patriotism; that the true love of country is a love for those institutions which make life in our country worth the living—opening wide to all the door of opportunity. In order that institutions shall be loved by the people they must be shown to be worthy

2 Henry F. Kohlmeyer, op. cit., p. 67.

of love. The beneficent influence of government and the especially favorable phases of our own government must be shown to the young. It is believed that this love of our institutions is so sacred in character, so like the love of a child for its father and mother, that it may be induced early in children; and that it may grow and keep pace with the development of intelligence in all directions."[3]

In his report for 1896–98, the Superintendent of Public Instruction of North Carolina said with respect to the introduction of civil government into the public schools of his state:

"I advise that we add Civil Government to our list of subjects to be taught in our Public Schools.

"It is singular, but nevertheless true, that so large a per cent. of our more intelligent people are so poorly informed upon matters pertaining to our government, both the National and the State Government.

"We want our children to be patriotic, to love our government, and one of the ways to do this is to teach them what our government is, and how our laws are made.

"Our children should know the duties required of the various State officers; how laws are enacted, repealed, or amended.

"Our children should know the duties of the President of the United States, and of the different Cabinet officers. They should be taught the duties of both Houses of Congress, and the various departments of our government.

"While we may not in many cases have regular classes studying this subject, yet the teachers should be well informed on this subject, and should give oral lessons at least once a

[3] *Forty-Third Annual Report* of the State Commissioner of Common Schools to the Governor of the State of Ohio, for the year ending August 31, 1896, p. 6.

week to the entire school, and even in this way our children may acquire a good general knowledge of our government." [4]

VALUES OF CIVICS PROPER

During the decade following 1910 there was an enormous amount of discussion of civics as a subject of study in elementary and secondary schools. The values proclaimed during these years by textbook writers, teachers, and educational administrators were not wholly unlike those advocated during the two decades prior to 1910. During the decade under review those interested in civics in the schools said that the subject was valuable to: acquaint citizens with the forms of organization and methods of administration of government in its several departments; make an individual a more intelligent, a more efficient, and therefore a better citizen and voter; promote social stability and progress; inculcate patriotism; give youth a knowledge of governmental institutions; support the study of history; aid in the translation of civic thought into action; teach an individual his relation to society; train one for participation in community life; awaken civic conscience; make an individual conscious of the relation between community welfare and himself; give an individual a proper sense of his own responsibility in making his government honest and efficient; discipline the mind; train in proper use of leisure time; teach the purpose of government; inspire citizens to perform their civic duties; inculcate political and social idealism; and create a deep interest in government.[5] Most emphasis was placed on Numbers 1, 2, 3, 7, and 8 of this list. The majority of the writers of textbooks felt that

[4] *Biennial Report* of the Superintendent of Public Instruction of North Carolina for the Scholastic Years 1896–97 and 1897–98, p. 47.
[5] Kohlmeyer, *op. cit.*, p. 70.

the value of civics in acquainting youth with the functions of government was paramount. Teachers emphasized the value of the subject in aiding pupils to translate civic thought into action. Educational administrators failed to rally around any one of the foregoing values.

"Training for effective citizenship" was a slogan much used during the late 1910's. In analyzing the values claimed for civics in a program intended to put this slogan into action one teacher suggested that civics possessed large value as a tool for use in training for intelligent and conscientious participation in civic activities; bringing persons into intelligent relationship with the community about them; imparting a practical knowledge of American politics, political party platforms, and the management of political parties; encouraging independent thinking and independent voting; seeing all sides of a public question and weighing the *pros* and *cons* before coming to a decision; affording an acquaintance with the functions of national, state, and city government; getting individuals to see what the nation, the state, the city, the town, and the country are actually doing for them daily; and promoting in young people a willingness to contribute their share toward securing the proper type of citizenship.[6] The efforts to translate these values into the everyday life of the pupils were nation-wide during the fifteen years after 1910. The success attending these efforts was by no means astounding. The fact that it was easier to state high sounding values of a subject of study than to achieve them in actual practice became evident to many. "To do" was by no means as easy as "knowing what were best to do." Indeed, had it been so, desirable changes in many phases of social living would have occurred over night.

[6] J. M. Gathany, "Practical Aims and Methods in the Teaching of Civics," *History Teacher's Magazine*, IV (1913), 20.

Since 1925 civics as an individual subject of study in the elementary and secondary schools has been on the defensive. Whereas the values proclaimed in the eighteen nineties served to secure the subject a place in the program of studies, the values claimed for civics since 1925 have been expected to aid in keeping it in the schools. Whether civics as an independent subject can be or should be kept in the schools are matters which have not yet been objectively determined. Even so, in an effort to meet the demands made on it during the years following 1907 civics became differentiated into social civics, vocational civics, economic civics, international civics, advanced civics, and community civics. When this differentiation took place the word "civics" passed out of use as a single word to name a body of material taught in the schools. Those who used the word at all, after about 1920 had to accompany it with a qualifying adjective. After this date, values were stated in terms of community civics, vocational civics, governmental civics, and the like. For this reason it is proper to end a historical treatment of values claimed for civics as a school subject with the year 1920.

II

THE ENTRANCE OF MATERIALS FROM THE FIELD OF POLITICAL SCIENCE INTO THE SCHOOLS: THE CONSTITUTIONAL PERIOD

Materials from the field of political science gradually found their way into the academies and high schools of this country during the generation prior to the Civil War. The extent of the offerings of these materials cannot be stated in numerical terms except in a few isolated cases. The nature of what was offered may be determined from the textbooks in use. In the discussion which follows both of these aspects of the matter are treated in more or less detail, attention first being directed to the extent of the offerings.

THE EXTENT OF THE OFFERINGS PRIOR TO 1860

During the generation following the establishment of the first public high school in Boston in 1821 materials from the field of political science gradually found their way into the high schools and academies of this country. To what specific extent there seems to be no way directly to determine. Some indirect evidence in the form of textbooks published during the period is at hand. While the exact number of these texts is not known, there were at least as many as forty-five on the market in 1860—this being the number reported in use in the schools of New York under the heading "Constitution, Government, and Law." Fourteen texts were reported as early as 1834 and thirty in 1847.[7] Besides this indirect evidence of the early existence of materials from political science in the school there is some that is more direct. It is to the effect that of all pupils in regular attendance in the academies of New York in 1827, 8.2 per cent attended schools in which materials relating to the constitution, law, and government were offered. For 1830, the per cent was 17; for 1832, 27; for 1834, 41; for 1847, 25; and for 1860, 24.[8] Data are lacking relative to the exact number of pupils in each academy availing themselves of the opportunity to pursue these materials.

There is other evidence at hand regarding the prevalence of materials from the field of political science in the high schools

[7] W. E. Russell, "The Entrance of History into the Curriculum of the Secondary School," *History Teacher's Magazine*, V (1914), 315.
[8] *Ibid.*

and academies in the state of New York prior to 1860. In 1834, twelve of the sixty-three academies reporting included the constitution of the United States in their program of studies, and three, the constitution of the state of New York.[9] Furthermore, the increase in the per cent of academies (high schools included after 1850) offering materials from the field of political science was from less than 3 in 1826 to 25 in 1860, the per cents for the five-year periods between these two dates being: 1830, 8.77; 1835, 59; 1840, 33; 1845, 30.72; 1850, 18; and 1855, 20. The height reached in 1835 seems somewhat remarkable. No data are at one's command to account for the ups-and-downs of the per cents.[10]

Some evidence is available relating to the extent that such subjects as political philosophy, government of the United States, constitution of the United States, and constitution of Connecticut were pursued in the high schools of Connecticut and Massachusetts prior to 1860. The constitution of Connecticut was on the program of studies of the Hartford High School in 1859 and on that of the Waterbury High School in 1861. The constitution of the United States was among the subjects taught in the high school at Hartford in 1848 and government of the United States was among the subjects taught in Middletown in 1850. There were 22 pupils enrolled in a class studying the constitution of the United States in the public high school of Hartford in 1856. The total registration in the school at this date was 222.[11] In Massachusetts, there were in 1834, twelve towns claiming to offer in their schools

[9] Gideon Hawley, *Documents of the Senate of the State of New York*, I (1835), 17–21 and 32–35 of Document No. 70.

[10] The per cents in this paragraph were computed from data in Charles F. Wheelock's *Secondary Education*, pp. 122, 150, and 177. Albany, N. Y.: The University of the State of New York, 1922.

[11] Facts gathered from Silas Hertzler's *The Rise of the Public High School in Connecticut*. Baltimore: Warwick and York, 1930.

material that one writer has classified as political science.[12] In 1837, there were 9 towns making the same claim; in 1838, 29; in 1839, 29; and in 1840, 30. Since there were probably never over 18 actual high schools in Massachusetts between 1834 and 1841 some of these offerings had to be in grades below the high school. This is a somewhat significant fact. It evidences that in one state at least the subject now called "civics" was taught in the elementary grades as early as 1838.

A few other interesting items relating to the offerings in subjects within the field of political science remain to be mentioned. One of these is that the constitution of the United States was one of the subjects pursued by the lowest class in the English High School of Boston in 1827—political philosophy having been included among the list of subjects for the highest class since the beginning of the school in 1821. So it is correct to say that the career of material from the field of political science in the high schools of this country is almost co-existent with the high school itself. In 1857 Massachusetts by legal enactment placed "civil polity" on the required list of subjects for all high schools in towns of 500 families and over.[13]

In concluding this brief survey of the evidence relating to the extent of the offering of materials from the field of political science prior to 1860, reference will be made to some existing indirect evidence. A page or so back the number of textbooks in political science for use in schools below the college available prior to 1860 was cited—the texts cited having been used in the academies of New York. Now, there is no reason to believe that textbooks on the constitution, law, and government were published prior to 1860 for use in New York State alone. If records concerning the textbooks used were avail-

[12] A. J. Inglis, *The Rise of the High School in Massachusetts*, p. 75. New York: Bureau of Publications, Teacher's College, 1911.
[13] *Ibid.*, pp. 72 f.

able for every state in which academies and high schools existed in 1860 as they are for New York, there is no reason to doubt that they would contain proof that considerable attention was given to the constitution, law, and government in the academies and high schools outside of New York during the decades following 1820. Lacking data to verify it, this statement will have to remain in the realm of conjecture.

THE FIRST TEXTBOOKS CONTAINING MATERIALS FROM
POLITICAL SCIENCE

Indoctrination was a principle practiced by the writers of the first textbooks containing material from the field of political science to be used in the schools of this country below the college. During the late 1790's when the tide of Jeffersonian democracy was running high there appeared a text with the avowed purpose of instructing the youth of the land in sound principles of government as conceived by a staunch New England Federalist. The volume was writen by one Elhanan Winchester, its complete title being *A Plain Political Catechism Intended for Use in the United States of America, wherein the Great Principles of Liberty and of the Federal Constitution are Laid Down and Explained by Way of Question and Answer, Made Level to the Lowest Capacities.* This text was published in 1797 and as hinted above was written to stem the tide of the rising Jeffersonian democracy, which the author looked upon with fear and trembling. He saw in it a dangerous invasion of atheism and disorganization and wished to contribute his mite to the erection of safeguards against the devastations of these monsters. Questions such as the following were asked and answered in the text: (1) "What is man in a state of nature without society?" (2) "What makes government necessary?" (3) "Will the early knowledge of politics of our country tend to introduce disorder, discontent, division, animosity, and rebellion amongst the young people, as some persons pretend?" No data are available with respect to the extent that this little volume of about one hundred pages was used. Its use could not have been extensive because of the scant amount of attention in the schools of that day to the type of material it contained. In the matter of stemming the tide of the rising Jeffersonian democracy it was a complete failure inasmuch as the Jeffersonian Democrats took charge of the government in March, 1801, and remained in power for nearly a quarter of a century.

Winchester's signal failure to enhance the cause of federalism in the face of the rise of virile democracy seems to have acted as a deterrent to others who might have harbored a similar ambition, for it was almost a generation before another book in the field appeared. This offering was by one William Sullivan, a staunch opponent of Andrew Jackson and the kind of democracy he championed. It was published[14] in 1830 under the title *The Political Class Book, Intended to Instruct Higher Classes in Schools in the Origin, Nature and Use of Political Power.* According to Sullivan current provisions in the usual course of education for the training of those approaching manhood to discharge the political duties which they must later assume were wholly inadequate. He hoped that his modest little volume of 144 pages would do something toward supplying what he considered a grave need. Inasmuch as a second edition of the book appeared in 1831, the volume must have met with some success. It was still being reprinted in 1846.

[14] A volume had appeared in 1828, its author and title being A. J. Stansbury, *Catechism of the Constitution of the United States.* Boston: Richard, Gray, Little, and Wilkins, 1828.

Sullivan's volume contained material on the constitution and laws of the states and the United States; religion; education; banking, promissory notes, bills of exchange, and notaries; persons—their capacities, incapacities, and classification; laws which govern men in society; sources of knowledge; men considered individually and socially; means by which the order of society is preserved; property; and choice of employment.[15] To those acquainted with the contents of present-day texts in problems of American democracy, some of these topics will be familiar, for example, such topics as religion, education, banking, and property.

Sullivan was by no means the only individual who tried to stem the tide of Jacksonian democracy during the 1830's by appealing to the young through a textbook containing materials drawn primarily from political science. Others who joined him were James Bayard, E. D. Mansfield, and Andrew W. Young in 1833, 1834, and 1835. Bayard's volume was entitled *An Exposition of the Constitution of the United States*. It contained chapters on the Preamble of the federal constitution, the House of Representatives, the Senate, powers of Congress, limits on the powers of Congress, limits on the powers of the states, the executive, powers and duties of the President, judiciary, miscellaneous subjects, and amendments. Mansfield's work, *The Political Grammar of the United States* contained material on such topics as definitions of government, origin of the constitution, the constitution, ratification, theory of state government, relation between the general and state government, practical operations of the national constitution, and practical operations of state government.[16] The fact that the

15 Henry F. Kohlmeyer, *op. cit.*, pp. 7 ff.
16 W. H. Wheeler, "A History of the Content and Method of Teaching Civics in the High School Prior to 1910," p. 16. Unpublished Master's thesis, University of Chicago, 1924.

sixteenth edition of this volume appeared as early as 1849 is indicative of the extent of its use. The long and cumbersome title of Young's volume was *Introduction to the Science of Government and Compend of Constitutional and Civil Jurisprudence, Comprehending a General View of the Government of the United States and the Government of the State of New York Together with the Most Important Provisions of the Constitutions of the Several States: Adapted to Purposes of Instruction in Families and Schools.* Its four parts were devoted to the topics "Principles of Government," "The Government of the United States," Civil Jurisprudence of the United States," and "Political Economy." The Appendix contained the Declaration of Independence and the constitution of New York State. In commenting on Young's book an authority on political education on one occasion remarked, "The work of this author appeared under this [the foregoing] title or that of *The Political Class Book* in many editions by various editors. The most recent edition seems to have been that of 1901. But the book seems still to be taught in schools. . . . A book that could hold its own for three-quarters of a century, even with revisions and re-editing, was no lame or superficial effort." [17]

The writing and publishing of textbooks containing material primarily from the field of political science by no means ended with the passing of the administrations of Jackson and Van Buren—the output during the 1840's equaling or surpassing that of the 1830's. As the Civil War approached and the disruption of the Union became more and more feared by public minded individuals, materials for educating the young in the origin, meaning, and benefits of the then existing federal government never ceased to be offered to those in charge of the

[17] Edgar Dawson, "Beginnings in Political Education," *Historical Outlook,* IX (1918), 439 f.

schools. Consequently during the 1840's and 1850's a number of books on the United States constitution and the American government appeared. Mention can be made of but a few of these such as: (1) Charles Mason, *Elementary Treatise on the Structure and Operation of the National and State Governments of the United States*, 1842; (2) Peter Parley, *Young American* (Book of Government and Law), 1842; (3) Salma Hale, *The Constitution of the United States,* 1843; (4) John S. Hart, *A Brief Exposition of the Constitution of the United States,* 1845; (5) J. B. Shurtleff, *The Government Instructor,* 1845; (6) William Hickey, *The Constitution of the United States,* 1846; (7) Joseph B. Burleigh, *The American Manual,* 1848; (8) Joseph Story, *A Familiar Exposition of the Constitution of the United States,* 1849; (9) A. W. Young, *Citizen's Manual of Government and Law,* 1851; (10) D. R. Williams, *A Book of the Constitution,* 1852; (11) Furman Sheppard, *The Constitutional Text-book,* 1855; (12) A. W. Young, *The American Statesman,* 1856; and (13) Mordecai McKinney, *Our Government: An Explanatory Statement of the Government of the County, State, and Town,* 1856.

The foregoing list, of course, only approximates completeness. It contains, however, most of the titles that one meets in the literature of the period. There is evidence extant to the effect that some of the texts on the list and those previously mentioned were actually in use prior to 1860. In 1854, one academy in New York was using Bayard's volume. The texts by Burleigh and Sullivan were also used in one academy each at this date. Story's and Shurtleff's texts were used in two academies each and Young's (probably his *Introduction to Science of Government*) in twenty-one.[18] There is also some

[18] *Sixty Ninth Report of the Regents of the University of the State of New York*, pp. 322 ff.

evidence that Burleigh's text was used in Maryland, Michigan, and Ohio. The fact that Burleigh was a practical school man, being a teacher for a number of years in the schools of Baltimore, probably explains the success of his volume.

THE NATURE OF POLITICAL SCIENCE MATERIALS IN THE SCHOOLS PRIOR TO 1860

While objective data are lacking on the extent of the use in the schools of materials from the field of political science prior to 1860 there is evidence concerning the nature of this material, such evidence being found in the textbooks listed above. Generally speaking, the emphasis in these books was on the constitution, law, and government, the constitution of the United States being the chief center of interest. So strong and so general was this emphasis on the federal constitution that the period in the teaching of law and government ending with 1860 may be designated The Constitutional Period.

There seems to be no doubt that the agitation for the teaching of law and government in the schools during the eighteen thirties and forties had its roots in the despair of the educated classes and the guardians of conservatism. These individuals felt that the country in the hands of the Jacksonian Democrats was on the road to universal ruin. They felt that there was some hope of salvaging the republic through the education of the rising generation in the fundamentals of constitutional government and public law. The author of one of the most used texts of the period put the matter thus:

"Distinguished as the American people are for their comparative general intelligence, a large portion of them, it must be confessed, are greatly wanting in political knowledge. . . . Multitudes in this republic are annually arriving at that period of life, when they are to exercise, for the first time, their privileges as citizens. In the state of New York alone, the number is about *fifteen thousand,* and is composed, chiefly, of those whose education does not embrace even the first principles of political science. It is not to be expected that political power, in such hands, can be exercised with safety to the government, or with benefit to the community." [19]

While the chief emphasis in the teaching of law and government in the schools prior to 1860 was on the constitution of the United States, it was the custom of some authors to include material from the field of ethics, religion, international law, commercial law, and local government. Stansbury's, Sullivan's, and Burleigh's texts were sprinkled with material from the fields of ethics and religion. For example, Sullivan's analytical index (1830 edition) contained the following (Notice the Puritanic flavor): "Apocrypha; Bible; Blasphemy; Calvin; Catholic Church; Conscience; Dissenters; Dress, its proper use; Education of Females, its defects; Sanctity of Marriage; Ministers of the Gospels; Moral Sense; New Testament; Parishes; Pope, origin of; Protestantism; Puritans; Reason or Light of Nature; Quakers; Sabbath, duty on, etc." [20]

As early as 1836 Sullivan in his *The Political Classbook* began to include material from the fields now designated education, international law, commercial law, state government, local government, economics, and vocational guidance. In his *The American Manual* Burleigh made an effort to broaden the content of his subject by including material on the historical aspects of government and authority, international law, English origins of colonial institutions, and the duties of citizens, voters, and civil magistrates. These two texts seem to

[19] Quoted by A. W. Brown, *The Improvement of Civics Instruction,* p. 9. From the 1840 edition of Young's *Science of Government.*
[20] Cited by Wheeler, *op. cit.,* p. 17.

have been typical for the period. The one by Burleigh was used somewhat widely. It was the adopted text in three high schools of Baltimore in 1848; in the cities of Pittsburgh and Allegheny City, Pennsylvania, in 1849; in Norfolk, Virginia, and Ypsilanti, Michigan the same year; in Steubenville and Cincinnati, Ohio, in 1850; and in Indianapolis, Indiana, and Washington, D. C., the same year.

Two facts stand out with respect to the content of textbooks in law and government published prior to 1860. These are (1) the overshadowing emphasis on the constitution of the United States and (2) the overt propaganda for the Northern view of the nature of the constitution and the Union. Students of the history of the Jacksonian Era are not surprised to find those interested in material on law and government appropriate for schools turning to the most talked-of document of the day, the constitution of the United States. The constitutionality of internal improvements at national expense, the right of a state to nullify a federal law, and other constitutional questions were widely discussed during the period; and it is not surprising to find the spirit of the times reflected in the textbooks dealing primarily with the federal constitution.

On the matter of indoctrination some of the texts were outspoken in favor of the Northern view, for example, of secession. Bayard in his *Exposition of the Constitution of the United States* published in 1833 claimed that were the constitution merely a compact of states, no one of the parties would have a right to withdraw and added "we must indignantly frown upon the first dawning of every attempt to alienate any portion of our country from the rest, or to enfeeble the sacred ties, which now link together the various states." Small chance did Bayard's book have of state-wide adoption in South Carolina in 1833. The truth of the matter is had South Carolina desired a book on law and government for use in her schools even as late as 1860 there would have been few available ones entirely free from the type of indoctrination found in Bayard's text. Excepting Burleigh and Mansfield, the authors of text-books on the constitution, law, and government published prior to 1860 for use in the elementary and secondary schools lived east of Pittsburgh and north of Baltimore, hence reflected in their works in most cases the Northern view on the controversial issues of the day—a view which was in a large measure the New England view.

III

THE ESTABLISHMENT OF MATERIALS FROM THE FIELD OF POLITICAL SCIENCE IN ELEMENTARY AND SECONDARY SCHOOLS, 1860-97

It seems clear from the available evidence that materials from the field of political science taught under such captions as science of government, United States constitution, civil government, political science, state constitution, parliamentary rules, civics, and American politics, became fairly well established in both elementary and the secondary school during the forty years following the Civil War. The evidence to substantiate this statement is presented below.

THE PREVALENCE OF MATERIALS FROM POLITICAL SCIENCE IN SECONDARY SCHOOLS

Political-science materials taught in secondary schools between 1860 and 1900 existed as hinted above under a number of titles, such as science of government, United States constitution, civil government, political science, and others. The extent of the offerings under each of these titles in a group of states is shown in Table I. It will be observed from the data

TABLE I

NUMBER AND PER CENT OF SCHOOLS IN THE NORTH CENTRAL ASSOCIATION TERRITORY OFFERING COURSES CONTAINING MATERIALS FROM THE FIELD OF POLITICAL SCIENCE, 1860–1900*

SUBJECTS	1860–65 20 Schools		1866–70 20 Schools		1871–75 20 Schools		1876–80 20 Schools		1881–85 25 Schools		1886–90 30 Schools		1891–95 40 Schools		1896–1900 40 Schools	
	NO.	%	NO.	%	NO.	%	NO.	%	NO.	%	NO.	%	NO.	%	NO.	%
Science of Government	3	15	2	10	3	15	3	15	2	8	1	3⅓	..	..	..	...
United States Constitution	8	40	4	20	5	25	4	20	4	16	6	20	..	..	2	5
Civil Government	..	..	8	40	7	35	8	40	15	60	23	85	25	62½	24	60
Political Science	..	..	1	5	1	5	..	..	..	..	11	..	..	..	..	...
State Constitution	..	..	..	..	1	5	..	..	..	..	2	6	..	..	1	...
Parliamentary Rules	..	..	..	..	..	..	1	5	..	..	..	..	..	..	..	...
Civics	..	..	..	..	..	..	..	..	..	..	1	3⅓	7	17½	10	25
United States and State Constitutions	..	..	..	..	..	..	..	..	..	..	..	..	1	2½	..	...
United States Civil Government	..	..	..	..	..	..	..	..	..	..	..	..	1	2½	..	...
State Civil Government	..	..	..	..	..	..	..	..	..	..	..	..	1	2½	..	...
American Politics	..	..	..	..	..	..	..	..	..	..	..	..	..	..	1	2½

* John E. Stout, *The Development of High-School Curricula in the North Central States from 1860 to 1918*, pp. 62–68 and 73 f. Chicago: The University of Chicago Press, 1921.

herein that science of government, United States constitution, and civil government were the three most frequently used titles of the courses in the field of political science offered between 1860 and 1900 in the schools in the North Central Association territory. The fact that civil government had come to be the most used title of the course even as early as 1866 should be noted, because of its subsequent popularity. It will be observed that the word "civics" was not used prior to 1884. An explanation of this occurrence is found in the fact that the word "civics" used to designate those aspects of political science that pertain to the elevation of citizenship did not come into use until about 1885. Credit for using the word in this connection first seems to belong to Henry Randall Waite, who was born in New York in 1845. During 1885-86, Waite edited a magazine called *The Citizen*. Later he became editor of another magazine which circulated under the title *Civics*. In 1885, Waite founded the American Institute of Civics. So it seems evident that by 1886 he had brought the word "civics" into somewhat general use. This fact is substantiated by reference picked up here and there during the middle 1880's. For example, the following definition of civics appeared as early as 1886: "Civics is the science of citizenship—the relation of man, the individual, to men in organized collections—the individual in his relation to the state." [21] A year later in an article entitled "American History in Preparatory Schools" reference was made to the recent appearance of the word "civics." [22] This same year the following elaborate definition of the word appeared.

"In a word, the minimum of what the citizen should know, in addition to the ordinary compulsory branches, that he may be reasonably prepared for his civil duties, is the fundamental or rudimentary facts and principles of these five subjects— Ethics as pertaining to government, Civil Polity, Economics, History, at least of his own state and country, and Law or

[21] C. F. Creshore, "The Teaching of Civics in the Schools," *Education*, VII (1886-87), 264.
[22] G. W. Rollins, *Academy: A Journal of Secondary Education*, I (1887), 133-139.

Jurisprudence. These I would include in this new science of civics, and they should all be taught in some regularly graduated system in all public schools." [23]

It is evident from Table I that the interest in the type of subject matter represented by the titles of the courses listed therein increased after 1880. This increase in interest indicates that the recovery from the relapse that occurred between 1860 and 1875 was under way. In all probability the revival of interest in materials from the field of political science on the part of school people was hastened by the activities of certain groups of individuals which strenuously advocated the inclusion of these materials in the program of studies of all schools. For example, the National Teachers' Association (now the National Education Association) at its fourth annual meeting in 1863 appointed a committee of five to consider and report on what the times and the conditions of the country demanded relating to the teaching of the principles of government. Before final adjournment of the Association this Committee brought in a report which was unanimously adopted. After the vote was taken the audience united in the singing of "America." The report of the Committee follows.

"Whereas, in a Democratic Government, wherein the people are, of necessity, the sovereigns, it is indispensable to the prosperity and perpetuity of such government that these sovereigns, the people, understand the principles of said government, and

"Whereas, the exigencies of the times, demand the highest intelligence, the purest patriotism, therefore,

"*Resolved*, 1. That it is imperative, that the History, Polity,

[23] James E. Vose, "Methods of Instruction in Civics," *Education*, VII (1886–87), 530 f.

and Constitution of our Government be taught in all our schools, wherein the maturity of the pupils is equal to the subjects.

"*Resolved, 2.* That this Association earnestly commends this subject to the attention of teachers, trustees, and committeemen, throughout the nation.

"*Resolved, 3.* That this teaching should never be prostituted to the inculcation of merely partizan sentiments and principles." [24]

In spite of these resolutions and the efforts of well-meaning individuals, it was not possible for the study of the principles of government to make headway throughout the sixties and most of the seventies. Signs of a revival, however, began to appear in the middle seventies. In 1875, an important textbook in the field was published[25] and in 1876 a report of the National Educational Association was made touching the subject. By 1885 an enthusiastic supporter of the teaching of political science in the schools felt justified in saying to the members of the Philadelphia Social Science Association:

"In few countries in the world is the study of Political Science so universal as in America. It is represented in some of its branches in all grades of educational institutions, from the elementary school of the rural district to the college and university. It is studied not only by those boys who expect to make a profession of law and politics, but by those who intend to follow other professions and callings as well. The future

24 "National Teachers' Association," *Barnard's American Journal of Education,* XIV (1864), 41 f.

25 George H. Martin, *A Textbook on Civil Government in the United States.* New York: A. S. Barnes and Co., 1875. A text by Joseph Alden for use in the elementary grades was published in 1867. It was entitled Alden's *Citizen Manual.*

clergyman, physician, merchant, college professor—of whatever
branch—have all studied Political Economy and Constitutional
Law, if they finished a college course before taking up their
professional study. The future civil engineer, chemist, geolo-
gist, and mining engineer have all given more or less attention
to these subjects if they prepared themselves for their work in
a higher technical school or college. The artisan, carpenter,
mason, cabinet-maker, and clerk, so far as they have finished
the average high school course in our towns and cities, are
also acquainted with the elements of the same subjects, and in
some of our states even the ungraded country schools offer a
certain amount of instruction in these branches. Nor do our
schools rest content with offering such instruction to the boys,
but, so far as they are mixed schools, the same advantages are
open to the girls, and even the schools exclusively for girls
nearly all incorporate these subjects in their curricula." [26]

The author of this very optimistic statement gave no facts to
support his musings. It seems evident now that he could
not have found facts sufficient to support his fine statements;
for during the very year in which James made his statement
there were in Ohio but 2411 out of a total of 30,372 high school
pupils pursuing the science of government. Corresponding
numbers for other years of the eighteen eighties and nineties
are presented in Table II, which shows that the so-called revival in interest in the science of government as a school subject was not a revival at all in Ohio, but a more or less gradual
gain in per cent of pupils pursuing the subject from year to
year. While the gain between 1882 and 1897 in the per cent
of pupils pursuing the science of government was a substantial

[26] E. J. James, *Instruction in Political and Social Science*, p. 3. Philadelphia:
Philadelphia Social Science Association, 1885.

one, there was no large increase in any one year prior to
1896. Evidence is available, however, that there actually was
a revival in New York. Between 1860 and 1890 the per cent of
academies and high schools of this state offering material from

TABLE II

NUMBER AND PER CENT OF PUPILS IN THE PUBLIC HIGH SCHOOLS
OF OHIO PURSUING SCIENCE OF GOVERNMENT, 1882–97 *

YEAR	TOTAL HIGH-SCHOOL ENROLLMENT	NUMBER PURSUING	PER CENT PURSUING
1882	27,920	1,571	5.63
1883	27,471	1,980	7.20
1884	29,697	2,073	6.98
1885	30,372	2,411	7.93
1886	30,419	2,282	7.50
1887	30,706	3,418	11.13
1888	31,430	3,098	9.85
1889	31,709	3,482	10.98
1890	33,572	5,364	15.98
1891	24,731	4,997	20.20
1892	35,182	5,744	16.32
1893	36,784	6,169	16.77
1894	40,577	7,899	19.46
1895	44,008	9,217	20.94
1896	44,610	10,815	24.24
1897	52,751	18,596	35.25

* Data, except those in the last column, are from the reports of the State Commissioner of Common Schools and Superintendent of Public Instruction for the years indicated.

the field of political science increased from 23.95 to 94.02.
During the 1880's the increase was from 52.32 to 94.02 per
cent.[27]

Throughout the 1890's over half of the districts in Michigan
offered civil government in their schools. Beginning with
55.96 per cent of the districts in 1890, the per cent offering this
subject increased to 80.93 in 1900. The details for the intervening years are included in Table III.

[27] Charles F. Wheelock, *op. cit.*, pp. 122 and 177.

An investigation in Illinois for the year 1892 disclosed the fact that 45 out of 65 high schools reporting maintained courses in civil government, 39 for three months and 6 for eight months. Eleven out of 47 of these schools offered civil

TABLE III

NUMBER AND PER CENT OF DISTRICTS IN MICHIGAN OFFERING INSTRUCTION IN CIVIL GOVERNMENT, 1890–1900 *

YEAR	NUMBER OF DISTRICTS MAINTAINING SCHOOLS	Number and Per Cent Offering Instruction in Civil Government	
		NUMBER	PER CENT
1890	7074	3959	55.96
1891	7132	4339	60.83
1892	7130	4370	61.29
1893	7066	4417	62.51
1894	7069	4181	59.14
1895	7078	5135	72.54
1896	7046	5395	76.56
1897	7083	5527	78.03
1898	7083	5444	76.86
1899	7091	5673	80.00
1900	7124	5758	80.82

* Reports of the Superintendent of Public Instruction of the State of Michigan, for the years indicated. Percentages were calculated by the author.

government during the first year; 16, the second; 9, the third; and 11, the fourth.[28]

Some idea of the content of the course in civil government in one city in 1886 is attained from the following comment:

"At Frankfort, Ind., recognizing that social instability comes from popular ignorance of law, of rights, of persons and property, of the sound principles of political economy, the following work has been mapped out, and was done during the last

[28] C. W. Groves, "Unification and Consolidation in the High School Courses," *Academy: A Journal of Secondary Education*, VII (1892), 106–112.

year: 1. A study of local government—officers, institutions, elections, local improvements. 2. A study of State government —officers, educational, benevolent and penal institutions, elections, legislature. 3. A study of National Government—legislature, judicial, executive; comparison of, and relation between State and National Government; process of law-making; reasonableness of obedience to authority; national institutions and improvements. 4. A study of business relations, wealth, exchange." [29]

STATUS OF CIVIL GOVERNMENT IN ELEMENTARY SCHOOLS

To this point in the discussion of materials from the field of political science in the schools from 1860 to 1897 attention has been directed primarily to the situation in secondary schools. Inasmuch as this type of material was included in the program of studies of some elementary schools, a review of the evidence relating thereto is apropos here.

In the report of the United States Commissioner of Education for the year 1888–89 there appeared a somewhat lengthy summary of the status of civil government in elementary schools. The important phases of this summary are quoted below.

"Civil government is a separate branch of instruction in twenty-two of the eighty-two cities [reporting]; its principles are taught in many more—nearly all, perhaps—incidentally in connection with history, geography, or like science and general history, as a part of the supplementary reading. The object of such instructions is declared to be better preparation for the duties of citizenship. In its usual application the subject em-

29 U. S. Comr. of Educ., *Rep. for 1886–87*, p. 239.

braces only the nature and forms of government, and the provisions of the Constitution of the United States, and that of the pupils' own State; but the study may be, and sometimes is, so broadened that it not only covers the elements of political science, but also trenches upon the domain of ethics. Several excellent textbooks have been prepared but they are not extensively used except as books of reference, the instruction being chiefly oral—frequently in accordance with a general plan or a syllabus prepared by the superintendent. One of the best of these syllabuses is that which appears in the Manual of the Course of Instruction in the grammar department of the Philadelphia public schools.[30] The instruction in that city is given in one year only, the eighth, and follows the topical method throughout. No text-book is used, but each pupil has constant access to the Declaration of Independence, the Constitution of the United States, and the Articles of the State Constitution. . . .

"Mr. R. W. Stephenson, in his report for 1887–88, as superintendent of public instruction of Columbus, Ohio, very thoroughly discussed the importance of training for citizenship, laying particular stress upon the cultivation of the virtues of obedience to rightful authority, integrity, industry, and patriotism. He would have instruction also in the forms and methods of government, but he believes that the possession of the virtues named is more necessary to the citizen than a mere knowledge of any particular system of laws. He therefore urges that the teachers aim particularly at the inculcation of these desirable qualities in order that their pupils may be the better as citizens. . . .

"As to the time for beginning, we find that in Denver, Washington, Detroit, East Saginaw, Minneapolis, Camden,

---

[30] This is the syllabus that appears on pp. 250 f. below.

Brooklyn, Milwaukee, and Philadelphia, only the pupils of the eighth-year class are permitted to pursue the study. In San Francisco, Cal., Atchison, Kans., Lynn, Mass., and Salt Lake City, Utah, two years are given to the subject. In Quincy, Ill., West Des Moines, Iowa, Baltimore, Md., Lawrence, Mass., and Jersey City, N. J., three years. In Wichita, Kans., and New Orleans, La., four years.

"The time per week varies from a half hour in San Francisco, New Orleans, and Baltimore, to 3½ hours in Detroit and 3 4/5 hours in Milwaukee. As a rule, the time per week is short where the number of weeks is great and vice versa, so that the total time given to the subject is remarkably uniform." [31]

The syllabus in civil government in use in Grade VIII in Philadelphia mentioned above was unique in more ways than one. It was probably one of the first ever used in this grade in any city. Because of its historical value it is reproduced below.

A SYLLABUS IN CIVIL GOVERNMENT USED IN GRADE VIII IN THE
CITY OF PHILADELPHIA IN 1888

Nature and Forms of Government.

I. Government: What is meant by the term; social nature of man; necessity of civil government; what is meant by the constitution of a nation; what a law is.

II. Different forms of government: (1) Monarchical; (2) aristocratic; (3) democratic; (4) republican; combinations of different forms.

Colonial Government.

I. Political Organizations of the colonies: Three forms of colonial government: (1) Provincial (royal); (2) proprietary; (3) charter.

II. Differences produced by these forms of government; superiority of political institutions resulting from the charter form

[31] U. S. Comr. of Educ., *Rep. for 1888–89,* I, 384–87.

of government; town system of New England a pure democracy; a local legislature, with one branch elected by the people, common to all three forms.

First Attempts of the Colonies at Union.

I. Absence of Political connection between the colonies.

II. The first Continental Congress, 1774; necessity of association; steps taken.

III. The second Continental Congress, 1775; (1) Duration; (2) measures adopted.

IV. The Declaration of Independence, July 4, 1776. Its contents and object.

Articles of Confederation.

I. Difficulties of carrying on the Revolution resulting from the absence of union between the States; necessity for a general government.

II. The Articles of Confederation; principal features.

Constitution of the United States of America.

I. Circumstances which led to the adoption of the Constitution; (1) defects of the Articles of Confederation; (2) functions performed by the Articles of Confederation in accustoming the States to associated action, and in leading to "a more perfect union."

II. Convention of delegates for the purpose of "revising the Articles of Confederation," etc.; different plans suggested; discussion of these; final completion of the Constitution.

III. Constitution of the United States of America adopted to go into effect when ratified by nine States; order in which the States acted.

IV. Preamble of the Constitution.

Branches of the United States Government—(1) Legislative; (2) Executive; (3) Judicial.

LEGISLATIVE BRANCH

I. Vested in Congress, consisting of (1) House of Representatives. (2) Senate.

II. House of Representatives: (1) Composition. (2) Powers: (a) Legislative—concurrent, exclusive; (b) impeachment; (c) elective—officers, President of the United States.

III. Senate: (1) Composition. (2) Presiding officer. (3) Powers: (a) Legislative; (b) executive—appointments, treaties; (c) elective—officers, Vice President of the United States; (d) judicial.

IV. Law-making: Methods; orders; resolutions; votes.

V. Powers granted to Congress.

VI. Powers denied to Congress.

VII. Powers denied to the several States.

Executive Branch

I. In whom executive power is vested; term of office, salary, oath.

II. Eligibility.

III. How elected: (1) By electors; (2) by the House of Representatives.

IV. How removable.

V. Powers and duties of President: (1) Military; (2) Civil.

VI. Vice President: (1) Eligibility, term, oath; (2) how elected; (3) powers and duties.

Judicial Branch

I. Where vested: (1) Supreme Court. (2) Inferior courts: (a) Circuit; (b) district.

II. Judges: (1) How appointed; (2) term of office, salary, oath; (3) how removable.

III. Jurisdiction: (1) Limitation; (2) original; (3) appellate.

Relations Between the States and the Federal Government.

I. Public acts, records, and judicial proceedings of States.

II. State citizenship.

III. Fugitives from (1) justice, (2) service.

IV. Formation and admission of new States (territories).

V. Guaranty and protection to the States.

Miscellaneous Provisions.

I. Supremacy of the Constitution.

II. Guarantee of personal rights.

III. Abolition of slavery.

IV. Enfranchisement of Negro citizens.

V. Validity of the public debt.

Constitution of the Commonwealth of Pennsylvania.
I.   Historical notes.
II. General analysis.
III. Analogies between the Federal and the State government.[32]

Large gains were made in the establishment of civil government in the upper-elementary grades between 1887 and 1897. Evidence of these gains is found in the fact that at the latter date the teaching of civil government in the elementary schools was required by law in eleven states, namely, Maryland, West Virginia, Kentucky, Missouri, Tennessee, South Carolina, Michigan, Wisconsin, Kansas, Colorado, and California.[33]

THE CONTENT OF COURSES IN THE CONSTITUTION, LAW, AND GOVERNMENT AS REFLECTED IN THE TEXTBOOKS OF THE PERIOD

Inasmuch as syllabi, laboratory methods, and classroom libraries were more or less in the realm of the unknown so far as the subject of civil government in elementary and secondary schools was concerned between 1860 and 1897, it is necessary to go to the textbook in use to find the content of this subject during the period. Besides the texts carried over from pre-Civil War days, there was available a number of new ones published from time to time. The following is a partial list of the new texts.

1. Henry Flanders, *An Exposition of the Constitution of the United States,* 1860.
2. Elisha P. Howe, *The Young Citizen's Catechism, Explaining the Duties of District, Town, City, County, State, and United States Officers,* 1860.
3. Joseph P. Alden, *The Science of Government,* 1866.

[32] *Ibid.,* pp. 385 f.
[33] T. R. Croswell, "Courses of Study in the Elementary Schools of the United States," *Pedagogical Seminary,* IV (1896), 295.

4. Joseph P. Alden, *Alden's Citizen's Manual*, 1867.

5. Israel W. Andrews, *Manual of the Constitution of the United States*, 1874.

6. George H. Martin, *A Text-book on Civil Government in the United States*, 1875.

7. Charles Nordhuff, *Politics for Young Americans*, 1875.

8. David Northam, *Manual of Civil Government*, 1877.

9. Anna Dawes, *How We Are Governed*, 1885.

10. Jesse Macy, *Our Government: How It Grew, What It Does and How It Does It*, 1886.

11. W. A. Mowry, *Studies in Civil Government*, 1887.

12. W. H. Rupert, *Guide to the Study of the History and Constitution of the United States*, 1887.

13. Luther H. Porter, *Outlines of the Constitution of the United States*, 1887.

14. Paul L. Ford, *American Citizen's Manual*, 1887.

15. James T. McCleary, *Studies in Civics*, 1888.

16. James Thorpe, *Government of the People of the United States*, 1889.

17. B. A. Hinsdale, *The American Government*, 1889.

18. John Fiske, *Civil Government in the United States With Some Reference to Its Origins*, 1890.

19. Charles F. Dole, *The American Citizen*, 1891.

20. A. L. Peterman, *Elements of Civil Government*, 1891.

21. A. O. Wright and W. D. Kuh, *Civil Government in the United States*, 1893.

22. Noah Brooks, *How the Republic Is Governed*, 1896.

There were, of course, books originally published prior to 1860 that were reprinted and used during the period under review. Inasmuch as these contained the old type of material which was prevalent before 1860, their inclusion here would add nothing to the discussion. Prevailing trends are found in current publications and not in earlier ones merely reprinted or even revised and reused.

Two facts conspicuously stand out in the content of the books in the foregoing list, namely, the reactionary nature of those published prior to 1875 and the portends of a revolution in some of the books appearing after this date. The textbooks published soon after 1865 were so reactionary in their content that it is proper to say that the material of the 1830's was revived in them. This means that the United States constitution and the national government got the lion's share of attention. It is not surprising to find soon after a war to save the union writers of textbooks on law and government treating the national aspects of their subject rather than the local. Three of these reactionary texts were those by Alden, Townsend, and Andrews (see list for titles and dates of publication). These individuals respectively devoted to the national government 70, 80, and 85 per cent of their space. The use of historical material and material on state and local matters that had appeared a few years before 1860 was not characteristic of these three books. The chapter headings of one of them will illustrate their reactionary nature.

CHAPTER HEADINGS IN ISRAEL W. ANDREWS' *Manual of the Constitution of the United States*, 1874

Chapter 1. Civil Government—Its Object, Origin, and Nature—Different Forms of Government—Peculiarity of that of the United States—Not a Consolidated Republic, nor a League of States.

Chapter 2. The Colonial Governments—Royal, Proprietary, and Charter—The Causes of the Revolution—The Continental Congress—The Declaration of Independence.

Chapter 3. The Articles of Confederation—Their Failure—The Convention to Form a Constitution.

Chapter 4. The Constitution of the United States.

  Article I.   The Legislative Department.
  Article II. The Executive Department.
  Article III. The Judiciary.
  Article IV. Various Subjects.
  Article V.   Mode of Amending the Constitution.

Article VI. Supremacy of the Constitution.
Article VII. Ratification of the Constitution.

Chapter 5. The Ratification of the Constitution by Conventions of the Several States.
Chapter 6. The Admission of New States—The Territorial Governments.
Chapter 7. Practical Operation of the Constitution.
Chapter 8. The State Governments.

It should be pointed out that Andrews was a little less reactionary than Townsend and Alden. His descriptive form of treatment, his slight emphasis on the historical aspects of the subject, and his material on state government indicated that he looked backward less continuously than did Townsend and Alden. Andrews devoted much space to an analysis of the federal constitution. In addition he allotted eleven pages to its ratification in the several states, forty-six to its practical operation, and seventy-six to the historical background of the government of the United States, the admission of states, and state government.

It was evident in 1875, when a *Textbook on Civil Government in the United States,* by George H. Martin appeared, that the reactionary days were passing. Textbooks in civil government devoted largely to the federal constitution had had their inning. Henceforward other aspects of the field were to be emphasized. In seeking the three books that carried most of the burdens of the reform movement between 1875 and 1897, those by Martin, Macy, and Dole probably deserve first rank. Martin inaugurated the reforms by devoting about one-fourth of his book to historical content; by incorporating considerable material on state and local government; by including some material on international and commercial law; by treating state and local government before treating national government; and by placing heavy emphasis on the principles underlying government, and the definition of terms. Martin himself was wont as some of the outstanding features of his work to call attention to (1) the full statement of principles contained therein; (2) the comprehensive plan, embracing the state, county, city, and town organizations as well as that of the United States; and (3) the historical method.

The main body of Martin's book contained 302 pages, distributed among four parts. Topics such as "Definition of Terms," "Sources of Authority in the State," "The Government: Its Functions and Departments," "Forms of Governments," and "Nature and Duties of Citizenship" were treated to the extent of 54 pages in Part I. The second part consisting of 95 pages was devoted to civil government in the states before their independence. Constitutional government in Massachusetts was treated in the third part, consuming 78 pages. The last part, consisting of 75 pages, was concerned with constitutional government in the United States. Notice that this topic was treated last—an important innovation in textbooks in civil government.

It was evident on the appearance of *Our Government: How It Grew, What It Does and How It Does It,* by Jesse B. Macy in 1886 that the old formal type of material from the field of political science was changing to a new functional type. While high-school courses in civil government in 1886 were doomed to be confined largely to a dry-as-dust treatment of the machinery of the federal government for at least two decades longer in the majority of cases, the reforms which Macy's little book initiated were destined to be generally adopted by those interested in dynamic civics teaching.

While Macy discussed the national government and the federal constitution, these topics were not treated at the expense

of other important ones. Other governments and constitutions
were also discussed. School, township, county, state, and territorial governments received due consideration. His volume
as a whole was divided into six parts. The first part was entitled "Historical and Introductory"; the second, "Matters
Chiefly Local"; and the third, "Administration of Justice."
The topics "The Postal Service," "Money," "Banks and Paper
Money," "The Treasury Department," "The Foreign Service,"
"The Interior Department," and "The War and Navy Departments" were treated in Part IV. Law making in early
times and in our own time was discussed in Part V. Constitutions of societies, townships, cities, states, and the nation
were treated in the last part. The new material in Part II
related to such topics as "Education," "Highways," "Care of
the Poor and Other Unfortunate Classes," "Taxation," "Incorporated Town and Cities," and "The Choice of Public
Servants."

The remaining of the three innovating books mentioned
above was a little volume by Charles F. Dole entitled *The
American Citizen.* The contents of this forward-looking book
appear below.

THE CONTENTS OF CHARLES F. DOLE's *The American Citizen,* 1891

PART FIRST.   THE BEGINNINGS OF CITIZENSHIP

CHAPTER

It was a far cry between the contents of this volume by Dole and that of some of the earlier texts of this period, for example, the book by Andrews, the contents of which are given a few pages back. The center of gravity in Dole's volume was "The Citizen" while the center of attention in the volume by Andrews was the federal constitution. The former was functional and dynamic, the latter, analytic, formal, and static. The latter was civil government of the old type, the former was not civil government at all. It might have been named "civics," a word that had been in use but a short time in 1891.[34]

In closing this treatment of the subject-matter of civil government between 1860 and 1897, it seems fair to warn the reader against accepting the ideas of reformers as representing the actual situation. In spite of the forward-looking books by Martin, Macy, Dole, Fiske, and Peterman, the principal con-

[34] Other texts about as forward-looking as Dole's and appearing near the same time were *Civil Government in the United States* by John Fiske and *Elements of Civil Government* by A. L. Peterman.

tent of courses purporting to deal with materials from the field
of political science throughout the years between 1860 and 1897
was the constitution of the United States. The study of the
national government took precedence over that of state and
local. The actual revolution foreshadowed in the foregoing
texts had not arrived even as late as the year 1900. The following quotation from an address before the National Education
Association in 1889 is indicative of the thinking of many
people at this date relative to the subject-matter of civil government.

"To instruct in the rights and the duties of citizenship is one
of the chief aims in the study of civil government. In a
course in civil government in the high school, the constitution
of the United States should have the most prominent place.
Too much time should not be spent in studying about the
constitution, but the text of this document itself should be
studied and learned word for word. Great attention should be
paid to the meaning of words and explanation of the text, and
the constitution of the United States and that of the State
should be frequently compared by the teacher. The work
should be made as real as possible by showing to the pupils
the different kinds of money, bonds, revenue stamps, postage
stamps, naturalization papers, etc. Special days should be set
apart for the discussion of such questions as taxation, repre-
sentation, protection, free trade, right of trial by jury, and
suffrage." [35]

[35] Laura Donnan, "The High School and the Citizen," *National Education
Association Proceedings*, 1889, p. 516.

IV

THE AGE OF CIVIL GOVERNMENT IN THE SCHOOLS, 1897-1915

Prior to 1890, the subject-matter from the field of political science which was taught in the schools was chiefly the constitution of the United States. Here and there a state constitution was added. The term "science of government" was occasionally used to name the course; civil government also appeared here and there, as was the case with civics. After 1895, civil government became the term most generally used to name the content which had broadened somewhat. This broadening as has already been shown began as early as 1875. It never ceased. After 1907, it took a different turn, the turn that completely dominated the period after 1915. On the whole the civil-government period is a transitional one, a transition from the "old civics" to the "new civics."

EVIDENCE OF THE EXISTENCE OF CIVIL GOVERNMENT IN SECONDARY SCHOOLS

Fortunately for this discussion the United States Bureau of Education included for the year 1897-98 civil government in its list of subjects about which information was gathered relative to the number of pupils pursuing. During the years between 1897 and 1914 the expression civil government was used in the blank calling for information relating to the number of pupils pursuing certain subjects. In 1914-15, both civil government and civics were used. So, according to the title used in the reports of the United States Commissioner of Education it seems true to the facts to say that "civil government" was the term used most generally to name the content from the field of political science which was taught both in the elementary and secondary schools between 1897 and 1915. The per cent of pupils in public high schools and private high schools and academies pursuing the subject by states for certain years between 1897 and 1915 is shown in Table IV. In interpreting this table the fact must be kept in mind that not all of the high schools and academies in existence during the years represented are included, probably not over 60 per cent of them in 1900 and about 85 per cent in 1910. Furthermore, there should be kept in mind the additional fact that beginning with 1909–10 the per cents are based on the total number of pupils in schools reporting on subjects pursued and not on the total enrollment in all schools reporting to the Bureau as they are for the years before 1909. As explained in Division Two in connection with the per cents of pupils pursuing history during the 1890's, the per cents for the years prior to 1909 are too low because of the base used in calculating them. With these preliminary remarks out of the way attention may now be directed to an analysis of the data in the table.

Speaking for the country as a whole the per cents for the years included in Table IV vary but slightly, the range being from a fraction less than 16 per cent to a little over 21. Just why the per cent dropped from 21.41 in 1897–98 to 16.11 in 1914–15 is not easy to account for. One explanation is that more schools dropped civil government than added community civics between 1910 and 1915. This fact seems to be substantiated by the data in the last two columns. On the whole the general evenness of the per cents throughout the states and throughout the years is somewhat remarkable. While the number of pupils pursuing civil government was never large in any state, there were always a few in every state and territory

TABLE IV

PER CENT OF PUPILS PURSUING CIVIL GOVERNMENT IN PUBLIC
HIGH SCHOOLS AND PRIVATE HIGH SCHOOLS AND ACADEMIES,
1897–1915*

STATE OR TERRITORY	Per Cent Pursuing in						PER CENT PURSUING CIVIL GOVERNMENT, 1914–1915	PER CENT PURSUING CIVICS, 1914–1915
	1897–1898	1900–1901	1903–1904	1905–1906	1909–1910	1914–1915		
Continental U. S........	21.41	20.60	18.51	16.65	15.99	16.11	8.81	7.20
Alabama...............	17.82	19.28	24.32	21.72	14.52	19.77	11.67	8.10
Arizona...............	29.88	41.45	15.89	12.69	8.14	18.45	7.89	10.67
Arkansas.	21.31	30.43	30.47	29.81	30.20	30.74	24.54	6.21
California.............	17.15	15.50	14.33	12.62	14.02	13.76	7.86	5.91
Colorado..............	16.99	15.64	13.09	10.23	9.44	10.92	4.78	6.14
Connecticut...........	11.10	11.76	10.66	11.34	7.88	13.09	6.76	6.34
Delaware..............	17.85	25.54	15.37	12.22	36.91	22.23	12.10	10.53
District of Columbia....	4.19	3.84	18.81	2.25	2.72	6.91	2.55	4.36
Florida...............	24.31	28.29	39.46	34.99	38.20	24.60	17.61	7.00
Georgia...............	9.15	12.39	17.29	27.35	25.93	19.90	14.29	5.61
Idaho.................	37.55	40.81	26.91	20.84	14.96	9.65	4.80	4.85
Illinois...............	21.39	16.36	13.58	13.51	13.23	13.02	5.95	7.01
Indiana...............	25.98	17.88	15.25	13.38	18.40	20.87	10.70	10.18
Indian Territory.......	16.93	17.94	32.87	35.72	.....	.....	.....	.....
Iowa.................	30.46	27.26	23.22	21.56	24.53	20.37	10.65	9.73
Kansas...............	36.80	33.33	25.49	17.59	9.97	15.24	6.97	8.28
Kentucky.............	26.01	28.67	24.72	22.71	16.67	16.03	11.20	4.84
Louisiana.............	22.68	17.90	21.16	20.67	23.80	17.09	8.00	9.09
Maine................	15.59	15.71	16.15	14.61	10.82	15.70	10.95	4.75
Maryland.............	11.79	24.61	25.64	22.36	16.40	23.07	10.85	13.03
Massachusetts.........	12.84	11.20	9.29	10.13	7.82	13.31	6.79	6.52
Michigan.............	24.90	20.49	18.49	17.27	14.38	13.16	7.73	5.43
Minnesota............	14.52	11.01	12.33	12.46	15.08	12.68	6.00	6.64
Mississippi...........	28.20	41.31	39.15	44.38	35.53	30.71	21.68	8.71
Missouri..............	27.59	24.33	17.30	16.57	12.05	11.21	7.63	3.58
Montana..............	35.10	22.81	12.01	8.83	11.57	11.07	4.02	7.06
Nebraska.............	35.65	33.11	31.62	32.52	38.57	22.49	12.78	10.12
Nevada...............	40.47	48.54	43.52	43.64	9.50	16.76	10.68	6.08
New Hampshire........	12.33	11.42	6.91	9.83	15.94	14.02	8.55	5.47
New Jersey............	15.82	15.64	13.65	9.92	12.37	10.80	4.52	6.28
New Mexico...........	22.77	33.98	28.73	19.22	27.19	26.70	15.53	11.13
New York.............	17.52	16.26	14.28	23.87	10.03	10.98	5.76	5.21
North Carolina........	14.20	26.87	18.65	23.79	20.24	17.98	13.42	4.56
North Dakota.........	33.05	20.74	17.09	17.53	11.04	17.87	9.23	8.65
Ohio.................	24.00	23.19	22.49	20.12	17.90	17.85	9.21	8.51
Oklahoma.............	24.74	38.18	27.93	28.82	26.10	18.38	9.53	8.86

STATE OR TERRITORY	Per Cent Pursuing in						PER CENT PURSUING CIVIL GOVERNMENT, 1914–1915	PER CENT PURSUING CIVICS, 1914–1915
	1897–1898	1900–1901	1903–1904	1905–1906	1909–1910	1914–1915		
Oregon...............	16.99	27.43	21.38	15.01	14.34	17.55	10.20	7.35
Pennsylvania...........	23.56	25.20	26.36	26.11	24.86	23.68	14.84	8.84
Rhode Island...........	12.02	15.28	11.74	12.94	13.28	13.08	4.38	8.73
South Carolina.........	14.35	20.62	22.97	25.30	25.86	29.78	22.40	8.16
South Dakota..........	32.80	35.05	35.15	31.46	16.36	19.37	9.44	9.95
Tennessee..............	16.33	21.16	20.58	18.77	18.53	18.67	10.81	7.87
Texas..................	33.61	34.47	29.41	30.15	23.36	19.18	12.08	7.10
Utah..................	10.65	5.64	7.94	6.70	7.76	9.95	5.91	4.04
Vermont..............	19.25	19.59	16.53	13.78	10.62	12.36	6.94	5.43
Virginia..............	7.81	16.15	15.07	19.93	17.81	19.06	11.32	7.80
Washington...........	20.37	15.46	12.58	9.65	10.02	14.21	3.17	11.04
West Virginia.........	27.78	32.82	21.91	22.41	21.20	18.72	8.04	10.68
Wisconsin.............	23.04	21.22	17.09	13.91	15.23	16.29	8.28	8.02
Wyoming.............	42.12	25.64	23.77	32.11	11.51	16.56	9.29	6.75

* Compiled from data in the reports of the Commissioner of Education for the years indicated.

enrolled in the subject. In some states the number thus enrolled approximately equalled the total number of pupils in the first year of the high school; while in others it scarcely equalled the total number in the fourth year. For the country as a whole the total enrollment in civil government during each year represented in the table was approximately the same as the total enrollment in the third year of the high school. This statement is based on the distribution of pupils in 1910 which was 42.9 per cent in the first year; 27.1 per cent in the second year; 17.8 per cent in the third year; and 12.1 in the fourth. These per cents varied very little during the decade prior to 1916.[36]

There is a little evidence at hand which indicates that the per cents in Table IV are too high, considerably so in some

[36] U. S. Comr. of Educ., *Biennial Survey of Education,* 1920–22, II, 535.

instances and slightly in others. According to the reports of the High School Inspector of Minnesota the per cent of high school pupils pursuing civil government in 1899–1900 was 15.81; in 1904–05 it was 10.47 per cent; in 1909–10, 11.51; and in 1914–15, 9.72[37]—in general a little lower than those in Table IV for approximately the same years. In the case of Missouri the per cent of high school pupils pursuing civil government during the years 1907–15 averaged but 3—an insignificant number when compared to any of those for this state in Table IV. There is a way, however, to explain this difference. In 1905–06, 27.31 per cent of the pupils in the fourth class high schools in Missouri were pursuing civil government and 11.29 per cent of those in the second class high schools. It is not beyond the realm of possibility that the reports from these two classes of schools to the United States Commissioner of Education outnumbered those from the first and third class schools for the years represented in Table IV, especially after 1905.[38]

CIVIL GOVERNMENT IN ELEMENTARY SCHOOLS

Evidence of the existence of civil government in elementary schools during the eighteen-year period following 1897 is by no means overwhelming. That the subject was taught in Grades VII and VIII here and there in the large cities seems reasonably certain. In a study published in 1905 it was revealed that material that could be classified as civil government was taught in Grades VII and VIII of eight of fifty selected cities. This study also revealed that four of these

[37] Annual reports of the Inspector of Minnesota High Schools for the years indicated.
[38] Facts relative to Missouri are from *Fifty-Seventh, Sixty-Second and Sixty-Sixth Reports* of the Public Schools of the State of Missouri, 1906, 1911, and 1915.

cities included similar material in Grades I and II; three, in Grades III, IV, and V; and seven, in Grade VI.[39] Five years later, a study of the subjects included in the offerings in the elementary schools of fifty of the largest cities in the country revealed that eighteen of these cities included civics in the program of studies for Grade VIII and six for Grade VII. In no grade below Grade VII was civics included.[40] A survey in 1910–11 of the offering by grades of 259 schools and school systems revealed that out of 224 reporting on civics but 7 included the subject in Grades I, II, and III; 12, in Grade IV; 16, in Grade V; 24, in Grade VI; 31, in Grade VII; and 91, in Grade VIII—not an especially flattering showing.[41] According to the findings of this study, the interest in civil government as a separate subject of study in the elementary grades was certainly at a low ebb in 1910–11. It should be remarked, however, that at this date there was a good deal of civics taught in connection with history. A canvass of the opinion relative to this type of combination revealed that of the 229 persons reporting on the matter, 130 favored a combined course in civics and history; 61, a separate course; and 31, combination at times and separation at other times. Regardless of whether taught with history or as a separate subject the evidence is lacking to show that there was any great demand in 1910–11 for civics in the elementary schools. It will be recalled that the Committee of Eight of the American Historical Association reporting in 1909 made specific recommendations concerning the teaching of civics in the grades. No effects of these recom-

39 Bruce R. Payne, *Public Elementary School Curricula*, p. 21. New York: Silver, Burdett and Co., 1905.

40 Cleveland Public Schools, *Annual Report of the Superintendent of Schools, 1909–1910*, p. 15. Cleveland, Ohio: Board of Education, 1910.

41 Rolla M. Tryon, *Materials, Methods and Administration of History in the Elementary Schools of the United States*, p. 23. Bloomington, Ind.: Indiana University, 1912.

mendations can be detected in the foregoing data for the scholastic year 1910–11.

THE CONTENT OF CIVIL GOVERNMENT IN SECONDARY SCHOOLS, 1897–1915

For the major content of the courses in secondary-school programs of study circulating between 1897 and 1915 under the titles "civil government," "government," "civics," "advanced civics," and "American government" one must go to the text-books of the period. While there are no data with respect to the exact circulation of any text, one is reasonably sure of discovering what was taught by examining a few typical ones. On the whole these texts were so much alike that a detailed analysis of all of them would not yield results proportionate to the time necessary for such an analysis. Even though not analyzed, a representative list of texts in civil government and kindred subjects published during the period under review seems worth including here. This list follows, chronologically arranged.

1. W. W. Willoughby, *The Rights and Duties of Citizenship*, 1898.

2. Laura Donnan, *Our Government*, 1900.

3. Edward Schwinn and W. Wesley Stephenson, *Civil Government*, 1901.

4. Frank Strong and Joseph Schafer, *The Government of the American People*, 1901.

5. J. A. James and A. H. Sanford, *Government in State and Nation*, 1901.

6. Lyman B. Kellogg and A. R. Taylor, *The Government of the State and Nation*, 1901.

7. J. W. Smith, *Training for Citizenship*, 1902.

8. Salter S. Clark, *The Government*, 1902.

9. Robert Lansing and G. M. Jones, *Government: Its Origin, Growth, and Form in the United States*, 1902.

10. Frank D. Boynton, *School Civics*, 1904.

11. S. E. Forman, *Advanced Civics: The Spirit, the Form, the Function of American Government,* 1906.

12. R. L. Ashley, *The American Federal State,* 1906.

13. Arthur W. Dunn, *The Community and the Citizen,* 1907.

14. Roscoe L. Ashley, *American Government for Use in Secondary Schools,* 1908.

15. Paul S. Reinsch, *Civil Government,* 1909.

16. William A. Miller and W. S. Hornor, *Civil Government, State and Federal,* 1910.

17. Bernard Moses, *The Government of the United States,* 1910.

18. Crittenden Marriott, *How Americans Are Governed in Nation, State, and City,* 1910.

19. Wm. B. Guitteau, *Government and Politics in the United States,* 1911.

20. James W. Garner, *Government in the United States,* 1913.

In the foregoing list there is a group of texts that hewed pretty closely to the line of formal civil government, emphasizing machinery of government rather than function and service. In this group should be placed the texts by James and Sanford, Ashley, Boynton, Moses, Forman, Lansing and Jones, and Strong and Schafer. A few texts in the list broke away from the traditional civil government and included new and forward-looking material. These were the volumes by Clark, Smith, Willoughby, and especially Dunn. The formal nature of the contents of the books in the first of these groups is shown in the Table of Contents of one of them.

CHAPTER HEADINGS IN F. D. BOYNTON's "SCHOOL CIVICS," 1904

    I. Government: Its Origin, Necessity, Objects and Function
   II. Forms of Government
  III. Colonial Government in America: Its Origin and Development in the Constitution
  IV. Attempts at Union (1643–1777)
   V. The Articles of Confederation (1781–1789)
  VI. The Constitution: Its Formation and Adoption
 VII. The Constitution: Its Origin and Nature

As early as 1910 there were at least seven books on the market which made a radical departure from the old order in the realm of civil government in the secondary school. Four of these have been mentioned above, the other three being texts from the period ending in 1897. Reference is here made to volumes by Fiske, Dole, and Peterman, published in the early 1890's. Lack of space precludes a detailed consideration of each of these. For this reason extensive notice is restricted to the most outstanding one in the list, *The Community and the Citizen,* by A. W. Dunn, published in 1907. In this little volume intended primarily for Grades VIII and IX Dunn broke away from the old order almost completely as shown in the following chapter headings.

CHAPTER HEADINGS OF A. W. DUNN'S "THE COMMUNITY AND THE CITIZEN," 1907

It will be observed that the community was the center of
interest in Dunn's volume, the word appearing in its singular

or plural form in sixteen of the twenty-five chapters. It will also be noted that the material on government proper appeared in the last chapters, the approach being from the local to the national government. While this approach was not entirely new when this book was published, no other volume that preceded it made the approach in exactly the same way that it did. When Dunn's book appeared, it was clear to everybody that a revolution in the realm of civics in the schools had been inaugurated. The volume enjoyed a large and enthusiastic following. Its influence on texts in the field published after 1915, especially for Grades VIII and IX, would be difficult to over-estimate.

The revolutionary aspects of Dunn's volume were (1) heavy emphasis on the community in all of its various aspects, (2) emphasis on participation in community life on the part of the pupils, (3) the claim that the pupil is a citizen hence should participate in the life of the community as such, (4) emphasis on the physiology rather than the anatomy of the government of county, state, and nation, and (5) the claim that civics is not something in a textbook to be memorized and recited in a memoriter fashion but something to be lived in one's daily life. The important fact about the revolution that Dunn inaugurated is that it succeeded. Civics in the grades for which it was intended was sure to be different in all schools using it as a text. The formal analysis-of-the-constitution days were over in these schools. For them were substituted days of working with material dealing with the practical affairs of daily living in one's own surroundings.

Evidence is available that by 1913 many people had made up their minds forever to banish the "old civics" from the schools. For example, at its November meeting of this year even an association of history teachers passed the following set of resolutions relating to civics in elementary and secondary schools.

1. The order of teaching should be from the functions to the machinery of government, with special emphasis on function rather than machinery.

2. The work should be based on the pupils' experience and immediate surroundings.

3. There should be a continual connection of civics with current events, and the student should be made to form the habit of keeping up with the news.

4. The keynote of the course should be the obligation of the citizen to serve the community.

5. Means should be found for the actual participation of the students in civic activities. This means more than the usual visits to courts and public buildings. They should do something to help, either as individuals or through civic associations.

6. Civic training should be secured through the organization and discipline of the schools. If the organization is such as to develop in the pupils personal responsibility, initiative, a social conscience, and high ideals of conduct, the best civic lesson has been learned.

7. Civics should be given a place of its own separate from history.

8. This Association should take steps to secure separate examinations for United States History and Civics. Examination questions in civics should call for something besides a knowledge of the machinery of government.[42]

The foregoing resolutions were prompted by two addresses

[42] "Resolutions Adopted by the Association," *The Association of History Teachers of the Middle States and Maryland,* 1913, p. 73.

delivered before the Association. In one of these addresses the speaker remarked as follows with respect to what the "new civics" would be when it arrived:

"To those who, like the prodigal son, came to themselves, the paleolithic age seemed as unreal as the eolithic, and then we passed on to the new age, known as neolithic. We are entering upon this epoch just now. Signs of change are visible all about us. The neolithic civics will be historical, because it will show that government is an evolutionary process, not a static system unchanging as the hills—even the hills are drawn down to the sea. It will be constitutional, because it will expound the great political principles which lie at the basis of American government. *The Federalist* will be read again throughout the length and breadth of the land. It will be 'actual' for it will show how the principles of government were worked out in concrete form in party practice and statutory details. But it will be more. It will treat the government as an instrument of public service and show how the government comes into contact with the lives of men and women at a thousand points. It will stress the economic functions of the government rather than its machinery. It will give more attention to a railway tariff sheet made out under the supervision of the Interstate Commerce Commission than to tally sheets. It will devote more pages to public franchises than to ballot legislation. It will show what is being done in other states and other countries to make the government a more efficient and a nobler servant of democracy. It will give to women that place in civics to which their position in the economic and intellectual life of our age entitles them. It will teach that the character of the government and its work will depend upon what the people want the government and its work to do, rather than upon any changes in the structure of the machinery of government. It will seek above all to interest students in the government and its work, and trust that they will find their way to the polling booths on election day. In short, the rights and duties of citizens, and the functions of government will occupy the first place in the neolithic civics, and political machinery will be reduced to about one-third its former domain." [43]

THE CONTENT OF CIVICS IN THE ELEMENTARY GRADES, 1897–1915

There was published during the years between 1897 and 1915 a number of textbooks containing materials primarily from the field of political science intended for the last four grades in the elementary school. Most of these texts were for the two upper grades. The following is a partial list of those available in 1915: (1) Charles F. Dole, *The Young Citizen*, 1900; (2) Charles D. Hoxie, *How the People Rule, Civics for Boys and Girls*, 1903; (3) Roscoe L. Ashley, *Government and the Citizen*, 1904; (4) Mabel Hill, *Lessons for Junior Citizens*, 1906; (5) Frances G. Jewett, *Town and City*, 1906; (6) Charles D. Willard, *City Government for Young People*, 1906; (7) S. E. Foreman, *Essentials in Civil Government*, 1908; (8) Paul S. Reinsch, *The Young Citizen's Reader*, 1909; (9) Arthur T. Gorton, *Elementary Civics for the Fifth and Sixth Years*, 1912; (10) W. B. Guitteau, *Preparing for Citizenship*, 1913; (11) Charles A. Beard and Mary R. Beard, *American Citizenship*, 1914. Some of these texts might just as well have been placed among the texts for use in the secondary school, as was done in the case of Dunn's little volume. For instance, the texts by Willard, Forman, Ashley, Guitteau, and the

[43] Charles A. Beard, "Training for Citizenship," *The Association of History Teachers of the Middle States and Maryland*, 1913, p. 56.

Beards could have been and were used in the top grade of the grammar school or in the bottom grade of the traditional four-year secondary school. The remainder of the volumes in the list were intended for Grades V to VIII inclusive, one (Gorton's) being especially planned for Grades V and VI. Three of them (Hill, Willard, and Jewett) were devoted entirely to matters pertaining to the town and city. No book on the list emphasized the machinery of government at the expense of functions and services. Annexing Dunn's volume to the list, one may say that by the time 1915 had come there was available for use in the top four elementary grades material in textbook form to meet at least some of the demands of the times for dynamic civics in the schools.

It is one thing to talk about the excellent material available at a certain date in a specific field, but a very different thing to face what was actually going on in the schools. In 1910-11 the actual situation in the elementary schools of the country with respect to the content of courses in civics was somewhat deplorable. The returns from 224 schools and school systems revealed that the general topic, "National Civics and United States Government" was included in the program of studies of 37 schools or school systems; "State Civics and Government" in 25; "Local Civics and Government" in 22; and "Home Civics" in 6. Eleven of these schools or school systems based their work in civics on Dunn's *The Community and the Citizen;* 3, on *The American Citizen,* by Dole; 2, on *Town and City,* by Jewett; 2, on *Junior Citizen,* by Mabel Hill; and 1, on *Essentials of Civil Government,* by Forman.[44]

The demand for material devoted to matters pertaining to the pupils' own state or city resulted in the appearance of three types of texts prior to 1915. These types were (1) texts de-

[44] Tryon, *op. cit,* p. 22.

voted primarily to materials applicable to a particular state, for example, *Civics: Texas and Federal*;[45] (2) texts devoted primarily to the general field with material relating to a specific state included therein, for example, *Government Class Book,* Illinois edition,[46] the material on Illinois being placed after the general index; and (3) texts devoted largely to a specific city with material relating to county and state added, for example, *A Civic Manual for Chicago, Cook County, and Illinois.*[47] On the whole one may say that after 1915 those interested in what came to be called the "new civics" were primarily engaged in putting into practical operation the ideas that germinated during the ten years prior to this date.

V

COMMUNITY, VOCATIONAL, ECONOMIC, AND ADVANCED CIVICS IN THE SCHOOLS, 1915–1933

The revolution in subject-matter, spirit, and method of civics below Grade XII which Dunn inaugurated in 1907 when he published *The Community and the Citizen* came to fruition during the 1920's. The progress of the revolution was evidently accelerated by the publication of two significant reports in 1916. These were entitled *The Social Studies in Secondary Education* and *The Teaching of Government,* the former by a committee of the National Education Association and the latter by a committee of the American Political Science Association. Inasmuch as both of these reports have been consid-

---

[45] By Henry F. Triplett and Ferdinand A. Hauslein. Houston, Texas: Rein & Sons Co., 1912.

[46] By Andrew W. Young and Harry P. Judson. New York: Maynard, Merrill & Co., 1900.

[47] By S. R. Winchell. Chicago: A. Flanagan Co., 1910.

ered in detail in Division One, the only comment necessary here is to the effect that the latter made an appeal for more attention to material somewhat of civic nature in the primary and intermediate grades and the former accelerated the community civics movement which had been slowly gaining momentum since about 1907. Soon after the appearance of these two reports courses of study in civics for each of the eight elementary grades began to appear. The courses for the city of Philadelphia and the state of Iowa are excellent examples of what happened. However, before considering the details of courses such as these, it seems appropriate to survey some of the existing evidence of the prevalence of civics in the schools between 1915 and 1933. Attention is first directed to the traditional four-year high schools and academies.

PREVALENCE OF CIVICS IN TRADITIONAL FOUR-YEAR HIGH SCHOOLS AND ACADEMIES, 1915–1933

The United States Commissioner of Education collected data by states concerning the number and per cent of pupils pursuing civics in public high schools and private high schools and academies for the years 1921–22 and 1927–28. Table V contains the data on civics and community civics for these years. For the scholastic year 1921–22 the forms used in collecting the data included civics only; in 1927–28 they included community civics and civics other than community. It is significant to note that the days of civil government were over by 1920 and that the term "civics" was in general use. The number and per cent of pupils pursuing the subject in 1921–22 were certainly not large. A fraction over 18.59 per cent meant but about 18 pupils in each 100 enrolled in the schools represented in the table. While the number, 444,306, seems large, it is in

TABLE V

NUMBER AND PER CENT OF PUPILS IN PUBLIC HIGH SCHOOLS AND PRIVATE HIGH SCHOOLS AND ACADEMIES PURSUING CIVICS DURING THE SCHOLASTIC YEARS 1921-22 AND 1927-28*

STATE	Civics 1921-22		Community Civics 1927-28		Civics Other than Community 1927-28		All Types of Civics 1927-28	
	NUMBER	%	NUMBER	%	NUMBER	%	NUMBER	%
Continental U. S.	444,306	18.59	412,418	13.11	206,784	6.57	619,202	19.69
Alabama	6,606	21.75	7,860	22.64	2,285	6.58	10,145	29.22
Arizona	979	16.79	929	8.04	1,087	9.41	2,016	17.45
Arkansas	5,460	31.09	4,736	18.39	1,202	4.66	5,938	23.06
California	16,435	14.42	13,248	6.56	17,104	8.47	30,352	15.04
Colorado	3,123	12.04	2,841	8.27	1,453	4.23	4,294	12.50
Connecticut	4,607	12.88	5,833	13.63	1,323	3.09	7,156	16.72
Delaware	786	17.90	451	8.07	199	3.56	650	11.64
District of Columbia	433	3.35	489	2.96	811	4.92	1,300	7.88
Florida	1,576	13.14	5,677	18.08	2,531	8.06	8,208	26.15
Georgia	6,065	19.88	6,060	17.92	1,563	4.62	7,623	22.55
Idaho	1,553	12.86	1,135	5.81	943	4.82	2,078	10.63
Illinois	21,309	13.15	22,968	10.64	15,518	7.10	38,486	17.84
Indiana	11,159	12.89	8,582	8.05	10,396	9.75	18,978	17.81
Iowa	19,879	26.16	10,171	11.60	8,317	9.48	18,488	21.09
Kansas	10,683	15.99	9,474	12.66	10,099	13.49	19,573	26.15
Kentucky	3,138	11.37	4,577	11.64	2,052	5.21	6,629	16.86
Louisiana	1,986	10.26	2,996	9.25	2,612	8.06	5,608	17.32
Maine	3,596	15.24	5,955	25.21	1,449	6.13	7,404	31.35
Maryland	3,444	15.79	5,466	16.81	3,015	9.27	8,481	26.09

TABLE V—Continued

NUMBER AND PER CENT OF PUPILS IN PUBLIC HIGH SCHOOLS AND PRIVATE HIGH SCHOOLS AND ACADEMIES PURSUING CIVICS DURING THE SCHOLASTIC YEARS 1921–22 AND 1927–28*

STATE	Civics 1921–22		Community Civics 1927–28		Civics Other than Community 1927–28		All Types of Civics 1927–28	
	NUMBER	%	NUMBER	%	NUMBER	%	NUMBER	%
Massachusetts	19,769	11.89	17,928	13.55	5,102	3.87	23,030	17.54
Michigan	13,022	14.11	12,209	9.14	6,491	4.86	18,700	14.01
Minnesota	9,219	13.76	7,606	8.57	4,156	4.68	11,762	13.25
Mississippi	2,106	8.69	2,357	20.16	1,252	10.70	3,609	30.86
Missouri	12,640	16.38	15,501	17.16	4,648	5.14	20,149	22.31
Montana	2,239	12.96	1,405	7.41	1,158	6.11	2,563	13.53
Nebraska	6,210	14.98	5,500	11.04	3,747	7.52	9,247	18.56
Nevada	172	10.40	287	14.99	66	3.44	353	18.44
New Hampshire	1,245	11.33	1,287	7.78	2,299	13.91	3,586	21.71
New Jersey	22,684	31.13	22,317	22.19	2,973	2.95	25,290	25.15
New Mexico	612	14.48	523	6.11	671	7.85	1,194	13.97
New York	69,956	30.40	88,089	22.42	5,794	1.98	93,883	23.89
North Carolina	10,526	30.06	15,066	24.94	2,860	4.73	17,926	29.68
North Dakota	3,227	17.92	2,544	14.05	1,555	8.58	4,099	22.64
Ohio	28,876	18.91	17,239	8.99	16,990	8.86	34,229	17.86
Oklahoma	3,837	8.98	2,917	5.69	2,485	4.85	5,402	10.55
Oregon	5,266	18.39	1,640	4.72	5,097	14.67	6,737	19.40
Pennsylvania	51,072	27.55	33,584	14.42	25,091	10.77	58,675	25.19
Rhode Island	1,611	12.93	1,158	7.64	929	6.12	2,087	13.77
South Carolina	2,802	21.06	2,198	13.76	977	6.12	3,175	19.88

TABLE V—Continued

NUMBER AND PER CENT OF PUPILS IN PUBLIC HIGH SCHOOLS AND PRIVATE HIGH SCHOOLS AND ACADEMIES PURSUING CIVICS DURING THE SCHOLASTIC YEARS 1921–22 AND 1927–28*

STATE	Civics 1921–22		Community Civics 1927–28		Civics Other than Community 1927–28		All Types of Civics 1927–28	
	NUMBER	%	NUMBER	%	NUMBER	%	NUMBER	%
South Dakota	7,072	43.95	1,246	5.57	2,611	11.69	3,857	17.27
Tennessee	3,488	13.23	4,766	13.88	2,279	6.64	7,045	20.52
Texas	9,358	12.28	5,109	5.51	6,395	6.90	11,504	12.41
Utah	2,964	19.52	1,881	11.95	1,302	8.27	3,183	20.23
Vermont	1,814	19.20	1,099	14.49	408	5.38	1,507	19.88
Virginia	5,287	14.00	3,122	6.89	4,096	9.05	7,218	15.95
Washington	5,366	10.97	4,720	7.55	4,081	6.42	8,801	14.08
West Virginia	3,418	14.39	6,303	21.98	2,195	7.65	8,498	29.63
Wisconsin	19,063	27.27	14,139	17.05	3,854	4.64	17,985	21.69
Wyoming	910	16.41	927	11.88	564	7.22	1,491	19.11

* Compiled from data in *Biennial Survey of Education* for the years indicated. In 1921–22, 15,598 schools, enrolling 2,335,623 pupils reported on subjects pursued; in 1927–28, 16,941 schools, enrolling 3,144,645 pupils reported on subjects pursued. In 1921–22 a total of 16,019 schools enrolling 2,416,048 pupils reported. These figures for 1927–28 were 20,564 schools and 3,614,722 pupils.

reality small when thought of in relation to 2,335,623, the number in the schools that could have been pursuing civics in 1921–22.

The distribution of the pupils in terms of community and other civics for the year 1927–28 indicates that there were almost twice as many pursuing community civics as there were pursuing civics other than community. This fact is due to the practice of teaching the former in the bottom grade of the high school and the latter in the top grade. It is evident that some states in 1927–28 were more enthusiastic over community civics than others. Observe the high per cents in Alabama, Arkansas, Florida, Georgia, Maine, Mississippi, Missouri, New Jersey, New York, and North Carolina. While there were significant increases in the per cents in some states during the period represented in Table V the increase for the country as a whole was insignificant.

There is some evidence at hand which shows that the per cents for 1927–28 in Table V are too high. Some of this evidence is contained in the reports on the subjects pursued in the high schools of the states comprising the territory of the North Central Association of Colleges and Preparatory Schools. In 1929–30 there were twenty states in this territory. The number of high schools in each of these states which offered during this year community civics and government and the per cent of the total enrollment pursuing these subjects are shown in Table VI. When the per cents herein are compared by states with those in Table V it is observed that those in the latter case are generally somewhat higher. One reason for this fact is that in the report to United States Commissioner of Education there was an opportunity to include all types of civics while in the North Central reports no such opportunity was present. For example, one might with propriety ask, Where

were vocational civics and economic civics included in the
North Central reports? That many types of civics could have
been omitted in these reports is evidenced by the situation in

TABLE VI

COMMUNITY CIVICS AND GOVERNMENT IN 2226 OF THE NORTH
CENTRAL ASSOCIATION HIGH SCHOOLS IN 1929–1930*

STATE	NUMBER OF SCHOOLS	Community Civics		Government	
		NUMBER SCHOOLS OFFERING	PER CENT OF TOTAL ENROLLMENT PURSUING	NUMBER SCHOOLS OFFERING	PER CENT OF TOTAL ENROLLMENT PURSUING
1. Arizona........	35	12	7.0	26·	17.5
2. Arkansas.......	58	34	11.7	16	4.8
3. Colorado.......	92	53	9.0	34	4.2
4. Illinois.	313	111	6.7	166	5.2
5. Indiana........	100	37	7.5	87	8.7
6. Iowa..........	137	37	4.7	99	10.9
7. Kansas.........	147	62	7.3	123	16.2
8. Michigan......	183	84	4.4	71	2.8
9. Minnesota.....	99	14	7.0	33	8.4
10. Missouri.......	120	86	19.0	28	1.8
11. Montana.......	44	19	6.5	20	4.5
12. Nebraska......	114	42	7.9	71	4.0
13. New Mexico...	28	8	5.2	13	4.9
14. North Dakota..	73	51	13.1	4	3.2
15. Ohio..........	295	144	7.4	191	9.3
16. Oklahoma.....	107	47	9.2	30	2.3
17. South Dakota..	67	15	2.3	43	11.5
18. West Virginia..	71	47	18.6	21	3.8
19. Wisconsin......	116	91	16.9	21	2.2
20. Wyoming......	27	15	11.8	5	8.4

* Charles C. Brown, "Proceedings of the Commission on Secondary Schools," *North
Central Association Quarterly*, V (1930), 99, 111, 112.

California in 1927–28. Although not in the North Central
territory, the situation in this state with respect to differentiation in courses in civics was by no means exceptional. For
example, there were, out of a total of 274 high schools reporting in 1927–28, 188 which offered courses in civics. There

were also 44 which offered courses named citizenship; 41, community and vocational civics; 27, occupational and economic civics; 16, American government and social problems;

TABLE VII

CIVICS IN THE ELEMENTARY SCHOOLS OF OHIO 1915-19*

SCHOOL YEAR	Number and Per Cent of Pupils Pursuing						Total	
	Cities		Villages		Rural			
	NUM-BER	PER CENT	NUM-BER	PER CENT	NUM-BER	PER CENT	NUM-BER	PER CENT
1914–15.........	29,788	7.90	5,295	4.04	7,313	2.30	42,396	5.13
1915–16.........	43,816	11.10	6,666	5.36	9,098	2.92	59,580	7.08
1916–17......,..	48,246	11.54	7,482	5.23	9,144	3.00	64,872	7.49
1917–18.........	50,053	11.76	7,886	5.54	8,666	2.89	66,605	7.68
1918–19.........	50,034	11.55	9,622	6.38	10,512	3.53	70,168	7.97

* Based on data from the annual reports of the Superintendent of Public Instruction of Ohio for the years indicated.

8, social civics; 4, constitution; 3, civil government; and 2, development of modern democracy.[48] A situation of this character would certainly make accurate reports improbable, especially when restricted to the two categories that were included in the blanks used in assembling the data for the North Central Association reports.

EVIDENCE OF THE EXISTENCE OF CIVICS IN ELEMENTARY SCHOOLS, 1915–1933

For a few years after 1914 the Superintendent of Public Instruction in Ohio collected data concerning the number of pupils in the elementary schools pursuing civics. These data are presented in Table VII. They may or may not represent

[48] Junior Jennings Collins, "Development of the Social Sciences in the Secondary Schools of California," pp. 104–106. Unpublished Master's thesis, Leland Stanford Junior University, 1927.

the situation in the country at large. If they do, the number of elementary-grade pupils pursuing civics during the latter half of the 1910's was certainly not large, ranging from about five to almost eight in each one hundred pupils.

The study of forty-four state courses of study for rural elementary schools, from which data were used in Division Two, included civics as well as history. Very little emphasis was placed on civics as a separate subject in these courses. Among the 44 courses analyzed, 14 contained general suggestions relating to civics; 3 provided an outline for Grade I; 4, for Grade II; 5, for Grade III; 6, for Grade IV; 9, for Grade V; 10, for Grade VI; 20, for Grade VII; and 27, for Grade VIII.[49] There were among the 44 courses some which deliberately tried to provide for civics in connection with history, especially in the two upper grades. Because of this fact, one must not conclude from the meager showing in the foregoing tabulation that civics was more or less neglected in the elementary grades as a whole. Desirable or undesirable as the case may be, it must be said that in the rural elementary schools of the country in about 1920, the attention given to civics as a separate subject was almost negligible. However, in city school systems at about this date civics seems to have been fairly well cared for. In a study, the results of which were made generally available early in 1924, facts relative to the grade placement of civics in the elementary grades of 273 city school systems were revealed. Some of these facts are found in Table VIII. It seems very clear from the data herein that civics was largely an eighth-grade subject in 1924 and that the increase in the per cent of cities teaching the subject was

[49] Charles M. Reinoehl, *Analytic Survey of State Courses of Study for Rural Elementary Schools*, p. 33. Department of the Interior, Bureau of Education Bulletin, 1922, No. 42. Washington, D. C.: Government Printing Office, 1923.

somewhat gradual from grade to grade. There is no way to determine from the data whether the subject was coming into or going out of the grades below the eighth at this date.

Time-allotment studies are more valuable than grade-place-

TABLE VIII

NUMBER AND PER CENT OF 273 CITIES TEACHING CIVICS IN THE VARIOUS ELEMENTARY GRADES, 1923–24*

GRADES	Cities Teaching Civics in	
	NUMBER	PER CENT
I–B.........................	53	19.41
I–A.........................	54	19.78
II–B........................	58	21.24
II–A........................	59	21.61
III–B.......................	64	23.44
III–A.......................	66	23.80
IV–B........................	76	27.83
IV–A........................	78	28.57
V–B.........................	96	35.16
V–A.........................	105	38.46
VI–B........................	125	45.78
VI–A........................	125	45.78
VII–B.......................	144	52.74
VII–A.......................	143	52.38
VIII–B......................	192	70.32
VIII–A......................	219	80.21

*J. R. McGaughy, "Distribution of Grades in Which Elementary Subjects Are Taught in 375 Cities," *Second Yearbook*, Department of Superintendence, 1924, p. 152.

ment studies for determining the actual attention given to a subject at any particular date. During the 1920's at least two time allotment studies which included civics were made. One of these studies used data from 49 cities and the other from 444. It was found that 9 of 49 cities over 100,000 in population in about 1922–23 allotted an average of 49 minutes a week to civics in Grade I; 10, an average of 55 minutes in Grade II; 10, an average of 54 minutes in Grade III; 11, an average of 51, in

Grade IV; 12, an average of 54, in Grade V; 13, an average of 55, in Grade VI; 14, an average of 70, in Grade VII; and 12, an average of 81, in Grade VIII.[50] It will be observed that the number of 49 cities allotting time to civics in any grade, even the eighth was not large, only about one-fourth of the entire number. Speaking of the cities as a whole, it seems that civics as an independent subject of study got but scant attention in them. Nor did the subject receive any more liberal treatment in the 444 cities studied, the average number of minutes a week allotted to civics and citizenship being 11, in Grade I; 12, in Grade II; 14, in Grade III; 16, in Grade IV; 19, in Grade V; and 21, in Grade VI.[51] Commenting on the general situation revealed by his study Mann said:

"Only 1 per cent of the total time in grades 1-6 is given to citizenship and civics; this is the average for 444 cities. Of this group only 233 cities report time allotted specifically for this purpose. In addition, the authorities in 49 cities report that citizenship and civics are included in history; 5, in social science; 3, in 'other subjects'; and in 4 cities it is 'taught incidentally.' One hundred fifty cities of the entire group apparently do not include citizenship and civics as a part of the curriculum of grades 1-6.

"Among those that allot time to citizenship and civics, the range of total time is very wide. The maximum total time in grades 1-6 is more than 100 times as great as the minimum. The median time allotment for the 233 cities is 154 minutes per week in all grades, and the range of the middle 50 per cent

[50] Fred C. Ayer, *Studies in Administrative Research*, p. 15. Department of Research, Seattle Public Schools, Bulletin No. 1. Seattle, Washington: Public Schools, 1924.

[51] C. H. Mann, *How Schools Use Their Time*, p. 23. Teachers College, Columbia University Publication, No. 333. New York: Bureau of Publications, Teachers College, 1928.

is from 83 to 245 minutes. Within the middle 50 per cent of the group some schools allot three times as many hours for instruction in citizenship and civics as do others. A greater percentage of small than of large communities report time allotments. In fact the percentage of cities which allot time to this subject decreases regularly as the size of city increases, from 63.5 per cent in the 2,500 to 5,000 population group, to 35 per cent in the largest group which includes cities with a population of 100,000 or over. However, among those cities which do allot time, with the exception of the 10,000 to 30,000 group, the larger the city, the larger the amount of time given to citizenship and civics. The median amount of time for the smallest group is 129 minutes per week in grades 1–6, as compared with 240 minutes for cities of the largest group.

"It is significant that citizenship and civics has been carried down into the curriculum of the kindergarten by 28 out of 115 cities reporting kindergarten allotments. The amount of time given to this subject by the kindergartens varies from 10 to 50 minutes per week." [52]

CIVICS IN JUNIOR HIGH SCHOOLS, 1915–33

Civics has enjoyed considerable prestige in the junior high schools of the country, especially since 1920. It will be recalled that the program in civics suggested for the junior high school by the Committee on the Social Studies in Secondary Education of the National Education Association was a very generous one, provision being made for the subject in each of the three years—one-half of the time devoted to the social sciences in the eighth grade being allotted to the subject and all of the time in the ninth. These recommendations were subsequently

[52] Mann, *op. cit.*, pp. 99 and 104.

wholeheartedly accepted by many junior high school program-makers.

There is an abundance of evidence to justify the statement that both community civics and vocational civics were generally required in junior high schools during the 1920's. Throughout these years some type of civics was fairly well entrenched in Grade IX. After the appearance of the so-called unified courses in the social sciences civics along with history lost its identity as a separate subject. By 1930 a number of junior high schools throughout the country had adopted the principle of unification. Few, however, at this date had satisfactorily applied it.[53]

After 1915 the word "civics" lost the definiteness in meaning that it had previously enjoyed. Originally civics was used as a name for material from ethics, civil polity, governmental machinery, and the history of political institutions. During the 1920's the word "civics" did not mean the same to any two people who used it. To some it meant a discussion of the sociological aspects of the divorce problem; to others a consideration of economic organization and control. In fact it meant anything that anybody wanted it to mean. For this reason, the content taught after 1915 has to be considered in terms of specific courses such as community civics and American government, the former being taught in the bottom grade of the four-year high school, the top grades of the eight-year elementary school, and the top two grades of the junior high school and the latter in the top grades of the four-year and three-year high school. Along with community civics, vocational or economic civics went hand in hand. Advanced civics and social civics were terms occasionally used instead of American government.

[53] Bessie P. Erb and Howard E. Wilson, "A Survey of Social Studies Courses in 301 Junior High Schools," *School Review*, XXXIX (1931), 504.

COMMUNITY CIVICS

The exact date of the appearance of the expression "community civics" in the educational literature of this country has never been determined. As early as 1910 an article appeared with the following title: "Why Teach Community Civics?" The following is an excerpt from this article:

"Why teach community civics? In the language of the day, to train for social efficiency; for the same reason that we have introduced manual training, domestic science, vacation schools, continuation schools, playgrounds, into our city school system; to adapt the individual to an urban environment; to give him an understanding of the dangers and opportunities of urban life; to show him that the welfare of the individual and of the community depends on what he and his fellows do for the general good; in order to preserve the very life of the city, physically, intellectually, morally." [54]

Arthur W. Dunn, the author of *The Community and the Citizen,* probably should be given sole credit for originating the community-civics movement, even though he may not have first used the expression. To him certainly belongs wholesale credit for the able guidance the movement had in its infancy. He worked year in and year out to make people understand what community civics meant. In 1915, he wrote an article in which he attempted to elucidate the meaning of a much abused expression, even at this early date. The following excerpt contains the substance of this article:

"The aim of community civics is to help the child to 'know

[54] Frank P. Goodwin, "Why Teach Community Civics?" *Ohio Educational Monthly,* LIX (1910), 415.

his community'—not merely a lot of facts about his community, but the meaning of his community life, what it does for him and how it does it, what the community has a right to expect from him and how he may fulfill his obligations, meanwhile cultivating in him the essential qualities and habits of good citizenship.

"Community civics by no means minimizes the importance of government. It describes and emphasizes government at every step as the chief means by which the citizens of a community co-operate. It seeks to give a perspective to government that the older 'civil government' did not give. It approaches the mechanism of government through its relations to the immediate interests of the citizen.

"Community civics does not mean local civics merely. There is some confusion about this. Some seem to fear that community civics will displace an adequate consideration of the national and state governments. Sometimes there is talk about community civics in one grade and national civics in another. This is a misapprehension of the significance of the term.

"It is true that community civics lays emphasis upon the local community because (1) it is the community with which every citizen, especially the child, comes into most intimate relations, and which is always in the foreground of experience; (2) it is easier for the child (as for any citizen) to realize his membership in the local community, to feel a sense of personal responsibility for it, to enter into actual co-operation with it, than is the case with the national community.

"But our nation and our state are communities, as well as our city or village, and the child is a citizen of the larger as of the smaller community. The significance of the term 'community civics' does not lie in its geographical implications, but in its implication of community co-operation through government, and so on. It is possible even to study one's own town without having the point of view or the spirit of community civics. It is a question of point of view and this attitude to the study of the national community as well as to the study of the local community." [55]

In spite of Dunn's extreme care in explaining the meaning of community civics the term continued to be a much-abused one. In making a plea for community civics one writer made reference to this fact when he wrote as follows:

"The work in every year of the course should be presented in terms of community service. A few words of explanation relative to the meaning of the much abused term 'community civics' may not be out of place. Community civics teaching, especially in the more advanced grades which focus the attention on purely local problems, is pernicious. Community civics in a broad sense stresses civic and social relations in an ever-widening circle through home, town, county, state and nation, applying to the problems of each larger community group the principles involved in the smaller community group. The latter conception is vital if pupils are to develop a national consciousness.

"The recent national crisis has demonstrated our individualistic tendencies, our lack of common ideals of government. Community civics must teach that we are a nation of community groups united for common purposes, not that we are a nation separated into community groups, with attention centered upon local affairs.

"The subject-matter must be comprehensive and simplified

[55] "Communuity Civics—What It Means," *History Teacher's Magazine*, **VI** (1915), 52.

to come within the understanding of the pupil. It must also make a definite and conscious appeal to the pupil's interest." [56]

Prior to about 1925 the content of the courses in community civics in the upper elementary grades and bottom high school grades was largely that which appeared in 1915 in a bulletin of the United States Department of Education.[57] As outlined in this bulletin community civics meant "a study of the ways in which people do, and should, co-operate in order to secure the various elements of common welfare, such as community health, protection of life and property, etc." Soon after this bulletin appeared, the expression "the welfare topics" came into general use as a brief description of the content of community civics. The so-called welfare topics listed in the bulletin were health, protection of life and property, recreation, education, civic beauty, wealth, communication, transportation, migration, charities, correction, and government.

It would be difficult to exaggerate the influence of the pamphlet in which the foregoing welfare topics appeared. Courses of study throughout the country were patterned after the set-up found in this pamphlet. Textbooks were written to conform to its recommendations. The list of these texts is too long to include here. However, to make no extended mention in a discussion of the content of community civics of textbooks in the field would certainly be omitting the main part of the story. Fortunately some of these texts have been analyzed. The results of one of these analyses appear in Table IX. Granting that the fourteen textbooks represented in this table

[56] *Twenty-Fourth Annual Report for the School Year Ending July 31, 1917, Inspector of State High Schools, State of Minnesota*, p. 17. Minneapolis, Minn.: Syndicate Printing Co., 1917.

[57] J. Lynn Barnard and others, *The Teaching of Community Civics.* United States Department of Education, Bulletin, 1915, No. 23. Washington, D. C.: Government Printing Office, 1915.

—five of which having the word "community" in their titles —was representative of the general content of the civics that was taught during the 1920's in the top grades of the elementary school and in certain grades of the junior high school,

TABLE IX

AVERAGE PERCENTAGE OF SPACE IN FOURTEEN INTRODUCTORY TEXTBOOKS IN CIVICS GIVEN TO CERTAIN TOPICS*

TOPICS TREATED	NUMBER OF TEXTS ALLOTING SPACE TO	AVERAGE PERCENTAGE OF SPACE GIVEN TO IN BOOKS TREATING
1. Community activities............	9	16.7
2. Citizenship....................	8	8.9
3. State government...............	13	37.3
4. National government............	14	27.7
5. International relations..........	7	3.8
6. American ideals................	8	9.0
7. Industrial society..............	9	8.32
8. Political parties................	12	2.9
9. Social problems................	10	9.0

* Eleanor McFarling, "Trends in the Teaching of the Introductory Courses of Civics in the Public Schools," p. 9. Unpublished Master's thesis, University of Southern California, 1926.

it is necessary to examine the content of these texts more in detail in order to determine the specific nature of the subject-matter of elementary civics. In the composite outline of the fourteen texts which appears below are shown the topics treated under each of the large divisions included in Table IX.

COMPOSITE OUTLINE OF FOURTEEN TEXTS IN ELEMENTARY

CIVICS

I. *Community Activities.*—Health; police; fire; streets; transportation; parks; libraries; beauty centers.

II. *Citizenship.*—Rights of; duties of; meaning of.

III. *Functions of State Government.*—Elections; taxation; education; state constitution; executive department; judicial department; legislative department; local government; relation of state to national government; subdivision of state government—county, township, municipal or city.

IV. *National Government.*—Structure; constitution; executive department; legislative department; judicial department; finance department; territories and dependencies.

V. *U. S. International Relations.*—International law; commerce; war and peace.

VI. *American Ideals.*—Honesty; reverence; thrift; industry; freedom; justice; patriotism; vocational guidance.

VII. *Industrial Society.*—Work; worker; labor; wages; capital; unions; communication and transportation.

VIII. *Political Parties.*—History of; organization; government.

IX. *Social Problems.*—Crime; poverty; charity; liquor; immigration; conservation.[58]

According to the composite outline above, the content of civics in the junior high school in about 1925 was concerned with varied aspects of social living. It is evident from the outline that the political, economic, social, and governmental aspects of group life were definitely provided for. The emphasis on community activities, citizenship, and American ideals reflected the spirit of Dunn's *The Community and the Citizen,* published in 1907.

AMERICAN GOVERNMENT OR ADVANCED CIVICS

Since 1915 the course based on certain materials from the field of political science and usually offered in the top grade of the traditional four-year high school has been chiefly known

[58] Eleanor McFarling, *op. cit.,* pp. 5a, 5b, and 5c.

as American government or advanced civics. After the rise
and spread of community civics, it became necessary to differentiate the material intended for the senior high school from
that used in the junior high school. The differentiation that
was attempted was frequently one in name only. This means
that in an effort to differentiate it from community, vocational,
and economic civics the senior high school course was christened advanced civics or American government (rarely political science for some unknown reason).

Prior to 1915 the chief faults found with the courses in
civics taught in the top grades of the high school were that
they dealt too largely with the lifeless machinery of federal,
state, county, and municipal government and that they were
unrelated to the activities and problems of every-day life. Finding fault with what was contained in these courses was in
most cases finding fault with the textbook in use; for courses
in civics in the top grades of the traditional high schools of
this country have always been very largely textbook courses.
It follows from this fact that, if one desires to know the content of courses in advanced civics at any particular date such
may be found in the textbook in use at that date. In 1915,
the most widely used textbooks in the field were: (1) James
and Sanford, *Government in State and Nation;* (2) Garner,
Government in the United States; (3) Ashley, *American
Government;* (4) Forman, *Advanced Civics;* (5) Beard,
American Citizenship; (6) Moses, *The Government of the
United States;* (7) Boynton, *School Civics;* (8) Hinsdale,
The American Government; and (9) Guitteau, *Government
and Politics in the United States.*[59]

Between 1915 and 1924 a new appraisal of the content of

[59] *The Teaching of Government,* p. 51. New York: The Macmillan Co.,
1916.

senior high-school civics was made. New textbooks appeared along with completely revised editions of old ones. The allotment of lines in five of these texts was as following: average number of lines devoted to form of government, 5886; to function of government, 4359; to theory and principles of government, 1487; to historical data, 1126; to constitutions, 1762; to responsibilities and rights, 331; to such topics as public finance, money and banking, commerce, labor, and conservation, 1628; to topics such as education, home, charities, prevention of crime, health, races, immigration, conditions of labor, liquor, and recreation, 1128; and to political parties and party organization, 962.[60]

It will be observed from these data that five texts analyzed devoted most of their space to the form, function, theory, and principles of government. The topics in the list having an economic or a sociological flavor represent the new material that was trying to find its way into the course. Judging from the total of the average number of lines devoted to this material it seems clear that textbooks in senior high school civics had not gone far in the early 1920's toward introducing social and economic content into the course. Be this as it may, "Old Civics" had at least been reduced to the status of "King" by this date. Prior to 1915 it was "Emperor."

In 1922 the Committee of the American Political Science Association published the outline of its proposed course in civics for the senior high school.[61] The extent to which this outline was in agreement with certain textbooks is shown in Table X, which contains the results of an analysis of four textbooks in advanced civics published before the report of the

[60] From a number of tables in "A Comparison of the Content of Civics Texts with Aims of Education," by J. L. Cobb. Unpublished Master's thesis, University of Illinois, 1925.

[61] *American Political Science Review*, XVI (1922), 119–124.

TABLE X

THE NUMBER AND PER CENT OF PAGES IN FIVE REPRESENTATIVE
TEXTBOOKS IN ADVANCED CIVICS DEVOTED TO THE TOPICS IN
CIVICS PROPOSED BY THE COMMITTEE OF THE AMERICAN
POLITICAL SCIENCE ASSOCIATION IN 1922*

TOPICS PROPOSED BY THE COMMITTEE	Number and Per Cent of Pages Devoted to in							
	Text No. V		Text No. VI		Text No. VIII		Text No. IX	
	PAGES	PER CENT	PAGES	PER CENT	PAGES	PER CENT	PAGES	PER CENT
1. Human Society........	21	6.58	..	....	..	....	..	....
2. United States.........	9	2.82	11	2.50	15	3.71	8	2.72
3. Peoples, Races, and Racial Problems.......	8	2.50	9	2.04	..	....	..	....
4. American Home and Community.........	27	8.46	..	....	..	....	..	....
5. Economic Factors and Organization	4	1.25	11	2.50	11	2.72	..	....
6. Nature and Forms of Government........	..	....	15	3.40	12	2.96	19	6.46
7. Citizen, Rights and Duties..............	25	7.83	..	....	..	....	7	2.38
8. Popular Control of Government........	..	....	12	2.72	1	.24	..	....
9. Suffrage and Elections .	15	4.70	10	2.27	16	3.96	23	7.82
10. Party Organization and Machinery..........	16	5.01	24	5.46	8	1.98	11	3.74
11. Counties and Rural Communities	5	1.56	18	4.09	20	4.95	22	7.48
12. City Government	7	2.19	22	5.00	30	7.42	11	3.74
13. Municipal Problems...	10	3.13	11	2.50	..	....	6	2.04
14. State Government.....	13	4.07	10	2.27	27	6.68	19	6.46
15. Legislature	4	1.25	25	5.68	10	2.47	11	3.74
16. Governor.............	2	.62	8	1.81	8	1.98	8	2.72
17. Courts and Law (Local and State).......	1	.31	15	3.40	12	2.96	8	2.72
18. National Constitution.	15	4.70	34	7.73	35	8.66	19	6.46
19. Congress.............	10	3.13	23	5.22	40	9.90	24	8.16
20. President and Cabinet..	10	3.13	39	8.86	37	9.14	53	18.02
21. Courts and Law (National).............	8	2.50	6	1.36	11	2.72	10	3.40
22. National Resources, Conservation and Public Domain......	8	2.50	9	2.04	..	....	..	....
23. Agricultural Interests..	4	1.25	..	....	..	....	..	....

TOPICS PROPOSED BY THE COMMITTEE	Number and Per Cent of Pages Devoted to in							
	Text No. V		Text No. VI		Text No. VIII		Text No. IX	
	PAGES	PER CENT	PAGES	PER CENT	PAGES	PER CENT	PAGES	PER CENT
24. Encouragement and Regulation of Commerce............	15	4.70	6	1.36	16	3.96	5	1.70
25. Industry and Labor....	17	5.32	11	2.50	..	....	..	....
26. Currency, Banking and Credit..............	8	2.50	16	3.63	17	4.20	..	....
27. Public Utilities........	7	2.19	11	2.50	..	....	..	....
28. Public Finance.........	16	5.01	28	6.36	30	7.42	14	4.76
29. Public Health.........	5	1.56	9	2.04	..	....	2	.68
30. Poor Relief, Correction and other Welfare Problems...........	10	3.13	26	5.90	15	3.71	2	.68
31. Education............	7	2.19	10	2.27	13	3.21	12	4.08
32. National Defense......	8	2.50	9	2.04	10	2.47	..	....
33. Foreign Relations.....	4	1.25	3	.68	10	2.47	..	....
Total pages of subject matter....................	319	....	440	....	404	....	294	....

* Arnold W. Brown, *The Improvement of Civics Instruction in Junior and Senior High Schools*, pp. 61, 62, 63, 64, 65. Ypsilanti, Mich.: Standard Printing Co., 1929. Texts Nos. I, II, III, IV and VII in Brown's table are omitted here.

committee was well known. The content of each book was analyzed in terms of the outline proposed by the committee. The thirty-three topics in the table are intended to include all but three of the main ones in the Committee's outline. Book No. V, published in 1917, contained some material on thirty-one of these topics; book No. VI devoted some space to twenty-nine of them; book No. VIII, to twenty-three; and book No. IX, to twenty-one. According to these data the Committee was not much in advance of at least two books in the market when its report appeared. As early as 1922 a text[62] appeared which was intended actually to embody the outline

[62] W. B. Munro and C. E. Ozanne, *Social Civics*. New York: The Macmillan Co., 1922.

more or less completely. This text in a way set the standard for subsequent ones.

VOCATIONAL, OCCUPATIONAL, AND ECONOMIC CIVICS

In its report in 1916 the Committee of the National Education Association on the Social Studies in Secondary Education listed a course to be given in the ninth year, as follows: "Civics: Economic and Vocational Aspects." Later in its report the expression "vocational civics" was used. Before 1916, the expressions "vocational guidance," "vocational enlightenment" and "a survey of vocations" were in general use. While the foregoing committee did not feel that the expression "vocational civics" was adequate for what it had in mind, namely, the civic relations of vocational life, it seems to have adopted it for lack of a more satisfactory term.

Those who taught vocational guidance prior to 1920 became teachers of vocational civics soon after this date. In fact one of the first, if not the first, textbooks using the expression "vocational civics" in its title was simply a systematization and elaboration of notes that had formerly been collected for a course in vocational guidance.[63] This fact explains the failure of the book to live up to the standard proposed by the committee mentioned above. One searches in vain for the civic relations of vocational life in it. On the whole this bad start was very unfortunate for vocational civics; for it caused the course when taught to drop to the level of a forensic treatment of occupations in terms of classification, qualification, preparation, opportunities, advantages, and disadvantages. In other words, the course became little more than a treatment of occupations, pure and simple. This was far from what the com-

[63] Frederick N. Giles and Imogene K. Giles, *Vocational Civics*, p. vii. New York: The Macmillan Co., 1919.

mittee proposing the course had in mind as will be observed from the statement below.

"The chief purpose of the phase of the ninth-year work now being emphasized should be the development of an appreciation of the social significance of all work; of the social value and interdependence of all occupations; of the social responsibility of the worker, not only for the character of his work but for the use of its fruits; of the opportunities and necessity for good citizenship in vocational life; of the duty of the community to the worker; of the necessity for social control, governmental and otherwise, of the economic activities of the community: and of the part that government actually plays in regulating the economic life of the community and of the individual. In other words, the work here proposed is an application of community civics to a phase of individual and community life that is now coming into the foreground of the pupil's interest." [64]

After 1920 textbooks in economic and vocational civics which attempted to embody the spirit of the committee mentioned above began to appear. The nature of the content included in two of these texts[65] is portrayed in their chapter headings which are listed in parallel columns below.

CHAPTER HEADINGS IN TWO TEXTBOOKS IN ECONOMIC
AND VOCATIONAL CIVICS

ECONOMIC CIVICS	VOCATIONAL CIVICS
I. The Things We Need	I. Earning a Living
II. The Things We Want	II. Saving and Thriving

[64] *The Social Studies in Secondary Education*, p. 27. Department of the Interior, Bureau of Education, Bulletin, 1916, No. 28.

[65] R. O. Hughes, *Economic Civics*. Boston: Allyn and Bacon, 1921; Howard C. Hill, *Vocational Civics*. Boston: Ginn and Co., 1928.

ECONOMIC CIVICS	VOCATIONAL CIVICS
III. What Government Does for Us	III. Buying and Selling
IV. Our Duty to Our Government	IV. Sending Messages and Distributing News
V. The Machinery of Government	V. Transferring Goods
VI. Foundations of Our Nation's Life	VI. Problems in Working Together
VII. Producing Things	VII. Choosing One's Work
VIII. Modern Business	VIII. Gaining a Living from the Earth
IX. The Producers	IX. Manufacturing and Building
X. Carrying Goods	X. Shipping and Transporting
XI. Conveniences of Trade	XI. The Store, the Bank, and the Office
XII. Making Living Conditions Better	XII. Working for the State
XIII. Making Industry Better	XIII. Serving the Public
XIV. Making Government and Society Better	XIV. Succeeding in One's Work

While the foregoing books were not the only ones used in courses in economic and vocational civics during the 1920's, their contents represent fairly accurately what was taught in these courses throughout the country in 1933.

In the late 1920's two books appeared which attempted to fuse all of the prevailing notions of community, vocational, and economic civics. The sub-titles of these books were *A Textbook in Social and Vocational Citizenship*,[66] and *A General Social Science*.[67] Should these texts and others like them become the rule independent courses in community, vocational, and economic civics will pass out of the picture.

[66] T. R. Williamson, *Civics at Work*. Boston: D. C. Heath and Co., 1928.
[67] G. N. Carver and Gladys M. Adams, *Our Economic Life*. Philadelphia: The John Winston Co., 1929.

THE CONTENT OF CIVICS IN THE ELEMENTARY GRADES

After 1915 it became more and more common to plan courses in civics for each of the eight elementary grades or for groups of grades such as the primary, the intermediate, and the grammar. One of the first large cities to evolve and publish an eight-year course in civics was Philadelphia. In July, 1916, and in January, 1917, the Board of Public Education of this city authorized a course[68] in civics for Grades I–VI inclusive and a course for Grades VII and VIII. In the first of these courses the work of the primary grades was centered on the so-called civic virtues, such as obedience, cleanliness, orderliness, courtesy, helpfulness, kindness to animals, punctuality, truthfulness, care of property, fair play, safety, thoroughness, honesty, and respect. In the last half of Grade III, provision was made for a study of people who look after the needs of a community along the lines of food, clothing, shelter, fuel, and medical care—the baker, the tailor, the carpenter, the coal man, and the physician. It should be noted in passing that material of this type was definitely recommended for the primary grades by the Committee of the American Political Science Association in its volume entitled *The Teaching of Government,* published in 1916.

The content of the Philadelphia course for the intermediate grades consisted primarily of material relating to the policeman, the fireman, the street cleaner, the garbage collector, the ash collector, the rubbish collector, water, gas, electricity, telephone, the neighborhood, the city beautiful, safety first, industries of Philadelphia, occupations, and ethics of

[68] *The Course of Study in Civics, Grades One to Six for Public Schools of Philadelphia,* and *The Course of Study in Civics, Grades Seven and Eight for the Public Schools of Philadelphia.*

business. Content similar to this also appeared in the report mentioned in the paragraph above and in the report of the Committee of Eight of the American Historical Association, entitled *The Study of History in the Elementary Schools* and published in 1909.

Philadelphia's course for Grade VII and VIII was based on the welfare topics suggested by the Committee on the Social Studies in Secondary Education and elaborated in *The Teaching of Community Civics,* a pamphlet sponsored by this committee. Inasmuch as the welfare topics have been listed elsewhere,[69] they need not be repeated here.

The influence of the foregoing courses in civics for the elementary grades was significant. For example, a *Course in American Citizenship in the Grades* for use in the schools of Iowa and published in 1921 centered the content of the primary grades on the civic virtues and that of the intermediate and grammar grades primarily on the welfare topics. So it may be said that the early 1920's found some content from the field of civics in all of the grades of the elementary school. Furthermore, there is evidence at hand relative to the actual topics found in thirty-five state courses of study for rural schools for the year 1919–20. The tabulation below supplies this evidence.

TOPICS IN ELEMENTARY SCHOOL CIVICS ARRANGED IN THE ORDER
OF THEIR FREQUENCY OF APPEARANCE IN THIRTY-FIVE STATE
COURSES OF STUDY FOR RURAL SCHOOLS

I. *Appearing in 80 Per cent or More of the Courses.*—State government; rights and duties; government; national government; county government; national constitution; school district government.

[69] See p. 313.

II. *Appearing in 60 to 80 Per Cent of the Courses.*—Home and family government; officers, public office; village, town government; elections, nominations; comparison of governments; legislative department; courts, trial by jury; executive department; laws, lawmaking; judicial department; city government; township, town government; education, schools.

III. *Appearing in 40 to 60 Per Cent of the Courses.*—Departments of government; taxation; political parties; powers of government; public health; money, coinage system; army, navy; senators, representatives; protection, life and property; constitutional amendments; revenues, expenditures; community civics; how a bill becomes a law; patriotism; roads and bridges; post office, postal system.

IV. *Some Suggestive Topics Appear in Fewer than 40 Per Cent of the Courses.*—Banks, banking; care of poor; character lessons; churches; citizenship clubs; work of Congress; current events; fire protection; food inspection; initiative; referendum, recall; naturalization; parcel post; parks, playground; police systems; property rights; public improvements; public institutions; public property.[70]

It is to be noted that the topics appearing in fewer than 40 per cent of the courses indicate a tendency to give less attention to civil government as such and more attention to civics which concerns home and community life. On the whole, however, the civics in the majority of the courses was largely of the old type.

During the 1920's civics largely lost its identity in the primary grades in all places operating on the unified-program plan. Even when a completely unified scheme was not in operation the differentiation in the aspects of the subject-matter in the field of the social sciences disappeared. Thus there was no longer in some schools any content labeled civics in the primary grades. However, in the school systems where no attempt was made to unify the curriculum, civics remained

[70] Charles M. Reinoehl, *op. cit.*, p. 84.

TABULAR VIEW OF THE PENNSYLVANIA COURSE OF STUDY IN CIVICS FOR THE FIRST SIX ELEMENTARY GRADES*

GRADES I AND II	GRADE III	GRADE IV	GRADE V	GRADE VI
The family. Team work between school and home. Protection and care the home gives. Protection and care the school gives.	Home and school in contact with activities in the neighborhood. Service, dependence, Interdependence. Adult embodiment of civic virtues. (Success in life is due to good habits formed early in life.) Servants who furnish us food, clothing, fuel, shelter, medical aid.	The servants of the neighborhood: Policeman. Fireman. Postman. Engineer. Conductor. Motorman. Brakeman. Switchman. Road mender. Watchman. Lamplighter Wireman. Scoutmaster. Game warden. Constable. Justice of Peace. Forester.	Our neighborhood: 1. Growth of the town. 2. Service rendered by the following: a. School. b. Library. c. State house. d. Court house. e. Post office. f. Hospitals. Churches. Community centers. 3. Roads, streets. 4. Parks, playgrounds, the public square. 5. Water supply. 6. Lighting: a. Gas. b. Electricity. 7. Police protection. 8. Fire protection. 9. The telephone. 10. Means of communication with nearby localities.	Industrial co-operation. Fair play in business and community life.
	The school: Working and playing together. Obedience.			

* Manual for Elementary Schools for the State of Pennsylvania, p. 110. Harrisburg: State Department of Education, 1922.

TABULAR VIEW OF THE PENNSYLVANIA COURSE OF STUDY IN CIVICS FOR THE FIRST SIX ELEMENTARY GRADES*

GRADES I AND II	GRADE III	GRADE IV	GRADE V	GRADE VI
Courtesy. Helpfulness. Cleanliness. Orderliness. Kindness to animals. Continue work of first grade. Add: Fair play. Promptness. Truthfulness. Care of property. Safety First.	Continue work of first two grades. Add: Thoroughness. Honesty. Respect.	Continue work of first three grades. Add: Courage. Self-control. Thrift. Perseverance.	Continue work of first four grades. Add: Helpful initiative. Self-reliance.	Continue work of first five grades. Add: Broadmindedness. Sense of civic responsibility.

* Manual for Elementary Schools for the State of Pennsylvania, p. 110. Harrisburg: State Department of Education, 1922.

as an independent subject in the program of studies during all of the 1920's. A representative example of its content in the six elementary grades during the 1920's is found in the *Manual for Elementary Schools for the State of Pennsylvania*—a tabular view of which appears on pages 326 f.

Content similar to that in the foregoing tabulation found its way into the elementary grades of more and more schools after 1922. In fact a quiet revolution in this realm of the curriculum had been going on since about 1909. The aspects of this revolution were well summarized in 1929 by one thoroughly conversant with the situation. His summary follows:

"In none of the social studies have the changes of the last twenty years been so marked as in the field of civics. A generation ago this subject, when it was given recognition in the elementary school curriculum, was limited to a simplified study of government. Usually this study was restricted to the upper grades and took the form of verbatim memorization of the Constitution of the United States.

"In comparison with this narrow interpretation of the subject, the connotation of the term 'civics' has, in more recent years, broadened out of all recognition. Today civics includes the whole body of material which relates to preparation for citizenship. And citizenship is interpreted by the schools to cover not only the various relations that obtain between the individual and his government, but to embrace as well all those activities which bring him into relation with his fellow-men. More than that, citizenship is not an attribute peculiar to adults. The child also is a citizen, and has rights, duties, and privileges in relation to the community of which he is a member, whether that community be regarded as his home, his school, or any other social group in which he lives.

"This broadening of the conception of civics has been reflected in the elementary school curriculum. In the last two decades city after city, State after State, has incorporated into its school program definite provision for citizenship training. Civic virtues, such as obedience, respect for authority, reliability, and the like find a place in many courses of study, and definite suggestions are given the teacher as to how they may be inculcated. In general, preachment is avoided; instead, advantage is taken of the many opportunities offered by school situations and of the reference found in the stories and poems of the grade to build up proper attitudes and wholesome habits. On this foundation a graded program is constructed stressing the fundamental ideas of service and interdependence. Consideration of service leads to a review of vocations and occupations, including a study of thrift, and these in turn to a simplified survey of governmental agencies, first local, then State, then national. Such in brief is the outline of a typical elementary course in civics, the topics being carefully graded and distributed over the six years of the elementary school.

"In the modern school civics is taught as a 'doing' subject, rather than as a body of information to be learned. From the very beginning, the classroom situation offers abundant opportunity for the building up of wholesome relationships and the creation of a dynamic appreciation of the individual's obligations to the group to which he belongs. Throughout the grades this concept is developed and elaborated, socialized classroom activities, school play, and pupil government all making significant contributions. The modern school is consciously directing its efforts toward the building up of that group of civic habits and attitudes which has come to be

known as 'school citizenship.' It is not too much to say that
nowhere in the schools of America has a more valuable piece
of constructive work been attempted." [71]

71 Armand J. Gerson, "The Social Studies in the Grades—1909–1929,
Historical Outlook, XX (1929), 272.

DIVISION FOUR

ECONOMICS, SOCIOLOGY, AND SOCIAL SCIENCE
AS SCHOOL SUBJECTS

DIVISION FOUR

ECONOMICS, SOCIOLOGY, AND SOCIAL SCIENCE AS SCHOOL SUBJECTS

I. ECONOMICS AS A SUBJECT OF STUDY IN THE SCHOOLS.—Values
   Claimed for Political Economy and for Economics; the
   Long Struggle of Political Economy for a Place in Academy
   and High-School Programs of Study; the Content of Po-
   litical Economy in Secondary Schools; the Establishment of
   Economics as an Independent Subject of Study in the
   Schools and the Nature of Its Content, 1900–1920; the
   Maturing of Economics as a Subject of Study in Acade-
   mies and High Schools and the Nature of Its Content,
   1920–1933.

II. SOCIOLOGY AS A SUBJECT OF STUDY IN ACADEMIES AND HIGH
   SCHOOLS.—Values Claimed for Sociology as a Subject of
   Study; the Career of Sociology in the Schools; the Con-
   tent of Sociology on the Secondary-School Level.

III. SOCIAL SCIENCE AS A SUBJECT OF STUDY IN ELEMENTARY AND
   HIGH SCHOOLS.—Uses of the Expressions "Social Science,"
   "Social Sciences," and "Social Studies"; the Movement to
   Establish Social Science as a Special Discipline; the movement for the Establishment of Social Science as a Subject
   of Study in Elementary and Junior High Schools; the Unification of the Social Sciences Other than History.

The two social sciences which have always received the bulk
of attention in both elementary and high schools are history
and civics. These subjects have had in this country an independent existence in the schools for over one hundred years.
Economics excepted, this statement cannot be made relative to the careers of the other social sciences. Even though
economics was early recognized as a school study under the
name political economy, the subject never received widespread

333

recognition until after 1916. So it is within the bounds of truth to say that the history of the social sciences other than history and civics as subjects of study in elementary and high schools begins about 1916. Because of the brevity of their life lines, it seems advisable to treat all of them in a single division of this volume. They are so considered below, in the order of their general acceptance in the schools.

ECONOMICS AS A SUBJECT OF STUDY IN THE SCHOOLS

Economics, formerly political economy, as an independent subject of study in academies and high schools has a history that extends in this country over a period of time almost equal in length to that of the academy and the high school. In one sense it is by no means a new subject in these schools and in another sense it has always been a new subject. These statements are explained by the fact that the subject gained ground so slowly as a school study it remained until somewhat recently in the stage of infancy in so far as the extent of its existence in the school is concerned. It may be that one of the reasons for the slow establishment of the subject in the school is to be found in the fact that the values claimed for it were not sufficiently impelling to attract the attention of school authorities. What some of these claimed values have been is revealed below, first for political economy and then for economics.

VALUES CLAIMED FOR POLITICAL ECONOMY AND FOR ECONOMICS AS SCHOOL SUBJECTS

Prior to 1900 the values claimed for political economy as an independent subject of study in the schools were more or less in harmony with the pedagogical thinking of the time. This means that those who had values to state expressed them in terms of the categories of educational values in common use. For example, throughout the nineteenth century heavy emphasis was placed on the disciplinary value of subject-matter. So when the protagonists of political economy enumerated their claims for it as a school subject chief among these claims was the disciplinary value. They insisted and probably rightly so, according to the manner of teaching the subject in common use prior to 1900, that political economy possessed disciplinary value for pupils in academies and high schools which could scarcely be equaled by any other subject. In placing so much emphasis on this value, these well-meaning individuals made the same mistake that was made by the protagonists of history. They fastened a method of teaching political economy upon the school which was extremely detrimental to the subject. It may be that the disciplinary value and the formal method of teaching which it dictated had something to do in causing the subject to be nicknamed the "dismal science." It seems that by emphasizing the disciplinary value of their subject at the expense of other values the protagonists of political economy as a school subject prior to 1900 were attempting to fit the value of political economy to the times rather than to the subject or to those pursuing it.

Another thoroughly respectable value of political economy in schools put forward by those interested in the subject was the cultural. In suggesting this value these individuals were as much in harmony with the pedagogical thinking of the time as they were in proposing the disciplinary value. Inasmuch as the general implications of this value have been considered in some detail in the discussion of the values claimed for history, no further attention needs to be given it here, except to say that those interested in political economy were able to make a strong case for the cultural contributions of the subject to the lives of those who pursue it.

The citizenship value of political economy was by no means neglected by those who wished to see the subject take its place among subjects such as history and civics, which relied so heavily on their training-in-citizenship qualities. The champions of the cause of political economy argued that it was equally as important for the cause of effective citizenship for practitioners of the art to be well informed on the multifarious and complex economic topics upon which a citizen must pass as a voter as it was for him to be informed relative to the past of his country and the laws governing it. It seems reasonable to believe that had those who were interested in securing for political economy a prominent place in the sun of high-school subjects emphasized the citizenship value of the subject much more than they did, it would not have remained in the entrance stage as long as it did.

It was also in harmony with the pedagogical thinking of the nineteenth century in this country for those interested in political economy in the schools to claim that the subject inherently possessed outstanding ethical values. In some of the texts in political economy in use before 1860 the ethical value was strongly emphasized. In two of these early texts were expressions such as, "This science protests against *distilling* and *brewing* on the same principles as it protests against *gambling* and *war*" and "A nation to become prosperous and great must be a virtuous nation."[1] These texts were *Elements of Political Economy,* by S. P. Newman, published in 1835; and *Political Economy: Its Objects, Uses, and Principles*

[1] Quoted by E. J. Dougherty "An Historical Consideration of Economics in the Secondary School, 1821 to 1824," p. 15. Unpublished Master's thesis, University of Chicago, 1924.

Considered with Reference to the Conditions of the American People, by A. Potter, published in 1841. In both of these books the moral tone was prominent, especially in Potter's volume in which ethics and political economy were inseparable.

After about 1900 the term political economy was generally displaced by economics. For this reason it is proper to speak of the values claimed for economics from 1900 on. The change in the subject's name carried with it a change in the values claimed for it. For example, those interested in economics as an independent subject of study in the secondary school stated values more specifically than they had been stated prior to 1900. Those who stated these specific values made an effort to set up worthwhile values that could be achieved only or at least primarily through a study of economics. Out of these efforts came the claim that a systematic pursuance of the subject of economics would be useful in giving the pupils: (1) an understanding of the processes by which one gets a living; (2) the ability to form intelligent judgments on economic issues; (3) a vivid awareness of economic problems and of the rôle played in economic thinking by prejudice and special interests; (4) a clear conception of the meaning of economy; (5) an understanding of fundamental economic generalizations or laws; (6) an understanding of the weak and the strong aspects of our present-day economic order and an unselfish desire to assist in creating an economic order in which the weak aspects will be reduced to the minimum; (7) the habit of refusing to accept unsound principles of business; (8) the power to resist high pressure salesmen either in a personal interview or over the radio; (9) a correct understanding of money, capital, and distribution and the ability to detect and the willingness to combat the many dangerous fallacies connected with them; and (10) economic intelligence—meaning the ability to do productive thinking on economic matters.

One fails to meet in this list the old standby values such as cultural, ethical, citizenship, and disciplinary which were so universally proclaimed for political economy prior to 1900. Of course, no teacher of economics in the high school, although well equipped for the job, has ever been able to attain a 100 per cent realization of all the values in the foregoing list, and no mathematics, modern language, and natural science teacher who has in the past taught classes in economics in high schools because he happened to have a little time to spare has probably ever achieved even a few of them.

THE LONG STRUGGLE OF POLITICAL ECONOMY FOR A PLACE IN ACADEMY AND HIGH-SCHOOL PROGRAMS OF STUDY

Political economy as an independent subject of study in academies and high schools made little headway during the first seventy-five years of its existence. The small advance it made during these years was primarily in the realm of content. After 1875 textbooks began to appear written with the secondary-school pupil in mind—those previous to this date being double-purpose ones, that is, intended for both college and secondary pupils. In the matter of the number of schools offering the subject and the number of pupils pursuing it, the increase was painfully slow as will be subsequently shown, along with the advance in the character of the content.

Writing in 1885 J. Lawrence Laughlin at the beginning of his distinguished career as an economist, a career which has but recently ended, said, "Although Adam Smith wrote his *Wealth of Nations* in 1776, it is a mortifying fact that political economy was practically an unknown science to the American people before 1860." [2] One searching for evidence of the existence of political economy in schools during the forties and fifties can well appreciate the truth of this statement. While scattered bits of evidence are picked up here and there, no substantial amount seems available. If it were permissible to base a generalization on the absence of data, one would be justified in saying that the number of pupils in academies and high schools who were exposed to political economy during the first half of the nineteenth century must have been pitiably small. Be this as it may, Professor Laughlin's sweeping statement quoted above probably deserves to stand.

Some evidence is at hand with respect to the number of academies and high schools in Massachusetts and New York offering courses in political economy prior to 1860. According to Inglis, political economy first appeared in the curriculum of Massachusetts high schools in 1842 and by 1860 it was offered in sixteen high schools of this state.[3] The law of 1857 requiring the teaching of the subject in the high schools of towns of 4000 inhabitants accounts for its presence in these sixteen schools.

Political economy seems to have invaded the academies of New York about 1832, this being the date that the subject first appeared in the Regents' report. During the late 1840's political economy was offered in most of the academies and high schools of this state, there being 163 out of 166 reporting which offered the subject, whereas but 7 out of 153 academies were offering it in 1845. In 1835 but 2 of the 66 academies reporting offered it. The pace set during the late 1840's was maintained throughout the 1850's, there being 163 of the 164

2 *The Study of Political Economy*, p. 20. New York: D. Appleton & Co., 1885.
3 *Rise of the High School in Massachusetts*, pp. 82 f. New York: Teachers College, Columbia University, 1911.

reporting in 1855 offering political economy and 187 of the 192 reporting in 1860.[4] According to these data the subject must have been generally recognized in the academies and high schools of New York after 1845. No data are available relative to the number of pupils in these institutions who were actually exposed to the subject of political economy.

Passing to the forty-year period after 1860 one finds evidence that political economy during these years slowly gained admission to a limited number of secondary schools throughout the United States. As more and more high schools were established, the field for political economy became larger and larger. Furthermore, the subject became firmly established in colleges and universities during these years, there being 66 out of 83 of these institutions in 1888 offering, in the course leading to the A.B. degree, political economy and three economics. Furthermore, between 1885 and 1895 economics became a profession in the United States to which more and more individuals devoted their talents and their time. In 1885 the American Economic Association was organized and *The Journal of Political Economy* was launched in 1892, the American Academy of Political and Social Science having been founded two years previously. With all of these happenings in the field of political economy on the college level, it is reasonable to believe that their influence was felt in a small way at least in the secondary school. In fact there is evidence that at least one high-school principal had caught the spirit of the time as early as 1880. Note his plea for political economy in the high·school in the following excerpt:

"We believe that political economy should occupy a promi-

[4] C. F. Wheelock, *Secondary Education,* pp. 122, 177, 186. Albany: University of the State of New York, 1922.

nent place in the curriculum of our high schools and academies; first, because from these institutions four-fifths of those
who receive higher education go out, and, secondly, because
the principles which it teaches are such as every self-govern-
ing people must understand.

"In these high schools the masses not only get their culture
and store of knowledge, but their ideas, their inspirations,
their habits of reading often, and methods of thought. The
common schools give the rudiments merely, and these too
often in but an indifferent way, and the college and the university are beyond the reach of many.

"From the high schools then must multitudes go out into
life, with or without correct ideas of the relations of capital
and labor, of wealth and its true sources, of extravagance and
its results, in a word, of all these fundamental principles which
underlie the structure of society, and regulate the conduct of
men in the most common affairs of life." [5]

For the country as a whole there is little available evidence
relative to the extent to which political economy found its way
into academies and high schools during the forty years following 1860. On one large group of states meager data
are at hand. These relate to a few schools in the North
Central States between 1860 and 1900. Between 1860 and
1865 four of twenty schools in this region included political
economy in their programs of studies. Between 1866 and
1870 this number increased to six in twenty schools. Between
1871 and 1875 it was five in twenty schools; 1876–80, three in
twenty schools; 1881–85, eight in twenty-five schools; 1886–90,

[5] Levi D. Miller, "Political Economy in High Schools," *Ninety-Third Annual Report*, Regents of the University of the State of New York, p. 547.
Albany: Weed, Parsons and Co., 1880.

eleven in thirty schools; 1891–95, eleven in forty schools; and 1896–1900, sixteen in forty schools.[6]

There is evidence that political economy was fairly well

TABLE I

NUMBER AND PER CENT OF TOTAL HIGH-SCHOOL ENROLLMENT PURSUING POLITICAL ECONOMY IN THE STATE OF OHIO, 1882-1900.*

YEAR	TOTAL HIGH-SCHOOL ENROLLMENT	Number and per cent pursuing	
		NUMBER	PER CENT
1882	27,920	338	1.21
1883	27,471	215	.78
1884	29,697	442	1.49
1885	30,372	667	2.19
1886	30,419	725	2.38
1887	30,706	277	.90
1888	31,430	769	2.44
1889	31,709	515	1.62
1890	33,572	799	2.37
1891	24,731	694	2.80
1892	35,182	885	2.51
1893	36,784	698	1.89
1894	40,577	1534	3.78
1895	44,008	1122	2.54
1896	44,610	1152	2.58
1897	52,751	1219	2.31
1898	55,452	1656	2.98
1899	57,031	1346	2.36
1900	56,932	1744	3.06

* Based on the reports of the State Commissioner of Common Schools and Superintendent of Public Instruction for the years indicated.

represented in the program of studies in the high schools and academies of New York between 1865 and 1900, there being 185 of 202 schools reporting in 1865 that offered the subject. In 1870, 171 of the 182 reporting offered it. In 1875, 196 of

[6] John E. Stout, *Development of High School Curricula in the North Central States from 1860 to 1918*, pp. 62–68. Chicago: University of Chicago Press, 1921.

216; in 1879, 205 of 237; in 1890, 109 of 335; and in 1900, 211 of 705.[7]

Space is available for the presentation in some detail of the situation with respect to political economy during a part of the

TABLE II

NUMBER AND PER CENT OF TOTAL HIGH-SCHOOL ENROLLMENT PURSUING POLITICAL ECONOMY IN THE STATE OF MINNESOTA, 1894-95 TO 1900-01.*

YEAR	TOTAL HIGH-SCHOOL ENROLLMENT	Number and per cent pursuing	
		NUMBER	PER CENT
1894-95	9,402	182	1.93
1895-96	10,143	255	2.51
1896-97	11,218	300	2.67
1897-98	11,377	344	3.02
1898-99	11,742	252	2.14
1899-00	12,802	299	2.33
1900-01	14,170	304	2.14

* Based on the annual reports of the Inspector of State High Schools, State of Minnesota, for the years indicated.

period under review in but two more states, namely, Ohio and Minnesota. Table I contains the data from 1882 to 1900 inclusive for the state of Ohio and Table II exhibits similar facts for Minnesota for the years 1894-95 to 1900-01 inclusive. It will be observed that the per cents in these two tables do not vary to any great extent, except for two years in Ohio. Some increase in the per cent of pupils pursuing the subject occurred in Ohio, but there was no general increase in Minnesota. At no time during the period was the number of pupils pursuing political economy large, on the average less than three in one hundred.

[7] C. F. Wheelock, *op. cit.*, p. 175. In 1900 the subject was reported under the caption Economics.

If the subject of political economy existed in the academies and high schools of this country to any great extent in 1900 the evidence seems lacking to prove that it did. In fact there is a bit of evidence available which at least indicates that it was taught in only a few of the large cities. For the year 1900–01 the United States Commissioner of Education reported that in 146 public high schools in the fifty largest cities there were but 897 pupils enrolled in economics. This was but .82 per cent of the total enrollment in these schools. However, it should be said in this connection that there were during this same year 104,101 pupils in public high schools outside of the fifty largest cities pursuing economics. This number was 24.06 per cent of the total enrollment in these schools.[8]

It must have been evident to those interested in political economy as an independent subject of study in high schools and academies in 1900 that the subject would have to overcome some of the handicaps under which it was trying to operate before it could command of school people the attention which it inherently deserved. One of these handicaps was the name "political economy" under which the subject was circulating. This name harked back to a traditional subject-matter which was national in character. The center of gravity was national economy. Those who taught this subject-matter had in mind the making of good housekeepers of the nation. While this was a worthy ambition, there was also grave need in 1900 of good housekeepers in trade, in industry, and in personal affairs. So the demand for a new deal in political economy arose. This demand resulted in the substitution of "economics" for "political economy" and the introduction of a content much less national in character. The chief credit for the change in name probably belongs to Alfred Marshall, the famous English

[8] U. S. Comr. of Educ., *Rep. for 1900–01*, II, 1907.

economist, whose *Principles of Economics* appeared in 1890.

Some of the other handicaps under which political economy was operating in 1900 were (1) an already overcrowded curriculum; (2) lack of prepared teachers; (3) the claim on the part of some that the subject-matter was too abstract and too difficult to be easily grasped by high-school pupils; (4) the dogmatic content and the philosophical approach found in many current textbooks; (5) the refusal of many colleges to allow entrance credit for political economy; and (6) the claim that the content of the subject could best be treated in connection with history, commercial law, and civil government. To overcome some and if possible all of these handicaps, and to secure for economics a significant place in the high schools and academies of the land was the ambition of those interested in the subject at the beginning of the present century. Before presenting the evidence revealing the extent to which this ambition was realized during the first two decades of the century, a brief exposition of the content of political economy prior to 1900 will be presented.

THE CONTENT OF POLITICAL ECONOMY IN SECONDARY SCHOOLS

The content of the political economy that was taught in high schools and academies during the first sixty years of its existence as an independent subject of study in these schools was the *verbatim* content of the current textbooks. Indeed, had there been no textbooks in the subject it is beyond one's imagination to conceive how the subject could ever have found its way into the secondary school. Thus a discussion of the content of political economy in high schools and academies prior to 1900—and after this date too for that matter—must be in terms of the available texts in use from time to time.

Prior to 1875 textbooks in political economy as has been noted above were of the double-purpose type, that is, they were intended for use in both the secondary and the college levels. The demand for texts in the field was so small at first that neither authors nor publishers could afford to write or publish books for the college alone and even less could they afford to place a book on the market solely for the secondary school. After 1875, however, textbooks in political economy, written especially for pupils in high schools and academies, began to appear. The discussion below considers these two types of books separately, first the double-purpose type and then the type especially intended for the secondary level.

A brief list of the textbooks available for classes in academies primarily, for there were comparatively few high schools in the country prior to 1865, were (1) S. P. Newman, *Elements of Political Economy*, 1835; (2) E. P. Smith, *Manual of Political Economy*, 1853; (3) A. Potter, *Political Economy: Its Objects, Uses, and Principles*, 1841; (4) Francis Bowen, *Principles of Political Economy*, 1856; (5) J. B. Say, *Treatise on Political Economy*, 1821 (translated edition); (6) Francis Wayland, *Political Economy*, 1853; and (7) Andrew Young, *National Economy*, 1864.

The general content of three of these texts will serve to illustrate the nature of the materials of political economy prior to 1865. Newman's *Elements of Political Economy* was divided into two parts, one treating production and circulation of wealth and the other distribution and consumption of wealth. In his heavy emphasis on wealth, Newman was following Adam Smith whose *Wealth of Nations* had long been in circulation. Under the heading "Production and Circulation of Wealth," Newman devoted a chapter each to definition of terms, economic arrangements for production, human in-

dustry, natural aids for production, productive capital, circulation of wealth, price, agriculture, manufacture, commerce, the
restrictive system, and different classes of productive labor.
Under the topic "Distribution and Consumption of Wealth"
there were chapters on distribution of wealth, wages, interest
or profit of capital, rent or profits of natural agency, profits of
the undertaker, fees and salaries, consumption of wealth, and
national expenditure.

The 1841 edition of the text by Potter contained but eleven
chapters, one each devoted to definition of the science, definition of wealth and labor, conditions of the production of
wealth, wages, land, capital, value, distribution of wealth,
production, interest, and conditions of labor. Smith's small
volume, which appeared in 1853, contained chapters on laws
of endless circulation of matter, gratuitous co-operation of
the natural agents with human value, formation of soil,
rent, wages, profits, exchange, money and prices, and government.

It will be observed that much emphasis was placed in these
books on production and distribution and of these the former
got the lion's share of space, Potter devoting about three-
fourths of his text to it. Besides this heavy emphasis on two of
the traditional divisions of the subject, textbooks in political
economy prior to 1865 had the following general characteristics: 1. Their contents were taken almost wholly from the
works on political economy written in England. 2. The
principles of political economy were given much attention. 3.
The discussions of current economic issues were partisan in
character, the authors definitely settling all controversial questions. 4. The ethical aspects of the principles of political
economy were not overlooked.

The close following of the theories set forth in English

political economy is illustrated in the text by Newman above
and the emphasis on ethical material in the volume by Potter.
The breaking away from both of these tendencies is well
portrayed in the text by E. P. Smith, *Manual of Political
Economy,* published in 1853. Small reliance was placed in
this book on material from English political economists, the
author relying almost wholly on the works of H. C. Carey,
the leading American political economist of the time. Inasmuch as Smith attempted to consider political economy as a
pure science, he had little use for ethical values in his scheme.

The partisan aspects of these early texts in political economy
remain for consideration. Their authors certainly did not
hesitate to include vital issues of a controversial nature and to
express their personal opinions regarding them. They knew
how all questions relating to the tariff, slavery, trade-unions,
communism, radicalism, and socialism ought to be settled and
stated their solutions dogmatically. They defended men of
wealth and the system of private property against all attacks.
There is no evidence to prove that the notions expressed in these
books ever got wide circulation. Fortunately few pupils in
high schools and academies were ever exposed to them. Their
theoretical character, their abstract material and the didactic
methods used in presenting it, their involved sentence structure, their technical vocabulary and vague meaning made them
books to be avoided rather than used by young people. They
were more a detriment than an aid to the emerging subject of
political economy and to effective training therein. However,
one must not forget that these authors were pioneering and
their efforts ought to be judged by the standards of their day
and not by those of our time.

Between 1865 and 1900 the writers of textbooks in political
economy were by no means idle. Of course, some of the books

produced prior to this period were carried over into it, yet
enough new ones appeared to change the character of the
content considerably. It was during this period that the "systematic" and finished texts in political economy appeared.
They were systematic in the sense that they treated the chief
divisions of the subject, namely, production, distribution, consumption, and exchange in a very logical and systematic fashion. Note the contents of one of the leading texts for use in
secondary schools during the 1880's.

Part I.   Production.
   Chapter   I.   Labor.
   Chapter   II.   Capital.
   Chapter III.   Co-operation of Capital and Labor.
Part II.   Consumption.
   Chapter   I.   Involuntary Consumption.
   Chapter   II.   Voluntary Consumption.
   Chapter III.   Public Consumption.
Part III.   Distribution.
   Chapter   I.   Remuneration of Labor.
   Chapter   II.   Remuneration of Capital.
   Chapter III.   Distribution of Profits.
   Chapter IV.   Revenue of the Government.
Part IV.   Exchange.
   Chapter   I.   Nature, Necessity and Agents of Exchange.
   Chapter   II.   Money an Instrument of Exchange.
   Chapter III.   Credit an Instrument of Exchange.
   Chapter IV.   Banks and Paper Money.
   Chapter   V.   International Trade.[9]

Some of the other texts in use during the period were:

[9] Aaron L. Chapin, *First Principles of Political Economy Concisely Presented.*
New York: Sheldon & Co., 1879.

350   SOCIAL SCIENCES AS SCHOOL SUBJECTS

1. J. T. Champlin, *Lessons in Political Economy*. New York: American Book Co., 1868.

2. Millicent G. Fawcett, *Political Economy for Beginners*. London: Macmillan & Co., 1870.

3. A. B. Mason and J. J. Lalor, *The Primer of Political Economy in Sixteen Definitions and Forty Propositions*. Chicago: A. C. McClurg Co., 1875.

4. A. L. Perry, *An Introduction to Political Economy*. New York: Scribner, Armstrong Co., 1877.

5. M. R. Leverson, *Common Sense, or First Steps to Political Economy*. Denver, Colo.: Chain and Handy, 1876.

6. Joseph Alden, *First Principles of Political Economy*. New York: Davis, Bardeens & Co., 1879.

7. Aaron L. Chapin, *First Principles of Political Economy Concisely Presented*. New York: Sheldon & Co., 1879.

8. J. M. Gregory, *A New Political Economy*. New York: Van Antwerpt Broog Co., 1882.

9. Simon Newcomb, *Principles of Political Economy*. New York: Harper, 1885.

10. E. B. Andrews, *Institutes of Economics*. Boston: Silver, Burdett & Co., 1889.

11. J. L. Laughlin, *The Elements of Political Economy*. New York: American Book Co., 1887.

12. R. T. Ely, *An Introduction to Political Economy*. New York: Hunt and Eaton, 1889.

13. F. A. Walker, *First Lessons in Political Economy*. New York: Henry Holt, 1889.

14. S. M. Macvane, *The Working Principles of Political Economy*. New York: E. Maynard & Co., 1890.

15. G. Steele, *Rudimentary Economics for Schools and Colleges*. Boston: Leach, Sewell and Sanborn, 1890.

16. C. J. Bullock, *Introduction to the Study of Economics.* Boston: Silver, Burdett & Co., 1897.

While each of the texts in this list was not organized as systematically as the volume by Chapin cited above, their authors seemed to have looked upon political economy as a subject compressed in a neatly rounded-out set of "general propositions, universally accepted, which could be set forth in a textbook and learned like the multiplication table," with the emphasis on "learned like the multiplication table." Furthermore, some of these authors looked upon their work with a certain degree of finality. In his Preface Perry said: "I have endeavored in this book so to lay the foundations of Political Economy in their whole circuit, that they will never need to be disturbed afterwards by persons resorting to it for their early instruction, however long and however far these persons may pursue their studies in this science. It seems to me no advantage for any young person to gain a conception of a science that will have to be discarded afterwards for a better one." [10]

The fact has already been mentioned that after 1875 textbooks in political economy written primarily for use in high schools and academies began to appear. The volume by Chapin, the contents of which are exhibited above, was one of the first purely secondary texts to be written. Others followed, so by the end of the century there was available a number similarly written, for example, the volumes by Macvane, Laughlin, Walker, and Bullock in the foregoing list. The appearance of texts in political economy especially adapted to pupils in secondary schools was the one big happening in

[10] *Introduction to Political Economy,* Preface, p. v.

the field of political economy as a school subject during the later half of the nineteenth century.

Before passing to a summary of the character of the subject-matter of high-school political economy during the generation prior to 1900, particular mention ought to be made of one book in the foregoing list. This is the volume by Mason and Lalor. These authors had in mind a volume suitable for use in elementary schools. In the Preface they said, "This little book is simply a primer. We have written it in the hope that it may be used as a textbook in the common schools of the country." The sub-title of the little volume indicates the nature of its contents, *Sixteen Definitions and Forty Propositions*. Some of the propositions in the volume read "Production and Consumption benefit labor;" "It is a bad policy to strike;" "A tariff should be for revenue alone." This last proposition suggests that the book might have been used as a Democratic handbook in the campaign of 1876. Inasmuch as the last edition seems to have appeared in 1914, some use must have been made of the volume over a considerable period of years. It is known to have been used in a few of the academies in New York during the first five years after its appearance. The fact that pupils pursuing elementary-grade subjects attended some of these academies probably explains its use in them.

Certain generalizations may now be made with respect to the subject-matter of political economy during the forty years following 1860. In the first place, material written especially for high-school pupils appeared. In presenting this material the authors attempted to overthrow the tradition that political economy was too difficult for pupils of high-school age. As an example of the sort of argument used to set aside this tradition an excerpt from the Preface of one of the texts written especially for pupils fifteen and sixteen years of age is cited here. It read: "For one, I am fully persuaded that it is as easy to teach political economy to students of fifteen, sixteen, or seventeen years of age, as it is to teach geometry or quadratic equations, which are actually taught, and with complete success, within that period of life."[11]

Other generalizations that may be made concerning the content of high-school political economy during the period under review are: 1. The systematically organized content was generally in terms of production, distribution, consumption, and exchange. 2. After 1875 material relating to current economic problems was increasingly included in textbooks —in other words, attempts to make the subject of immediate practical value. For example, in his Preface the author of a volume which appeared in 1889 said: "In the first place, I wished to show that the principles of Political Economy may be developed in such a form as to bring out their close and vital connection with every-day industry. . . .

"Political Economy is among the most practical of sciences, yet it is made to look very much like an abstract philosophy. . . . In the little book here offered the attempt is made to work out the leading principles of economics with a constant eye on actual affairs."[12] 3. Barring most of the texts published prior to 1875, the partisan nature of the content of texts in political economy disappeared before 1900. The spirit of these non-partisan texts is well embodied in the following brief excerpt from one of them: "It is eminently proper on questions that divide public opinion both sides should have a fair hearing, in order that the immature student may understand the grounds of belief on which either party rests its faith. This,

[11] F. A. Walker, *First Lessons in Political Economy*, Preface, p. iv.
[12] S. M. Macvane, *The Working Principles of Political Economy*, Preface, pp. v f.

too, has been the purpose of the author. Questions just now agitating the public are freely discussed with the main arguments sustaining the different doctrines briefly, but it is hoped clearly, presented." [13] 4. The recognition of the social nature of economic activity especially in texts published after 1892. Inasmuch as this idea came to fruition after 1900, no further attention needs to be given it here.

Thus in 1900, the typical content of a course in political economy in the high school or academy was a content based on a textbook which contained material organized in terms of the four traditional divisions of political economy suggested by French and English economists such as J. B. Say and James Mill. In addition to material on production, consumption, distribution, and exchange there usually appeared in a text a separate division on practical economics, the material being presented in a fair and impartial manner.[14]

THE ESTABLISHMENT OF ECONOMICS AS AN INDEPENDENT SUBJECT IN THE SCHOOLS AND THE NATURE OF ITS CONTENT, 1900-20

During the first two decades of the present century economics gained a very respectable foothold in he program of studies of academies and high schools. While the subject was increasing in popularity, its content was also changing—just how will be pointed out in the second half of this section, the first being devoted to factual evidence of the existence of the subject in the schools.

Prior to 1910 the evidence of the existence of economics in the high schools is very fragmentary. In 40 high-school programs for the year 1906-11 examined there were 18, or 45 per

[13] G. Steele, *Rudimentary Economics for Schools and Colleges,* Preface, p. v.
[14] For much of the data in the foregoing six or eight pages reliance was placed in E. J. Dougherty, *op. cit.*

cent of the total, which provided for economics.[15] This fact is somewhat significant when thought of in connection with the 27.5 per cent of 40 schools making such a provision about ten years earlier. However, one must guard against overstating the situation with respect to economics in the high schools during the first decade of the century. A study of 137 high schools for the year 1908–09 revealed that the subject was offered in not over five of them.[16] At this date the departments of the social sciences were exhausting all of their energy in attempting to conform to the letter of the report of the Committee of Seven of the American Historical Association. They had little time or energy for subjects not recommended by this Committee.

If one were permitted to estimate the situation in the country as a whole from what was happening in one state with respect to economics in the high school, the basis for his estimation exists in certain data for the state of Ohio, covering the years 1900–09. These data tell an interesting story. They are presented in Table III. By way of comparison it may be stated that the per cents pursuing the science of government during the same even years included in Table III were as follows: 30.70, 27.14, 28.03, 24.42, and 22.28. It will be observed that these per cents are from about ten to nearly twenty times greater than those for political economy. It would seem from this showing in one state that the subject had not succeeded, at least by 1910, in overcoming the handicaps previously pointed out. Furthermore, there is no reason to believe that the situation in Ohio was unusual in either direction, that is, too favorable to the subject, or not sufficiently favorable to it. The scattered available data indicate that Ohio was giving

15 Stout, *op. cit.*, p. 217.
16 Oscar Williams, *History Teaching in the High School.* Indiana University Bulletin, Vol. VII, No. 8, p. 7. Bloomington, Ind.: Indiana University, 1909.

more attention to economics in the high schools than many other states of the Union at this date, certainly more than Indiana and Wisconsin.

There are at hand data relative to the status of economics in the country as a whole for the years 1914–15 and 1918–19.

TABLE III

NUMBER AND PER CENT OF TOTAL HIGH-SCHOOL ENROLLMENT PURSUING POLITICAL ECONOMY IN THE HIGH SCHOOLS OF OHIO, 1900-09.*

YEAR	TOTAL HIGH-SCHOOL ENROLLMENT	Pursuing Political Economy	
		NUMBER	PER CENT
1900............	56,952	1744	3.06
1901............	58,099	1406	2.42
1902............	58,511	2128	3.63
1903............	57,649	1782	3.09
1904............	57,632	1728	2.99
1905............	60,748	2275	3.74
1906............	64,166	2212	3.44
1907............	65,681	1272	1.93
1908............	68,431	1623	2.37
1909............	73,317	1362	1.85

* Based on the reports of the State Commissioner of Common Schools and Superintendent of Public Instruction for the years indicated.

Those for the former of these dates show that of the 7197 high schools reporting 2064 or 28.67 per cent were offering economics either as a required or an elective subject. In 498 schools the subject was required.[17] For the year 1918–19 of the 5054 high schools reporting, 1824 or 36.09 per cent included economics in their program of studies.[18] An increase between 1915 and 1920 from 28.67 per cent to 36.09 per cent in the schools offering economics indicates that the subject was rapidly becoming one of the recognized offerings in the high

[17] U. S. Comr. of Educ., *Rep. for 1914–15*, II, 121.
[18] "The Present Status of Social Studies in the High Schools of the United States," *Historical Outlook*, XI (1920), 88.

schools of the country. The rise of commercial high schools no doubt accounts for some of this increase. As early as 1915 there were 208,605 pupils enrolled in commercial high schools. There was an increase of 1,270.5 per cent in the enrollment in these schools between 1893 and 1915.[19]

TABLE IV

NUMBER AND PER CENT OF HIGH SCHOOLS BY STATES IN THE NORTH CENTRAL ASSOCIATION OFFERING ECONOMICS, 1916-17.*

STATE	NUMBER OF HIGH SCHOOLS	Offering Economics	
		NUMBER	PER CENT
1. Arizona	6	2	33.33
2. Colorado	36	19	52.77
3. Illinois	135	85	62.96
4. Indiana	79	14	17.72
5. Iowa	76	76	100.00
6. Kansas	67	30	44.77
7. Michigan	112	35	31.25
8. Minnesota	67	45	67.16
9. Missouri	52	27	51.92
10. Montana	25	15	60.00
11. Nebraska	57	13	22.80
12. New Mexico	4	1	25.00
13. North Dakota	30	15	50.00
14. Ohio	165	68	41.21
15. South Dakota	24	11	45.83
16. Wisconsin	92	51	55.43
17. Wyoming	5	2	40.00
Total	1032	509	49.32

* Calvin O. Davis, *Accredited Secondary Schools of the North Central Association.* United States Bureau of Education Bulletin, 1919, No. 45, p. 94. Washington, D. C.: Government Printing Office, 1919.

For the high schools belonging to the North Central Association there are data on economics for the years 1916–17 and 1919–20. For the first of these years there is available the number of high schools by states offering economics. Table IV contains these data. For the year 1919–20 the report of the

[19] L. S. Lyon, *A Survey of Commercial Education in the Public Schools of the United States,* p. 1. Chicago: University of Chicago Press, 1919.

Association did not include by states the number of high
schools offering economics. Only gross totals were given.
These totals show that of the 1180 schools reporting 696, or almost 59 per cent, claimed to offer economics. It will be observed that this is the highest per cent that had ever been
reported for these schools as a whole. In 1916–17 as shown in

TABLE V

ECONOMICS IN HIGH SCHOOLS OF OHIO, 1914-19.*

SCHOOL YEAR	Number and Per cent Pursuing in						TOTAL	
	Cities		Villages		Rural			
	NO.	%	NO.	%	NO.	%	NO.	%
1914-15.........	1146	1.89	872	2.71	392	3.21	2410	2.29
1915-16.........	1214	1.98	1332	3.83	495	3.66	3041	2.77
1916-17.........	1522	2.37	1724	4.80	741	4.76	3987	3.45
1917-18.........	2005	2.68	1945	5.50	841	5.31	4791	3.80
1918-19.........	2179	2.69	2466	6.97	1261	7.67	5906	4.45

* Based on the reports of the Superintendent of Public Instruction to the Governor
of the State of Ohio for the years indicated.

Table IV it was but 49.32 per cent. So the evidence seems
ample from two sources to justify the statement that economics
had become fairly well established in the high schools of the
country by 1920. That the subject was taught in city, village,
and rural high schools in at least one state is indicated by the
material in Table V. It is evident from the data in this table
that the village and rural high schools of Ohio between 1914
and 1919 enrolled in their classes in economics a higher per
cent of the total school population than did the city high
schools, the difference in the per cents being significant during
most of the years represented in the table. These data refute
the statement that one meets again and again that economics
has been taught primarily in the large industrial cities; for it

is evident that in Ohio from 1914 to 1919 inclusive the subject was pursued by a higher percentage of the pupils in village and rural schools than in city schools.

Fragmentary evidence picked up here and there, such as 79 out of 103 schools in Ohio in 1917 were offering economics, and in 78 out of 101 in 1920 the subject was offered, the per cents being 43 in 1917 and 56 in 1920, could be included here to prove that by 1920 economics as a high school subject had become fairly well established in the schools of this state. Inasmuch, however, as enough evidence has already been presented to show that economics was an established subject in the high schools of the country in 1920, the discussion will now turn to the content during the first two decades of the present century.

The content of economics as a subject of study in high schools and academies underwent certain fundamental changes between 1900 and 1920. Chief among these changes were: 1. The content was broadened by the addition of material from the fields of sociology, political science, industrial history, and economic geography. 2. The attempt to formulate, as was the practice prior to 1890, a systematic science with emphasis on the laws and principles of the subject was abandoned. 3. The social point of view in economic activities was mildly stressed, an innovation that had begun to appear prior to 1900. 4. The emphasis on problems which illustrate the practical application of theory was noticeably increased, an innovation also begun in a feeble way prior to 1900. 5. The name of the subject was changed from political economy to economics. 6. In a few cases the traditional divisions of political economy in the organization of the content were completely disregarded. 7. A forward look was incorporated into the content by the inclusion of a section on economic reforms. These innovations seem to justify speaking of them as revolutionary. However, in spite of all of the new features, many old ones remained, so the changes must be considered evolutionary rather than revolutionary.

It would be incorrect to leave the impression that all of the foregoing changes occurred soon after the opening of the present century, because they did not. The text most used during the first decade of the century, namely, *First Lessons in Political Economy,* by F. A. Walker, was originally published in 1889. This text along with *Elementary Principles of Economics,* by R. T. Ely and J. R. Wicker, published in 1904, probably dictated the content of most of the courses in high-school economics during the early years of the century. The content dictated by them was far from being ultra modern.

To illustrate each of the innovations mentioned above would carry this discussion far beyond the limits of a mere overview of the subject. Because of its significance, however, some additional attention is here bestowed upon one of these innovations, namely the stressing of the social point of view in economic activities. The social point of view is exemplified in some of the texts of the period in their emphasis on the idea that the activities connected with making a living are carried on in an organized society. Furthermore, a few of these texts stressed the interdependence evident in modern society and pointed out that the welfare of society should be placed above that of any individual. This social point of view was probably the paramount innovation in economics as a high-school subject during the first two decades of the present century.

No attempt will be made here to list the numerous texts in economics that appeared during these two decades. In lieu of such a list, an analysis of nine texts published between 1900 and 1922 along with one published in 1887 and still in use in 1923 is offered. Table VI contains this analysis in terms of the per cent of the total words in all books devoted to each main division of the content and to each sub-division under the same. According to the data in this table the introductory material in the texts analyzed consumed 5.80 per cent of the total words. Consumption got 6.25 per cent; production, 39.56; exchange, 21.94; distribution, 21.48; and programs of economic reform 4.97. Distributed in terms of days in a one-semester course these per cents would mean about 5 days for the introductory material, 6 for consumption, 36 for production, 20 for exchange, 19 for distribution, and 4 for programs of economic reform. The data in the last column of the table make very clear where the emphasis was placed within each large division of the content.

THE MATURING OF ECONOMICS AS A SUBJECT OF STUDY IN ACADEMIES AND HIGH SCHOOLS AND THE NATURE OF ITS CONTENT, 1920–33

During the 1920's economics held the ground it gained during the five years preceding this date. By 1930 it had reached a maturity for which its supporters had been working for thirty years. Of course, maturity does not mean that it was offered in 100 per cent of the high schools and academies of the country. It simply means that the subject was no longer a new one in the curriculum. Furthermore, the ideas with respect to the content of the course which had been floating around for about a generation found practical application in both textbooks and syllabi. In some quarters the course was elevated to a full year standing, a movement that had been a long time in culminating. The brief survey below of the

TABLE VI

THE PER CENT OF THE TOTAL WORDS DEVOTED TO CERTAIN TOPICS IN ECONOMICS BY NINE TEXTBOOKS IN THE FIELD.*

TOPICS	PERCENTAGE OF TOTAL WORDS DEVOTED TO	PER CENT OF TOTAL WORDS IN EACH LARGE DIVISION DEVOTED TO EACH TOPIC THEREIN
A. Introductory Material.........	5.78	
1. Nature of Economics........	.92	15.86
2. Divisions of Economics......	.26	4.54
3. The Social Sciences.........	.20	3.47
4. Wealth and Welfare........	.51	8.91
5. What Makes a Nation Prosperous..................	2.78	47.98
6. Miscellaneous.............	1.11	19.22
B. Consumption.................	6.24	
1. Nature of Consumption.....	1.66	26.54
2. Laws of Consumption.......	.62	9.94
3. Demand, Supply, Price......	1.41	22.63
4. Kinds of Consumption......	1.22	19.65
5. Standard of Living.........	.94	15.02
6. Miscellaneous Material......	.39	6.22
C. Production..................	39.52	
1. Meaning of Production......	.98	2.49
2. Agents of Production.......	11.80	29.84
3. Organization of Production..	12.33	31.17
4. Transportation.............	2.25	5.71
5. Economic History..........	5.67	14.33
6. Specialization in Production..	2.12	5.36
7. Laws of Production.........	1.50	3.79
8. Miscellaneous..............	2.87	7.27
D. Exchange....................	21.95	
1. Money.....................	5.52	25.16
2. Credit....................	1.11	5.04
3. Banking...................	4.32	19.70
4. Domestic Commerce........	1.03	4.68
5. International Trade.........	4.50	20.48
6. Value.....................	2.08	9.47
7. Price.....................	.79	3.64
8. Miscellaneous Material......	2.60	11.81
E. Distribution.................	21.46	
1. Nature of Distribution......	1.93	8.01
2. Rent.....................	2.26	9.51
3. Wages....................	3.24	14.10

TOPICS	PERCENTAGE OF TOTAL WORDS DEVOTED TO	PER CENT OF TOTAL WORDS IN EACH LARGE DIVISION DEVOTED TO EACH TOPIC THEREIN
4. Interest.....................	2.24	10.31
5. Profits......................	1.24	5.70
6. Government's Share in Distribution................	3.23	14.95
7. Labor Problems............	3.66	16.93
8. Experimental Programs......	1.74	8.02
9. Miscellaneous Material......	1.92	8.85
F. Programs of Economic Reform..	4.96	
1. Socialism..................	2.69	54.20
2. The Single Tax.............	.82	16.61
3. Communism...............	.40	8.15
4. Constructive Liberalism.....	.39	7.79
5. Anarchism.................	.26	5.18
6. Social Progress............	.40	8.06

* Data from a number of tables in "The Content of Economics as Taught in Secondary Schools," by Guy Thompson. Unpublished Master's thesis, University of Illinois, 1923.

evidence relative to the existence of the subjects in the schools during the 1920's and the general description of its content indicate the nature of the maturity which economics attained between 1920 and 1933.

There is an abundance of data on the status of economics in secondary schools during the 1920's. Out of the existing mass of these data three types have been selected as representative, namely, material from the reports of the United States Commissioner of Education on the number of pupils pursuing economics in 1921–22 and 1927–28, facts from special studies which include schools in more than one state, and data from studies each of which include but one state. These three types of data are presented below in the order named here.

In 1921–22 economics was for the first time included in the list of subjects on which data relative to the number of pupils pursuing subjects have been collected at various dates since

TABLE VII

ECONOMICS IN THE PUBLIC HIGH SCHOOLS AND PRIVATE HIGH SCHOOLS AND ACADEMIES OF CONTINENTAL UNITED STATES DURING THE SCHOLASTIC YEARS ENDING IN 1922 AND 1928*

STATE	Schools Reporting on Studies Offering Economics				Pupils Pursuing Economics in Schools Reporting Studies			
	NUMBER		PER CENT		NUMBER		PER CENT	
	1922	1928	1922	1928	1922	1928	1922	1928
Continental U. S........	4,587	5,316	29.4	31.3	107,642	153,848	4.6	4.8
Alabama..............	77	63	34.2	27.6	1,827	1,340	6.6	3.8
Arizona..............	21	24	50.0	47.0	478	896	8.2	7.7
Arkansas.............	50	74	25.1	29.1	1,014	1,601	5.7	6.2
California.............	113	186	30.1	36.8	4,081	7,416	3.5	3.6
Colorado.............	44	54	30.1	29.5	838	1,472	3.2	4.2
Connecticut...........	30	38	26.1	27.3	678	1,316	1.8	3.0
Delaware.............	2	10	7.4	37.0	14	155	.3	2.7
District of Columbia ...	11	8	37.9	20.5	366	468	2.8	2.8
Florida...............	11	30	10.0	17.4	468	600	3.9	1.9
Georgia..............	17	29	7.0	11.2	425	680	1.3	2.0
Idaho................	51	85	41.8	55.9	819	1,487	6.8	7.6
Illinois..............	359	440	41.6	47.8	7,072	10,066	4.3	4.6
Indiana..............	82	332	11.8	50.4	1,767	7,065	2.0	6.6
Iowa................	557	508	69.5	61.4	9,901	11,810	13.0	13.4
Kansas..............	227	220	39.2	35.7	3,563	3,427	5.6	4.5
Kentucky.............	43	98	12.6	20.9	651	1,641	2.3	4.1
Louisiana.............	29	12	13.8	4.7	255	579	1.3	1.7
Maine...............	27	36	12.2	17.1	1,110	761	4.7	3.2
Maryland.............	23	15	15.3	8.3	668	560	3.0	1.7
Massachusetts.........	74	96	20.3	24.8	2,827	4,153	2.5	3.1
Michigan.............	123	273	22.9	42.7	3,407	7,018	3.6	5.2
Minnesota............	217	112	45.5	21.3	4,787	4,254	6.9	4.7
Mississippi............	37	131	20.3	46.1	985	1,921	6.4	8.8
Missouri.............	223	93	37.7	12.5	2,767	2,486	3.5	2.7
Montana.............	78	96	43.8	56.8	1,189	1,548	6.8	8.1
Nebraska.............	77	101	16.6	21.9	1,177	2,468	2.8	4.9
Nevada..............	5	3	29.4	13.6	43	27	2.5	1.4
New Hampshire........	36	40	40.4	29.4	672	1,001	6.1	6.0
New Jersey...........	55	88	26.4	35.4	2,022	3,828	2.7	3.8
New Mexico..........	8	21	13.3	22.1	133	308	3.1	3.6
New York............	106	206	11.8	21.7	10,779	25,193	4.6	6.4
North Carolina........	15	28	4.0	5.4	296	864	.8	1.4
North Dakota.........	197	84	61.5	24.7	2,837	1,286	15.7	7.1
Ohio................	430	301	44.2	32.8	9,230	8,046	6.4	4.1
Oklahoma............	130	153	34.4	33.9	2,098	2,726	4.9	5.3

STATE	Schools Reporting on Studies Offering Economics				Pupils Pursuing Economics in Schools Reporting Studies			
	NUMBER		PER CENT		NUMBER		PER CENT	
	1922	1928	1922	1928	1922	1928	1922	1928
Oregon..............	29	82	13.1	38.1	765	1,424	2.1	4.1
Pennsylvania..........	230	210	22.6	20.7	8,492	10,215	4.5	4.3
Rhode Island..........	12	7	33.3	20.0	344	338	2.7	2.2
South Carolina........	....	30	....	21.4	.....	605	...	3.7
South Dakota.........	81	152	28.9	57.3	899	2,013	5.5	9.0
Tennessee.............	26	69	10.4	21.3	468	1,425	1.7	4.1
Texas................	94	178	16.4	34.7	3,537	4,852	4.6	5.2
Utah.................	26	22	45.6	37.3	870	1,131	5.7	7.1
Vermont.............	24	17	26.0	20.0	398	847	4.2	11.1
Virginia.............	119	24	28.7	7.6	1,488	552	3.9	1.2
Washington..........	83	117	28.2	40.2	2,217	3,018	4.5	4.8
West Virginia.........	53	67	29.6	31.3	1,177	1,953	4.9	6.8
Wisconsin............	211	232	51.5	58.0	4,584	5,097	6.4	6.1
Wyoming.............	14	21	29.1	29.5	168	326	3.0	4.1

* Based on data in *Biennial Surveys of Education* for 1920-22, 1926-28.

1889 by the United States Bureau of Education. The facts relative to economics for the years 1921-22 and 1927-28 are set forth in Table VII, which reveals the fact that in 1928 economics was pursued in some of the secondary schools of every state in the Union. In a few states the number of pupils pursuing the subject was of minor importance, while in others it was of near major importance, for example, Iowa and Vermont. In the country as a whole economics made a slight gain between 1921 and 1928 in the per cent of schools offering, but practically no gain in the per cent of pupils pursuing—4.6 per cent in 1921-22 and 4.8 per cent in 1927-28. In fifteen states the per cent of pupils pursuing the subject in 1927-28 was lower than in 1921-22. In North Dakota the per cent of pupils pursuing economics dropped from 15.7 in 1921-22 to 7.1 in 1927-28, a drop which is explained by the adoption of the course in problems of American democracy in this state. The per cent of high schools offering economics was lower in 1927–28 in each of twenty states than it was in 1921–22. It is certainly evident from the data in Table VII that economics as a

TABLE VIII

STATUS OF ECONOMICS IN CERTAIN HIGH SCHOOLS DURING THE 1920'S AS REVEALED IN SPECIAL REPORTS AND INVESTIGATIONS

SOURCE OF DATA	DATE	NUMBER OF SCHOOLS	Offering Economics	
			NUMBER	PER CENT
1. H. H. Moore, *Status of Certain Social Studies in High Schools*	1921–22	6624	2707	40.86
2. W. S. Monroe, and J. O. Foster, *The Status of the Social Sciences in the High Schools of the North Central Association*	1921–22	475	316	66.52
3. Edgar Dawson, *The History Inquiry*	1923–24	2404	1014	42.17
4. C. O. Davis, "The North Central Association Quinquennial Study," *School Review*, XXXIII (1925)	1924–25	1571	672	42.77
5. Emery N. Ferris, *The Rural High School* (Rural and semi-rural)	1924–25	404	194	48.01
6. Joseph Roemer, *Secondary Schools of the Southern Association*	1926–27	849	73	8.59
7. C. C. Brown, "Proceedings of the Commission on Secondary Schools," *North Central Quarterly*, V (1930).	1929–30	2226	1151	51.70

secondary-school subject gained little ground during the 1920's.

Data of a similar character to those in Table VII were collected from year to year during the 1920's by certain individuals and associations. Some of these data apply to the country as a whole and others to groups of states or to high schools in a number of individual states. They serve as a check on the facts in Table VII. It will be observed that all of them relate to number and per cent of public high schools offering economics. They are embodied in Table VIII. The data in studies Nos. 1 and 2 in this table included schools from the country at large. The per cent of high schools represented in these two studies offering economics is considerably higher than the per cent of schools represented in Table VII offering the subject. In fact, except in one group of high schools included in Table VIII, the per cent of high schools represented therein offering economics is significantly higher than it is in the schools included in Table VII. Judging from the data in study No. 6, the high schools of the Southern Association had little interest in economics as a high-school subject in 1926-27.

In order to portray the status of economics in a large group of states at the middle and the end of the decade of the 1920's, the number and per cent of high schools in the North Central Association for the years 1924-25 and 1929-30 are presented in Table IX. Placing the two years in the same table in close juxtaposition affords a convenient device for the making of specific comparisons. While the schools in Tables VII and IX are not the same ones, those in Table IX could have been included in the reports on which Table VII is based. When the per cents in the twenty states of the North Central Association are compared in the two tables few startling differences are found. For this reason it seems reasonable to conclude that the picture of economics in the secondary schools of the country portrayed in Table VII and IX closely approximates the actual situation. Speaking for the country as a whole about five of each one hundred pupils in the secondary schools during the 1920's were pursuing economics. There is certainly no guarantee in this fact that the generation of the 1940's will know a great deal about the economic order.

Before passing to a consideration of the content of economics during the 1920's, one more type of evidence relative to the existence of the subject in high schools will be presented. During the 1920's special investigations of the status of the social sciences in a number of states were made. The data in ten of

TABLE IX

ECONOMICS IN THE PUBLIC HIGH SCHOOLS BELONGING TO THE NORTH CENTRAL ASSOCIATION, 1924-25 AND 1929-30.*

STATE	Number and per cent Offering Economics				Number and per cent of Pupils Pursuing			
	NUMBER		PER CENT		NUMBER		PER CENT	
	1925	1930	1925	1930	1925	1930	1925	1930
1. Arizona..............	9	16	33.33	45.71	171	979	2.41	8.2
2. Arkansas............	15	32	48.38	55.17	550	1132	6.58	8.1
3. Colorado............	26	31	39.39	33.69	734	884	3.29	2.7
4. Illinois..............	119	182	56.93	58.14	3924	6540	2.93	3.3
5. Indiana.............	34	63	40.00	63.00	1155	2749	2.28	4.1
6. Iowa................	89	115	81.65	83.94	4128	5337	10.37	10.5
7. Kansas.............	62	75	55.35	51.02	1437	1872	3.76	4.1
8. Michigan...........	35	118	28.68	64.48	1441	4223	2.25	3.8
9. Minnesota..........	46	35	58.97	35.35	1876	2225	5.71	4.5
10. Missouri...........	†	47	†	39.16	1106	1824	2.97	3.1
11. Montana...........	16	29	50.00	65.90	477	915	4.47	6.0
12. Nebraska...........	†	27	†	23.68	528	1068	2.20	3.0
13. New Mexico........	7	12	23.33	42.85	138	224	2.64	3.3
14. North Dakota.......	†	4	†	5.47	1559	116	14.53	.9
15. Ohio...............	103	162	50.24	54.91	4020	5674	3.95	3.7
16. Oklahoma..........	33	49	40.74	42.52	989	1392	3.52	3.6
17. South Dakota.......	16	44	42.10	65.82	279	950	3.04	6.8
18. West Virginia.......	‡	38	‡	53.23	‡	1682	‡	6.7
19. Wisconsin..........	50	62	53.12	53.44	1768	2180	3.67	3.3
20. Wyoming...........	12	10	54.54	37.03	271	250	4.91	3.4

* Charles C. Brown, "Proceedings of the Commission on Secondary Schools," *North Central Association Quarterly*, V (1930), 99, 112; and Calvin O. Davis, *Our Secondary Schools* (1925), pp. 24, 45, and 76.
† Data imperfect.
‡ West Virginia not yet a member of the Association.

these investigations are comparable and seem worth presenting here. They appear in Table X in which eight states are represented—six of them in the North Central Association territory, which fact makes possible a comparison of the findings of these special studies with those in Tables VIII and IX. In one of these states, Iowa, the data in Tables VIII, IX, and X on the number and per cent of high schools offering economics are

TABLE X

NUMBER AND PER CENT OF PUBLIC HIGH SCHOOLS IN CERTAIN STATES OFFERING ECONOMICS AT VARIOUS DATES DURING THE 1920's.*

STATE	DATE	NUMBER OF SCHOOLS	Offering Economics	
			NUMBER	PER CENT
1. Missouri..........	1920–21	384	136	35.41
2. Wisconsin.........	1921–22	295	159	53.89
3. Minnesota.........	1921–22	246	155	63.00
4. Illinois (community high schools)....	1922–23	259	236	91.11
5. Minnesota.........	1923–24	255	159	62.35
6. Iowa..............	1924–25	577	216	37.43
7. Pennsylvania.......	1926–27	161	45	27.95
8. California.........	1926–27	274	142	51.82
9. Kansas...........	1927–28	700	349	49.85
10. Iowa..............	1928–29	253	168	66.40

* Based on data in: (1) Caroline E. Hartwig, "The Place of the Social Studies in the High Schools of Missouri," pp. 32 f. Unpublished Master's thesis, University of Missouri, 1922; (2) M. A. Fisher, "The Study of the Social Studies in the Public Accredited High Schools of Wisconsin," p. 3. Unpublished Bachelor's thesis, University of Wisconsin, 1922; (3) Minnesota, *Second Report of the State Department of Education* (1921-1922), p. 49; (4) Department of Superintendence, Sixth Yearbook (1928), p. 103; (5) Minnesota, *Third Report of the State Board of Education* (1923-24), p. 42; (6) Ray C. Hurd, "Status of Social Studies in the High Schools of Iowa, Grades Nine to Twelve," p. 68. Unpublished Master's thesis, University of Iowa, 1924; (7) Barbara C. Fretz, "A Survey of the Teaching of History in the High Schools of Pennsylvania," p. 49. Unpublished Master's thesis, Cornell University, 1927; (8) Junior J. Collins, "Development of the Social Sciences in the Secondary Schools of California," pp. 108 f. Unpublished Master's thesis, Leland Stanford Junior University, 1927; (9) Ethel S. Crowell, "Status of Social Science in Kansas High Schools," pp. 39-43. Unpublished Master's thesis, University of Kansas, 1928; (10) Byron L. Braman, "Trends in the Social Science Programs in Iowa High Schools," p. 47. Unpublished Master's thesis, University of Iowa, 1929.

for approximately the same year. Comparing the per cent of high schools represented in each of the three tables offering economics one finds but little difference in the 66.4 per cent for the year 1928–29 and 61.4 per cent for the year 1927–28, the former determined by a special investigation and the latter by reports to the United States Bureau of Education. However, when the high schools in Iowa belonging to the North Central Association are considered separately, the per cent of schools offering economics in 1929–30 increases to 83.94. So it would seem that in this state the per cent of high schools offering economics during the 1920's was greater in the high schools belonging to the North Central Association than in the general run of high schools. This situation was not found in all of the states represented in Table X. In Illinois in 1922–23 economics was offered in 91.11 per cent of 259 community high schools while in 1921–22 the subject was offered in but 41.6 per cent of the high schools reporting to the United States Commissioner of Education. On the basis of the data in Tables VIII, IX, and X one may conclude: (1) that during the 1920's economics was offered in approximately one-third of the high schools in continental United States; (2) that the general status of the subject changed little during the decade; and (3) that the subject was probably offered in a larger proportion of small than of large high schools.

Turning now to the content of economics during the 1920's it seems apropos to remark that those interested in economics as a subject of study in high schools and academies were so busy maturing the innovations that were under way in the early years of the decade that they had little time to propose others. A few new textbooks appeared and those available in 1920 continued to be used. The practice of holding on to what was good was much in vogue in 1920 in the realm of high-school textbooks in economics. Inasmuch, however, as the 1920's saw a good deal of curriculum revision, many courses in economics appeared which were not wholly in terms of a given text. For example, a full year's course in the subject was organized during the late years of the decade in the University of Chicago High School. It was based on the following units of understanding and christened Economic Society.

Unit   I. Why People Work.
Unit   II. How We Produce Goods.
Unit III. Buying and Selling.
Unit   IV. Facilitating Exchange.
Unit   V. Dividing the Product.
Unit   VI. Saving and Thriving.
Unit VII. Managing One's Income.
Unit VIII. Earning a Living.[20]

As an example of what some states were doing, the one-semester course in economics proposed for the state of Washington may be cited. It was based on the following general topics and shows that the shades of the 1890's were still hovering around.

I. Introduction—Preliminary Survey of Economics.
II. Consumption of Economic Goods.
III. Production.
IV. Exchange.
V. Distribution.[21]

When those responsible for the teaching and the administration of the course in high-school economics took charge of its content, uniformity disappeared, especially in the large cities. It is, of course, true that some State Departments of Education or other agencies in the state attempted to secure

[20] "Work Reports," Secondary, Vol. IX, Part 5, 1927–28. The University of Chicago, The Laboratory Schools, 1928.
[21] *High School Social Science*, pp. 110–114. Olympia, Washington: State Department of Education, 1930.

a cerain amount of uniformity. For example, in the state of
Iowa an every-pupil test has been conducted since 1931 in
the major subjects taught in the high schools. To give the
teachers an idea of the content on which the tests would be
based, outlines of the subjects on which pupils were to be
tested were supplied. The outline in economics for 1932 contained the following large divisions:

    I. Elementary Concepts.
   II. The Evolution of Economic Society.
  III. Division of Labor and Control of Production.
  IV. Business Organization.
   V. Large Scale Production, Combination and Monopoly.
  VI. Price—Supply and Demand.
 VII. Cost of Production and Price.
VIII. Money.
  IX. Money and Prices.
   X. Principles of Banking.
  XI. The History of American Banking.
 XII. The Federal Reserve System.
XIII. International Trade.
XIV. Rent.
 XV. Wages (Price paid for human services).
XVI. Interest (Price paid for use of capital).
XVII. Profits.

Nothing of significance would be gained in a further pursuance of the content of high-school economics during the
1920's. The foregoing three examples indicate the nature of
this content in two states and one private school. By referring
to Table VI it may be seen that the content in the two states
mentioned above was about what was contained in the text-

book in high-school economics in 1922. The course in the University of Chicago High School was typical of those organized independently of textbooks in the field and to which a full year was devoted.

II

SOCIOLOGY AS A SUBJECT OF STUDY IN ACADEMIES AND HIGH SCHOOLS

Sociology is still young as a special discipline and younger still as an independent subject of study in academies and high schools. In both of these capacities it has most of its life yet to live. The history that it has made is an important aspect of the development of high-school studies; the values that have been claimed for it are in some respects unique; its career in the schools has been somewhat uneventful; and its content is still very much unsettled as the discussion below indicates.

VALUES CLAIMED FOR SOCIOLOGY AS A SUBJECT OF STUDY

In a study of textbooks in sociology for use in secondary schools and material from State Departments of Education relative to sociology in the schools certain values of sociology as a school subject were brought to light. Standing at the top of the list of thirty-eight values discovered in this study was one stated as follows: "Sociology is valuable for the understanding it gives to those who pursue it of their individual membership in society and the consequences and responsibilities of such membership." Next to this value was "Sociology is valuable for the understanding it gives of current social problems and conditions." Other values for sociology as a subject of study that were mentioned in the twenty texts analyzed and the twenty-seven state outlines examined[22] were: provides contact with great social issues; trains for social life after school age; gives an understanding of the nature and function of social institutions; aids in the recognition of social leadership and inspires one to follow the same; promotes constructive criticism of the social order; stimulates interest in social problems; furnishes an understanding of the current functionings of society; affords valuable lessons in tolerance; aids one to function normally in society; and makes clear the complexity of social life. Citing these claimed values does not imply that they are all realized in present-day courses in high-school sociology. In the minds of those who proposed them they were objectives to be accomplished or ends to be sought. Thought of as values, they furnish a point of departure for the setting up of objectives.

Besides the claimed values of sociology that may be assembled from textbooks and state outlines there are those proposed by individuals who write on the specific topic "Values of Sociology." For example, in summarizing a short article on the subject one writer said:

"Finally to summarize: the study of sociology has real cultural value and it helps prepare the students for effective citizenship. It promotes culture and has practical worth for life because, as already stated, it has a direct bearing on the conduct and problems of life. There are four important things that the study of sociology will do for the student. It will (1) help him to enjoy life; (2) prepare him for duty; (3) give him a desire to participate intelligently in the world's

22 John C. West, "An Analysis of Senior High School Sociology." Unpublished Doctor's dissertation, University of North Dakota, 1930.

work, and (4) help him to render genuine social service. And what else can the study of sociology give that can in any way compare with a sincere desire to have even a small share in solving some of the problems of civilization?" [23]

When asked to write specifically of the values of a course in social problems for the secondary schools, the author of a much used book in the field said with respect to the values of the subject:

"First: It should have a disciplinary value. If the student is held strictly accountable for definite assignments; if he traces through the relation between cause and effect in the social phenomena; and if he searches out, classifies and analyzes obtainable facts, there is no reason why this course should not have just as great disciplinary value as any other course in the curriculum. . . .

"Second: It should have a cultural value. In showing the weaknesses and injustice in our social order, the amount of poverty, the sorrow and suffering of our dependent classes, the serious consequences of child labor, it should develop our sympathy for the less fortunate, give us a kindlier feeling toward our fellowmen, and prompt us to make every effort to right these wrongs, and alleviate these sufferings. It should give us a broader outlook upon life, and develop a more altruistic spirit toward others. . . .

"Third: It should familiarize the student with the sources of information on the various subjects. . . .

"Fourth: It should give the student a better understanding of the present. These are all live, vital questions today, and questions directly affecting the lives of every one of us. To

[23] Ransom A. Mackie, "The Value of Sociology," *Science*, LXIII (1926), 94.

understand them, one must study them carefully and intensively.

"Fifth: It should give a clearer comprehension of the movements of the social forces. It is only by studying such questions historically, tracing through the different stages in their development, that we can see the workings of the great forces in our social life. If we are to control and direct these forces, we must first understand them.

"Sixth: It should give us a constructive viewpoint in our attitude toward society." [24]

The foregoing, of course, does not exhaust the list of values that have been claimed for sociology since it joined the ranks of high-school subjects. Inasmuch as the life line of the subject in the schools is so short, a treatment of the values claimed for it must be more descriptive than historical, for the reason that the values now prevalent are mostly those that have existed since the subjects entered the high-school program of studies about a quarter of a century ago.

THE CAREER OF SOCIOLOGY IN THE SCHOOLS

Sociology as a subject of study in the high school has had a short career. It is one of the newest of the new subjects which have taken up their abode in the high-school program in recent years. The available evidence seems to establish the fact that sociology was introduced into two high schools of the middle west during the same school year, 1911–12. One of these courses was offered in the high school of Hammond, Indiana and the other in the high school of Jacksonville, Illi-

[24] E. T. Towne, "A Course in Social Problems for Secondary Schools—Content, Method, Aims," *Historical Outlook,* XVII (1926), 185 f.

nois. Writing in 1913 of his experience with the course in the high school of Hammond, the teacher said: "My experience in teaching sociology has been very satisfactory. We have had a course in the high school for two years. It has been required of all seniors. The work has been rather difficult, owing to the fact that it is an abstract subject. As to the advisability and value of the subject in high school, I believe that there is no question. An elementary course should be given in every high school of any size." [25]

The teacher in charge of the course in the high school of Jacksonville wrote about the same time that the foregoing comment was made as follows:

"This is only our second year at giving sociology but the results last year cause us to offer the course without any hesitation. If the aim of the instructor is to give a course the object of which is to start the boys and girls to thinking along this line, the course can be of unquestionable value in the community. (An effective and usable text should be one that is simple and very readable, yet presenting some of the underlying scientific facts in readable form.) We are using Ellwood's *Sociology and Modern Social Problems.* I find it necessary to use a text at least as elementary as this in high school. An effective text is one that will keep the student interested and that may be done by presenting the social problems as in Ellwood." [26]

The facts that the high school is over a century old and that sociology as a subject of study did not enter it until it was

[25] Quoted by John M. Gillette, in "Sociology as a High School Subject," *Educational Review,* XLV (1913), 261.
[26] *Ibid.*

about ninety years old might provoke the inquiry, "Why was sociology so late in entering the high-school program of studies?" For an answer to this question one has but to go to the history of sociology as a college subject in this country. Writing in 1926 on the development of sociology in the United States a sociologist commented as follows on the entrance of sociology into the colleges and universities:

"It is just fifty years since Professor Sumner at Yale gave what is usually thought of as the first course in sociology in the United States. However, Thorpe, in his *Benjamin Franklin and the University of Pennsylvania,* says that Professor Thompson gave such a course at that institution in 1874. As a text Sumner used Spencer's *Sociology* (probably his *Principles of Sociology,* not his *Introduction to the Study of Sociology*), which was then appearing in parts. After a year or so the course disappeared to appear again about 1885 as 'Social Science,' under which title sociology has been given at Yale to the present time. In 1881 Professor Dunstan offered a course called 'social science' at Michigan. It was not until 1883 that the first American book on sociology, Lester T. Ward's *Dynamic Sociology,* appeared. In 1885 Professor Woodford gave a course in sociology at Indiana. In 1889 President Albion W. Small started a small class in sociology at Colby University. In the same year Professor Frank W. Blackmar introduced sociology at the University of Kansas. In 1890 Professor Franklin H. Giddings announced a course on 'Modern Theories of Sociology' at Bryn Mawr College. In 1891 Professor Edward A. Ross gave his first course in sociology at University of Indiana. In 1892 appeared Ward's *Psychic Factors of Civilization,* and in 1893 the Department of Sociology was opened at the new University of Chicago. In 1894 a chair of sociology was established at Columbia University, and Professor Giddings was invited to occupy it."[27]

From the feeble beginnings recorded above the course in sociology rapidly invaded the colleges and universities throughout the United States. Thus by the time the subject entered the high school it was being taught in about 370 higher institutions of learning in this country.[28]

To the foregoing reason, namely, recent appearance of sociology in higher institutions of learning, for the late entrance of sociology into the high-school curriculum two others should be added: (1) the lack of education in sociology on the part of high-school teachers, and (2) the belief current in 1913 among most sociologists that the subject was too difficult for high-school pupils. In due time the colleges took care of the first of these two reasons and the textbook writers attempted to prove that the subject could be made easy enough for high-school pupils to comprehend.

To say that, after being enrolled in 1911–12 among the elderly and highly respectable social sciences already in the high-school program of studies, sociology at once sprang into popularity and was rapidly introduced into all of the high schools of the land would be a gross exaggeration. Proof of this statement is at hand in a study that was completed in 1917.[29] This study canvassed the status of sociology in the high schools of the country at large. Sixty-seven secondary courses in sociology were found, most of which were in the

27 J. L. Gillin, "The Development of Sociology in the United States," *Publication American Sociological Society*, XXI (1926), 1 f.

28 Paul Monroe, Editor, *Encyclopedia of Education*, V, 359.

29 Theron Freese, "The Teaching of Social Problems Courses in High Schools," Unpublished Master's thesis, University of Southern California, 1917.

states of Minnesota and California. In commenting on the length of time certain courses had been given in 1917, the author of the report said:

"The oldest courses mentioned are six years old. These are given in Hammond (Indiana) High School and in the Preparatory School of the University of Utah. Social economics has been given in Long Beach High School eight times, evidently being repeated each semester. Social problems has been given nine semesters at Los Angeles High School. One course has been offered for six semesters; two, for two semesters. One course has been given for four years; two, for three years; one, for two years; two, four times; nine, twice; eight, once; one, for 'several years'; another, no data given. Probably two courses have been given during one or both semesters for six years; one, for four and one-half years; four, for four years; three, for three years; ten, for two years; ten, for one year."

During the first decade of its existence as an independent subject in academies and high schools, sociology made fairly respectable progress at least in some sections of the country. For example, in the high schools belonging to the North Central Association of Colleges and Secondary Schools there were but 41 out of 1119[30] that reported a course in sociology for the school year 1916–17. In 1919–20 there were 298 out of 1180 high schools in this Association reporting such a course.[31] Granting the accuracy of this latter report, it is correct to say that so far as the high schools of the North Central Asso-

[30] Calvin O. Davis, *Accredited Secondary Schools of the North Central Association.* United States Bureau of Education Bulletin, 1919, No. 45, p. 93.
[31] C. O. Davis, "Training for Citizenship in the North Central Association of Secondary Schools," *School Review,* XXVIII (1920), 271.

ciation were concerned, sociology had gained considerable recognition by 1920—nearly one-fourth of the schools in the Association territory offering a course in sociology at this date. So speaking for this territory alone, it is within the bounds of truth to say that the increase between 1911 and 1920 in the number of high-school courses in sociology was somewhat remarkable—from two in 1911–12 to 298 eight years later.

Some evidence is available relative to the number of pupils in the high schools throughout the country pursuing sociology during the school years 1921–22 and 1927–28. This evidence indicates that the situation with respect to the subject in the North Central territory in 1920 was not peculiar to this region. Table XI exhibits the number of academy and high-school pupils pursuing sociology during the scholastic years 1921–22 and 1927–28. It will be observed from the data for 1921–22 that there was a sprinkling of pupils in public high schools and private high schools and academies pursuing sociology in every state in the Union except South Carolina. The data for 1927–28 show that South Carolina later got on the band wagon. During the years represented in Table XI there was a very slight gain in the per cent of pupils in the country at large pursuing sociology. In two states, South Dakota and Oregon, the gain in per cent of pupils pursuing the subject was remarkable and in fifteen states the per cents were less in 1927–28 than in 1921–22. The per cents in two states, Georgia and Mississippi, remained the same. On the whole this table offers no encouragement to the proponents of sociology as an independent subject of study in academies and high schools.

During the 1920's certain studies of the social sciences in the schools were made by individuals and by associations. The findings of these studies supplement the data in the Biennial Surveys of the Office of Education. Table XII contains the

TABLE XI

SOCIOLOGY IN THE PUBLIC HIGH SCHOOLS AND PRIVATE HIGH
SCHOOLS AND ACADEMIES OF CONTINENTAL UNITED STATES
DURING THE SCHOLASTIC YEARS ENDING IN 1922 AND 1928.*

STATE	Schools Offering Sociology				Pupils Pursuing Sociology in Schools Reporting Studies			
	NUMBER		PER CENT		NUMBER		PER CENT	
	1922	1928	1922	1928	1922	1928	1922	1928
Continental U. S.	2327	3088	14.9	18.2	52,853	80,375	2.2	2.5
Alabama......	38	69	16.9	30.2	948	1,644	3.4	4.7
Arizona.......	6	11	14.3	21.5	142	161	2.4	1.3
Arkansas......	25	66	12.5	25.9	523	1,412	2.9	5.4
California.....	39	91	10.4	18.0	1,508	7,736	1.3	3.8
Colorado......	20	60	13.7	32.7	353	3,383	1.3	9.8
Connecticut....	23	11	20.0	7.8	359	293	1.0	.7
Delaware......	1	3	3.7	11.1	7	65	.1	1.1
Florida........	10	44	9.0	25.5	219	760	1.8	2.4
Georgia.......	5	1	2.0	.4	81	84	.2	.2
Idaho.........	46	77	37.7	50.6	740	1,438	6.1	7.3
Illinois........	53	58	6.1	6.3	2,371	1,636	1.4	.7
Indiana.......	29	116	4.1	17.6	578	2,061	.6	1.9
Iowa.........	226	311	28.2	38.3	3,861	5,913	5.0	6.7
Kansas........	50	227	8.5	36.7	1,178	4,240	1.8	5.6
Kentucky.....	20	90	5.9	19.1	276	1,477	1.0	3.7
Louisiana......	6	13	2.8	5.1	57	155	2.9	.4
Maine........	5	6	2.2	2.8	72	267	3.0	1.1
Maryland......	17	13	11.3	7.2	391	278	1.7	.8
Massachusetts..	6	9	1.6	2.3	146	414	.1	.3
Michigan......	36	83	6.7	13.0	544	2,895	.5	2.1
Minnesota.....	175	157	36.7	29.9	2,447	5,326	3.5	6.0
Mississippi....	4	25	2.2	8.8	103	134	.6	.6
Missouri......	257	90	43.4	12.0	3,303	2,565	4.2	2.8
Montana......	70	93	39.3	55.0	635	1,498	3.6	7.3
Nebraska......	24	58	5.1	11.6	632	1,263	1.5	2.5
Nevada.......	1	8	5.8	36.3	21	46	1.2	2.4
New Hampshire	2	17	2.2	12.5	53	374	4.8	2.2
New Jersey....	35	11	16.8	4.4	2,030	630	2.7	.6
New Mexico...	6	23	10.0	23.1	105	336	2.4	3.9
New York.....	6	14	.6	1.4	129	980	.05	.2
North Carolina.	3	8	.8	1.5	46	212	.1	.3
North Dakota..	166	76	51.9	22.3	2,482	982	13.7	5.4
Ohio.........	299	254	30.8	27.7	6,102	7,043	3.9	3.6
Oklahoma.....	78	150	20.7	33.2	1,218	2,757	2.8	5.3
Oregon........	24	58	10.9	26.9	511	8,551	1.7	24.6
Pennsylvania...	135	97	13.3	9.6	6,334	5,422	3.4	2.3

STATE	Schools Offering Sociology				Pupils Pursuing Sociology in Schools Reporting Studies			
	NUMBER		PER CENT		NUMBER		PER CENT	
	1922	1928	1922	1928	1922	1928	1922	1928
Rhode Island...	2	3	5.5	8.5	90	41	7.2	.2
South Carolina.	0	3	0	2.0	0	80	0	.5
South Dakota..	53	156	18.9	58.8	724	2,375	4.5	10.6
Tennessee......	15	3	6.0	.9	226	69	8.5	.2
Texas.........	15	23	2.5	4.4	255	1,301	.3	1.4
Utah.........	32	28	56.1	47.4	1,034	1,233	6.8	7.8
Vermont......	5	8	5.4	9.4	179	223	1.8	2.9
Virginia.......	67	28	13.7	8.9	991	755	2.6	1.6
Washington....	25	82	8.5	28.1	1,137	2,152	2.3	3.4
West Virginia..	51	74	28.5	34.6	1,149	1,998	4.8	6.9
Wisconsin.....	109	162	26.6	40.5	2,284	3,070	3.2	3.7
Wyoming......	14	20	29.1	28.1	198	355	3.5	4.5

* Based on data in *Biennial Survey of Education* for 1920-22 and for 1926-28.

data on sociology which six of these studies revealed. It will be observed that the per cents herein are much more favorable to sociology than those in Table XI. It is difficult to explain the discrepancy in per cent in study No. 1 in Table XII and reports for the country as a whole for 1921–22 in Table XI, the same year and the same general territory being represented in each. According to other existing data the per cent in study No. 1 in Table XII is more representative of the actual situation. There are at hand facts on the number of high schools in the North Central Association offering sociology and the number of pupils pursuing the subject for the years ending in 1925 and 1930. These data are exhibited in Table XIII. They show that in general the per cent of high schools in the North Central Association offering sociology was considerably higher in 1929–30 than it was for the country at large in 1927–28. Furthermore, Table XIII shows that there were but three states, Arizona, Missouri, and North Dakota, in which the per cent of pupils pursuing sociology decreased between 1924-25 and 1929-30. In North Dakota and Missouri the decrease was caused by the introduction of a course in problems of American democracy which course it may be remarked was

TABLE XII

SOCIOLOGY IN CERTAIN HIGH SCHOOLS DURING THE 1920'S AS REVEALED IN SPECIAL REGIONAL AND STATE INVESTIGATIONS

SOURCE OF DATA	DATE	NUMBER OF SCHOOLS	NUMBER OFFER-ING	PER CENT OFFER-ING
1. H. H. Moore, *Status of Certain Social Studies in High Schools* . .	1921-22	6624	1666	25.15
2. W. S. Monroe and J. O. Foster, *The Status of the Social Sciences in the High Schools of the North Central Association* . . .	1921-22	475	156	32.84
3. Edgar Dawson, *The History Inquiry*	1923-24	2404	276	11.48
4. C. O. Davis, "The North Central Association Quinquennial Study," *The School Review*, XXXIII (1925)	1924-25	1571	282	17.95
5. Emery N. Ferris, *The Rural High School* (Rural and semi-rural schools)	1924-25	404	179	44.30
6. C. C. Brown, "Proceedings of the Commission on Secondary Schools," *North Central Quarterly*, V (1930)	1929-30	2226	675	30.32

by no means void of material from sociology. So it seems within the bounds of truth to say that in 1930 sociology as an independent subject of study in academies and high schools was still struggling to hold its own, gaining ground in some states and losing in others.

Even though sociology as an independent subject of study in the high school had attained voting age by 1933, it had not taken on the attributes of maturity when judged by the num-

ber of high schools in which it was offered or by the number
of pupils pursuing it. As long as less than three pupils in a

TABLE XIII

SOCIOLOGY IN THE PUBLIC HIGH SCHOOLS IN THE NORTH CENTRAL
ASSOCIATION IN 1925 AND 1930.*

STATE	Number and Per Cent Offering Sociology				Number and Per Cent of Pupils Pursuing			
	NUMBER		PER CENT		NUMBER		PER CENT	
	1925	1930	1925	1930	1925	1930	1925	1930
1. Arizona......	1	5	3.7	14.2	52	78	.73	.6
2. Arkansas....	9	18	29.0	31.0	247	614	2.95	4.3
3. Colorado....	14	39	21.2	42.3	523	821	2.34	2.5
4. Illinois......	19	35	9.0	11.1	804	1337	.60	.6
5. Indiana......	15	16	17.6	16.0	461	669	.91	1.0
6. Iowa........	24	57	22.0	42.1	691	1702	1.68	3.3
7. Kansas......	24	64	21.4	43.5	555	1876	1.45	4.1
8. Michigan....	12	50	9.8	27.3	365	1323	.57	1.2
9. Minnesota...	23	30	29.4	30.3	1201	1996	3.65	4.0
10. Missouri.....	†	44	†	36.6	1392	1634	3.74	2.8
11. Montana.....	14	25	43.7	56.8	341	828	3.20	5.4
12. Nebraska....	†	17	†	14.9	301	598	1.25	1.6
13. New Mexico.	4	13	13.3	46.4	100	252	1.91	3.5
14. North Dakota	†	2	†	2.7	795	40	7.40	.3
15. Ohio........	64	124	31.2	42.0	2851	5015	2.80	3.3
16. Oklahoma...	21	35	25.9	32.7	392	984	1.39	2.5
17. South Dakota	20	42	52.6	62.6	477	550	5.21	3.9
18. West Virginia	‡	37	‡	52.1	‡	1380	‡	5.5
19. Wisconsin....	11	25	11.4	21.5	313	866	.65	1.3
20. Wyoming....	7	7	31.8	25.9	118	218	2.13	3.0

* Charles C. Brown, "Proceedings of the Commission on Secondary Schools," *North Central Association Quarterly*, V (1930), 99, 113; and Calvin O. Davis, *Our Secondary Schools* (1925), pp. 24, 45, and 76.
† Data imperfect.
‡ West Virginia was not yet a member of the Association.

hundred, considering the country as a whole, were being exposed to it yearly, the sum total of its influence remained very
small. To account for these facts the youthfulness of sociology
as a discipline must be considered. When the subject entered
the high school as an independent subject of study it had not

been taught at all in the colleges and universities of this country more than thirty-five years and to any great extent over ten years. Other factors tending to slow up the progress of sociology in the schools were (1) the lack of teachers prepared to teach the subject; (2) the contention among college people that the subject was too difficult for high-school pupils; (3) the general lack of understanding among school boards and school administrators as to the true nature of the subject; (4) the overcrowded condition of the high-school curriculum when sociology sought admittance thereto; and (5) especially since 1920, the fact that sociology had to dwell in the same house in which community civics and problems of American democracy lived. As has been pointed out elsewhere, these two subjects, both popular in some parts of the country, drew very heavily on the field of sociology for their content. When state departments of education recommended, as sixteen were doing in 1930,[32] the course in problems of American democracy, nothing was said about a course in sociology. So with all of these handicaps to overcome, it may be said that sociology as a high-school subject has had to struggle along with the cards stacked against it. While it has achieved some success, it has touched the lives of relatively few high-school pupils.

THE CONTENT OF SOCIOLOGY ON THE SECONDARY-SCHOOL LEVEL

From the very beginning of sociology as a high-school subject, suitable content for young people of high-school age has been one of the chief considerations of those interested in the subject. Certain almost insurmountable difficulties with respect to content have been encountered. One of these is the differentiation of the course in sociology from the course in

[32] John C. West, *op. cit.*, p. 61.

community civics generally offered in the top grade of the traditional eight-year elementary school or the bottom year of the traditional four-year high school. Before this difficulty can be appreciated, it is necessary to know the general nature of the content of some of the first courses in high-school sociology. Fortunately there is at hand an outline of one of the first courses in sociology ever given in a high school in this country. While the outline as it appears below was in use in the high school of Mankato, Minnesota, during the school year 1914–15, it is substantially the one used three years previously in the high school of Jacksonville, Illinois. The reader will discover in the outline many topics usually found in a present-day course in community civics.

THE MAIN FEATURES OF A COURSE IN HIGH–SCHOOL SOCIOLOGY
GIVEN IN MANKATO HIGH SCHOOL, MANKATO, MINNESOTA,
DURING THE SCHOOL YEAR, 1914–15

I. Introduction.—Reasons for studying sociology.

II. Institutions of Society.—Family; government; church; school.

III. The Family.—Historical development; importance as primary social organization; training of the individual in the home; importance of stability in the home; divorce and its evils.

IV. Growth of Population.—Old theories; economic basis of growth; social basis of growth.

V. Population in the United States.—Rate of increase, present and past; distribution and density; rural and urban; races and sexes; present tendencies.

VI. Immigration.—Causes in general; immigration to the United States; restrictions on immigration.

VII. The Problem of the City.—Causes of growth of large cities; moral conditions in city life; social life in the great city; political conditions; proposed remedies.

VIII. Child Labor.—Extent; history; causes; effects; remedies; present tendencies.

IX. Poverty and Pauperism.—Extent; causes; prevention through education; direct relief and indirect relief.

X. Dependents and Defectives and their Care.—Blind; deaf; feeble-minded; insane.

XI. Crime and its Punishment.—Definition of crime; extent and cost of, in the United States; causes; methods of treatment; reform in prison management; juvenile offenders and their care.

XII. The Liquor Problem.—Present status of the traffic and the industry; effects of the traffic; control and abolition; the temperance movement.

XIII. Education and Social Progress.—Education for life and its meaning; the efficient man and his relation to progress; education and prevention of social problems; education and progress in the past; present demands of society upon the individual.[33]

There would be little left of the foregoing set-up if all of the material generally included in a present-day course in community civics were extracted therefrom. Should one do this, it would all go but the Introduction. However, inasmuch as the outline was made in the days of pioneering in high-school sociology, one should not be too critical of it. As time passed and a small demand was created for texts in the field, a few began to appear. After they did appear, the content of sociology in the high school was largely dictated by them. For this reason one must go to the available texts in elemen-

[33] W. G. Bate, "An Experiment in Teaching a Course in Elementary Sociology," *School Review*, XXIII (1915), 337–340.

tary sociology for a picture of the content of courses on the high-school and academy level at any specific date.

In 1929, two independent analyses of textbooks in sociology intended for use in high schools and academies were made. Nine texts were used in one of these analyses and thirteen in the other. The topics revealed and the number of pages and

TABLE XIV

NUMBER AND PER CENT OF PAGES DEVOTED TO CERTAIN TOPICS BY NINE TEXTBOOKS IN SOCIOLOGY*

TOPICS	TOTAL PAGES DEVOTED TO	PER CENT OF GRAND TOTAL OF PAGES DEVOTED TO
1. General, social theory and origins.......	476	15.03
2. Economics.............................	459	14.49
3. Defectives, crime, poverty..............	384	12.12
4. Civic problems........................	362	11.43
5. Growth of the population..............	349	11.02
6. Family origins and problems............	309	9.76
7. Education.............................	297	9.38
8. Government...........................	235	7.42
9. Race problems........................	108	3.41
10. Rural problems........................	78	2.46
11. Heredity and environment..............	63	1.99
12. Evolution and psychology..............	47	1.48

* John Crouch, "The Results of an Objective Test in High School Sociology in the State of South Dakota," p. 3. Unpublished Master's thesis, University of Colorado, 1929.

per cent of total pages devoted to each in the nine texts analyzed are shown in Table XIV. With respect to the topics in this table, the investigator remarked as follows:

"In addition to the above classifications there are two hundred seventeen pages of introductions and similar material that were not classified. They are therefore left out of the reckoning in figuring percentages.

"Under the first heading there is a considerable range of material. Social theories, origins, objectives and subject-matter are usually discussed. . . .

"Material that is classified as economics forms one of the

TABLE XV

GRAND TOTAL AND PER CENT OF GRAND TOTAL OF PAGES DEVOTED TO EACH OF CERTAIN TOPICS IN THIRTEEN TEXT-BOOKS IN SOCIOLOGY.*

TOPICS	GRAND TOTAL PAGES DEVOTED TO	PER CENT OF GRAND TOTAL OF PAGES DEVOTED TO
1. Population.............................	350.5	11.34
2. Immigration...........................	380.0	12.30
3. Child Labor............................	56.5	1.82
4. Women in Industry.....................	35.5	1.15
5. Sweating System.......................	19.5	0.63
6. Labor.................................	54.5	1.76
7. Unemployment.........................	54.0	1.74
8. Blind and Deaf........................	28.5	0.92
9. Feeble Minded.........................	100.0	3.23
10. Crime.................................	161.0	5.21
11. Marriage and Divorce..................	165.0	5.34
12. Liquor................................	55.5	1.79
13. Poverty...............................	129.5	4.19
14. Conservation of Natural Resources......	41.5	1.34
15. Conservation of Plant and Animal Life...	16.5	0.53
16. Conservation of Human Life............	22.5	0.72
17. Family................................	159.0	5.14
18. Races.................................	244.0	7.89
19. Education.............................	112.5	3.64
20. City..................................	68.0	2.20
21. Child Welfare.........................	46.5	1.50
22. Social Progress.......................	130.5	4.22
23. Crowds and Mobs......................	9.0	0.29
24. Sectionalism..........................	9.0	0.29
25. Industrialism..........................	111.5	3.60
26. Law Obedience........................	19.0	0.61
27. Personal Competition..................	9.0	0.29
28. Religion..............................	82.5	2.67
29. Social Classes.........................	17.5	0.56
30. Wealth Distribution...................	18.0	0.58
31. Social Control........................	83.5	2.70

TOPICS	GRAND TOTAL PAGES DEVOTED TO	PER CENT OF GRAND TOTAL OF PAGES DEVOTED TO
32. Morality............................	13.0	0.42
33. Alien Americanization.................	9.0	0.29
34. Community and State..................	25.0	0.80
35. Woman Suffrage......................	39.5	1.28
36. Beauty..............................	1.5	0.05
37. Communication......................	7.5	0.24
38. Transportation.......................	4.5	0.14
39. Illegitimacy..........................	25.0	0.80
40. Rural Life...........................	30.0	0.97
41. Public Health........................	105.0	3.39
42. Use of Leisure Time..................	19.0	0.61

* J. Kynett Haeheln, "The Construction of X Units in Social Problems," pp. 6 f. Unpublished Master's thesis, University of Iowa, 1929.

largest items. In several cases a chapter or more is devoted directly to economics. In others, it is used as a background to various social problems such as poverty and dependence. . . .

"Under the topic, 'Growth of Population,' migration, immigration, birth and death rates and the growth of cities are treated. In considering cities, only the factors bearing upon the congestion of the population are considered. Social problems caused by overcrowding, the ability of man to live in great cities and problems peculiar to urban populations are considered under civic problems.

"The negro problem constitutes the large part of the pages allotted to race problems. In one text the Chinese and Japanese problem is considered under race problems, in other texts it is treated under migration.

"Evolution and psychology are found in a separate heading in only one text. They are used as a background for social origins and customs.

"Education and government are considered largely as social agencies. Their connection with social problems is very close but the difference was great enough to warrant a separate classification."

From the analysis of thirteen texts in sociology, the topics listed in Table XV, along with total pages and per cent of grand total pages devoted to each, were revealed. Four of the texts included in this analysis were among those in the analysis mentioned above. One of the books used was a volume of readings in social problems. Eight of the others had the expression "Social Problems" in their titles. It is interesting to note the relatively heavy emphasis in the texts on population and immigration—almost 24 per cent of the total pages in them being devoted to these topics. Crime, marriage and divorce, the family, and races combined received a total of 23.4 per cent of the pages. Thus it turns out that 47 per cent of the pages in the thirteen texts represented in Table XV was devoted to but six of the 42 topics therein. It seems from these data that the authors of these books wrote a little about many things and a little more about a few things.

On the basis of the results obtained in the foregoing analysis of thirteen texts in sociology and social problems the following large divisions of a course in high-school sociology were proposed.

     I. The Study of Society.
    II. Problems of Population.
   III. Problems of the Family.
   IV. Problems of Sanitation and Health.
    V. Problems of the State.
   VI. American Race Problems.
  VII. Problems of Organized Industry.
 VIII. Problems of Poverty.

Twelve of the fourteen divisions in this proposed course in sociology are concerned with material frequently found in courses in problems of American democracy. In fact the protagonists of the course in problems of American democracy would accept the foregoing proposals for a course in sociology *in toto*. Thus it seems that those in search of suitable content for a course in high-school sociology during the 1920's were between the devil and the deep sea. They could get little respect for a course which was a repetition of the content of community civics and they could get less respect in some quarters at least for a course in sociology made up almost wholly of the customary content of problems of American democracy.

One more analysis of textbooks in sociology for the secondary schools remains to be presented. This analysis was completed in 1931 and included eight texts, all of which except one were published or revised between 1925 and 1930. In this analysis, then, one has a late edition of the content of high-school sociology. The topics discovered in this investigation along with the emphasis in terms of total pages devoted to each appear in Table XVI. It seems from this and the foregoing analysis of textbooks in sociology for use in the secondary school that a distinctive content for the subject has never been found. Should what is now taught in economics, community civics, and problems of American democracy be

TABLE XVI

TOTAL NUMBER OF PAGES AND PER CENT OF GRAND TOTAL OF
PAGES DEVOTED TO CERTAIN TOPICS IN EIGHT TEXTBOOKS IN
SOCIOLOGY.*

TOPICS	TOTAL PAGES DEVOTED TO	PER CENT OF GRAND TOTAL PAGES DEVOTED TO
1. Society and its Background, Social Processes, Origins, Organization, etc.	665	22.46
2. The State as an Institution	324	10.94
3. Industry, Child Welfare, Women in Industry	283	9.56
4. The Family as an Institution	238	8.04
5. Poverty and Pauperism	151	5.09
6. Population	127	4.29
7. Crime	127	4.29
8. Education	118	3.98
9. Dependents, such as Feebleminded, Insane, etc.	117	3.95
10. The City Problem	112	3.78
11. Immigration	102	3.44
12. The Negro Race Problem	77	2.60
13. Prohibition	54	1.82
14. The Rural Problem	53	1.79
15. The Church, Religion	45	1.51
16. Socialism, Anarchism, Communism	40	1.35
17. Moral Problems	22	.74
18. Miscellaneous	306	10.33

* A. B. Grimes, "The Sociology of Newspapers," p. 101. Unpublished Master's thesis, State University of Iowa, 1931.

deleted from the content of high-school sociology as revealed
in textbooks, there would be little left.

III

SOCIAL SCIENCE AS A SUBJECT OF STUDY IN ELEMENTARY AND HIGH SCHOOLS

During the second half of the nineteenth century social
science dreamed of becoming a special social discipline. The

sudden rise of sociology kept such a dream from coming true. In recent years social science has attempted to become an independent subject of study in elementary and high schools under such captions as "unified social science," "integrated social science," "exploratory social science" and the like. The outcome of both the dreams and the attempts of social science since about 1850 are briefly considered below.

USES OF THE EXPRESSIONS "SOCIAL SCIENCE," "SOCIAL SCIENCES," AND "SOCIAL STUDIES"

Since 1920 there has arisen much confusion in the field of the social sciences because of the indefinite meanings which have been attached to the expressions "social science," "social sciences," and "social studies." During these years each of these expressions has been used with a variety of meanings attached thereto.

There are at hand examples in which the expression "social science" has been used: (1) interchangeably with sociology; (2) co-ordinately with social studies; (3) co-ordinately with history; (4) interchangeably with social sciences; (5) as a name for a so-called unified course in the social sciences; (6) as an encyclopedic term for all of the social disciplines; and (7) interchangeably with social sciences and social studies.

It has long been the practice of some well informed individuals to use the expression "social science" interchangeably with sociology. Writing in 1899 a teacher of economics commented as follows:

"One proposed disposition of economic study requires incidental notice at this point. It is to put social science into the curriculum, displacing economics or allowing it to remain only as a division of social science. There are several textbooks on social science for high-school use, and the study is required in the normal schools of Minnesota. This movement must meet all the arguments that are made against teaching economics in the schools, and its means of defence are at present scanty. Sociology as a coherent science began only with Herbert Spencer; it is still in the formative stage; that which is of permanent value cannot easily be distinguished from the rubbish; and the literature available for students is limited." [34]

In a book by two well-known English sociologists, published in 1932, one finds the expression, "But social science or sociology is neither so clearly marked off as chemistry. . . ." [35] Tradition is a powerful determinant.

The use of social science synonymously with social studies is found in a chapter in the *Fourth Yearbook*[36] of the Department of Superintendence which opens thus: *"Social Science—* the science of getting along with people—is coming to be recognized as an essential part of every child's education." At another place in this chapter is this expression: *Social Science Department*—"A *social studies* department in junior high school should . . . etc."

The use of the expression social science co-ordinately with the word "history" is not at all uncommon. One writer says, "The increasing dissatisfaction with the traditional formulations of the facts of history and social science has stimulated a search for causes in the human motives that make history and determine the phenomena of social science." [37]   In a

[34] Frederick R. Clow, "Economics as a School Study," *Economic Studies,* IV (1899), 223.

[35] Sidney and Beatrice Webb, *Methods of Social Study,* p. 1. New York: Longmans, Green and Co., 1932.

[36] Pp. 323 and 354.

[37] James Williams, *The Foundations of Social Science,* p. vii. New York: Alfred A. Knopf, 1920.

twelve-year program in the social sciences for the state of Pennsylvania published in the early 1920's appeared this statement: "This program insists that history and social science are of co-ordinate rank and importance; the one giving us a perspective as to how mankind has slowly and painfully learned to lead the group life; the other giving us a sort of cross-section view of how man is now leading the group life, through the various organizations and activities that together constitute present-day civilization." [38]

It is difficult to conceive of the expression "social science" being used interchangeably with "social sciences." Be this as it may, such a use is to be found. In a discussion of the topic "The Social Sciences and Education" appears this statement: "The main endeavor in this chapter is to exhibit the interrelations of Social Science with education by presenting briefly the current treatment of certain educational problems which are outstandingly social in nature. In certain instances education leans so directly on the social sciences that little more can be attempted than a bare statement of the educational problem with the appropriate reference to the social science treatment." [39]

The use of the expression "social science" as a name for a so-called unified course in the social sciences is very common. Many examples of this use are at hand. In a study of ninety-five junior high schools in Ohio in 1927–28, it was found that twelve of them had adopted a unified course in the social sciences and were calling it "Social Science." [40]

[38] Edgar Dawson, *The Social Studies in Civic Education.* United States Bureau of Education Bulletin, 1923, No. 23, p. 3.

[39] W. F. Ogburn and Alexander Goldenweiser, *The Social Sciences and Their Interrelations,* p. 414. Boston: Houghton Mifflin Co., 1927.

[40] Clarence L. Stingley, "Curriculum Practices in Ninety-Five Junior High Schools of Ohio," pp. 18 f. Unpublished Master's thesis, The Ohio State University, 1928.

Speaking of the use of social science as an encyclopedic
term for all of the social disciplines a sociologist once remarked, "Social Science is preferable to sociology as an encyclopedic term for all of the social disciplines and is now used
by the best authorities." [41] An example of the use of the expression "Social Science" interchangeably with social sciences
and social studies is found in a recent monograph in which
the various courses offered in the social sciences appear as
"Social Science." The first item in the Table of Contents is
"General Introduction to the Social Sciences." The first item
under the Introduction is "Present Tendencies in the Teaching
of the Social Studies." [42]

In the use of the expression "social sciences" there seems to
exist the same general confusion that is exhibited above with
respect to the use of the expression "social science." One of the
common uses of the expression is as a co-ordinate with history.
For example, "History and the social sciences, directly concerned with human affairs, should be adapted to the full for
the development of the balanced life of the individual and
the community." [43] Also "The contention that the historian
must be thoroughly equipped with knowledge of the social
sciences is a much more recent position. The social sciences
have only recently arrived at that state where their subject-
matter is sufficiently reliable to serve as a dependable foundation for historical insight and analysis." [44]

Other uses of the expression "social sciences" met in the
literature on various aspects of social living are (1) as an

[41] C. A. Ellwood, *Sociology and Its Psychological Aspects,* p. 4, note 1.
[42] *Social Sciences.* Senior High School, Grades Ten, Eleven, and Twelve.
Denver, Colo.: Public Schools, 1931.
[43] Thomas J. Jones, *Essentials of Civilization,* p. 150. New York: Henry
Holt and Company, 1929.
[44] Harry E. Barnes, "The Essentials of the New History," *Historical Outlook,* XVIII (1927), 202.

encyclopedic term for all of the sciences concerned with sociological phenomena, and (2) as the name of a course of study in which the individual social sciences maintain their identity, meaning a course in which no deliberated attempt is made to unify the various social sciences. For example, *A Course of Study in the Social Sciences*[45] means a course in which civics, history, and commercial geography keep their identity. An example of the encyclopedic use of the expression reads: "The *social sciences* are those sciences which are devoted to the investigation of particular classes of sociological phenomena, or, to particular aspects of these phenomena."[46]

The uses that have been made of the expression "social studies" since its first appearance in this country have been as varied and even more confusing than the uses of the expressions "social science" and "social sciences." During the middle 1880's two books, each with the expression "social studies" in its title were copyrighted.[47] In both of these volumes the expression was used to name a body of somewhat heterogeneous material, ranging from women as nurses to the religious aspects of socialism. There is certainly nothing in the original use of the expression in this country that suggests a clear-cut meaning. When the expression first appeared in the vocabulary of education it was used as an encyclopedic term to include civics, economics, and sociology. As early as 1905 there appeared an article in the magazine, *Southern Workman,* in which the work done in civics, economics, and sociology in Hampton Institute, Hampton, Virginia was described under

[45] Chicago Public Schools, Bulletin SS-789, Junior High School. Chicago: Board of Education, 1931.

[46] I. W. Howerth, "Sociology in a Teachers College Curriculum," *Education,* XLVIII (1928), 562.

[47] Sarah K. Bolton, *Social Studies in England.* Boston: Lathrop and Co., 1885; and R. H. Newton, *Social Studies.* New York: G. P. Putnam's Sons, 1886.

the title "Social Studies." At this date, the title of the individual in charge of these subjects in this school was "Instructor in Social Studies." [48] In 1911, the expression was also used as an encyclopedic term to include history, civics, commercial geography, economics, politics, and sociology. In a paper read at this date is found this expression: "In a four-year high-school course, on the four-study program, give one period for the four years to language and literature; one to science and mathematics; one to history, civics, commercial geography, economics, politics, and sociology, and one period to various electives. That gives to required *social studies,* including history, one-fourth the time; and they deserve it." [49]

In 1915, there was published by the state of North Dakota a course of study entitled, *An Outline of Social Study for Elementary Schools.* The object of this outline was to suggest and organize a body of material from the field of the social sciences similar in purpose and spirit to that very generally found in an outline of nature study. To those who made the outline "social study" was to the field of the social sciences what nature study was to the fields of the natural and physical sciences. The outline was not intended to displace history and civics, but rather to supplement them.[50]

A knowledge of the fact that the chairman of the Committee on Social Studies of the Commission on the Reorganization of Secondary Education of the National Education Association was the instructor in social studies at Hampton Institute in

[48] Thomas J. Jones, *Social Studies in the Hampton Curriculum.* Hampton, Va.: Hampton Institute Press, 1908.

[49] O. L. Manchester, "A High School Course in Economics," *Papers Presented at the Second Conference on the Teaching of Economics,* p. 52. Chicago: The University of Chicago Press, 1911.

[50] "An Outline of Social Study for Elementary Schools," *Course of Study for the Elementary Schools of South Dakota,* pp. 139 ff. Pierre, S. D.: State Supt. of Public Instruction, 1915.

1905, makes it easy to account for the use of the expression "social studies" in naming the Committee. On the publication of the final report of this Committee in 1916 the expression the "social studies" passed into general circulation. The meaning attached to it by this Committee was practically the same as that illustrated in the quotation from Manchester above, except that geography instead of commercial geography was included in the list of social studies.

It will be observed that the meaning attached to the expression "social studies" by the Committee mentioned above permits the individual subjects of history, civics, geography, economics, and sociology to maintain their identity. Interesting to relate, the expression finally came to mean exactly the opposite, namely, to denote a body of integrated material in which all subjects lost their identity. Note the following statement: "More recently, in recognition of the fact that under modern conditions a citizen cannot be intelligent upon the problems he is forced to meet in daily life without at least an elementary knowledge of the social sciences, the term social studies has come into use, to designate an integrated program of history, economics, and geography, which will enable pupils to comprehend life in Society." [51]

The use of the expression "social studies" to name an integrated course of study became more or less common during the 1920's. For example, one notes the following titles of courses of study in which no subject maintains its identity, *The Social Studies for Grades V, VI, VII, and VIII*[52] and *Social Studies for the Schools of Ann Arbor, Michigan, Grades Three to Six*[53] and *Social Studies for Kindergarten and Grades*

[51] Gertrude Hartman, "The Social Studies," *Progressive Education,* II (1925), 208.
[52] Curriculum Bulletin, No. 5. Dayton, Ohio: Public Schools, 1927.
[53] Ann Arbor, Mich.: Board of Education, 1929.

I–VI.[54] It would seem from these examples that contradictions are no deterrent to individuals who wish to put a fairly new expression to work. No one to date, however, has ever been able to explain how the same expression can legitimately have two meanings that are exactly opposite.

As used by some the expression "social studies" has recently overstepped the boundary of the social sciences proper and taken the entire curriculum for its field. When the expression is made to include all those studies which are the products of social co-operation its boundaries have been immensely enlarged.[55] Used thus the expression "the social studies" becomes a synonym for the curriculum. Inasmuch as the meanings of the expression have actually become contradictory in practice it would seem that the time has arrived for those interested primarily in the social sciences to quit using it to mean primarily history, civics, economics, and sociology, for evidently such a use is too restricted. If the social studies are all of the studies in the curriculum, the expression certainly cannot be correctly applied solely to one group of studies.

With respect to the expressions "social science" and "social sciences" it would seem that a distinction in their use ought to be made. When John Stuart Mill originated the expression "social science" about 1836 he declared that the time was ripe for marking off from scientific and philosophical subjects a general social science. As a name for this new subject Mill suggested such expressions as "natural history of society," "social philosophy," "speculative politics," "social economy," and "social science." [56] It is not possible to go back to what Mill had in mind; for, if one did, the expression social science

---

[54] St. Louis, Mo.: Board of Education, 1926.

[55] C. H. Judd, "Social Studies in the High School," *Junior-Senior High School Clearing House*, IV (1930), 572–574.

[56] *Encyclopædia Britannica* (14th ed.), XX, 911.

at the present time would have no meaning at all. Should one confine its meaning, as Mill did, to the common matrix out of which the individual social sciences originally have come, there would be no matrix left after the last individual social science arose, therefore no social science. For this reason it seems that a use other than the historical one needs to be found for the expression. Such a use might be discovered in the field of the natural sciences. If the expression could always be used to mean in the field of the social sciences what biology means in the field of the natural sciences, much confusion would be avoided. Or one could stick to the generic use of the expression and use it as the words "fruit," "vegetable," or "animal" are used. Used thus one would speak of social sciences and a social science just as one speaks of fruits and a fruit. This use would at the same time take care of the expression "social sciences," which would simply become the plural of a social science just as fruits is the plural of a fruit.

THE MOVEMENT FOR THE ESTABLISHMENT OF SOCIAL SCIENCE
AS A SPECIAL DISCIPLINE

Social science as the name of a special discipline actually had its beginning in this country with the publication in 1859–60 of H. C. Carey's *Principles of Social Science* in three volumes. In these volumes the author now and then formally defined social science. For example, in Volume I, page 63, he said, "Social science treats of man in his efforts for the maintenance and improvement of his condition, and may now be defined to be the science of the laws which govern man in his efforts to secure for himself the highest individuality, and the greatest power of association with his fellow-men." The last chapter of Volume III is entitled "Of Social Science." Near the close of this chapter is this significant statement:

"Science, as we are told, is the interpreter of nature. It reverently inquires, what there is, and why it is that such things are. It listens that it may know. It seeks for light. It knocks, that it may obtain communication—its duty being then performed when it has recorded the processes of nature, and accepted them as true. That department which is denominated Social Science, treats of the laws which govern man in the effort for developing his own powers, and thereby obtaining entire control over the great forces of nature—at each step gained, turning her batteries against herself, with a view to make her subjugation more complete. The object of its teachers is that of indicating what have been the obstacles which, thus far, have prevented progress, and the means by which they may be diminished, if not removed."

Carey was much concerned over what he felt that a study of the laws of social science would do. In commenting on this aspect of the matter he said:

"Careful study of those laws would satisfy—
"SOVEREIGNS, that the maintenance of peace, and a studious respect for the rights of others, was the surest road to power and influence for the communities in whose lead it is their fortune to be placed:
"NATIONS, that every invasion of the rights of others must be attended with diminished power to protect their own:
"LEGISLATORS, that their duty was limited to the removal of obstacles to association among the people with whose destinies they were charged, among the most prominent of

which would be found those resulting from the failure to recognize the existence of a perfect harmony of international interests:

"FARMERS, that the road to prosperity for themselves and their children, was to be found in the adoption of measures looking to their emancipation from the oppressive tax of transportation, and to the development of the powers of their land:

"WORKINGMEN, that the more perfect their own respect for the rights of property, and the greater the tendency towards harmony and peace, the more rapid must be the growth of the productive power, with correspondent increase in their own *proportion* of the larger quantity of commodities produced:

"FREEMEN, that true liberty is inconsistent with interferences with the rights of others, and that in the most perfect subordination is to be found the road to harmony, peace, and freedom:

"FREE-TRADE ADVOCATES, that the more varied the production of a community, the greater must be the commerce in the bosom of nations, and the greater their power to maintain commerce with the world:

"ADVOCATES OF WOMEN'S RIGHTS, that the road towards elevation of the sex, lies in the direction of that varied industry which makes demand for all the distinctive qualities of woman:

"ANTI-SLAVERY ADVOCATES, that freedom comes with the diversification of pursuits which make demand for all the various human powers, and that slavery is the necessary consequence of a system which looks to an exclusive agriculture:

"DISCIPLES OF MR. MALTHUS, that the Creator had provided self-adjusting laws, regulating the movement of population; that the treasury of nature was unlimited in extent; that demand produced supply; and, that the power to make demand increased with increase in the number of mankind:

"PHILOSOPHERS, that war, pestilence, and famine, were the result of man's errors, and not of errors of the Creator—the Great Being, to whom we are indebted for existence, having instituted no laws tending to thwart the objects of man's creation:

"REFORMERS, that nature always works slowly and gently, when she desires that man shall profit by her action, and that man would do well to follow in the same direction—one of the greatest of all precepts being found in those two most simple words—*festina lente:*

"STATESMEN, that power and responsibility went hand in hand together; that upon their action depended the decision of the great question, whether those whose destinies had been committed to their care, should go forward in the direction of the real MAN, master over nature and master of himself, or decline in that of the mere animal having the form of man, treated of in Ricardo-Malthusian books; and that failure to qualify themselves for the proper exercise of the powers confided to them, was a crime, for the effects of which they must answer to their fellow-men, and to Him from whom that power had been derived:

"CHRISTIANS, that the foundation of Christianity and of Social Science is found in the great precept—ALL THINGS WHATSOEVER YE WOULD THAT MEN SHOULD DO TO YOU, DO YE EVEN SO TO THEM." [57]

In going through these rambling and repetitious volumes it

[57] *Principles of Social Science,* III, 469 ff. Philadelphia: Carey and Hart, 1860.

is evident to the reader that Carey was not dealing with what is now orthodox history, economics, or political science. (There was no sociology when he wrote.) In the treatments of such topics as "Man, the Subject of Social Science," "The Occupation of the Earth," and "The Formation of Society" one finds material that could be designated historical. Subjects like "Wealth," "Production and Consumption," "Distribution," and "Competition" suggest present-day economics. The fact that Carey had published a book entitled *Principles of Political Economy* in 1837 explains the large emphasis on economic topics in these volumes under consideration. There are, moreover, materials included in the volumes that seem foreign to present-day economics, sociology, political science, and history. For example, the whole of Volume II was devoted to "Vital Changes in the Form of Matter" and "The Instruments of Association." In Volume I considerable space was devoted to "Changes in Matter in Place."

While Carey's volumes must have been abstract, heavy and uninviting to the general reader of the 1860's, they seem to have been read by the *intelligentsia* of the day. In their attempts to put Carey's ideas into practice his followers organized in 1865 an association known as "The American Social Science Association," the objects of which, as set forth in the constitution being:

"To aid the development of social science, and to guide the public mind to the best practical means of promoting the amendment of laws, the advancement of education, the prevention and repression of crime, the reformation of criminals, and the progress of public morality, the adoption of sanitary regulations, and the diffusion of sound principles on the questions of economy, trade, and finance. It will give attention to pauperism and the topics related thereto; including the responsibility of the well endowed and successful, the wise and educated, the honest and respectable, for the failures of others. It will aim to bring together the various societies and individuals now interested in these objects, for the purpose of obtaining, by discussion, the real elements of truth; by which doubts are removed, conflicting opinions harmonized, and a common ground afforded for treating wisely the great social problems of the day." [58]

Soon after the organization of the foregoing association, a disciple of Carey, R. E. Thompson, began in 1868 an independent course in social science at the University of Pennsylvania. Professor Sumner established a similar course at Yale in 1872 and like courses were offered in the University of Missouri in 1876, Columbia University in 1878, University of Michigan in 1880, and Cornell University in 1885.[59] This movement for setting up courses in social science in higher institutions of learning reached its zenith about 1890. It could not survive the competition of the new subject known as sociology. When this subject annexed to its domain courses on criminology, charities, immigration, labor problems, and social legislation, the courses in social science no longer had an independent content.

Before the movement for social science as an independent discipline collapsed there was formulated an elaborate outline of the content in which it was interested. In 1886, a special committee of the American Social Science Association reported the following topics as suitable for university and college lectures as well as conferences on social science. The

[58] F. B. Sanborn, "The Work of Social Science, Past and Present," *Journal of Social Science*, VIII (1876), 25.
[59] Edwin R. A. Seligman, *Encyclopædia of the Social Sciences*, I, 339.

topics were organized in terms of the five departments of the association.

I. Department of Public Education.
   1. The Relation of Government to Education.
   2. The Course and Object of Education.
   3. Institutions of Education.
   4. Pedagogy as a Social Science.
   5. Moral Education as a Social Result.

II. Department of Public Health.
   1. Sanitation in the Broad Sense.
   2. Birth, Marriage, and Death.
   3. General and Specific Diseases.
   4. Sanitary Necessities.
   5. Relation of the Medical Profession to the Public.

III. Department of Finance and Political Economy.
   1. Relation of the State to Economic Questions.
   2. National, State and Local Debt.
   3. The Right of Property, Individual and Corporate.
   4. Labor and Wages.
   5. Railroads and Machinery in Relation to Labor.
   6. The Problems of Pauperism Economically Considered.
   7. Banking, Landlords, Rent, and Interest.
   8. Value, Exchange, Money.

IV. Department of Social and Domestic Economy.
   1. Two Aspects of Economic Questions—one looking towards Wealth, the other towards Welfare.
   2. Civilization and the Social Whole.
   3. In Social Economy the Mass of the People are to be Considered.
   4. Financial Aspects of Social Economy.
   5. Art in Education and Amusement.

6. Domestic Economy.

7. Holidays and Observances.

V. Department of Jurisprudence.

1. Law in Ancient and in Modern Times.

2. The Penal Law.

3. Legislation and Vice.

4. The Amendment of Laws.

5. The Administration of Law.

6. Legal Education.

7. The Relation of Jurisprudence to Modern Civilization.[60]

The foregoing topics make it clear that social science as conceived by those who suggested them was not in a state of depression in 1886. The subject's chief difficulty seems to have been an over-supply of content from other fields. Its supporters realized this but did little to rectify it. Speaking to this point a decade before the outline appeared one of the most enthusiastic advocates of the subject said:

"Do not expect me to define the phrase (social science), however, even negatively, by stating what Social Science is not. I have never seen or heard of a person who could concisely define what it is we call social science, or state wherein it differs from other branches of human knowledge. It seems, indeed, to be neither a science nor an art, but a mingling of the two, or of fifty sciences and arts, which all find a place in it. Whatever concerns mankind in their social, rather than in their individual relations, belongs to this comprehensive abstraction, and social science shades off easily and

[60] "Methodical Education in Social Science," *Journal of Social Science,* XXI (1886), 13–20.

imperceptibly into metaphysics on one side, philanthropy on another, political economy on a third, and so round the whole circle of human inquiry. Pope advises us 'to grasp the eel of science by the tail.' Now to deal with a science so fleeting, so fluctuating, and Protean as this in a country like ours, where everything fluctuates and glides into every other thing, is to grasp the most elusive of eels by the most tantalizing of tails; it slips from our hold and defies all attempts to classify it." [61]

THE MOVEMENT TO ESTABLISH SOCIAL SCIENCE AS A SUBJECT OF STUDY IN ELEMENTARY AND JUNIOR HIGH SCHOOLS

It is interesting to relate that in recent years efforts have been made to do over again the job that Carey did, although imperfectly. Carey was trying to bring together in one treatise in an integrated form the significant factors involved in the molding of human society. In our day, individuals are attempting to determine the critical issues and significant problems in social living and organize them for teaching purposes in the grades and the high school irrespective of subject-matter boundaries. This is called unification of the existing social sciences. Those attempting such a set-up seem to think that, if some way can be found to eliminate subject boundaries, all will be glorious. It is too early in the life of this reactionary movement to predict that a new synthetic subject of social science will emerge from it.

To chronicle in detail the history of the movement for the creation and establishment of social science as a subject of study especially in the primary, intermediate, and junior high-school grades, would require much more space than is

[61] F. B. Sanborn, "The Work of Social Science in the United States," *Journal of Social Science*, VI (1874), 36.

available here. Because of its newness the junior high school early became the experimenting ground for the course in social science. It seems that the first serious attempt to create and establish social science as a subject of study in these grades was made by the city of Denver, Colorado. As early as the autumn of 1924 there was ready to place in the hands of the teachers of history, civics, and geography in the junior high schools of this city a monograph which contained a tentative course of study in social science for these schools. The fact that the title of the monograph was *Social Science, Grades Seven, Eight and Nine, Junior High School* is significant, for it seems to have been the first course for these grades issued under such a title. There was no recognition of history, geography, and civics as independent subjects in the main body of the monograph—a tabulation under the categories of history, geography, and civics of the main facts used from these subjects being furnished the teachers. According to this tabulation material from the field of geography received chief emphasis in Grade VII; material from the field of history, in Grade VIII; and material from the field of civics, in Grade IX. Two revisions of this original course have appeared, one in 1926 and the other in 1931. In the last revision the individual subjects were restored—Old World background of American history in Grade VII A, United States history in Grade VIII, and governmental civics and international relations in Grade IX A. Present-day problems of a modern community was the content of Grade IX B and the constitution of the United States and changing civilizations in a modern world formed the basis for the work in Grade VII B. Whether or not the cities that followed the lead of Denver in the matter of unification will also return to the individual subject remains to be seen.

The city of Denver also attempted to make social science an independent subject of study in the first six grades, the published material being placed in the hands of the teachers in September, 1926. No specific recognition was given the subjects of geography, history, and civics as individual subjects in the monograph which was issued under the title *Social Science, Elementary Schools, Grades I–VI*. The revised edition of this monograph which appeared in 1931, contained no material for Grades I and II. No attempt was made in Denver to make social science an independent subject in the senior high school. Those responsible for the course in the social sciences on this level of instruction seemed content to leave this job to more daring experimenters.

It should be remarked in passing that Denver got both much inspiration and many ideas from an experiment in unifying the social sciences on the junior high-school level that was launched in the Lincoln School of Teachers College, Columbia University, during the early years of the 1920's. The results of this experiment and the volumes resulting from a number of investigations connected with it have received wide publicity. In fact they have become so well and generally known that further consideration of them seems unnecessary here.[62]

Other cities followed the lead of Denver in the movement for unifying the social sciences, especially on the junior high-school level. A list of these cities would be out of date before it could get into print; for this reason it would be an uneconomical use of space to include such a list here. Suffice it to say, however, that as the movement progressed subjects

[62] In all, no less than fifty individual volumes resulted from the investigations connected with the experiment. It would require more space than is available here even to list these volumes. For a brief account of the enterprise see the Preface of Harold Rugg's *Changing Government and Changing Civilizations*, published by Ginn and Co., in 1933.

outside the field of the social sciences were included, for example, art and English.[63] Just what turn the movement will take next no one but an infallible seer can tell. It seems evident, however, that the end of the movement is not yet in sight. It is logical to believe that, if a few subjects in the present curriculum can be unified there is a possibility of unifying all of them. Indeed, such has been accomplished in the primary grades in a number of cases. So it is no longer a problem of unifying the social sciences in the primary grades, but rather one of unifying all of the traditional subjects formerly taught therein.

THE UNIFICATION OF THE SOCIAL SCIENCES OTHER THAN HISTORY

While the movement for the unification of all of the social sciences was sluggishly moving along, receiving a set-back here and there, another movement for unification of a somewhat different type was slowly accumulating momentum. Reference is made here to the unification of the social sciences other than history. This movement took cognizance of the facts that there are fundamental differences in the subject-matter of history and that of the other social sciences and that there is value to be attained from the study of the individual social sciences. Accepting these facts as fundamental the big quest then became one of finding the most effective approach to history and to the social sciences other than history, especially in the junior and senior high school. In the junior high school this quest ended in an approach in terms of an exploratory course in both history and the social sciences other

[63] See *Western Youth Meets Eastern Culture*. A Study in Integration of Social Studies, English, and Art in the Junior High School, by three teachers in Lincoln School of Teachers College, Columbia University. New York: Bureau of Publications, Teachers College, Columbia University, 1932.

than history. As early as 1917 these exploratory courses were well under way. At this date in 259 junior high schools general history was offered as an exploratory course in 29 schools in Grade VII, 28 in Grade VIII, and 56 in Grade IX. Likewise general social science was offered in 9 of the 259 schools in Grade VII, 27 in Grade VIII, and 21 in Grade IX. General science and composite mathematics were far in the lead of general history and general social science in these schools. Should one consider the course in community civics as it has been taught since 1917 as a course in general social science, these differences would by no means be so great at the present time.

The idea back of the exploratory or introductory course both in history and the social sciences other than history seems to be a thoroughly sound one. It has invaded the universities with more or less success and bids fair to enjoy increasing application. Administrators of junior high schools are highly in favor of it. In speaking to this point one of these administrators on one occasion said:

"The second type of exploratory course (the one to which the word 'exploratory' more properly belongs) represents an attempt to introduce a new field by giving a simple, general survey of the field as a whole in order to lay open the field and to enable the pupil to orient himself in it. The pupil studies *about* the field rather than *in* it. Such a course, to be sure, often reveals the field more fairly than a sampling would, but the main purpose is to give the pupil an insight into a field of human endeavor—an insight which is educationally justifiable in itself and only incidentally propædeutic. Such a course is pedagogically and psychologically sound as a prerequisite for specialized courses and—what is more important—is peculiarly adapted to the mental capacities of the early adolescent. The dangers in such courses are that they may not reveal specifically enough future activities nor discover specific interests and that they may be so general as to be vague or difficult of comprenhension." [64]

The case for an exploratory or introductory course both in history and the social sciences other than history was briefly stated as early as 1913 as follows:

"History may or may not be a social science. This is a question we need not discuss here. At any rate, it is obviously in a somewhat different status from the other social sciences, since it is devoted primarily to recording events, while the other social sciences are devoted to the description and analysis of social phenomena. For this reason a general introductory course to social science could not hope to replace the introductory course in history, whatever that course may be. For example, if this course is modern European history it is obvious that such a general introductory course would in nowise replace it. But a general introductory course to social science might nevertheless furnish very excellent general preparation for the study of history in a way which will be indicated later." [65]

On the traditional four-year and senior high-school level an

[64] E. C. Cline, "Some Problems Relating to Exploratory Courses," *School Review*, XXXVIII (1930), 208.

[65] Maurice Parmelee, "An Introductory Course to the Social Sciences," *American Journal of Sociology*, XIX (1913), 238 f. Some attempts have been made in textbook-form to cater to the demand for a general course in the social sciences. See David Snedden and Genevra Snedden, *Basal Social Sciences*. New York: Charles Scribner's Sons, 1932; Ross Finney, *General Social Science*. New York: Macmillan Co., 1926; and H. P. Fairchild, *Elements of Social Science, An Introduction to the Study of Human Society*. New York: Macmillan Co., 1924.

exploratory course has been in vogue for over a century. At first it was called general history. Since about 1916 world history has been its name. Inasmuch as general history has been previously considered in some detail, it is not necessary to reconsider it here. Should a course in world history ever reach the stage of permanency in the junior high school and be required of all pupils, the need for it in the senior high school would probably be satisfied. There are few signs that such a permanency will be attained soon.

A course also appeared in the senior high school soon after 1916 which attempted to unify content from the social sciences other than history. This course was not intended as an introductory or exploratory course as was the course in general social science cited above. On the contrary, it was expected to serve as a culminating course in the social sciences. It was included in the recommendations of the Committee on Social Studies of the National Education Association. The name suggested for the course by this Committee was "Problems of American Democracy—Economic, Social, Political." The general nature of this course and its justification by the Committee have been considered in Division One, so they need not be repeated here. One comment, however, seems apropos. It is to the effect that the idea was not original with the Committee; it had been floating around for at least fifteen years prior to 1916. Note the following which was written about 1900:

"In the higher grades, formal instruction in political science by the use of elementary text-books, or by the pursuit of a well-defined plan, should be commenced. The process of observation begun in the lower grades should be continued; for there are political and social phenomena as well as natural phenomena to be observed and classified. The work in the high school should embrace History, Elementary Political Economy, Elementary Civil Government, Sociology, and a systematic study of the problems of modern society." [66]

The point should be made that the author of this statement had a much larger vision of the work in the social sciences in the high school than the Committee on Social Studies had. He desired a course in problems of modern society in addition to courses in economics, civics, and sociology, while the Committee was satisfied with a single course made up of material drawn from these three fields. Professor Blackmar's program was certainly an ambitious one for the year 1900. The fact of the matter is that few schools much more than approximate it even today. In proposing this program at this early date Professor Blackmar was certainly "hitching his wagon to a star."

The values that have been claimed for the course in problems of American democracy are so much like those discussed elsewhere under civics, economics, and sociology that they do not need to be reviewed here. The chief value claimed by the supporters of the course that could not be achieved through the study of any one of the social sciences alone was that of "laying a foundation in the social sciences both for those who go to college and for those whose academic education ends with the high school." It was believed by those who sponsored the course that such a value could not, because of time limitations, be attained through the offering of the social sciences other than history as independent subjects.

The year 1916 seems to have been a good one in which to propose an innovation in the offerings in the social sciences

[66] Frank W. Blackmar, *The Study of History, Sociology, and Economics*, p. 105. Topeka, Kansas: Crane and Co., 1901.

in the senior high school, for the innovation proposed by the Committee on Social Studies at this time met with considerable favor. Between 1916 and 1922 four other committees, all of national scope reported on certain phases of the social sciences in the high school. Three of these, the Committee on History and Education for Citizenship, the Committee on the Teaching of Sociology in the Grades and High School, and the Committee on Social Studies of the National Association of Secondary School Principals favored a course for the last year of the senior high school very much like the one proposed in 1916 by the Committee on the Social Studies in Secondary Education. Another committee, representing the American Political Science Association, opposed a course in problems of American democracy to take the place of civics. While two of the foregoing reports were not formally adopted by the bodies sponsoring them, it is very evident that by 1922 the suggestions made by the Committee on Social Studies in 1916 had been favorably received in many quarters.

With the backing of four committees of national scope, representing four strong organizations, the course in problems of American democracy made considerable headway during the 1920's. There seems to be no official record of the time and place the first course in the subject was offered. This event probably happened in the state of New Jersey, wherein as early as 1919 a law was enacted requiring instruction relative to the privileges and responsibilities of citizenship as they related to community and national welfare. In an attempt to comply with this law two courses were set up and required of all pupils in approved high schools, one in community civics and one in problems of American democracy. Twenty-five minutes a week in Grades IX and XII respectively were allotted to these subjects at first. Later the time was changed to at least sixty full hours in periods of not less than forty minutes each.[67] This schedule went into effect in the autumn of 1920, a syllabus having been prepared during the summer for the problems course.

During the 1920's the idea back of the course in problems of American democracy spread with a fair degree of rapidity. The Department of Education of the state of Pennsylvania accepted the course in 1921. As early as 1926 at least twelve state departments of education were recommending it and by 1929 this number had increased to twenty-three. The names of these states and certain details about the course are shown in Table XVII. It should not be concluded from the data in this table that when a state department of education outlined or suggested a course that it was immediately required in all of the high schools of that state. Eight of the states in the foregoing list are located in the territory of the North Central Association. In 1925, out of 1571 public high schools in this Association, but 150 or 9.5 per cent were offering a course in problems of American democracy. In 1930 in this same territory 450 or 20.2 per cent of the 2226 schools reporting offered the course. Except in the four states in which the course is required, there is no available evidence to show that it is extensively offered. Furthermore, it is losing ground rapidly in at least one state, Michigan. Between 1925 and 1930 the subject suffered a loss of 21.9 per cent in the North Central high schools of this state, while sociology gained 135.7 per cent, economics 141.3 per cent, government 39.2 per cent, and community civics 11 per cent.[68]

Before passing to a consideration of the content of the

[67] *Problems in American Democracy.* High School Series, No. 8, p. 9. Trenton, New Jersey: State Department of Public Instruction, 1920.
[68] George E. Carrothers, "High School Curriculum Revisions and Innovations," *Junior-Senior High School Clearing House*, VI (1932), 268.

course in problems of American democracy, brief reference
will be made to the variety of names under which the content
has been taught. It will be recalled that the title of the course

TABLE XVII

PROBLEMS OF AMERICAN DEMOCRACY IN 23 STATE COURSES OF
STUDY IN 1929*

	DATE OF COURSE	REQUIRED OR ELECTIVE	YEAR TAUGHT	AMOUNT OF CREDIT
Alabama.............	1924	Elective	4	1 unit
Arkansas...........	1925	Elective	4	1 unit
Florida.............	1926-28	Elective	4	1 unit
Indiana.............	1928	Elective	4	½ unit
Kansas.............	1925-28	Required	3	1 unit
Kentucky...........	1927	Elective	4	1 unit
Maine..............	1927	Not stated	4	½ unit
Maryland...........	1927	Elective	4	1 unit
Massachusetts.......	1927	Elective	4	½ unit
Mississippi..........	1928	Elective	4	½ unit
Missouri............	1928	Elective	4	1 unit
Nebraska...........	1928	Elective	4	
New Jersey.........	1922-25	Required	4	1 or ½
North Carolina......	1926	Elective	4	1 unit
North Dakota.......	1926-28	Required	4	1 unit
Ohio...............	1929	Elective	3 or 4	1 unit
Oklahoma..........	1924	Elective	4	1 or ½
Pennsylvania........	1925-27	Required	4	1 unit
Tennessee..........	1928	Required	4	½ unit
Virginia............	1925	Elective	4	½ unit
West Virginia.......	1925-27	Elective	4	1 unit
Wisconsin..........	1924	Elective	4	
Wyoming...........	1929	Not stated	3 or 4	1 unit

* Frances Purves Taylor, "Problems of American Democracy as a High School
Subject," p. 38. Unpublished Master's thesis, University of Chicago, 1929. According
to an investigation completed in 1930, Colorado, Delaware, Minnesota, New Hampshire, and Vermont should be added to the foregoing list of states to bring it up to date.
—John C. West, op. cit., p. 61.

suggested by the Committee proposing it read "Problems of
American Democracy—Economic, Social, Political." This
name proved too lengthy for most people. Furthermore, some
desired to change the "of" to "in," the title of the New Jersey
course being "Problems in American Democracy." An exam-

ination of fifty-one city and twenty-three state courses of study in 1928 revealed that thirty-eight of them used the title "Problems of Democracy" or "Problems of American Democracy." Seven of the city courses used "American Problems" and one each "Present Day Problems," "Advanced Social Science," "Current Problems," "Modern Problems," "Social Problems," and "Modern History Problems." [69] The state of Missouri also used in 1928 the name "American Problems"; Indiana, "Advanced Social Science"; and Ohio, "Problems of the Modern Nation or National Problems."

The content of the course in problems of American democracy was first outlined in the New Jersey syllabus mentioned above. Three years after the appearance of this syllabus one was issued by the State Department of Pennsylvania.[70] These two syllabi probably played a significant rôle in the determination of the content of problems of American democracy outside of these states. Inasmuch as the New Jersey syllabus was something new in the educational world in 1920, special notice of its contents seems worth while. Speaking generally the course was divided into two parts, one-third of the time allotted to it being given to the first part and the remaining two-thirds to the second. The first part was intended to supply an historical background and principles against which to project the specific problems outlined in the second part of the course. Four main topics were included in the introductory work, namely, "The Meaning of Democracy," "Fundamental Principles of Democracy," "Forms of Government Defined and Illustrated," and "Our Civilization Chiefly Anglo-Saxon in Origin." Following these introductory topics there appeared in this first syllabus an outline in considerable detail

---

[69] Frances Purves Taylor, *op. cit.,* p. 49.

[70] *Syllabus on Problems of Democracy.* Harrisburg, Pa.: State Department of Education, 1923.

of each of the following so-called problems: private property, capital and labor, communication and transportation, conservation, immigration and Americanization, education, political problems, and international relations.

Prior to 1922 all of the courses in problems of American democracy taught in the country had to depend on a syllabus for their general outline. Beginning with this year, however, there have been available textbooks purporting to conform to the ideas expressed by the Committee originating the course. Three of these texts appeared in 1922, two in 1923, two in 1924, two in 1928, one in 1929, and one in 1932, eleven in all. Inasmuch as there were in existence at least fifty-one city and twenty-three state courses of study in problems of American democracy in 1929, it would not seem fair to those who made courses to say that textbooks solely determined the content of the subject during the 1920's. Granting that the content was determined probably as much by the courses of study available as by the textbooks in the field the following topics are presented as indicative of this content. They appear in the order of their frequency in fifty-one city and twenty-three state courses of study in problems of American democracy in use in 1929: education, conservation, international relations, capital and labor, poverty, the family, immigration, defectives, dependents and delinquents, how we are governed, production, distribution, race problem, crime, city problems, money and banking, transportation, rural problems, population, communication, charity, commerce, public opinion, principles and ideals of democracy, business, political parties, how government is financed, child labor, health, prohibition, unemployment, industrial reform, socialism, taxation, civil and political rights, child welfare, private property, direct legislation, occupations of risk, elections, government ownership of public utilities, elevating American standards, making America prosperous, protection, growth of social and economic and political institu-

TABLE XVIII

NUMBER AND PER CENT OF LINES DEVOTED TO CERTAIN TOPICS
IN FOUR TEXTBOOKS IN PROBLEMS OF AMERICAN DEMOCRACY*

TOPICS	Number and Per Cent of Lines	
	NUMBER	PER CENT
1. Development of the principles of government.	1,541	2.70
2. Local government.	2,101	3.69
3. State government.	2,292	4.02
4. National government.	14,205	24.97
5. Political parties and elections	2,555	4.49
6. Government of territories and insular possessions.	712	1.25
7. Taxation.	1,640	2.88
8. International relations.	3,205	5.63
9. Industry.	5,743	10.97
10. Programs of industrial reform.	3,090	5.43
11. Transportation.	1,468	2.58
12. Labor relations.	3,338	5.86
13. Immigration.	1,488	2.61
14. Conservation.	1,684	2.96
15. Population.	3,324	5.84
16. Family.	2,720	4.78
17. Church.	1,045	1.83
18. Education.	2,894	5.08
19. Rural community.	1,209	2.12
20. Poverty.	2,914	5.12
21. Crime.	2,181	3.83
22. Health and care of defectives	1,203	2.11
23. Communication.	81	.14
24. Recreation.	158	.27
25. Liquor problem.	511	.89
26. Geographical features.	374	.65

* Oliver Reed Floyd, "Overlapping Between the Senior High School Courses in Problems of Democracy and American History," p. 23. Unpublished Master's thesis, University of Pittsburgh, 1928.

tions, government of dependencies, laws and courts, the ballot, civic duties, the constitution, foundations of American life, standards of living, co-operation and profit-sharing, the press, public service, the tariff, limitation of armaments, civil service, harmful drugs, recreation, budget, America's responsibilities, learning to live together, monopolies, wages, forces of control, Congress, president and cabinet, defense, the League of Nations, political and economic reconstruction, road to progress, and industrial economy.

Because there must have been a good deal of dependence on textbooks even though syllabi were available in the early twenties, it seems advisable to present the content of some of the early texts. Table XVIII contains the results of an analysis of the three texts published in 1922, the first ones in the field, and one published in 1924. It would seem from the data in this table and those revealed in the analysis of syllabi that the course in problems of American democracy has no content other than that included in economics, sociology, and political science. It may be that those who originated the course never intended that it should have a content any different from that portrayed above. It is clear from the data in Table XVIII that the writers of textbooks in problems of American democracy have heavily weighted the content on the side of government and politics, 41 per cent of their texts being devoted to these topics. Probably because of their inadequate training in sociology these authors actually constucted a stool with two legs instead of three. Evidence of this fact is exhibited in Table XVIII. The scant attention given to at least six of the sociological topics by the authors of four textbooks in American democracy is ample proof that they were overlooking the third leg of the stool which they were trying to construct.

DIVISION FIVE

ORGANIZING THE SOCIAL SCIENCES FOR TEACH-
ING PURPOSES IN ELEMENTARY AND
SECONDARY SCHOOLS

ORGANIZING THE SOCIAL SCIENCES FOR TEACHING PURPOSES IN ELEMENTARY AND SECONDARY SCHOOLS

I. INTRODUCTORY.
II. GENERAL APPROACHES TO A SOCIAL SCIENCE FROM THE STANDPOINT OF ORGANIZING IT FOR TEACHING PURPOSES.—The Chronological or Logical Approach; the Psychological or the Counter-Chronological Approach; the Spiral, Cycle, or Concentric Circles Approach; the Biographical Approach.
III. SCHEMES FOR ORGANIZING THE FIELD OF THE SOCIAL SCIENCES FOR TEACHING PURPOSES.—The Principle of Isolation; the Principle of Unification; the Principles of Correlation and Concentration.
IV. SPECIFIC WAYS OF ORGANIZING THE SOCIAL SCIENCES FOR TEACHING PURPOSES.—Organizing in Terms of Significant Topics; the Type-Study Plan of Organizing the Social Sciences; Organizing the Social Sciences in Terms of Problems; the Project as an Organizer of a Social Science; the Rôle of the Unit of Understanding in Organizing the Social Sciences; the Unit of Work; Organizing in Terms of Contracts.
V. REFLECTIONS AND CONCLUSIONS.

I

INTRODUCTORY

Before entering upon a systematic treatment of the subject of this division, it should be pointed out that there are individuals in charge of schools who do not feel that any predetermined organization of a field of knowledge for teaching purposes is needed. In certain so-called activity programs an almost utter lack of prearranged organization is found. This practice is in harmony with the notion held by many proponents of the activity program that the curriculum should be made by the pupils in terms of "leads" obtained in passing from one activity to another. It is evident that this view makes a predetermined organization of content both impossible and unnecessary. In fact it makes the content itself an unknown quantity. When it is accepted and applied in its extreme form traditional school subjects such as history, civics, geography, and arithmetic disappear; the need for the arrangement of a school program in an orderly systematic fashion passes away; and entire reliance is placed on what some have denominated "units of experience" actually encountered from day to day by those being educated.

Those who hold the foregoing doctrine seem to believe that systematic education as it has been practiced during the past generation has been a signal failure. They seem to desire a complete revolution in the realm of organizing subject-matter for teaching purposes even though they actually have no objective data to uphold their contention. To certain on-lookers they appear to act on the principle that whatever is novel, new, and untried is right. If this accusation is true, they are in direct opposition to the principle on which a scientist acts. It is said that the United States Weather Bureau always acts on the principle that the mistake of upholding old ideas too long is safer than the mistake of adopting new ideas before their validity is absolutely established. There are those who believe that present-day education could adopt this principle without any deleterious effects.

The antithesis of no predetermined organization is organization and the antithesis to no school subjects is history, geography, arithmetic, and the rest. The argument of those who believe in school subjects is based on the psychological explanation of how the mind apprehends an object. The three stages in the apprehension of an object suggested by the great German psychologist Wündt are vague apprehension, analytical study, and synthetic grasp.[1] According to the followers of Wündt there comes a time in the child's life when a desire to grasp the world more clearly and less vaguely matures. In order to do this the stage of analysis must be experienced. The learner must view the world from the standpoint of a good geographer, a good historian, a good chemist, or a good economist. So it comes about that school subjects actually belong to the analytical stage of mental growth,[2] and are necessary in order to assure a synthesis that is meaningful. It follows from this reasoning that, if school subjects are necessary in a scheme of education which aims to help the child "to see the world in all its fulness," some scheme for approaching these subjects and organizing them for teaching purposes is highly desirable. In the course of time, since the appearance of the social sciences as school subjects, many approaches and schemes of organization have been proposed and tried. In the discussion below consideration is first directed to some of these—leaving the systematic treatment of specific ways of organizing history and other social sciences for teaching purposes for later consideration.

II

GENERAL APPROACHES TO A SOCIAL SCIENCE FROM THE STANDPOINT OF ORGANIZING IT FOR TEACHING PURPOSES

Before one can deal effectively with the details of organizing a social science for teaching purposes, the problem of the gen-

[1] C. H. Judd, "The Training of Teachers for a Progressive Educational Program," *Elementary School Journal*, XXXI (1931), 580.
[2] *Ibid.*, p. 581.

eral approach to be used must be faced and solved. Speaking generally one has at least four possible approaches from which to choose when considering history and no less than three when considering a social science other than history. The four approaches applicable to history may be designated the chronological or logical, the psychological or counter-chronological, the cycle, and the biographical or individual. Each of these, except the last one, applies to any social science other than history. In order to portray clearly the characteristic features and specific applications of these approaches, a separate treatment in the order named above is accorded each.

THE CHRONOLOGICAL OR LOGICAL APPROACH

Prior to about 1920, the chronological approach to history was the prevailing one; since this date it has been losing ground very rapidly. Its long predominance was due to the influence of textbooks on history teaching. The authors of these textbooks in the majority of cases told their stories in a strictly chronological order. For example, the 1857 edition of Charles A. Goodrich's *History of the United States,* a much used text for a number of years, contained the following general organization:

Period First, from the Discovery of America by Columbus, 1492, to the first permanent English settlement in America, at Jamestown, Virginia, 1607.

Period Second, from the settlement of Jamestown to the French and Indian War, 1756.

Period Third, from the French and Indian War, 1756, to the commencement of the American Revolution, in the Battle of Lexington, 1775.

Period Fourth, from the Battle of Lexington, 1775, to the

Disbanding of the American Army at West Point, New York, 1783.

Period Fifth, from the Disbanding of the Army, 1783, to the Inauguration of George Washington as President of the United States, under the Federal Constitution, 1789.

Period Sixth, from the Inauguration of President Washington, 1789, to the Inauguration of John Adams, 1797.

Period Seventh, from the Inauguration of President Adams, 1797, to the Inauguration of Thomas Jefferson, 1801.

Period Eighth, from the Inauguration of President Jefferson, 1801, to the Inauguration of James Madison, 1809.

Period Ninth, from the Inauguration of President Madison, 1809, to the Inauguration of James Monroe, 1817.

Period Tenth, from the Inauguration of President Monroe, 1817, to the Inauguration of John Quincy Adams, 1825.

Period Eleventh, from the Inauguration of President Adams, 1825, to the Inauguration of Andrew Jackson, 1829.

Period Twelfth, from the Inauguration of President Jackson, 1829, to the Inauguration of Martin Van Buren, 1837.

Period Thirteenth, from the Inauguration of President Van Buren, 1837, to the Inauguration of William Henry Harrison, 1841.

Period Fourteenth, from the Inauguration of President Harrison, 1841, to the Inauguration of James K. Polk, 1845.

Period Fifteenth, from the Inauguration of President Polk, 1845, to the Inauguration of Zachary Taylor, 1849.

Period Sixteenth, from the Inauguration of President Taylor, 1849, to the Inauguration of Franklin Pierce, 1853.

Commenting on the edition which contained the foregoing organization, Goodrich remarked:

"The School History herewith presented to the public has

undergone such alterations as nearly to justify the announcement of it as a new work. The original division into periods, however, has been retained; the experience of teachers, for more than twenty years, having decided that, in this respect, it scarcely admits of improvement. And, in confirmation of the correctness of this judgment, it may be stated that every School History of the United States, published since the date of Goodrich's first edition, has been written, without exception, it is believed, upon the same general plan; and in some instances, so nearly identical with his, as in the estimation of some to justify a question of legality." [3]

Goodrich, of course, did not originate the chronological approach to history for teaching purposes. The complaint that he made against those who copied his general plan could likewise have been made against him. For example, in his organization of universal history for teaching purposes one author as early as 1808 used the following plan for the material prior to the birth of Christ.

First Period
From the Creation of the World to the Deluge, 1656 years.

Second Period
From the Deluge to the Calling of Abraham, 366 years.

Third Period
From the Calling of Abraham to the Law Given by Moses, 431 years.

Fourth Period
From the Law Given by Moses to the Taking of Troy, 347 years.

[3] Charles A. Goodrich, *History of the United States of America*, Preface. Boston: Hickling, Swan & Brewer, 1857.

Fifth Period

From the Taking of Troy to the Building of the Temple by Solomon, 192 years.

Sixth Period

From the Building of the Temple of Jerusalem to the Foundation of Rome, 239 years.

Seventh Period

From the Foundation of Rome to the Beginning of the Reign of Cyrus, 192 years.

Eighth Period

From Cyrus, First King of the Persians, to the Birth of Jesus Christ, 560 years.[4]

It would be difficult to exaggerate the tenacity with which writers of textbooks in history have held to the strictly chronological approach illustrated in the two foregoing examples. Until about 1910 textbooks in United States history for the intermediate grades, the upper-elementary grades, and the high school almost universally followed the strictly chronological approach. In presenting the material prior to 1789 each of the thirteen original colonies was given a separate consideration chronologically arranged. The Revolutionary War was treated by years. After 1789 each administration was discussed separately in chronological order, the events in each being arranged according to the principle of chronology.

It was evident in 1910, however, that the day was gone for writing textbooks in United States history for any level of in-

[4] Caleb Bingham, *A Historical Grammar or a Chronological Abridgement of Universal History.* Cited by W. F. Russell, "The Entrance of History into the Curriculum of the Secondary School," *History Teachers' Magazine,* V (1914), 312.

struction in terms of events arranged in rigid chronological sequence. Since this date chronology has not been ignored in the organization and the selection of the materials of textbooks, but it has been put to the useful work of securing continuity and development in the treatment of the materials.

Another influence favoring the chronological approach to history as a school subject was the belief of the American Herbartians in the culture epochs theory. This belief connected the chronological arrangement of historical material with the psychological and cultural development of children. It may be truthfully remarked that the chronological approach to history in the school never survived the blow that it received in the passing of the Herbartians, who had almost unlimited faith in the educative value of history and at the same time held a theory of child development that made chronology an essential aspect of the organization of history materials for teaching purposes. Even before 1910 at least five counts had appeared against the chronological approach. One of these said that those who organize history thus are interested in it chiefly for its own sake whereas they ought to be interested in the subject for the sake of the child. Other charges were: 1. Children from eight to thirteen years of age are unable to construct an orderly notion of temporal or logical relations. 2. The chronological approach assumes that the proper way to build up a knowledge of the past is through deduction rather than induction. 3. It is serviceable only to the trained historian as a structure about which to relate new information. 4. The recapitulation or culture epochs theory has no psychological basis in fact.

Advocates of the chronological approach to history for teaching purposes could not stem the tide of opposition which developed under the influences of the foregoing list of particulars against it. While chronology was not abolished from all of the history taught in the elementary and secondary schools after 1910, the use made of it was not as extensive after this date as it was prior thereto. Useful as the chronological approach was in organizing history for teaching purposes when the subject was new in the schools, the harm done to the cause of history as a school subject was probably greater than the good. The old type of history text was more or less formal because of its strict adherence to the exact order of events. When dissatisfaction arose with the results attained from instruction in history, the subject itself rather than the method of approach received the brunt of adverse criticism. Even to this day the adverse critics of history as a school subject have in mind the history that was generally taught in most of the schools prior to 1910. For this reason they are directing their tirades against a "has been" instead of an existing situation.

Before passing to a consideration of other major approaches to the social sciences as school subjects, mention should be made of the fact that the chronological approach and the logical approach are one and the same thing in history. To some the logical way to arrange the materials of history for teaching purposes is the chronological order. Outside the field of history, however, the logical approach is used by those who are mainly interested in an orderly arrangement of the material of a subject. For example, a logical approach to economics for teaching purposes is largely in terms of the traditional major divisions of the subject, namely, production, consumption, distribution, and exchange. A logical approach to advanced civics is in terms of local government, state government, and national government, or municipal government, county government, state government, and federal government, each of these divisions of government being considered under three heads, the executive, the judicial, and the legislative, with chief emphasis on the mechanical aspects of government.

The logical approach to economics and elementary political science was the dominant one in use in this country until about 1915. The first signs of its downfall began to appear on the horizon soon after the rise of community civics in 1907. Inasmuch as community civics was a subject that drew on so many fields of knowledge for its content, no logical organization of its subject-matter seemed possible. The fact that the subject of community civics has always defied logical organization has made it a leader in the movement to emancipate the social sciences from the grip of formalism represented in the strictly chronological approach to history and the logical organization of economics and elementary political science.

THE PSYCHOLOGICAL OR COUNTER-CHRONOLOGICAL APPROACH

Those who organize the social sciences as a field or by subjects for teaching purposes claim that they employ the psychological approach when the arrangement of the subject matter is made to fit the capacity, the interest, and the experience of the pupil. In history such an arrangement is not based on a forward-looking chronology, unless one accepts the recapitulation theory of the Herbartians, but a backward-looking one. For this reason the psychological approach to history may be termed the counter-chronological approach. Outside the field of history, however, the word "psychological" is used to describe the approach for teaching purposes to the field of the social sciences or a single social science when the learner instead of the subject is made the center of gravity.

Inasmuch as the counter-chronological approach to history as a school subject has been much discussed, *pro* and *con*, since about 1912, it seems to deserve consideration beyond mere mention, so attention will first be centered on its rise and original advocates. As early as 1896, arguments for its adoption began to appear. Writing at this date one of its ardent advocates commented as follows on certain of its aspects:

"No doubt the ordinary way of telling a story is to begin at the beginning, whether it be in the witness-box, in conversation with a friend, or in a three-volume novel. But that is because in these cases the starting-point and the terminus are equally familiar or equally unfamiliar. Where it is otherwise, we begin at the end. If an old friend turns up unexpectedly, the chances are that our first question will be, "How did you come here?" and that after explaining the immediate reason for his presence, he will go back to the date of his last meeting with us, and give an outline of his doings in the interval in chronological order. But in making a new acquaintance there is no last meeting to refer to, so conversation finds its starting-point in the incident which brought us together, or in the personality of the friend who introduced us, and thence travels back to earlier events connected with one or the other.

"Obviously the study of history resembles the second case rather than the first. There is no last meeting to refer to; no remote past already more familiar than the recent past. Each historical personage who comes on the scene is bound to justify his intrusion by tacking himself on to somebody of whom we have heard before; and who can the first introducer be, if not some living contemporary?" [5]

The appearance in this country of the teaching-history-backwards idea was in connection with the educational-psychology movement, a movement emphasizing the nature of the learn-

[5] Roland K. Wilson, "Should History Be Taught Backwards?" *Littell's Living Age*, XII (1896), 262 f.

ing process and the organization of subject-matter best suited
to it. As early as 1912, an educational psychologist in commenting on forward and backward chronology in their relation to the arrangement of historical materials for teaching
purposes said:

"To one who knows the history of a nation, the order in
which the facts most suitably arrange themselves is of course
the forward chronological order. All textbooks within my
knowledge unhesitatingly follow that order. It has, indeed,
seemed undubitable to teachers as well as writers of textbooks
that the students should begin where the country began. But
what has seemed so sure is very questionable. The pupil actually begins with knowledge of the present condition of his
own immediate environment plus a variable and chaotic acquaintance, through talk and books, with facts located vaguely
in other places and earlier times. Perhaps the story of the
voyage of the parents of some pupil in the class should precede
that of the voyage of Columbus; perhaps the date when some
house in the town was built, what was there before it, and
what was there in the boyhood of the grandfather of some
child in the class, should be studied before the dates of the first
colonies. Perhaps to work back from the Philippines to Alaska,
to the annexation of Texas, to the Louisiana Purchase, in a
study of the territory of our nation to-day, would be more
instructive than to begin with the Spanish, English, French
and Dutch settlements. The educational value of finding the
causes of what is, and then the causes of these causes, is so
very much superior to the spurious reasoning which comes
from explaining a record already known, or pretending to
prophesy what the wisest men of the past would not prophesy,
that the arrangement of the first part of the course in history

in the inverse temporal order, leaving the forward chronicle till later, deserves serious consideration." [6]

The foregoing quotations represent the ideas of specialists in a field other than history on the proper approach to history as a school subject. Specialists in history have also expressed their views on the proper way to approach history. In 1920, the author of a textbook in world history wrote:

"The merit of history is that it begins nowhere or rather that it begins everywhere. It does not matter where you make a start. You can read anything in which you are interested, a biography, an account of a movement, and from that you can proceed backwards or forwards. Indeed it is not a bad way to read all history backwards, passing from the known to the unknown. Many persons are choked off from the study of history at an early stage from the dullness of the beginning.

"The first chapter of any complete history is seldom interesting, origins are imperfectly known and much is left to conjecture; it is better to plunge into the middle. I have been told that Mr. Lecky, the historian, as a boy was very fond of reading, and that he generally began a new book from the second volume and worked back to the first after he had aroused his interest in the subject. Some persons are most interested in battles, some in institutions, some in men. To these last the biography of a great man, such as Frederick the Great, Peter the Great, or Napoleon, will stimulate where nothing else would have the effect." [7]

A concrete example of the point made in the foregoing

[6] Edward L. Thorndike, *Education, A First Book*, pp. 144 f. New York: Macmillan Co., 1912.

[7] Oscar Browning, "The Study of World History," *The Journal of Education and School World*, LII (1920), 730.

quotation is found in an historical treatment by an American historian[8] of the power of a court to declare a law unconstitutional. It is interesting to note that this essay appeared as early as 1912, a fact that helps to fix this date as an important one in the development of the counter-chronological approach to historical material. It will be recalled that the suggestion by an educational psychologist that such an approach might be used also appeared in print this same year.

In the treatment of his topic, Professor McLaughlin used the counter-chronological approach. While he did not begin with the most recent example of the declaring of a law unconstitutional, which a strict adherence to the counter-chronological approach dictates, he did use the approach very consistently from the case with which he began his discussion. Beginning with the decision in the case of *Marbury* vs. *Madison,* handed down in 1803, Professor McLaughlin went backward historically in his attempts to discover antecedents or foundations for this decision. While the subject is one particularly adapted to a backward historical treatment, the essay must be recognized as a concrete example of an effective use of the counter-chronological approach to an historical topic.

It is one thing to apply the counter-chronological approach to a treatment of the power of a court to declare a law unconstitutional, but a very different matter to apply it to organizing a field or a topic in history for teaching purposes. Few concrete examples of the application of the idea in this latter instance are available. One that has never reached the stage of publication seems worthy of inclusion here. It was developed in connection with an experiment in the teaching

---

[8] Andrew C. McLaughlin, *The Courts, The Constitution and Parties,* pp. 3–107. Chicago: The University of Chicago Press, 1912.

of history conducted in 1929.[9] One of the topics used in connection with the experiment was "Transportation," treated counter-chronologically. The general outline of this topic in reverse historical order is produced below.

1. *The American Eagle Uses Her Wings.*—Brock and Schlee at San Diego; Kingsford-Smith; Lindbergh's Visits as a Messenger of Good Will; the Lone Eagle (Lindbergh's flight to Paris); United States Mail Air Pilots; Magellan of the Air (Lowell Smith); Mixing Air and Water (Hydroplane); The Eagle's Claws (War planes); Day Dreams (Langley, Wright Bros., and Darius Green).

2. *On Rubber Wheels.*—the Pleasure Car; the Motor Bus; the Motor Truck; Auto in the World War; Goodyear and Pneumatic Tires; Early Attempts (Elwood Hayes).

3. *On Iron Rails.*—Transcontinental Service; the Freight Train; East Meets West at Ogden, Utah, in 1869; the Steam Car; Horse Drawn Cars; Cooper and Stevenson.

4. *Hoofing it Across Country.*—Harnessed Horses; Pack Animals; "Gee and Haw" with the Ox; Blazing Trails—hiking.

5. *Floating West.*—Modern Ocean Liner (the *Leviathan*); Steamboat (the *Clermont*); Sailing Vessels; Flat Boats; Canoes; Logs.

The reader will observe that an attempt is made in the outline above to keep the arrangement of the events in counter-chronological order. One conspicuous failure in this respect

[9] W. L. Walker, "An Experiment in Teaching History in Reverse Order." Unpublished Master's thesis, University of Southern California, 1929.

is noted under Arabic 5. This is in connection with the *Leviathan,* a modern ocean liner. While this type of ocean liner came after the steamboat in point of time, it did not antedate the items under Arabic 4. On the whole, however, the backward arrangement holds good in most of the items in the outline. Even though it is possible to arrange historical items in reverse order when organizing a topic for teaching purposes, it is difficult to point out the specific superiority of such an arrangement over the forward-looking one. As a general concept the counter-chronological approach seems to possess a degree of merit for those interested in organizing history for teaching purposes. However, when the notion is applied to a particular topic in history, it seems to have few, if any advantages, over the straight forward-looking arrangement. So one must conclude concerning it, that, as a general principle to follow, the idea seems sound, but in practical application unwieldy, illogical, and confusing.

As noted above, what is called the chronological approach in history is the logical approach in economics, sociology, and elementary political science. Likewise the counter-chronological approach is primarily applicable to history while the psychological is just as serviceable in the social sciences other than history as it is in history. Even though the counter-chronological arrangement is peculiar to history materials,[10]

10 It should be remarked in this connection that there is an approach designated by some as the semi-counter chronological. The following quotation from an advocate of this approach gives a hint of what it is. The comments in the quotation on the psychologically and chronologically written textbooks are also very pertinent here.

"A logically written textbook for the teaching of United States History in the junior or senior high school would begin with European backgrounds, somewhere about 1492. This is far away, both in time and place. A history textbook psychologically written begins with the near at hand, with the here and now. Children do not learn in the logical but in the psychological way; so logically written textbooks have certain limitations for young students. The psychologically written books have much in their favor for the best it does not follow that this type of arrangement is necessary when the psychological approach is employed in history. Furthermore, the point should be made that the psychological approach to history does not in itself debar the chronological arrangement of materials. The seemingly sane position for one to maintain in all of these matters is well expressed by an educational psychologist as follows:

"It may be found that the way of wisdom is to accept no general principle of order of arrangement of historical data. The reverse chronological order (frequently suggested heretofore) is in a measure defensible. It may be that a forward order is often desirable, whereas a reverse order may meet other cases more effectively. The suggestion here offered is this: We should begin with present interests and abilities. We need not employ the same order in all cases. We should select, from the past experiences of the nation or race, those data which may be brought to bear upon the present situation. What we shall then have are historical data related to—the kitchen range, the piano, the use of money, the street cars, eating out of dishes, using pencils and paper, reading books, building a kite, having a leader for 'sides' in 'dare-base,' obeying the leader, abiding by majority rule, saluting the flag, a holiday for Washington's birthday, the Fourth of July, having policemen, putting men in prison, etc., etc. The history teacher will

starting place in history is some present day event, situation, institution, or condition. A chronologically written book is a logical book, beginning in the past somewhere and coming up to the present. A counter-chronologically written book begins with the present and unfolds the story backwards. It is a psychologically written book. A semi-counter chronologically written book begins the story of each topic, as far as possible, with the here and now, and after giving the student a point of departure upon familiar grounds, a "toe-hold" so to speak, tells the story of the topic in a logical way."— Charles Vannest, "The Semi-Counter Chronological Approach in the Teaching of United States History Using the Topical Method," *Oregon Educational Journal*, III (1928). 5.

know the child's thinking, feeling and acting capacities and bring the fruits of past experience to nourish the present development in the projects of actual life." [11]

On reading the foregoing statement of the meaning and implication of the psychological approach to history as a school subject, one might be left with the impression that in order to employ such an approach one must select materials which are closely related to the temporal and spacial experiences of the pupil. While the material used when the psychological approach is employed must be in keeping with the present experiences of the pupil, time and space factors are not absolutely necessary. An organization of history for teaching purposes which includes a consideration of primitive life can be justified on the principle that it follows the psychological approach. Nearness in aspects other than space and time may be considered an attribute of the psychological approach. Indeed, if this were not the case, the material on primitive life now so prevalent in the primary grades would have difficulty in maintaining its present status.

The psychological approach is just as applicable to the organization of economics, civics, and sociology for teaching purposes as it is to the organization of history. When applied in these subjects the organization of the material is in terms of the capacities and interests of those for whom it is intended rather than in terms of a mature and logical organization. Instead of approaching economics from the standpoint of production, consumption, exchange, etc., as would be done when using the logical approach, an approach is made through items of current interest to pupils. Such an approach would

[11] Arthur I. Gates, "The Psychological vs. the Chronological Order in the Teaching of History," *Historical Outlook*, XI (1920), 229.

provide at the present time for a course in economics based on such topics as unemployment, government economy, inflation, farm relief, taxation, over-production, and business depressions. In sociology, such subjects as marriage and divorce, public charity, crime, illiteracy, and the like would be major aspects of the course. Some speak of the approach which turns up topics of this nature as the functional approach.

THE SPIRAL, CYCLE, OR CONCENTRIC CIRCLES APPROACH

Closely related to the psychological or functional approach to materials in the social sciences for teaching purposes is an approach which has circulated under such names as spiral, cycle, and concentric circles. In its practical application the idea means the teaching of the same general body of material at different levels of instruction, adapting it, at each level, to the interests, capacities, and psychological development of those for whom it is intended. Inasmuch as this idea of arranging materials of instruction was imported from Europe as early as or even before the eighteen eighties, it seems appropriate to cite an example of its application in the field of history from a syllabus of history used in the Prussian secondary schools in 1913.

Class	Content
V.	Stories from legends of classical antiquity: Greek up to Solon; Roman up to the War with Pyrrus.
IV.	Greek History up to the death of Alexander the Great; Roman History up to the death of Augustus.
III-B.	The Roman Empire under the Great Emperors; German History from the first contact of the Germans with the Romans up to the end of the Middle Ages.

III-A. German History from the close of the Middle Ages up to Frederick the Great, with particular attention to the History of Brandenburg and of Prussia.

II-B. German and Prussian from Frederick the Great to the present day.

II-A. The chief events of Greek History up to the death of Alexander the Great and of Roman History up to Augustus, with references to Oriental History.

I-B. The most important of the Roman Emperors; German History up to the end of the Thirty Years' War.

I-A. The History of Prussia and of Germany from the end of the Thirty Years' War to the present day.[12]

It will be observed that the foregoing course of study is arranged on a two-cycle plan, the same general field of history being covered twice. The plan is psychological only in the degree that the material in each cycle is adapted to the interests and the capacities of those for whom it is intended. Cases are on record of a three-cycle plan in history. For example, in their scheme for a twelve-year course of study of history for the schools of this country, many have included a three-cycle plan in the field of United States history, offering the subject first in one or more of the intermediate grades; second, in one or more of the junior high-school grades; and third, in one of the senior high-school grades. In the opinion of some this three-cycle scheme has never been satisfactorily worked out. In commenting on the matter the authors of a text for use in one of the cycles said:

"As thing. now stand, the course of instruction in American

[12] M. W. Keatinge, *Studies in the Teaching of History*, p. 155. London: Adam and Charles Black, 1913.

history in our public schools embraces three distinct treatments of the subject. Three separate books are used. First, there is the primary book, which is usually a very condensed narrative with emphasis on biographies and anecdotes. Second, there is the advanced text for the seventh or eighth grade, generally speaking, an expansion of the elementary book by the addition of forty or fifty thousand words. Finally, there is the high school manual. This, too, ordinarily follows the beaten path, giving fuller accounts of the same events and characters. To put it bluntly, we do not assume that our children obtain permanent possessions from their study of history in the lower grades. If mathematicians followed the same method, high school texts on algebra and geometry would include the multiplication table and fractions.

"There is, of course, a ready answer to the criticism advanced above. It is that teachers have learned from bitter experience how little history their pupils retain as they pass along the regular route. No teacher of history will deny this. Still it is a standing challenge to existing methods of historical instruction. If the study of history cannot be made truly progressive like the study of mathematics, science, and languages, then the historians assume a grave responsibility in adding their subject to the already overloaded curriculum. If the successive historical texts are only enlarged editions of the first text—more facts, more dates, more words—then history deserves most of the sharp criticism which it is receiving from teachers of science, civics, and economics." [13]

Adverse criticisms of the concentric-circles plan of organizing historical materials for teaching purposes appeared in this

[13] Charles A. Beard and Mary R. Beard, *History of the United States,* Preface, p. v. New York: Macmillan Co., 1921.

country long before the paragraphs quoted above were written. The Herbartians were severe critics of the plan. Writing in 1892, one of their number said:

"The disciples of Herbart, while admitting the merits of the concentric circles, have subjected the plan to a severe criticism. They say it begins with general and abstract notions and puts off the interesting particulars first and by a gradual process of comparison and induction reaches the general principles and concepts at the close. It inevitably leads to a dull and mechanical repetition instead of cultivating an interesting comparison of new and old and a thoughtful retrospect. It is a clumsy and distorted application of the principle of apperception, of going from the known to the unknown. Instead of marching forward into new fields of knowledge with a proper basis of supplies in conquered fields, it gleans again and again in fields already harvested. For this reason it destroys a proper interest by hashing up the same old ideas year after year. Finally the concentric circles are not even designed to bring the different school studies into relation to each other. At best they contribute to a more thorough mastery of each study. They leave the separate branches of the course isolated and unconnected, an aggregation of unrelated thought complexes. True concentration should leave them an organic whole of intimate knowledge relations, conducing to strength and unity of character." [14]

In spite of attacks like the two foregoing, the cycle plan of organizing material in history and the other social sciences is very generally used in this country. An example of its use in a course in citizenship for the first six grades is found in a

[14] Charles A. McMurry, *Elements of General Method*, pp. 86 f. Bloomington, Illinois: Public School Publishing Co., 1892.

little volume published in 1919.[15] The centers around which
the work of each of the six grades is focused in this example
are exactly the same. In the order of presentation they are
"Citizenship in the Home," "Citizenship in Recreation,"
"Citizenship in Work," "Citizenship in Social Intercourse,"
and "Citizenship in Organized Community Life." The psychological approach is plainly evident in the organization
which is set up under each of these centers for each of the
first six grades. It would be difficult to cite a better illustration
of the use of the psychological approach in organizing citizenship materials for teaching purposes and the arrangement of
the same in cycles.

THE BIOGRAPHICAL APPROACH

One general approach remains for consideration. It applies
to history alone and is known as the biographical. No single
approach has been more used in the United States since about
1909. Grades IV and V have been most utilized for its application. It would be difficult to overstate the emphasis that was
placed on the biographical approach in this country between
1909 and 1927. Since the latter date, there seems to have been
a diminution of interest in it. Oblivion is probably its near
doom.

The explanation of the wide use of the biographical approach in this country is found in the staunch backing it had
from renowned authority. For example, speaking as late as
1916, an eminent philosopher said, "The biographical method
is generally recommended as the natural mode of approach to
historical study. The lives of great men, of heroes and leaders,
make concrete and vital historic episodes otherwise abstract

---

[15] Arthur W. Dunn and Hannah M. Harris, *Citizenship in School and Out.*
Boston: D. C Heath and Co.

and incomprehensible. They condense into vivid pictures complicated and tangled series of events spread over so much space and time that only a highly trained mind can follow and unravel them. There can be no doubt of the psychological soundness of this principle." [16]

Long before the foregoing was written others had spoken on the value of the biographical approach. Because of their emphasis on the ethical value in education, the Herbartians were strong defenders of an approach which made much use of biographies of outstanding individuals. It was the contention of these reformers that pupils derive valuable ethical lessons from their study of the lives of eminent heroes and heroines. They felt that a completely developed and well-balanced biographical story was a powerful instrument in elementary education.

The more or less unmolested reign of the biographical approach to history in the United States extended from about 1885 to the close of the second decade of the twentieth century. During these years the approach was employed almost exclusively in one or more of the intermediate grades and occasionally in the primary grades, Grades IV and V being the chief victims of its devastations. The explanation of its overwhelming presence in these grades is found in such things as tradition, the tendency among educational practitioners to follow a certain type of leadership, the educational doctrine of the American Herbartians, and the theory of child development which made children of a certain age ardent hero worshipers.

The leadership in course of study making in history between 1890 and 1921 was furnished by the committees of

---

[16] John Dewey, *Democracy and Education*, p. 251. New York: Macmillan Co., 1916.

national scope that have been considered in some detail in Division One. Four of these committees, reporting in 1893, 1895, 1909, and 1921, advocated the biographical approach in one or more of the intermediate grades.[17] The recommendations of these committees were accepted by the makers of courses of study, textbook writers, and publishers without question or modification. Especially was this true of the recommendations of the Committee of Eight of the American Historical Association. It will be recalled that the report of this Committee was first published in 1909. Few textbooks or courses of study in history for the intermediate grades appeared during the decades following this date that did not acknowledge their indebtedness to this Committee. While the influence of this Committee was on the decline in 1920, the stand taken by the American School Citiznship League's committee on history in the elementary schools, reporting in 1921, acted to keep the biographical approach before the minds of curriculum makers a few years longer. However, it should be said in passing that the appearance also in 1921 of the unofficial report of the Committee on History and Education for Citizenship of the American Historical Association, which did not adhere to the biographical approach, acted as a deterrent influence on the report of the American Citizenship League and caused the educational practitioners feebly to turn away from the doctrine promulgated in 1909 by the Committee of Eight of the American Historical Association.

One of the chief factors in the overwhelming presence prior to 1920 of the biographical approach to history for teaching purposes, especially in the intermediate grades, remains to be considered. Many believe that children at a certain age have

17 Maude E. Doane, "Practices in History in Grade V," p. 23. Unpublished Master's thesis, University of Chicago, 1932.

a natural and healthy interest in biography and they naturally are strong supporters of the biographical approach. A few objective data are available to show that their contention is not wholly unfounded. In a study of the voluntary reading of pupils in Grades IV, V, and VI, covering a period of eight years in the same library, the following conclusion appears: "Children of all three grades show considerable interest in reading biography. More biography would be read if more were suitably written. During the months of March and April in 1924, 262 biographies were read by the sixth grade classes. This made an average of about three for each child." [18]

It would be contrary to existing facts to say that the biographical approach to history for teaching purposes has passed into oblivion. A survey in 1931 of fifty-seven courses of study in history for Grades IV, V, and VI, published during the years 1928–31 inclusive, showed that this approach was used in thirteen courses for Grade IV; eight, for Grade V; and one, for Grade VI. The older the course, the more likely was the biographical approach to be used.[19] But it seems evident from this study that it may be expected to pass ere long into the realm of "approaches that have been." Reasons for the evident passing of this method of approach may be pointedly stated as follows:

1. The enormous diminution in the influence of Herbartians on educational practices in this country.

2. The opposition of the specialists in history to the approach because of its strong emphasis on the now discredited "great man" theory of history.

3. The opposition of the makers of courses of study who

[18] Evangeline Colburn, *A Library for the Intermediate Grades*, p. 15. Chicago: Department of Education, University of Chicago, 1930.

[19] Hannah M. Lindahl, "History in the Intermediate Grades," *Elementary School Journal*, XXXII (1931), 260.

desire to emphasize continuity and development in the history course—important phases of history almost wholly ignored by the biographical approach.

4. The undesirable character of the biographical material available for use in the schools. Speaking to this point a historical scholar remarked:

"The question of motive is most prominent in biography. The difficulty has given rise to at least three forms of biographical writing. The simplest is epic in its nature. The biographer supplies the motive throughout and we have the simple personal, usually heroic, record. In the second form the biographer gives a history of the times, leaving to the reader to determine the part played by the subject. The third is documentary and usually is not very attractive. The first is used almost exclusively by the hero worshippers. It is to be found especially in the books intended for school children, where an attempt by the children to imitate the conduct of these hand-made heroes ultimately leads a large number of them into crime. The second form of biography finds its readers among the more intelligent class while discriminating scholars demand the third.

"In the first form the biographer allows his subject to hitch his wagon to a star and drive resistlessly over all surroundings and circumstances. This philosophy makes this form of biography the more pernicious in the hands of children. Whatever influence psychoanalysis, Freudianism, psychiatry, psychology, and other forms of determinism will have on biography, it is certainly sage to predict that human biography will not soon be reduced to a mathematical formula by any one of these processes. Perhaps there will be a compromise and instead of our conventional hero swimming majestically up current or drifting helplessly down he will lay a three-quarter course down stream and cross as sensible swimmers have always done."[20]

5. The passing of the belief that a story about a person is more interesting and appealing to children in Grades IV, V, and VI than a story of an incident connected with a great epoch in history. The number of those who accepted the doctrine that history to be worth while must deal with fundamental movements directly instead of approaching them indirectly and unhistorically through the biographies of outstanding leaders increased heavily after 1920. It was evident to all on-lookers even at this date that the advocates of the biographical approach to history as a school subject were on the road to historical oblivion.[21]

III

SCHEMES FOR ORGANIZING THE FIELD OF THE SOCIAL SCIENCES FOR TEACHING PURPOSES

On the basis of the relation of the social sciences to each other at least four general schemes of organizing the field for

[20] Logan Esarey, "The Outlook for History," *Indiana Magazine of History,* XXIII (1927), 373 f.

[21] For the sake of completeness attention is called here to the sociological approach which originated in the movement to socialize education. This movement has been prevalent since about 1900 in this country. Coupled with it was the conception of history held by the so-called new historians. When these two innovations found expression in the approach to history for teaching purposes much emphasis was placed on group life. Snapshot-views of life among various groups became common. In a course of study in history the material was organized in terms of primitive life, Indian life, life in Athens, life in Rome, mediæval life, and American Colonial life. No course of study in history for either the six or the eight elementary grades organized strictly according to the dictates of the sociological approach seems ever to have appeared in this country. Social history has been and now is emphasized in many courses. Such an emphasis, however, does not mean that the sociological approach has been or is now applied.

teaching purposes have arisen. Designating these in terms of the general principles embodied in each, one has the following categories: isolation, correlation, concentration, and unification. Figure 1 portrays these categories diagrammatically. Geography is included here among the social sciences because of its inclusion by those who originated and developed each

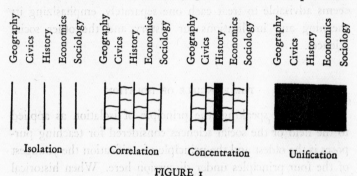

Isolation Correlation Concentration Unification

FIGURE 1

FOUR GENERAL SCHEMES OF ORGANIZING THE FIELD OF THE
SOCIAL SCIENCES

type of relationship shown in the figure. It will be noted that in the diagram illustrating the principle of isolation the lines representing the individual subjects are parallel and that no connecting rods between them are found. In the diagram illustrating the principle of correlation, the relations and connections among the individual subjects are indicated by the cross lines connecting the parallel ones which stand for subjects. The principle of concentration is more like the principle of correlation than any one of the others. The heavy line signifies that one subject becomes the center of attention and the other subjects are fused with it—in actual practice geography is made the center in one grade, history in another, and civics in still another. It will be noted that in the diagram illustrating the principle of unification all the lines standing for subjects have disappeared, leaving a unified body of material. Each of the principles illustrated above has had its staunch supporters in this country. Heated discussions have been waged over the merits and demerits of each. So much has been written and spoken concerning them since about 1890 that it seems advisable to treat each one separately, emphasizing its meaning and implications for history and the other social sciences.

THE PRINCIPLE OF ISOLATION

Historically speaking, the principle of isolation as applied to the field of the social sciences considered for teaching purposes is the oldest and the principle of unification the youngest of the four principles under discussion here. When historical material finally gained respectable notice in the school, it was in the form of a subject organized and taught under the caption "history." When material from the field of political science was introduced into the program of studies it too was a subject of study with an independent existence as was arithmetic, spelling, and reading. Similar statements are true of material from the fields of economics and sociology. Political economy or economics entered the schools as a subject of study with more or less definite boundaries. Material dealing with certain aspects of man in society appeared in programs of study under the caption "sociology." Inasmuch as these subjects grew up in isolation, they tended to maintain their autonomy even after it became very desirable that their interrelations be emphasized.

It is the opinion of many present-day educational reformers that isolation or departmentalization within the field of the social sciences is a very bad thing. They speak of it as the traditional way of organizing the field of the social sciences for teaching purposes. To label a thing "traditional" is one way of passing a very adverse judgment on it. Most persons prefer that the word "progressive" be applied to schemes they propose. However, in spite of the fact that one is spoken of as a reactionary in some quarter when one advocates the teaching of history, civics, and economics as independent subjects, there still remain in actual practice many examples of the principle of isolation, especially in its application to history and civics, not to mention geography. Prior to 1918, there appeared in this country eight-year courses of study in a social science other than history along with and independent of a history course of equal length. Philadelphia adopted in 1916 a course in civics and a course in history, each eight years in length. The state of Pennsylvania went over to the Philadelphia scheme a year or so later. Commenting on the Philadelphia plan, one writer remarked near the time of its adoption:

"The Philadelphia Plan is based on the idea that the work in civics will gain in effectiveness if it is regularly scheduled, by name, in every year of the elementary school, for at least two periods each week. The civic training thus becomes as steady and as cumulative as that in English or in mathematics. Moreover, this arrangement enables the distinctively civic material that lies scattered throughout the various subjects of the elementary curriculum, much of which would ordinarily be lost, to be gathered up and combined with the more strictly governmental concepts that enter into any course in civics. For example, 'public sanitation' is lifted bodily out of the course in physiology and hygiene and set down, gently but firmly, in the civics course. This results in confining hygiene to its individual application (personal hygiene), while community hygiene is given its appropriate social setting and application." [22]

The defenders of the principle of isolation are today and have been in the past chiefly found among subject-matter specialists who believe that the ability to solve contemporary social problems is best acquired through a systematic study of subjects such as history, civics, economics, and sociology. Concerning the advantage of treating economics as a separate subject one of these specialists has commented as follows:

"The advantage of isolating the economic aspects of society for separate study is that it conduces to clear thinking and a better understanding of the complexity of social relations. Its justification is the advance that has been made in the understanding of economic relations since Adam Smith made the study of them a separate science. In judicial procedure experience has taught the necessity of considering separately questions of fact and questions of law, although both are essential to the judgment; similarly in social study, it is a help to consider questions of economic fact and questions of moral right separately, although our action will be influenced by the two considerations jointly. The separation assists in the constructive handling of the mass of facts which bewilder us at our first attempt to discover the principles of the social organization. It prevents the confusion of thought and the argument at cross-purposes which inevitably result from the attempt to discuss *all* the aspects of a complicated question at once. Just as physiology, anatomy, and psychology study the

[22] J. Lynn Barnard, "Civics," *Teaching Elementary School Subjects,* edited by L. W. Rapeer, p. 474. New York: Charles Scribner's Sons, 1917.

same subject, man, from different points of view, so the social sciences, economics, ethics, politics, and law, study different aspects of the same subject, society. The method is simply an application of the common-sense principle, 'One thing at a time.' Specialization is as necessary in research as in industry; the progress of knowledge has been based on the same principle as the growth of the Roman Empire, *Divide et impera*. The method has its dangers, since aspects of a problem that can be separated for study cannot be separated for purposes of action; but the misuse of the conclusions of specialized study is no reason for giving up the study." [23]

The proponents of civics as a subject of study are able to assemble a challenging list of reasons for giving it an independent place in the program of studies. In the first place, they claim that an independent presentation makes it possible to recognize the fact that the child is a citizen when he enters school and continues to be one as long as he remains therein; and as a citizen he is a member of various communities such as the home, the school, the neighborhood, the city, the state, and the nation. Furthermore, the defenders of civics as an independent subject say that, to be of most value in the formation of the habit of being a good citizen, instruction in civics must be cumulative. To form the habit of good citizenship it is claimed that there must be given the opportunity for civic thinking, civic feeling, and civic acting not only on special occasions in the child's school career, but again and again throughout every year. These desirable ends are not according to the proponents of civics as an independent subject accomplished by incidental instruction in civics even though such

[23] Henry Clay, *Economics, an Introduction for the General Reader,* pp. 20 f. London: Macmillan and Co., 1916.

be given throughout the grades; neither are they satisfactorily achieved by devoting a half year to the civics at or near the end of the elementary course. Then, again, it is said, "If training in the practical phases of citizenship is as valuable as some of late have come to think it is, why deprive many pupils who never reach the seventh grade of formal instruction therein? Those who ask this question feel that there is but one'way to prevent the deprivation they have in mind and that is by giving civics a definite place in every year of the child's elementary-school life and high-school life too for that matter.

Those who argue for history as an independent subject say that the principle of isolation or separation gives the teacher (1) the occasion to teach to the child in an unhampered way the history that he needs for a comprehensive understanding of the life and institutions into which he is daily thrown and (2) the opportunity to teach the fundamental developments in the history of our own country in a systematic and connected way, thus making it possible to give the pupil a historical background against which he can throw a multitude of happenings that he daily meets.

While the ideal of the isolationists is a course in civics, history, and geography running parallel throughout at least the first eight grades, such an ideal has never been generally attained. The increase in individual subjects demanding an independent existence in the school has tended to react against the continuous offering of separate subjects in closely related fields. To prevent the neglecting of certain aspects of social living, the custom developed of alternating the individual social sciences in the schedule set up for all of the social sciences. For example, geography in Grade VII, history in Grade VIII, and civics in Grade IX. How this arrangement works out in the last six grades of a twelve-grade system is shown in the following set-up in use in the University High School, University of California in 1931:

Low Seven. The Americas.

High Seven. Our Country in the Making.

Low Eight. Nations as Neighbors.

High Eight. American Ideals and Government.

Low Nine. Life and Living in a Changing World.

High Nine. The Story of Human Progress.

Low Ten. Survey of the Development of World Civilization from the Days of Early Civilization to about 1815.

High Ten. Survey of the Development of World Civilization from 1815 to the Present Time.

Low Eleven. Survey of the Development of American Institutions—Emphasis Upon American History.

High Eleven. Survey of the Development of American Institutions with Emphasis Upon Government—World Relations Shown.

Low Twelve. Problems of American Democracy—Economic Problems, Their Social Phases and Political Relations.

High Twelve. Social Problems—Their Economic Phases and Political Relations.

Space does not admit of additional examples of the application of the principle of isolation to the organization of the social sciences for teaching purposes. However, the point ought to be made in closing this phase of the discussion that, in spite of the attempts of a number of people to discredit the principle, it seems to be very much alive. To say that it is holding its own against all new-comers would be making an untrue statement. There was a time when the principle was in universal use wherever materials from the social sciences were included in the program of studies. This, of course, is not the situation at the present time, because of the appearance in the educational horizon of other principles of organization, to which attention will now be directed.

THE PRINCIPLE OF UNIFICATION

The antithesis of the principle of isolation is the principle of unification. Those who believe in this latter principle speak of themselves as progressives. They are so certain that they are right that they have little patience with those who disagree with them. While they have no objective data to substantiate their position, they are very very certain that theirs is the only principle of organization for the field of the social sciences worthy of serious consideration. Their general viewpoint is well expressed in the following excerpt:

"The idea back of the fusion or unified course is that one can function effectively as a social human being only if one understands modern life and how it came to be. To understand the conditions and the institutions existing today, the mind must use facts, events, historical movements and generalizations, that come from all three subjects—geography, history and civics. Political history, how things happened, depends on economic history which tells why things happened. Or in other words, history and government are largely the story of the human race in terms of soils, harbors, oil, wheat, cotton and iron. For example, to understand the Westward Movement involves a study of North America and of the

United States; the influence of soil, rivers, harbors, mountains, deserts and climate upon how people live and where they locate and travel. How else can one get the why and where of the blazing trails, the development of new land and waterways and the rise of cities behind the frontiers? In the technique of government, the western drive is closely related to such democratic innovations as the direct election of United States senators, woman's suffrage, the initiative, referendum and recall, and to the growth of nationalism.

"The physiographic factors and natural resources must be brought into close relationships with man's social and political points of view and with the institutions he has developed, because they in large measure explain why these viewpoints and institutions obtain. This is, on the whole, the viewpoint of those who do not favor separate courses in geography, history, and civics." [24]

The idea of a unified social science is by no means indigenous to this country. August Comte and Herbert Spencer both attempted to evolve a unified social science. The early attempts to establish social science as a special discipline have been discussed in Division Four along with early adventures in the unification of the social sciences. In these discussions the chief interest was in the establishment of a social science as an independent subject of study while the present interest is in the most desirable adjustment between the social sciences themselves—a topic which has been in the minds of many people for a number of years. For example, as early as 1916, a professional historian was suggesting an adjustment between

[24] Bertha Montgomery, "Experimenting with a Fusion Course in Social Science in Grades VI, VII, and VIII," *Historical Outlook*, XXI (1930), 125. (Some writers use the expressions "fusion course" and "unified course" interchangeably. Such a practice certainly is not conducive to exact thinking in the field.)

history, economics, civics, and sociology on the high-school level that was virtually an application of the principle of unification. To a body of teachers this historian said relative to certain unsatisfactory conditions in the teaching of history as an independent subject in the high school:

"What is the result? The result is I think that high school students emerge from their history courses with a very slight and not very useful body of knowledge about the past, and with a capacity to think historically that is in no proper proportion to the time spent in such courses; for the most part they have memorized a few facts which mean little, or a few vague generalizations which mean even less.

"What is the solution for this fundamental difficulty in respect to the curriculum? Frankly, I do not know. But it seems clear that some radical reorganization of the curriculum is necessary. The value which the study of history undoubtedly may have, and which it therefore should have for high-school students, will not be obtained I am convinced until the student is made acquainted much more intimately with characters and events and those complex and concrete situations which alone make the past real and give to the study of it a practical and a disciplinary importance. This cannot be done without limiting the field covered. Perhaps the field should be contemporary history; perhaps it should be the history of our own country. In any case I doubt whether any satisfactory solution will be found so long as we continue to give distinct courses in history, economics, civics, and sociology. Why would it not be possible (it would be difficult certainly) to organize a single course, of one, two, three, or four years, which would embrace all that the high school gives in the so-called social sciences; a carefully coordinated course in which history, economics, civics, and sociology should all find their properly related place? Meantime, I am perfectly willing that someone else should attempt to organize this ideal course." [25]

The story of the pioneer effort of Denver, Colorado, to apply the principle of unification in the construction of a course of study in the social sciences has been told in Division Four. Inasmuch as the discussion of social science in Division Four as an independent subject of study in the schools and the present one are so closely related, further use will be made here of the work accomplished in Denver. In the previous discussion no mention was made of the details of the Denver set-ups in the first six elementary grades and in the junior high school. These set-ups are important for the present consideration. They appear below as first published during the summers of 1924 and 1926.

Social Science in the Elementary Grades
Denver, Colorado, 1926

Grade I–B. Home Life.

Grade I–A. Home Life.

Grade II–B. Community Life.

Grade II–A. Community Life.

Grade III–B. Indian Life.

Grade III–A. Child Life in Foreign Lands.

Grade IV–B. Colonial Life.

Grade IV–A. Westward Movement.

[25] Carl Becker, "History in the High School Curriculum," *Educational Administration and Supervision*, II (1916), 378.

Grade V. Interdependence: agriculture, irrigation, stock raising, fishing, lumbering, quarrying, and mining.

Grade VI. Interdependence: manufacturing, transportation, communication, invention and discoveries, recreation, and a survey of Denver.[26]

In the second revised edition of the foregoing set-up for Grades III, IV, V and VI, the material on Indian life and life in foreign lands was retained in Grade III. The general topic, "Satisfying Man's Need for Food, Clothing, Shelter, Transportation, and Communication" was allocated to Grade IV. Material relating to early explorations, Colonial life, pioneer life, Denver, and Colorado was located in Grade V. The work for Grade VI in the new set-up was based on economic life in the United States and our American neighbors and how they live.

The general set-ups for the junior high school, Grades VII, VIII, and IX appear below as published in 1924, 1926, and 1931.

In the Denver scheme no attempt was made to unify the social sciences in Grades X, XI, XII, separate courses in world history, American history, American problems, economics, and world relations being provided. No explanation appears in any of the published material why unification was not carried beyond Grade IX. Why a return to separation in the junior high school was made in 1931 is likewise not stated in the available published material.

To multiply examples of a so-called unified course in the social sciences would probably be an unprofitable use of space. The point, however, should be made that the grave difficulties

[26] *Social Science,* Grades One, Two, Three, Four, Five, and Six. Denver, Colo.: Public Schools, 1926.

THREE EDITIONS OF A JUNIOR HIGH-SCHOOL COURSE OF STUDY
IN SOCIAL SCIENCE, DENVER, COLORADO

GRADE	FIRST EDITION OF THE COURSE, 1924	SECOND REVISED EDITION, 1926	THIRD REVISED EDITION, 1931
VII	Unit I. Community Life Unit II. The Industrial Life of the American People Unit III. The Interdependence of Modern Industrial Nations Unit IV. The Changing Agricultural Nations	Unit I. The Commercial Development of the United States Unit II. The Interdependence of Modern Industrial Nations Unit III. The Changing Agricultural Nations	Constitution of the United States Changing Civilizations in a Modern World Old World Background of American History
VIII	Unit V. Westward Movement and the Growth of Transportation Unit VI. History of the Industrial Revolution Unit VII. Growth of American Democracy	Unit IV. The Westward Movement Unit V. The Industrial History of the American People Unit VI. The Growth of American Democracy	History of the United States
IX	Unit I. Forms of American Government and Outstanding Citizenship Problems Unit II. Waste and Conservation of America's Resources Unit III. Immigration and Americanization Unit IV. International Relations*	Unit VII. Group Life Unit VIII. Social and Civic Problems in the Community Unit IX. Economic Problems in the Community Unit X. Vocational Civics Unit XI. Governmental Civics Unit XII. International Relations	Present Day Problems of a Modern Community Governmental Civics and International Relations

* *Social Science*, Junior High School, Grades Seven, Eight and Nine, pp. 16, 68, and 115. Denver, Colo.: Public Schools, 1924; *ibid.*, second revised edition, 1926, p. 8; and third revised edition, 1931, pp. 9-12. In the 1931 edition the large phases of work in each grade were organized in terms of divisions and the divisions organized in terms of units.

inherent in the idea of unification soon became obvious as courses purporting to apply it began to appear here and there throughout the country. It was also evident in some of these courses that the friends of unification were determined to kill. These individuals were satisfied to stop with mere verbalism rather than to push on to pure and unadulterated unification if such could ever be attained. When these imitations once became evident, other schemes of utilizing the relations existing among these subjects began to appear. Those who opposed isolation and unification resurrected the Herbartians' principles of correlation and concentration, and in order to appear different used the words "integrated" and "fused" to characterize them. The implications back of the use of these two words are considered below in connection with correlation and concentration.

THE PRINCIPLES OF CORRELATION AND CONCENTRATION

The American Herbartians placed tremendous emphasis on correlation and concentration. By the latter they meant that one subject was made the core and all other subjects brought into close connection with it. A Herbartian's explanation of the term ran thus:

"By concentration is meant such a connexion between the parts of each study and such a spinning of relations and connecting links between different sciences that unity may spring out of the variety of knowledge. History, for example, is a series and collocation of facts explainable on the basis of cause and effect, a development. On the other hand, history is intimately related to geography, language, natural science, literature and mathematics. It would be impossible to draw real history out by the roots without drawing all other studies out bodily with it. Is there then any reason why school history should ignore its blood relationships to other branches of knowledge?

"In attempting to solve the problem of concentration the question has been raised whether a single study, the most important, of course, would constitute a concentrating nucleus, like the hub in a wheel, or whether all studies and experiences are to be brought into an organic whole of related parts. It is evident that history and natural science at least hold a leading place among studies and determine to some extent the selection of materials in reading and language lessons." [28]

There has been much talk since about 1920 of the necessity of making the social sciences the core of the curriculum in all grades. The only difference between the advocates of this notion and the Herbartians is that the latter used the term "history" instead of the expression "social sciences" to designate the core. In the middle eighteen nineties an American Herbartian proposed a plan for Grades IV, V and VI, which embodied the Herbartian idea of concentration. There is also illustrated in the plan the idea of correlation held by these reformers. The plan is presented here in full because of its historical importance.

FOURTH GRADE

"History: Frémont's Expedition.

"Geography: The country to which the class is introduced through the history, i.e., St. Louis, Mississippi River, Platte River, prairies of Kansas and Nebraska, animals, plants, and products of these states, Fort Laramie, Rocky Mountains in the region of Frémont's Peak, mountains, lakes, etc.; wheat

[28] Charles A. McMurry, *op. cit.,* pp. 69 f.

farms, cattle ranches, new Western cities, railroads, frontier facts, garrisons, Indian tribes, prairie fires, blizzards.

"Science: The Wheat plant, grasses of the West, rocks, fishes, birds, deer, buffalo, etc. If these animals are not all at hand, those most nearly related to them may be studied instead; for example, the sheep in place of the deer. Also instruments used by Frémont, i.e., the barometer, thermometer, compass (air-pressure and pneumatics).

"Arithmetic: Problems suggested by Geography and Science; compare lengths of rivers, for examples in division; value of wheat farms, quantity of wheat raised and its value at a certain number of bushels per acre; the values of hides and income of trappers from that source; value of cattle.

"Language: The thoughts expressed on paper are taken from History, Science, etc.

"Spelling: Words necessarily introduced by the other studies.

FIFTH GRADE

"History: Story of John Smith (his struggles with the shiftless colonists, his adventures with the Indians, and his expedition of discovery).

"Geography: Chesapeake Bay and vicinity; oyster-beds, tobacco-raising; coal and iron mines and fruit-growing in addition to study of climate, relief, soil, etc.

"Science: Tobacco plant, oysters, clams, snails, with other native plants and animals of Virginia.

"Arithmetic: Quantity of tobacco chewed by one person per year, in a lifetime; quantity smoked; its value; weight of ashes of cigar compared with weight of cigars; one is what per cent of the other, etc.

"Language: Compositions on the history of an oyster, the production of iron, John Smith's adventures, etc.

SIXTH GRADE

"History: Causes of the French and Indian War; Desire of France and England to secure the fur trade—differences in religion, etc.

"Geography: Valley of St. Lawrence, the Great Lakes, Ohio River, Nova Scotia, and New Brunswick, Lake Champlain, and Lake George, pineries of West and North, fisheries on coast.

"Science: Fur-bearing animals—beaver, otter, mink, bear, buffalo, raccoon. Also deer and moose.

"Arithmetic: Relative size of the lakes, expressed decimally; of the states in the once disputed territory; relative worth of various kinds of furs, and so forth." [29]

Instead of using the words "correlation" and "concentration" to designate a set-up very similar to the one above, current advocates of curriculum reforms use the words "integration" and "fusion." They do not deny the fact that *correlation* is a fundamental aspect of their proposed reforms, but insist that the correlation that they practice is natural and not forced as was the case all too frequently with the Herbartians. It will be observed in the foregoing example of concentration that the subject of history was made the center of gravity. In the scheme now frequently advocated under the words "integration" and "fusion," a unit of work, a problem, a project, a center of interest, or a unit of activity is usually made the basis for fusion or integration. The following set-up of a problem

29 Charles De Garmo, *Herbart and the Herbartians*, pp. 127–129. New York: Charles Scribner's Sons, 1895.

in history as carried out in Grade IV–B illustrates what occurs when the current notion of the principle of integration is actually applied. The problem was stated in the course of study in history thus: "How Europeans Came to Know the New World." The outline used by one teacher in directing a class in the solution of this problem is hereby submitted.

Problem: How Europeans Came to Know the New World

I. History

A. The topic was introduced to the children by a story of Marco Polo's adventures in China.

B. Stories of Columbus, Ponce de Leon, Cortez, and Balboa were used as work progressed.

II. Reading

A. History texts furnished material for reading lessons.

B. Books in the library corner furnished recreational reading on the history topic.

III. Geography

A. Countries and cities were located through map study.

B. Routes of explorers were traced on wall maps.

IV. English

A. Dialogues and explanations for an historical play growing out of the unit study and written by the class provided one type of constructive English.

B. Invitations to a performance of the play provided a letter-writing experience.

C. "Columbus," a poem by Joaquin Miller, gave worthwhile content for several literature periods.[30]

The outline below is submitted to show how a study of

[30] Mary S. Braun, "Intermediate Grade History Teaching," *Baltimore Bulletin of Education*, VIII (1930), 154 f.

water transportation served to integrate the work of a V-A grade. It will be observed that the integration in this case went much farther beyond the field of the social sciences than it did in the case above.

A Study of Water Transportation

I. History.—Ancient sea-trade; Study of early Phœnicia, Egypt, Rome, England, and Spain; Routes of early Explorers; Modern Trade Routes.

II. Geography.—The Characteristics of a Good Port; Important Ports and Dry Docks of the World; Various Imports and Exports which Pass through Ports in North and South America.

III. Composition.—Preparation of Written Reports; Letters to Mayor for Harbor Trip; Invitations to the Exhibition; Cooperative Paragraph for Sixth Grade Magazine; Making Arrangements for Trips; Original Poems; Words for Ship Song; Construction of Paragraphs to Accompany each Ship Model; Invitations to Parents.

IV. Reading.—Reference Reading for Reports; Sea Stories in and out of Class.

V. Spelling.—Correcting Misspelled Words in all Written Work; New Words Needed for Individual Use—Port, Signal, Seaward.

VI. Science.—Study of Constellations and Planets; Use of Compass; What Makes an Iron Boat Float.

VII. Manual Arts.—Wood for Block Prints; Stands for Finished Models; Mast Stands.

VIII. Music and Physical Education.—Sea Chanteys; Writing of Melody for Ship Song; Sailors' Horn Pipe; Steps to Sea Music.

IX. Art.—Linoleum Block Prints of Ships; Making of Books for Individual Logs; Lettering for Signs, Charts; Books for Poems, Songs.[31]

Evidence of pedagogical reversion is found in the two foregoing illustrations of present-day integration. Either of them would have been accepted during the 1890's as an application of the Herbartian doctrine of concentration. They are excellent examples of the sayings that the roots of the present lie buried in the past and that the present can be thoroughly understood only through a knowledge of the past. The roots of integration as preached and practiced today seem deeply buried in the doctrine of concentration as proclaimed in this country during the 1890's.

Those who use the word "fusion" to designate the kind of unification they have in mind say that its significance as over against either correlation or concentration is that it looks forward to a unity in which the distinctive subject-matter lines have disappeared. While the principles of correlation, integration, and concentration have been applied regardless of general subject-matter fields, fusion has been advocated largely by those interested primarily in the social sciences. The subjects to which the fusion idea has been applied most frequently are history, geography, and civics. One of the chief advocates and possibly the originator of fusion as applied to these fields commented not long ago as follows on how fusion actually works out in practice.

"As an illustration to show the naturalness of this fusion method, one of my groups set themselves to find an answer to

[31] A. Viola Lamm, "A Study of Water Transportation," *Baltimore Bulletin of Education*, VI (1928), 135–142.

this problem: 'How was Switzerland, situated in the midst of Europe, able to keep out of the World War?' One day, while this was under discussion, a visitor remarked at the end of the hour, 'I came in a little late, and although I have listened intently I do not know now whether this was a class in history, geography or civics.' We could not help much in giving him the proper label, but asked in turn if the problem could be answered without a study of the geography, history and government of this little Alpine state. At least we felt that they were all 'grist to our mill,' all necessary if we were to find the right answer. This points out, it seems to me, a perfectly natural and not a dragged-in correlation; in fact a 'fusion' of the significant and worthwhile materials from all three fields." [32]

The practice of fusing history, geography, and civics as suggested in this quotation has gained some ground since 1924. As early as 1926 a published account of how fusion had succeeded in one school appeared.[33] In commenting on the plan as he had observed it for two years the principal of this school remarked:

"This is not an attempt to correlate the history, geography, and civics usually taught in these grades. Correlation, however skillfully worked out never fully obviates the disadvantages of the water-tight compartment idea of subject matter. The name 'fusion' implies something more than finding points of contact between different fields of knowledge. In

[32] *Proceedings,* Twelfth Annual Meeting, New Jersey State High School Conference, p. 293. New Brunswick: The State University of New Jersey, 1930.
[33] R. W. Hatch and De Forest Stull, *The Social Studies in the Horace Mann Junior High School.* New York: Bureau of Publications, Teachers College, Columbia University, 1926.

this course of study certain desirable objectives and interests are introduced to the pupils and they are led to draw upon geography, history, or any other body of knowledge that may be necessary to develop the problems involved. Geography, history, and civics become not ends in themselves, but means to an end. The subject matter of these fields, therefore, has meaning to pupils because its relationship to a larger unit of knowledge becomes evident.

"To the principal of a school the fusion course has many administrative advantages, not the least of which is the economy of time involved. For instance, in our seventh grade, we have found that the four periods per week formerly given to geography and the three periods to history can be satisfactorily supplanted by a fusion course of six periods per week, one of which is devoted to current events." [34]

The first large school system to adopt the principles of fusion for Grades I–IX seems to have been that of Springfield, Massachusetts. As early as 1928 there began to appear in this city tentative courses of study under the general title "Social Studies." These were issued in terms of the Kindergarten and Grades I, II, and III; Grades IV, V, and VI; and Junior High School (Grades VII, VIII, and IX). In the Preface of each of the courses for the junior high school the word "fusion" was used in referring to the course in a certain connection. Nothing was said about unification, integration, correlation, or concentration. While the word "fusion" did not appear in the introductions to the courses for the two general levels below the junior high school, it is evident to one who merely scans the set-ups for these two levels that "fusion" was in the minds

[34] *Ibid.*, p. 1. For a critical analysis of fusion see Howard E. Wilson, *The Fusion of Social Studies in Junior High Schools*. Cambridge, Mass.: Harvard University Press, 1933.

of those responsible for them. For example, in the Kindergarten, Grades I, II, and III the expression "focusing point" is used in connection with the material proposed for each grade. The focusing point for each of the kindergarten-primary grades follows:

"Kindergarten. The Kindergarten Environment.
"Grade I-B. The School of the Immediate Neighborhood.
"Grade I-A. The Home and the Immediate Neighborhood.
"Grade II-B. Community Life in Relation to the Home.
"Grade II-A. Lives of Primitive Peoples in Relation to Present-Day Living.
"Grade III-B. City and Country Life with Emphasis on the Dependence of Each upon the Other.
"Grade III-A. Child Life in Other Lands." [35]

In the courses for all grades above Grade III the word "problem" was used instead of focusing point to name the center around which history and geography were fused. It is felt by some as hinted in the quotation above that the problem approach to fusion is the most natural and effective one now available.

It is possible to find examples of the application of the principles of integration, correlation, and concentration in unexpected places. For example, a study of the use made of geography, literature, economics, science and invention, and government and civics by the authors of six textbooks in United States history for the upper and junior high-school grades revealed some illuminating data. Contrary to the belief of some that when a pupil pursues a course in United States history based largely on a textbook, he is engulfed in

[35] *Social Studies.* A Tentative Course of Study for Kindergarten, Grades I, II, III, Table of Contents. Springfield, Mass.: Public Schools, 1931.

departmentalized history, this study proves that when a pupil
is studying any one of at least seven textbooks in United States
history, he is working in harmony with the principles of
integration, concentration, and correlation. Table I exhibits

TABLE I

CORRELATION WITH GEOGRAPHY, LITERATURE, ECONOMICS,
SCIENCE AND INVENTION, AND GOVERNMENT AND CIVICS
IN SEVEN TEXTBOOKS IN UNITED STATES HISTORY FOR JUNIOR
HIGH SCHOOLS.*

TEXTS	NET PAGES OF TEXT	Number of Items of Correlation with					Per Cent of Total Text					Total Per Cent
		GEOGRAPHY	LITERATURE	ECONOMICS	SCIENCE AND INVENTION	GOVERNMENT AND CIVICS	GEOGRAPHY	LITERATURE	ECONOMICS	SCIENCE AND INVENTION	GOVERNMENT AND CIVICS	OF SUBJECTS CORRELATED
1......	466	205	30	270	30	255	14.5	2.0	21.5	2.3	19.4	59.7
2......	379	135	5	200	30	160	13.6	.4	21.5	2.8	18.8	57.1
3......	480	175	40	230	40	255	13.5	2.4	15.6	3.5	20.8	55.8
4......	470	265	20	210	45	150	12.0	1.9	21.4	6.0	12.0	53.3
5......	380	120	5	180	30	135	12.6	.2	18.0	2.6	15.0	48.4
6......	410	115	25	175	65	80	8.3	2.4	14.5	6.8	9.0	41.0
7......	385	165	25	135	35	150	10.4	2.2	12.4	2.6	11.5	39.1
Median	410	165	25	200	35	150	12.6	2.0	18.0	2.8	15.0	53.3

* William L. Roach, "Correlation with Other Subjects in Junior High School United
States History Text-books," *School and Society*, XXXIII (1931), 178.

certain aspects of the findings of the study. Two items in this
table are of special interest, the total per cent of subjects correlated and the uniformity in the per cent of correlation with
geography, economics, and government and civics. In using
any one of the first four of the textbooks analyzed, the pupil
would be exposed to material other than historical more than
half of the time. In these texts he would be exposed to material from the fields of geography, economics, and government
and civics in more or less equal amounts. It would seem from

the results of this study that, if one wished to make history the center of integration or concentration, as did the Herbartians, it could be accomplished through the use of any one of the first four or five books represented in the table, as a basic text.

IV

SPECIFIC WAYS OF ORGANIZING THE SOCIAL SCIENCES FOR TEACHING PURPOSES

In their efforts to get a workable control over the subject-matter available for use in the schools, makers of courses of study have evolved a number of specific ways of organizing materials for teaching purposes. At least seven of these are especially applicable to the organization of one or more of the social sciences. These seven ways may be briefly denominated the topical, the type-study, the problem, the project, the unit of understanding, the unit of work, and the contract. Each of which is considered in turn below.

THE ORGANIZATION OF THE SOCIAL SCIENCES IN TERMS OF SIGNIFICANT TOPICS

The topical organization of a social science for teaching purposes has been advocated decade after decade in this country since about 1880. In the early years of this decade the argument in favor of organizing history for teaching purposes in terms of topics was stated by one of its defenders as follows:

"A merchant who wishes to learn the results of his business transactions at the close of the year, and to satisfy himself as to the comparative importance of his various trade enterprises, and their relative influence on each other, might possibly do so by examining his day-book alone, but it would require the labor of months to accomplish what he could do in a few hours by consulting his ledger. Histories are usually merely day-books of the business of nations, and so students read them through and through without remembering clearly the events narrated, their causes, or their immediate or ultimate bearing on any of the departments of national life or progress. The continuous concentration of thought which is so essential in the formation of correct conclusions concerning the effects of national customs or tendencies, is impossible when the attention is distracted by the presentation of so great a variety of unconnected events to the mind. If these events were grouped in ledger form so that they could be taught *topically,* the student would save much time and be able to make more satisfactory progress. Instead of giving facts relating to all kinds of events promiscuously, as they occurred, and as they would be recorded in a diary, they should be classified under a few leading heads, and the consecutive history of each class during the period under consideration taught independently. The chief elements that go to form the life and true development of a nation should be selected, and the history of each element narrated without reference to the others, except in so far as it is directly related to them. The historical topics should vary slightly for different periods and nations, but the following will generally include all that are necessary: 1. External History, including foreign relationships and wars, the loss or extension of territory, etc.; 2. Constitutional Growth; 3. Religion; 4. Literature; 5. Social Development; 6. Commerce; 7. General Progress." [36]

In the decade of the 1890's the argument for the topical

[36] J. L. Hughes, "The Topical Teaching of History," *Education*, II (1882), 410 f.

organization of United States history was defended by one of its advocates thus:

"The statement of the question on the programme, 'In cross sections or in parallels,' is significant. The mere anouncement is enough to attract the attention of all persons present interested in the teaching of history. Were I to ask those of you who are teaching United States history, if fifteen anecdotes were to be related by the same individual, and he would start in and give a little introduction to the first anecdote, and then drop it and take anecdote No. 2, and then pass to anecdote No. 3, and so on through to fifteen, with a slight introduction to each, and then return to the first and give a little bit more of it, and then to the second, and so on—would it be an interesting manner of relating anecdotes? Just think of this for a moment!

"United States history can be divided into ten or twelve parallel lines, or perhaps a less number. Certainly it is true that by studying history along parallel lines the striking facts in connection with each parallel can be easily strung together and better remembered. It is historical evolution. Ladies and gentlemen, I leave the question with you." [37]

There appeared the same year that the foregoing was written a textbook in United States history purporting to employ the topical organization. Because of its primacy in this field the list of topics used as chapter headings is included here. They were: "History Study and Teaching," "Pre-Columbian Discoveries," "Pre-Columbian Civilization," "Jesuits and Indians," "Colonial Government," "Growth of Government," "Making

[37] James M. Greenwood, "Shall American History be Taught in Cross Sections or in Parallels?" *Proceedings of the National Educational Association*, 1897, pp. 157 and 159.

and Ratifying the Constitution," "Judicial Department," "Congress," "Executive Departments," Elections," "Tariff and Revenues," "Paper Money," "Coin," "Banking," "Slavery," "Education," "Religion," "Journalism," "Diplomacy," "Political Parties," "Customs," "Amusements," "Sickness and Medicine," "Territorial Growth," "Manufactures," "Mail," "The Farmer," "The Laborer," "Lotteries," "Witchcraft," "Crime and Punishment," "Inventions," "Transportation," "State and Local Government," and "Governments of the World." [38] How extensively Joseph's book was actually used in the schools during the first ten years after its publication is unknown; but as only one edition, and probably a small one at that, seems ever to have been printed, it is safe to conclude that the volume was a failure when judged by its immediate influence.

During the first decade of the present century, proponents of the topical organization of history for teaching purposes were by no means modest in their claims for it. Relating his own experience with it, one of its advocates said:

"In my estimation our texts would do better if they would pursue what I think of as the continuous development method of presenting matters. I mean to take up one line of interest or activities and carry it through the course of a whole epoch or period without interjecting between its parts in the course of the period other kinds of interests and activities. I have tried this and found it works in an admirable fashion. To illustrate, I will name the topics I carried through continuously from 1789 to the Civil War, or such as extended through the whole of the period: Organization of government and parties; struggle for commercial independence; westward expansion

[38] J. A. Joseph, *Institutional History of the United States*, pp. ix–xii. Danville, Indiana: Indiana Publishing Co., 1897.

of territory, population, and transportation facilities; revolutionizing inventions and processes; political parties and doctrines; establishment and growth of protective tariff; some problems in finance and banking; development of the slavery issue; chief international problems.

"And when we reflect, we find that this continuous development of a single series of events or interests is just the sort of knowledge the citizen needs. He needs to know the tariff history in itself, and so on. He must know it this way in order to understand it. If it is not developed that way for him in school he is likely never to develop it, and, hence, always to be ignorant." [39]

The pleas for the topical organization, especially in the field of United States history, set forth in the foregoing quotations were as bread cast upon the pedagogical waters. In due time they returned in the form of topics more or less satisfactory to the proponents of organizing history in terms of significant topics. Between 1910 and 1920 at least four states adopted the topical idea in the field of United States history. For example, in their courses of study in United States history for the year 1915 for Grades VII and VIII the states of Kentucky and Idaho attempted to apply the topical-organization idea. Inasmuch as these efforts represent the status of the idea in the upper-elementary grades in 1915, the topics used in each of these courses seem worth including here.

TOPICS IN UNITED STATES HISTORY FOR PUPILS IN THE
UPPER-ELEMENTARY GRADES

"I. A list from the Kentucky Elementary Course of Study, 1915.

[39] John M. Gillette, "Reconstruction of History for Teaching Purposes," *School Review*, XVII (1909), 556.

1. Steps toward unity of the colonies.
2. Growth of religious toleration and the idea of suffrage.
3. Forms of government of the colonies as bearing on the Constitution.
4. International strife over the colonies, resulting in the triumph of England.
5. The commercial policy of England toward the colonies ending in the Revolution.
6. The introduction and development of the slavery system.
7. The labor systems in the colonies.
8. Organization of government and parties.
9. The struggle for commercial independence.
10. The Western expansion of territory.
11. The development of population and transportation facilities.
12. Revolutionizing inventions and processes.
13. Political parties and doctrines.
14. Establishment and growth of protective tariff.
15. Problems in finance and banking.
16. Development of the slavery issue.
17. Chief international problems, such as Monroe Doctrine.
18. The spoils system.
19. Financial panics.

II. A list from the Idaho Elementary Course of Study, 1915.

1. Portions of the country explored and settled by each nation.
2. Genesis of the colonies.

3. Territorial disputes between the great nations.

4. The French and Indian War.

5. Causes leading up to the Civil War.

6. Events about Boston till the evacuation.

7. Retreat of Washington through New York and New Jersey.

8. Burgoyne's Invasion.

9. Washington at Valley Forge.

10. Cornwallis' campaign in the South and at Yorktown.

11. State of money matters at the close of the Revolutionary War.

12. Growing hostility between the States.

13. Congress and the Articles of Confederation.

14. The Philadelphia Convention.

15. The Constitution before the people of the States.

16. Territorial Ordinance, by Nathan Dane.

17. Growth in territory.

18. Internal improvements.

19. History and extension of slavery.

20. Leading inventions and inventors.

21. Immigration.

22. The rise and influence of political parties.

23. The three departments of our government.

24. Our system of revenue.

25. Two leading campaigns of the Civil War.

26. Civil service reform."

As stated above the foregoing lists of topics were intended for the upper-elementary grades. It was not until about 1920 that a state-wide application of the topical idea to high-school history appeared. In the 1919 edition of the New York

State syllabus, American history was organized in terms of seven large and comprehensive topics as follows:

I. The Americans—A Nation of Immigrants.
II. The Rise and Progress of Democratic Institutions in the United States.
III. The Foreign Relations of the United States.
IV. Economic History of the United States.
V. Social Development in the United States.
VI. The Governmental Development of the United States.
VII. American Ideals.

Most of the gains made during the first two decades of the present century by the topical organization of history for teaching purposes were lost during the third decade. The rise of other ways of organizing material during this decade affected the topical organization adversely. In spite of the rise of other schemes, however, proponents of the topical system continued their agitation for it. Speaking to the point in 1921, one of this number said: "The only way we know anything is by the relation and connection of the parts. It is a mistake to study history as if it were a calendar, and all the events were strung on the thread of time. On the other hand, all the facts concerning one great subject should be grasped in one story though they cover a number of years. This is the topical as opposed to the chronological treatment." [40] Near the close of the 1920's the status of the topical organization was diagnosed as follows by a student both of history and the teaching of history.

"My suggestion is that a topical organization be adopted in-

[40] Lawton B. Evans, "History," *Public School Methods,* Project Edition, V, 153. Chicago: School Methods Co., 1921.

stead of a period organization, one in which certain major topics are organized into subject units which will run through the field of American history. That idea has been proposed before, and I claim no originality for it, but it has been much more discussed than applied. In fact, it has not been applied at all. One textbook writer twenty-five years ago attempted a partial application, but the volume went out of print some time ago. One or two brief outlines have been influenced by the topical idea. New York State in 1919 published a course of study built upon this plan. That course has been very little applied, chiefly I am told, because teachers hesitate to attempt it with existing textbooks without special assistance." [41]

Thus it may be said that, at least since the year 1882, there has been in this country a never ceasing demand for the adoption and use of the topical organization of history for teaching purposes. In spite of all of the agitation for it, however, there is not at hand objective evidence to prove that it has ever had a large following. While textbooks purporting to be organized in terms of topics are still appearing, one cannot be sure that they will not go the way of the one by Joseph cited above. Moreover, one thing seems very certain. It is that the topical organization is not apt to sweep the country in the near future. In all probability it will keep on making the same kind of history that it has always made, namely, continually threatening to arrive but actually never arriving.

The reader has noted running through all of the foregoing quotations dealing with the topical organization a healthy optimism in its favor. By way of summarizing this optimism

[41] J. Montgomery Gambrill, "What History Shall We Teach?" *Annual Ohio State Educational Conference,* IX (1929), 305.

the four chief advantages of the topical organization are listed below:

1. When a field of history is organized in terms of topics more continuity is achieved, provided the topics themselves are well organized for teaching purposes.

2. In actual practice, the teaching of one topic facilitates the teaching of other topics. For example, in tracing the history of household manufactures from the beginning of colonial times down to the Civil War, many aspects of the industrial revolution in the United States are unearthed. The same is true of topics such as transportation and the westward movement. Each cultivation of the historical ground makes subsequent cultivations easier.

3. When a straight chronological order has been used on one level and the same field is to be covered on a higher level, the topical organization helps to solve the problem of duplication. It was this consideration that led the state of New York to adopt the topical organization for the senior high school in the syllabus published in 1919.

4. When the topical organization is thought of in contrast to a straight chronological presentation of a field of history, it tends to make history something other than mere textbook history and to place the emphasis on knowing rather than rote memory.

The opponents of organizing history for teaching purposes in terms of topics include the following in their case of particulars against it: 1. The amount of duplication and confusion resulting from the topical organization is more than should be tolerated in a well organized program. 2. The topical organization is artificial; history is not actually made in terms of topics. 3. Historical topics are by their very nature frequently so large that to grasp them as connected stories is beyond the reach of pupils below the college level. 4. The lack of trained teachers and adequate library equipment precludes a wholesale introduction of courses in the social sciences organized in terms of topics.

Regardless of its advantages and disadvantages the topical organization has had so many handicaps to overcome that its progress has never been in proportion to its evident merits. Its chief handicap has always been the lack of a clear-cut conception of the nature of a topic. Some consider "The Battle of Bunker Hill" a genuine topic. Others claim that "The Economic and Social History of the United States" belongs in the same category. Still others insist that "Agriculture in American Life" is an ideal topic. In terms of sound reasoning it seems clear that but one of these conceptions of a topic, namely, "Agriculture in American Life," has any merit for one seeking examples of legitimate topics for use in organizing United States history for teaching purposes. "The Battle of Bunker Hill" is evidently more of an event than a topic. "The Economic and Social History of the United States" is too large to lend itself to easy comprehension. In compiling a list of topics adequately covering the various aspects of the past life of the United States in its bearings on present-day affairs, one certainly needs to avoid the pitfalls evident in so-called topics such as these two. A list of sixteen topics co-ordinate with "Agriculture in American Life" follows. The order in which the topics are listed is not important.

A Proposed Topical Organization of United States History for Teaching Purposes

    I. The Home and Home-Life in America.
    II. Travel, Transportation, and Communication.

III. Important Inventions and Scientific Discoveries.
IV. Commerce, Money, and Banking.
V. The Factory System and Manufacturing.
VI. Intellectual Life of American People.
VII. Agriculture in American Life.
VIII. Industrial Combinations and Trusts.
IX. Labor and Labor Organization.
X. International Relations.
XI. American Ideals.
XII. Immigration and Assimilation.
XIII. Crime and Punishment.
XIV. Religion and Religious Organizations.
XV. Amusements and Sports.
XVI. Humanitarian Reforms and Reformers.

Should the foregoing topics be used in the grades below the high school and a list were desired for use in the senior high school, the following might furnish a point of departure: (1) Political and Diplomatic Aspects of American Life; (2) Industrial and Commercial Aspects of American Life; (3) The Educational and Recreational Life of America; (4) The Church and Religion in American Life; (5) Social and Humanitarian Aspects of American Life; (6) Cultural and Æsthetic Aspects of American Life. While these topics are somewhat indefinite in scope and ill-defined in content, they do seem to cover all of the main aspects of American life both in the past and in the present.

THE TYPE-STUDY PLAN OF ORGANIZING THE SOCIAL SCIENCES FOR TEACHING PURPOSES

The originator in this country of the type-study plan of organizing subject-matter was Charles A. McMurry, Professor of Elementary Education at George Peabody College for Teachers, Nashville, Tennessee, from 1915 to 1929, the year of his death. The plan as evolved by Professor McMurry harked back to the Herbartian doctrine of concentration. So with due regard to Professor McMurry's indefatigable devotion to the plan and his never-ceasing activity in promoting it during the last twenty-five years of his life, it is correct to say that every fundamental idea in it is found in the doctrine promulgated by John Friedrich Herbart and his followers in Germany—Karl Stoy, Tuiskon Ziller, William Rein, and Otto Frick.[42] In treating the plan here, consideration is given to (1) its general nature as evolved in this country by Professor McMurry and his followers, (2) its application in the field of history, (3) its claimed superiority over other plans, and (4) its limitations.

In answering the question "What is a type study?" Professor McMurry on one occasion said: "What we call the type study is a demonstration of a principle discovered to be operative in a multitude of individual cases. A type study, in its first stage, is the dramatic setting for an idea and, in its second stage, it unfolds a constructive principle of broad application. To ignore the typical element in a large unit is to shut out the light, but to give it the full right of way opens a broad highway of knowledge. After this manner what often appears in our texts as a mere commonplace is seen to be a matter of importance in world business." [43] On another occasion when commenting on the meaning of type study McMurry remarked, "First of all, a type study is an important center

[42] Morris R. Mitchell, *A Critical Evaluation of the Type Study Plan as an Organizing Principle for Texts in American History*, pp. 10 f. Nashville, Tenn.: George Peabody College for Teachers, 1926.

[43] Charles A. McMurry, *Practical Teaching:* Book One, pp. 6 f. Richmond, Va.: Johnson Publishing Co., 1925.

of thought, a nucleus around which to group and organize a full body of knowledge. It develops with the growth of a dominant idea. A single idea rules a large topic such as a type study." [44]

It should be remarked in passing that type study was not the only name that Professor McMurry gave to what he defined in the foregoing statements. In browsing through his many discussions of the type-study plan one runs across at least ten other names. For example, expressions such as the following are frequently met: "important centers of thought," "big topics," "important units," "unit of thought," "standard units," "big teaching units," "large units of study," "central units," "controlling units," and "central topics." Inasmuch as all of these appear in a brief discussion of a course in geography and history it would seem that Professor McMurry was trying to avoid the monotony of using the same expression again and again. While the use of so many expressions to name a somewhat technical notion does avoid monotony, the practice certainly does not beget exact thinking and clarity of exposition. In all probability no two persons have ever attached the same meaning to any one of the synonyms Professor McMurry used so lavishly for the expression "type study."

Before passing to a consideration of the practical application of the type-study plan in one of the social sciences, attention will be called to the fact that Professor McMurry used two expressions synonymously with type study, each of which contained the word "topic." The use of the word "topic" synonymously with type study suggests this question: "What is the relation between the plan of organizing material for

[44] Charles A. McMurry, "Enrichment of the Course of Study," *Public School Methods: Teacher's Guide Index*, pp. 144 f. Chicago: School Methods Publishing Co., 1922.

teaching purposes in terms of topics and in terms of type studies?" Fortunately an answer to this question is available in the words of one of Professor McMurry's strong supporters. This answer follows:

"The use of topics, like that of periods, is not in opposition to the type study plan. Indeed as far as they go they are in strict accord with it. But there is this difference. The plan under discussion [the topical] reduces the chronological to the logical. The type study plan goes further in reducing the logical to the psychological. The plan of periods and topics is essentially one of division, of arrangement, of pigeon holing facts of like time and kind. This helps to bring order out of the chaos of the purely sequential collection of facts. But it does not eliminate save only as it disregards. And, as we have seen, tradition, public sentiment, and like forces, make such elimination almost impossible. The type study plan takes this logical arrangement, selects the significant ideas, breaks these up into the component topics, and presents these through a typical instance made clear by a wealth of detail. In this manner elimination takes place not by disregarding facts but by interpreting scores of them through comparison with the typical instance." [45]

Should one accept the foregoing distinction between topics and type studies, one would be doing an injustice to the latter in using the expressions synonymously, for few would deny the fact that the psychological approach to teaching material is superior to the logical. Even Professor McMurry himself recognized the impossibility of such a use when he wrote, "The familiar word 'topic' bears some resemblance to the *unit of study* [type study], but it fails to connote that progres-

[45] Morris R. Mitchell, *op. cit.*, p. 41.

sive organization around a center of thought, and it fails likewise to express the dynamic quality of growth and expression in thought." [46]

In working out a practical application of the type-study plan of organizing subject-matter for teaching purposes, its author found in it a way to put into concrete form the Herbartian notions of *concentration* and *correlation*. How the plan provides for the latter of these notions Professor McMurry as late as 1922 wrote:

"If we undertake to study the cotton industry in the South the mere list of sub-topics is a convincing proof of the necessary correlation of several studies. The cotton plant itself is a botanical specimen in its growth and life history. The cultivation of the crop is agriculture, the dealing with the boll-weevil is chiefly scientific, the cotton gin and the cotton press are scientific machines, the by-products of cotton are obtained by scientific processes, the shipment of cotton to the factories and markets is commerce and transportation, the study of labor problems in the cotton belt and the relation of whites and blacks is economics and sociology, the manufacture of cotton into textile fabrics with the numerous machines and inventions and its labor problems and mill-operatives, wages, hours of labor and factory sanitation deals with a large group of the varied subjects difficult to classify. In fact, there is no reason for attempting to classify and isolate these varied subjects. They belong together in one combined picture, one organized treatment of a practical occupation or group of occupations." [47]

In the application of the type-study idea to the organiza-

[46] Charles A. McMurry, *How to Organize the Curriculum*, p. 220. New York: The Macmillan Co., 1923.

[47] "Enrichment of the Course of Study," *Public School Methods: Teacher's Guide Index*, pp. 162 f. Chicago: School Methods Publishing Co., 1922.

tion of a course in history for teaching purposes one faces the problem of selecting and naming suitable type studies for a particular grade. On one occasion the author of the plan suggested the following list of type studies on the colonial period of United States history as suitable for a year's work in one of the upper-elementary grades: Virginia Plantation, Bacon's Rebellion, Government in Massachusetts, Governor Andros as an Illustration of Royal Governors, Early Dutch Settlements at New Amsterdam, Iroquois Indians, Life of Penn, Life of Benjamin Franklin During the Colonial Period, Last French War—Montcalm and Wolfe, and Shipbuilding and Commerce in New England During the Colonial Period.[48] On another occasion, the following types were suggested by Professor McMurry for Grades VII and VIII:

Grade VII—
1. The Constitutional Convention of 1787.
2. Hamilton's Financial Measures.
3. Anthony Wayne and the Indians.
4. Jefferson and the Purchase of Louisiana.
5. The Tariff of 1816.
6. Henry Clay and the Missouri Compromise of 1820.
7. The Monroe Doctrine.
8. Jackson and the New Democracy.
9. Webster, Calhoun and Nullification.
10. The Growth of Slavery.
11. Morse and the Telegraph and Other Inventions.
12. The Public Land System.

Grade VIII—
1. The Lincoln-Douglas Debate.

[48] "Teaching History by Type Studies," *Proceedings of the Mississippi Valley Historical Association* for the year 1911–12, p. 134.

2. Lincoln's Policy During the Civil War.
3. Reconstruction.
4. Education.
5. The Growth of Chicago and Western Cities.
6. Immigration.
7. Civil Service Reform.
8. The McKinley Tariff.
9. The Growth of Big Business.
10. The Spanish War and Our Colonial System.
11. Roosevelt.
12. Wilson and the Great War.[49]

It is not possible to portray the virtues of the type-study plan of organizing history for teaching purposes by the mere listing by name a number of type studies in history. To do justice to the plan its virtues must be scrutinized with care. Speaking generally, the supporters of the plan claim that one of its chief merits is that it reduces the number of isolated items or events commonly found in history courses on all levels of instruction. They say that the practice of centering attention on a few important type studies in a field of history eliminates many unimportant details. Instead of seeking order out of facts, the type study seeks the facts in terms of an organizing principle. Just how this process works out in practice has been explained thus: "First, an important historical development is perceived, such as the growth of the constitu-

---

[49] *A School Course in Geography and History.* The George Peabody College for Teachers, Type Studies and Lesson Plans, Vol. II, No. 5. Nashville, Tenn.: George Peabody College for Teachers, 1923. This is one of a series of pamphlets edited by Professor McMurry devoted to type studies and lesson plans. The titles of some others in the series dealing primarily with history are: (1) *Daniel Boone,* (2) *Benjamin Franklin and Social Service,* (3) *The Virginia Plantation,* and (4) *History and Geography.* For ten type studies in United States history worked out in detail by Professor McMurry see *Public School Methods,* V, 196–304. Chicago: School Methods Publishing Co., 1916.

tion, the growth and influence of slavery, the territorial expansion of the nation, the great westward movement of population in this country, the development of industry in the New England States, the influence of plantation life in the South. Second, a typical instance of the development to be taught is *sought* out and dramatically represented. Third, this instance is contrasted with others and the significance of the whole development is brought clearly to the child's mind." [50]

Should one desire a bill of particulars both for and against organizing history by type studies such is at hand from the pen of Professor McMurry himself. In summarizing the argument for and against the type-study plan he said as early as 1912:

"A number of arguments might be offered against this concentration upon a few topics: (1) it does not cover the ground of American history sufficiently, and consequently many of the common facts might not come into view; (2) it does not prepare properly for ordinary examinations and tests in American History; (3) children cannot well appreciate these large topics, for they need first to know the facts of history; (4) teachers cannot use such a plan because they have not been trained to it, and the prevailing text-books do not follow it.

"But the arguments in favor of concentration upon a few central type studies are quite as convincing. (1) a reorganization of the course of study in history is necessary, since the present course is impossible of proper treatment; (2) organization of facts upon central ideas greatly simplifies historical study and makes it intelligible and interesting; (3) the im-

[50] Morris R. Mitchell, *op. cit.*, p. 58.

portant facts of history are more easily learned and remembered when thus organized than when learned in such disconnected form as is usual; (4) the fundamental demand is for a far richer concrete treatment of topics than is possible with our present text-books; (5) the comparisons of the simple fundamental type with other examples of contrasts and with topics of opposite character set children to thinking, and give them a chance to see the far-reaching importance of the large and significant ideas in our history. A true interest is awakened by following the growth of important ideas." [51]

The plan was a one-man affair throughout its active career. Just why, no one has ever been able to explain. Outside of Professor McMurry's own writing, one finds practically nothing on the plan. No large school system has ever adopted it in toto and no textbook in history, civics, economics, or sociology has ever been written in conformity with its dictates. On the failure of even Professor McMurry's own colleagues to recognize the plan, one of his own students has commented thus:

"For some years there has been proposed a certain plan of curriculum organization and of instruction called the type study plan. The ideas involved have been woven into their present state of unity by Dr. Charles A. McMurry. He has been the undisputed protagonist of the plan and has devoted approximately a quarter of a century of almost undivided effort to its development.

"Year after year he has not only furthered his thinking on the problem but has engaged in teaching about the plan to scores of student teachers. Except for the ever loyal members

[51] "Teaching History by Type Studies," *Proceedings of the Mississippi Valley Historical Association* for the year 1911–12, pp. 134 f.

of his immediate family, however, the work has been practically single-handed. No others have written on the subject; no others have prepared actual subject-matter studies on the proposed basis; only very sparingly have the authors of standard texts adopted here and there an idea from the plan; and the other departments of Peabody College have never accepted the movement to the extent either of working out type studies or of teaching the subject matter to teachers on this basis of organization.

"There has been a consistently passive attitude toward the project as a whole as though all were waiting till Dr. McMurry got the plans well laid and the machinery all set to go; as though they would then either get behind it or oppose it. This, within limits, has been a desirable attitude. There had to be a leader, reasonably clear in his own thinking, before he could be helped either by followers or opponents." [52]

ORGANIZING THE SOCIAL SCIENCES IN TERMS OF PROBLEMS

It should be understood at the outset that the only interest this discussion has in the concept "problem" is in its utilization in organizing materials in the social sciences for teaching purposes. It is the problem organization and not the problem method that is being considered here. Furthermore, in the consideration below of the problem from its organizing-for-teaching purposes aspects, its utilization as a caption for the largest divisions of a course or year's work is always meant.

[52] Morris R. Mitchell, *op. cit.,* p. 3. One experiment is on record in which an attempt was made to determine the actual validity of the foregoing claims. It failed to do this inasmuch as the results obtained in two grades were but slightly better than those in another grade using a different plan of organization. In one grade the results were unfavorable to the organization of history by types. See Edwin L. Key, "An Experiment with the Type-Study," *Peabody Journal of Education,* VIII (1930), 157–159, 162.

Even though the words "problem" and "project" have been used synonymously by many in the voluminous mass of literature on the problem and project methods which has appeared since 1918, it seems best, when considering these concepts as organizing ideas, to treat them separately.

There seems to be no record of the first educational use of the term "problem"; neither does there seem to be any specific citation to the first use of the term as an organizer of a social science for teaching purposes. There is, however, enough evidence at hand to justify the statement that the idea of organizing history and some of the other social sciences in terms of problems had got pretty well under way by 1920. As early as 1917, there appeared concrete suggestions relative to organizing United States history in terms of problems. Note the following:

"How a subject of study may be pursued upon the basis of solving the problems which appear successively in the mastery of the subject may be illustrated briefly from United States history. In this illustration no effort is made to state accurately and inclusively all the problems which would be met in covering the period of United States history chosen for illustrative purposes. The illustration is intended to show the type of problem which should be in the minds of the children as the basis for effective work on their part. The large problem as here stated would break up into smaller ones from day to day, although care should be exercised constantly to have the children feel that they are working on problems rather than finding answers to little detailed questions. I suggest the following problems covering the work in United States history up to the opening of the national period:

1. How the Old World Came to Find the New.

2. The Attention the Old World Gave to the New after Finding It.

3. The Resulting Conflicts from the Settlements Made in the New World.

4. The Outcome of These Conflicts.

5. Why the Colonies Began to Dislike England.

6. The Result of the Dislike.

7. How the Colonies Organized Themselves for Work Following Independence.

8. The Weaknesses Which Appeared in Their Organization.

9. Why the Colonies Started a Movement for a Better Government.

10. The Results of Their Effort to Improve the Government.

11. How the New Plan of Government Started Off.

12. Some of the Difficulties of the New Government." [53]

The foregoing suggestions and comments appeared in print in June, 1917. There also appeared in this same month and year a state course of study in geography, history, and civics for the elementary grades[54] in which an attempt was made to organize some of the history materials in terms of problems. For example, United States history for Grade VII was organized in terms of the following problems:

Problem I. How America came to be discovered.

Problem II. What cause led to the settlement of the new world?

Problem III. What steps were necessary for establishing a claim in America and what nations satisfied these conditions?

[53] H. B. Wilson, "The Problem Attack in Teaching," *Elementary School Journal*, XVII (1917), 753 f. The problems are not numbered in the article.
[54] *The Teaching of Geography, History and Civics*. Trenton, N. J.: Department of Public Instruction, June, 1917.

Problem IV. What helps and hindrances did the American Indians offer to the colonists?

Problem V. Why was life in English colonies so difficult?

Problem VI. Why did the English colonies endure when Spanish and French failed?

Problem VII. Characterize home life in the colonies.

Problem VIII. How Englishmen in America became Americans.

Problem IX. How the Revolutionary War was fought.

Problem X. Why the first attempt of the United States to form a government was a failure—Articles of Confederation.

Problem XI. How our present form of government was obtained.

Problem XII. The nation's problems during the following forty years and how they were met.[55]

Subsequent development of the problem as an organizer of history materials for teaching purposes made the foregoing pioneer efforts seem somewhat feeble. It should be said, however, that their influence is clearly evident in organization in terms of problems which appeared during the early 1920's. For example, there was published in 1922 a course of study in United States history for Grades V–VIII. This course was supposedly organized in terms of problems. It was proposed by a committee representing nine cities in southern California. The indebtedness to previous efforts on the part of those who were responsible for the course, especially in the statement of the problems, may be seen in the following set-ups:

Grade V

Problem I. How our country began.

[55] *Ibid.*, pp. 157 ff.

Problem II. What great men and women have helped to build our nation.

Grade VI

Problem I. How our forefathers in Europe lived.

Problem II. How Columbus found a new world.

Problem III. How the bold explorers who followed Columbus revealed the nature of the new world.

Problem IV. How Spain gained her claim to California.

Grade VII

Problem I. How our early American ancestors lived.

Problem II. How our early American ancestors were governed.

Problem III. How the European countries fought for control of the New World.

Problem IV. How our forefathers gained their independence from England.

Problem V. How we planned the new government under which we began our life as a nation.

Problem VI. How the new government was put into effect.

Problem VII. How we got along with the other nations.

Problem VIII. How our country grew.

Grade VIII

Problem I. How the use of machinery changed the life of the people.

Problem II. How the people have come into control of their government.

Problem III. How education became recognized as a necessity for good citizenship.

Problem IV. How we met a great crisis in our development of a strong central government.

Problem V. The importance of all classes of workers in making our country a great industrial nation.

Problem VI. Our departure from the former policy of restricting our interests to the Western Hemisphere.

Problem VII. The struggle for self-determination by the people of the world.

Problem VIII. How the many great changes resulting from the war have caused us to make readjustments in our national life.[56]

The foregoing set-ups were more theoretical than practical. However, practice in this case was not far behind theory. During the school year 1922–23 there were in actual use courses in history and civics organized in terms of problems. For example, in the Oliver School, Lawrence, Massachusetts, the work in history and civics was organized in terms of problems as early as 1922. The following list includes some of the problems in history used in this school in Grades IV, V, and VI.

Grade IV. General Problem for the Year: How was liberty planted in America?

Problem 1. How did the region around Lawrence come to be settled?

Problem 2. How did the Pilgrims become Americans?

Problem 3. How did the people of Colonial Virginia become Americans?

Problem 4. How did Americans win liberty through the Revolution?

[56] Ernest C. Moore, Editor, *Minimum Course of Study*, pp. 237 ff. New York: The Macmillan Co., 1922.

Grade V. General Problem for the Year: How did the spirit of liberty grow stronger as the United States grew powerful?

Problem 1. Why did the American people make a strong union?

Problem 2. {
Why did the United States become a great nation?
How did the United States become a great nation?
}

Problem 3. Why was the Civil War another step toward liberty?

Problem 4. How did our great freedom-loving nation become "Big Brother" to small and weak peoples?

Grade VI. General Problem for the Year: How has liberty come to the whole world through the Great War? What is my part as a true American in helping this great cause of liberty?

Problem 1. To find out by a study of the World War:
  a. What brought it about?
  b. How was the world divided between the Allies and the Central Powers?
  c. How did this war differ from others in magnitude, use of science, trench warfare, employment of women, etc.?

Problem 2. What was our part in winning liberty for the world?

Problem 3. How was liberty brought to new Nations?

Problem 4. What is our present task?

Problem 5. What does it mean to be a true American?[57]

It seems evident that many of the so-called problems in the

[57] Blanche A. Cheney, "The Lawrence Plan for Education in Citizenship," *Journal of Educational Method*, II (1922), 198–200.

foregoing lists are not problems at all. They are simply topics stated in a challenging or a provocative form. For example, the general problem for Grade IV in the Oliver School as stated above reads "How was liberty planted in America?" Stated as a topic this so-called problem would read "The Planting of Liberty in America." After material of this character once got into print, it took little acumen to discover that those who were propagating it were simply applying a different name to a very old idea. It soon became evident that problems in the field of the social sciences would have to be more than topics stated in a challenging form, if they were to be problems at all. So it came about that problems began to be stated in terms of those who were expected to solve them, for example, "Prove that the Federal Convention of 1787 solved the difficulties existing under the Articles of Confederation by giving the people of the United States the National Constitution." Stated in this form the problem as an organizer of material in the social sciences began to assume an existence independent of the topic. It no longer had to carry the burdens that had been heaped upon the topic, for which it was at first another name, especially when used in printed courses of study.

As early as the school year 1908–09, some experimenting was going on with a problem organization of American history. In this experiment the problems were stated as follows:

First Problem. To trace the discoveries and explorations of the European countries in America.

Second Problem. To show the growth of colonization and the development of colonial institutions.

Third Problem. To show how the events of the Revolutionary period contributed to the growth of the Union.

Fourth Problem. To show how the government under the constitution was put into operation by the Federalists.

Fifth Problem. To show how the Republican party gradually became nationalized.

Sixth Problem. To trace the rise of the New Democracy.

Seventh Problem. To show how the slave question brought the secession of the Southern states.

Eighth Problem. To show the plan of the national government of forcing the seceded states back into the Union and the effect of war upon the economic, social and political conditions of the country.

Ninth Problem. To show how the plan of Reconstruction was worked out.[58]

Just why the form used above for stating a problem in history did not pass into common practice is difficult to say. It may be that the movement known as "objectives in education" played some part in the matter. When courses-of-study makers began to state objectives in history, they found the form occasionally used for stating a problem a convenient one, so they adopted it. Henceforth the protagonists of the problem-organization, who stated their problems in the *form* used immediately above, found themselves formulating objectives in history and the other social sciences rather than problems.

It is evident to one who takes an unbiased view of the problem as an organizer of the social sciences for teaching purposes that it has never succeeded and indeed probably never will succeed above the artificial level. It seems to belong primarily in the realm of method of instruction. The chief reason for its failure as an organizer of subject-matter in the field of the social sciences is found in the nature of the prob-

[58] E. D. Lee, "The Importance of Problems in Teaching American History," Unpublished Master's thesis, University of Missouri, 1909.

lems actually faced and solved by social groups in the past. After a problem has been solved by a group, its problematic nature disappears and when made a subject of study simply becomes a center about which to assemble information. On the other hand, if a social or political group has not solved an urgent problem facing it, such as the prevention of poverty, the only thing that a class in sociology can do about the problem is to gather information relating to proposed solutions in the past and to suggest solutions for the future. The class cannot actually solve the problem. Thus when a problem in the field of the social sciences is viewed as a situation or a circumstance in which a group is placed when some action is desirable and the specific nature of said action is unknown, it loses its organizing-for-teaching purposes value. For those who maintain that the problem is essentially a question involving doubt, its services seem to be almost *nil* in the realm of organizing subject-matter in the social sciences for teaching purposes. Especially is this true if pupils are expected to solve the problems set up in a particular course.

THE PROJECT AS AN ORGANIZER OF A SOCIAL SCIENCE FOR TEACHING PURPOSES

As now used in the literature of education the project may be defined as anything that anybody says it is. Why this deplorable situation exists has been explained thus: "When a word from the general vocabulary is carried over to a particular field, there is always the danger of confusion and misunderstanding, for it is rarely that the general concept can be applied ready-made to a specific field. The frequent result is that all shades of meaning are to be found, depending upon the stress which is placed in a given instance upon the original use of the term. The term, project, is a striking example of this kind." [59]

Historically speaking, the term project, used in an educational sense, has been circulating in this country for a generation or longer. Between 1900 and 1910 it was occasionally used to designate exercises in manual training such as making a coaster wagon, a library table, or a foot-stool. This means that when a boy was making a library table in his shop work he was working on the project "library table." The word was used in connection with the teaching of agriculture as early as the school year 1908–09 in Smith's Agricultural School at Northampton, Massachusetts, and in the vocational agricultural high schools in the same state. [60] Canning fruit, growing potatoes and fattening pigs were projects in an agricultural sense. After 1910 such expressions as "home projects" and "farm projects" passed into common use in the literature of vocational-agricultural education. The idea was so successful in this field that other fields soon began to adopt it. When taken over into the fields of history, literature, arithmetic, and other subjects of a similar nature, confusion arose as to its meaning and use. In fact so much confusion arose that in time the concept lost its original meaning, namely, a unit of educational work characterized by a positive concrete accomplishment such as the baking of a loaf of bread or the growing of a bushel of beans.

No comprehensive program in the social sciences seems ever to have appeared organized wholly in terms of projects. Examples of the use of the project in individual courses of study and for specific purposes are more or less abundant. Witness the use for experimental purposes that was made of a project-

[59] H. B. Alberty, *A Study of the Project Method in Education*, p. 17. Columbus: The Ohio State University Press, 1927.
[60] *Ibid.*, p. 18.

curriculum in a rural school in McDonald County, Missouri, during a four-year period ending September, 1921.[61] The projects used in this experiment were classified as excursion projects, hand projects, play projects, and story projects. Subject-matter divisions were ignored in executing these projects. Supposedly the entire content of this project-curriculum was selected from the purposes of the boys and girls in the life they were actually living. For this reason there was nothing fixed and stereotyped in it, hence of value to others only in its illustrative aspects.

While no course of study in history, civics, or economics organized wholly in terms of projects has yet appeared, much use has been made of the project idea in organizing courses of study in these subjects; in fact more than this brief discussion suggests and yet not enough to satisfy some. It was probably this dissatisfaction that led to the substitution during the 1920's of "activity" for project, especially in the kindergarten-primary grades. After 1921 courses of study for these grades in terms of children's activities began to appear.[62] The material in these courses was organized around what some called "activity units," merely another name for the project as used by some a few years before. Inasmuch as this discussion is interested in plans of organizing the social sciences for teaching purposes and the fact that courses of study based on children's activities disregarded departmental divisions, a systematic treatment of the activity movement would be a digression instead of a straight-line development. For this reason, the discussion of the project as an organizer of a social science for teaching purposes ends here.

---

[61] Ellsworth Collings, *An Experiment with a Project Curriculum.* New York: The Macmillan Co., 1925.
[62] Helen M. Reynolds, *A Course of Study in Terms of Children's Activities for Kindergarten and Primary Grades.* Seattle, Washington: The author, 1921.

THE RÔLE OF THE UNIT OF UNDERSTANDING IN ORGANIZING THE
SOCIAL SCIENCES FOR TEACHING PURPOSES

Just when the unit as an organizer of materials for teaching purposes was cast upon the sea of educational practices in this country is not definitely known. The American Herbartians made much use of the lesson unit in organizing a field of study. It was to this lesson unit that they applied in their everyday teaching practices the five formal steps, namely, preparation, presentation, comparison, generalization, and application. In the process of developing his type studies, McMurry made frequent use of such expressions as "important units," "units of thought," "standard units," "big teaching units," "units of study," "central units" and "controlling units." McMurry as shown a few pages above used all of these expressions synonymously with type studies and projects. He lived to see the ideas that he had been advocating for forty years centralize around two conceptions of the unit. One of these conceptions was captioned "unit of work" and the other "unit of understanding." Thus at the time of McMurry's death in 1929, courses of study in the social sciences were commonly organized either in terms of units of understanding or in terms of units of work.

The unit of understanding as an organizer of subject-matter for teaching purposes was introduced into the Laboratory Schools of the University of Chicago during the second half of the school year, 1920–21. While individuals might have organized certain courses in terms of units of understanding before this date, certainly no school system as a whole had organized the subject matter taught therein in these terms before 1920. Inasmuch as units of understanding were first used on a large scale in the foregoing schools, the nature of the original units in the field of the social sciences used therein merits attention here.

In the work reports of the high-school teachers of the social sciences for the year 1921–22 appeared for the first time the units of understanding then in use in courses in community life, modern problems, modern history, survey of civilization and ancient history. The units of understanding in the course in modern problems as given during the school year 1921–22 were—the first half of the year being devoted to the first four units:

Unit I. Liberty and Law.

Unit II. Congress at Work.

Unit III. The National Executive.

Unit IV. Federal Courts and Their Procedure.

Unit V. Modern Methods of Production.

Unit VI. Modern Methods of Buying and Selling.

Unit VII. Modern Methods of Dividing the Surplus Income.

Unit VIII. Taxation.[63]

The course in modern history was organized in terms of the following units of understanding:

Unit I. The Industrial Revolution.

Unit II. The French Revolution.

Unit III. The Era of Metternich.

Unit IV. The Development of Nationality.

Unit V. The Slavery Controversy.

Unit VI. The Westward Movement.

[63] "Work Reports," Secondary, Vol. III, Part 4. The University of Chicago, The Laboratory Schools, 1921–22.

Unit VII. Expansion of Industrial Nations.

Unit VIII. World War and World Reconstruction.[64]

In formulating the foregoing units of understanding those responsible for them were trying to put into practice the conception of a unit as a significant and comprehensive phase of a field of learning or of the environment of the learner. For example, the content suggested by the expression "French Revolution" is a significant and comprehensive phase of history, therefore rightly named a unit of understanding. After the publication of the theory back of the unit of understanding in 1926[65] the idea spread rapidly and was soon approximated in many courses of study throughout the country.

Mention has been made elsewhere in this Division of the early attempt of the schools of Denver, Colorado, to apply the unification-of-content idea in the junior high school. This was in 1924. At the same date this city also adopted the unit-of-understanding idea in organizing material for teaching purposes. In Grades VII, VIII, and IX, the organization of the content of a course named "Social Science" was in terms of eleven large units of understanding. When the material for the senior high school appeared in 1926 it too was organized in terms of units of understanding. Thus it may be said that as early as 1926 there was one large school system in the country that had adopted the unit-of-understanding idea throughout the work in the social sciences in all grades above the sixth. To say that the idea spread rapidly would be putting the matter very mildly. It simply swept the country during the three years following 1928. By 1932, it was a rare happening

[64] *Studies in Secondary Education*, I, pp. 103–115. Chicago: Department of Education, University of Chicago, 1923.

[65] H. C. Morrison, *The Practice of Teaching in the Secondary Schools.* Chicago: University of Chicago Press, 1926.

for a course of study in the social sciences to appear that made no use of the unit-of-understanding idea. While the courses of study in so-called social science for the junior and senior high schools published in 1924 and 1926 by the Denver Public Schools were organized in terms of units of understanding, the course for the elementary grades (one to six inclusive) made no use of the unit organization. Inasmuch as the units for the courses in the senior high school were certainly among the first ever published for use in these grades, those proposed for world history and American history and government are given below in order to show the character of one of the early attempts in the public high schools to apply the unit-of-understanding idea to courses in the social sciences.

Units of Understanding in World History, Grade X, 1926.
Unit I.   Primitive and Oriental Man.
Unit II.   The Greeks.
Unit III.   The Romans.
Unit IV.   The Middle Ages.
Unit V.   The Protestant Revolt.
Unit VI.   Political, Social, and Industrial Revolutions.
Unit VII.   Rise of Democracy.
Unit VIII.   Our World Today.

Units in American History and Government, Grade XI, 1926.
Unit I.   Establishment of the English in America.
Unit II.   Attaining Independence Through Revolution.
Unit III.   The New Nation Established.
Unit IV.   The Frontier Moves Westward.
Unit V.   The Unity of the National Government Assured.

Unit VI.   The United States Achieves Democracy.
Unit VII.   The United States Attains World Power.
Unit. VIII.   Development of Local Government.[66]

Soon after 1924 courses in one or more of the social sciences organized in terms of units of understanding began to appear here and there throughout the country. Those who were responsible for these courses did not always grasp the full meaning and significance of the unit of understanding. In their efforts to be up to date, they designated certain divisions of a course as units which did not contain even a semblance of unity. For example, a course in civics in use in 1930 contained a division entitled "Other Social and Civic Problems in the Community." This was Unit VI in a series of ten. One of the aspects of community life included in the word "other" could have been a unit of understanding; but certainly the expression as it stands suggests neither definiteness nor unity. Neophytes in the business of organizing history for teaching purposes in terms of units of understanding were apt to be caught in a pitfall similar to the foregoing.

Because the social sciences other than history are concerned largely with the present, the unit of understanding in them is primarily a significant aspect of the present social, political,

[66] *Social Science.* Senior High School, Grades Ten, Eleven, and Twelve. Denver, Colo.: Public Schools, 1926.

The fact should be mentioned here that by 1931 those in charge of the second revised edition of the 1926 senior high-school course of study in the social sciences in Denver had decided to discontinue the use of the word unit as it had been used in 1926. The largest divisions of a particular course in the 1931 revision were named "Parts," the same being organized in terms of units. In the third revised edition of the course for the junior high school appearing in 1931, the work for a grade was organized in terms of divisions which in turn were organized in terms of units. In the revised course for Grades III, IV, V, and VI appearing also in 1931 the material for each grade was organized in terms of units. It seems evident to one after reading these courses that those responsible for them must have believed that "variety is the spice of school life."

or economic environment of those seeking to understand it. In the field of history, the unit of understanding is a body of facts closely related which belong to the same chronological period. In other words it is the dominant idea or thought of the period, a generalization which sums up the most significant line of development of a period. In fact it may not be wholly unlike what was termed an epoch a generation ago. Note the thought in the following: "Now, the period of time during which some particular overshadowing, ruling, and pervasive thought and feeling governs the movement of the human race's life is an epoch in history. By seeing what is the common quality running through the entire movement we see the unity; by seeing what is variable in this common quality, we measure history off into epochs." [67] A similar view was expressed as follows:

"The period, or epoch, is the largest and most complex historical division. Fundamentally, it is one of the coordinate phases of institutional growth which go to make up the totality of a people's life. A period exists by virtue of the fact that a great movement in the life of the people dominates events for a given time. This epochal movement sets off its own time and events from those which precede and those which succeed it; it is, therefore, a differentiating idea. Were it not so, periods would be, in relation to each other, mere artificial inventions depending upon, and varying with, the whim of the writer or teacher. Not only does the dominant movement do this, but it also forms the common content of the facts of its own period, and thus performs the function of integration.

[67] Ellwood W. Kemp, *An Outline of Method in History*, p. 55. Terre Haute, Ind.: The Inland Publishing Co., 1897.

Fundamentally, an event without this common content does not belong to the period, even if it occurs within the usual chronological limits of that period." [68]

THE UNIT OF WORK

To some a unit of work means a large learning situation which makes use of all varieties of subject-matter and draws upon all phases of experience;[69] to others it means "a series of worthwhile experiences bound together around some central theme of child interest."[70] Other expressions frequently used synonymously with unit of work are "life situation," "center of interest," "unit of activity," "activity unit," "pupil enterprise," "unit experience," "social group project," "central activity," "central theme," and "work unit." When given actual concrete titles units of work read as follows: Animal life on the farm, a study of milk, a food study, water transportation, the school bank, how man has made records, the study of wheat, boats and boat-making, the aquarium, bulbs and bulb-planting, rocks and fossils, toys and toy-making, colonial life, the home, the garden and city market, the airplane, the park, the post office, Indian life, child life in China, child life in the jungles, child life in Switzerland, Indians of today, Armistice Day, Dutch colonial settlements, and others to the nth degree. One must say to the nth degree because units of work in reality are not things that teachers impose upon children; they arise out of the everyday experiences of pupils.

[68] William H. Mace, *Method in History for Teachers and Students*, p. 82. Boston: Ginn and Co., 1897.

[69] James S. Tippett and Others, *Curriculum Making in an Elementary School*, p. 29. Boston: Ginn and Co., 1927.

[70] Katherine L. Keelor and Mayme Sweet, *Units of Work*, p. 1. New York: Bureau of Publications, Teachers College, Columbia University, 1931.

Inasmuch as a complete list of the experiences of children in the elementary grades has never been compiled, no ultimate list of units of work is available. The number in actual use seems to be very large, in fact so large that a mere enumeration of the units of work in active service would require much more space than is available here.

Those who have been experimenting with units of work in recent years have felt the need of criteria for their selection. One set of such criteria is included here:

Criteria for Selecting Units of Work

1. The unit of work must be selected from real life situations and must be considered worth while by the child because he feels that he has helped select it and because he finds in it many opportunities to satisfy his needs.

2. The unit of work must afford many opportunities for real purposing and real projects, and it will be something which the child can carry into his normal activity.

3. The unit of work must stimulate many kinds of activities and so provide for individual differences.

4. The unit of work must make possible individual growth and at the same time provide for continuous group growth from one level to the next.

5. Each unit of work must furnish leads into other related units or must stimulate in the child the desire for a continued widening of his interests and understandings.

6. Each unit of work must help meet the demands of society and must help clarify social meanings.

7. Each unit of work must be accompanied by progress in the use of such tool subjects as contribute to that unit.

8. Each unit of work must lead to the development of desirable habits.[71]

In applying these criteria one school[72] selected and developed units of work in the field of the social sciences with titles as follows: animal life on the farm, wheat, milk, China, Indian life, water transportation, school bank, how man has made records, and others. To date, the kindergarten-primary grades have been the level for which units of work have been most frequently worked out. Explanation of this fact is found in the history of the unified-curriculum movement. A unified curriculum for the primary grades has been advocated for a number of years and has been actually achieved in many places. Above Grade III the unified-curriculum movement has not made conspicuous headway. Of course, units of work in the field of the social sciences are found in the intermediate grades, but not in the abundance characteristic of the lower group of grades. This fact is accounted for in the close relation between units of work and the activity curriculum, both of which have been running riot in the primary grades since about 1926.

Just what a series of units of work looks like when set up for kindergarten-primary grades may be observed from a recent course of study for these grades:

Units of Work in Kindergarten

1. Community: School and Immediate Neighborhood.
2. Apron.
3. Applesauce or Grape Jelly.

[71] James S. Tippett and others, *op. cit.*, chapter iii.
[72] *Ibid.*, p. v.

4. Circus or Zoo.
5. Playing Store.
6. Doll House or Play House.
7. The Farm.

Units of Work in Grade I

8. Community and Home.
9. Library.
10. Transportation.
11. Playing Store.
12. Community and Home.
13. Hens and Chickens.
14. The Farm.

Units of Work in Grade II

15. City—Relation to Farm and Food Supply.
16. Milk.
17. Eskimo Life.
18. Holland Life.
19. Indian Life.

Units of Work in Grade III

20. Japanese or Chinese Life.
21. Swiss Life.
22. Desert Life.
23. Early Cleveland.
24. Scandinavian Life and Viking Adventures.[73]

While the unit-of-work idea has been operating in the schools of this country off and on since at least 1900, it never

[73] *Elementary School Studies:* Kindergarten-Grade III. Cleveland Heights, Ohio: Board of Education, 1930.

threatened to sweep the country as did the unit-of-understanding idea until the activity-curriculum movement took a
new lease on life about 1925. In spite of the fact that the
activity curriculum is as old as the curriculum itself and has
had many advocates especially since the days of Pestalozzi,
nobody in this country seems to have become much excited
over it prior to the middle of the 1920's. The degree of the
excitement since this date may be judged from the number
of publications dealing with units of work and the activity
program since 1927. The list below certainly does not include
all of such publications.[74]

One of the strong features of the unit of work frequently
emphasized by its supporters is its integrating quality. Examples of units of work carried out in certain schools always
contain the related content in a variety of school subjects
which the unit is supposed actually to integrate. Some adverse
critics of the unit-of-work idea claim that this integrating
aspect is much over-worked. They contend that instead of

[74] Robert H. Lane, *A Teacher's Guide Book to the Activity Program.* New
York: The Macmillan Co., 1932; Katherine L. Keelor and Mayme Sweet, *Units
of Work.* New York: Bureau of Publications, Teachers College, Columbia
University, 1931; Lucy W. Clouser, Wilma J. Robinson, and Dena L. Neely,
Education Experience Through Activity Units. Chicago: Lyons and Carnahan,
1932; Lucy W. Clouser and Chloe E. Millikan, *Kindergarten-Primary Activi-
ties Based on Community Life.* New York: The Macmillan Co., 1929; Mary
M. Reed and Lula E. Wright, *The Beginnings of the Social Sciences.* New
York: Charles Scribner's Sons, 1932; *Activity Program for the Primary Grades.*
Honolulu, Hawaii: Department of Public Instruction, 1930; *Teachers' Guide
to Child Development.* Developed under the direction of the California Curriculum Commission. Washington, D. C.: Government Printing Office, 1930;
Marion Paine Stevens, *The Activities Curriculum in the Primary Grades.* Bos-
ton: D. C. Heath and Co., 1931; James S. Tippett and others, *Curricula Mak-
ing in an Elementary School.* Boston: Ginn and Co., 1927; Adolph Ferriere,
The Activity School. New York: John Day Co., 1928; Clyde Hissong, *The
Activity Movement.* Baltimore: Warwick and York, 1932; Alice C. Carey and
others, *Catalogue: Units of Work, Activities, Projects, etc. to 1932.* New York:
Bureau of Publications, Teachers College, Columbia University, 1932; Ruby
Minor, *Pupil Activities in the Elementary Grades.* Philadelphia: J. B. Lippin-
cott Co., 1929.

integration resulting from a unit of work, quite the opposite occurs. Note the contention in the following:

"Of the teacher-integrated type of activities the most conspicuous is that organization of school work about one topic called an activity. Furnishing a doll house is an example of such in Grades 1 and 2. This dates back a quarter of a century and more as exhibited in the New Paltz Normal School about 1900 and is still going strong east, west, north, south, differing but little from the New Paltz plan. For several weeks, a whole term, or a year, pupils work upon this doll house. How many tangents can be drawn to a given circle? Off on how many tangents can these pupils go when free to follow the many "leads" suggested? One has only to examine closely various courses of study outlined to see how far from the doll house these pupils go and then one wonders if they ever get back again. And one readily reads in these courses of study how all the conventional subjects are 'integrated' (a recent substitute for the old word correlated) about this one 'activity.' [75]

THE CONTRACT PLAN

Before passing to a final comment on organizing the social sciences for teaching purposes mention should be made of what has been denominated the "contract plan" as an organizer of materials for teaching purposes. It will be recalled that the contract idea was an integral part of the Dalton Plan, which originated in the Children's University School, New York, about 1913. Whether the contract plan is essentially method or a way of organizing a field of study is still unsettled. To

[75] Julius L. Meriam, "A Life Activity Curriculum," *Teachers College Record*, XXXIII (1931), 22.

some it is the former. Note the following long and cumbersome definition, "The contract plan is a means of instructional procedure which takes the individual approach to pupils by means of dividing up the subject matter into units of instruction, presenting these by means of the problem method and comprehension type questions, arranging the material for mastery on three or more accomplishment levels, placing the whole in definite copy form in the hands of each pupil, and allowing opportunity for discussion and individual or group testing to determine the degree of mastery."[76] This definition in spite of its length is probably too narrow, for some believe that the plan is more than a means of instructional procedure. They insist on organizing a body of social science material in terms of contracts. For example, there is in existence a four-year course in history, each year being devoted to one contract, which includes a year's work of ten assignments. The names given the four contracts are First Year Contract, Second Year Contract, Third Year Contract, and Fourth Year Contract.[77]

The chief proponent of the contract plan in this country during his lifetime was Harry L. Miller, principal of the University of Wisconsin High School, Madison, Wisconsin, 1912–1928. Inasmuch as the expressions, unit of learning and contract plan, were used synonymously by this authority, it would seem that all that has been said above under unit of understanding would apply to unit of learning. So one seems to be on safe ground when one says that the contract plan has both an organizing and a method of procedure aspect. The organizing aspect being practically the same as that of unit of

[76] W. Walker Brown, "What is the Contract Plan?" *Occasional Leaflet,* Southern California Social Science Association, IV (1928), 7.
[77] E. S. Marriott, *The "Individual" History.* London: George Philip and Son, Ltd., no date.

understanding, there seems to be no point in considering it further here.[78]

Perhaps the reader has found himself in a state of bewilderment on more than one occasion as he progressed through the material of this Division. That bewilderment exists in this particular realm of the social sciences as school subjects few would deny. To many, all of the specific ways of organizing materials in the social sciences for teaching purposes considered separately above seem to be the same. Just how a topic differs from a unit of understanding is not always clear from the examples taken from those who use the expressions. The same may be said concerning the type study and the project, the problem and the topic, and the unit of work and the type study. It is unfortunate for the reader that each of these expressions is not sufficiently restrictive in meaning to bar all of the others. Perhaps when users of these expressions resolve to do concise and exact thinking rather than indefinite and inexact, their utterances will be less confusing.

V

REFLECTIONS AND CONCLUSIONS

It is clear from the facts presented above that organizing the social sciences for teaching purposes has not yet passed out of the hypothetical stage. Long ago it was decided on the basis of *a priori* reasoning that, for purposes of research, education, and administration, the field of knowledge should be classified into large divisions and that these large divisions should be further classified into what are now known as sub-

---

[78] A year before his death Mr. Miller published *Creative Learning and Teaching*. New York: Charles Scribner's Sons, 1927. The first two chapters of this volume are devoted to the contract plan.

jects of study such as physics, chemistry, zoology, history, economics, and a multitude of others. Later, when the education of the oncoming generation became a paramount concern, it was decided, also on the basis of *a priori* reasoning, that it was best for all concerned to have a program of education formulated in terms of subjects and presented to those being educated in the form of subjects.

For a long, long time the educational world accepted these two hypotheses without serious questioning. In time, however, doubting Thomases appeared. Their questioning led to the hypothesis that individual subjects are hindrances rather than helps in the education of children and that the whole matter of the content of education should be determined by "leads" furnished by children during the course of their journey through the land of educational endeavor. It seems safe to conclude that objective data on which to base a program of action with respect to subjects of study or no subjects of study are too far in the future to make waiting for their arrival practicable. In view of this fact actual practice in the matter must continue to be dictated by reasoning of an *a priori* nature. In other words the end of controversy in this realm of educational procedure is fortunately not yet in sight.

As long as material from the field of the social sciences exists in the schools the quest for the most desirable adjustment between the subjects composing the field will continue. The day of isolation is probably gone in theory, even though it still remains in practice. The future will probably see more and more emphasis on the interrelations of the social sciences. This, of course, does not mean that history, political science, economics, and sociology will necessarily disappear as independent subjects of study in the schools. It simply means that as independent subjects each will be expected to live other than a hermitic life. The services of each to all of the others will be central in organizing them for teaching purposes. The principles of concentration and correlation bid fair to enjoy more and more application in the future, the ideas of fusion and integration being included therein.

In all probability the neophite in the realm of organizing the social sciences for teaching purposes will finish the reading of the material above on specific ways of organizing subject-matter with a feeling of bewilderment. He may conclude that the entire discussion is "much ado about nothing." In such a conclusion he may or may not be right, depending on the manner in which each of the ways of organizing a subject is viewed. Certainly, if they are considered merely on a super-ficial level, there is little use in discussing them. However, if the essential and fundamental meaning which the advocates of some of them have in mind is kept foremost in one's think-ing about them, the categories of the different ways of ap-proach will become something other than sounding brass and tinkling cymbals or pedagogical "clap trap" which disgusts the seeker after fundamentals.

The proponents of each of the ways of organizing the social sciences for teaching purposes discussed above may claim that the examples cited do not embody the fundamentals therein. If this is a valid claim, it explains why a topic in some of the examples looks so much like a unit of understanding and vice versa; why a contract so closely resembles a problem, a project a unit of work, a topic, or unit of understanding. The con-fusion found in these examples of ways of organizing the social sciences for teaching purposes possibly resulted from the lack of an actual understanding of the real implications of the terms on the part of those who formulated them. As long as the tendency to give old things new names exists in practical education, it will not be possible for one to get the full import of a new idea from the examples its well-meaning friends give of it. Therefore, in light of the existing confusion and lack of objective data with respect to organizing the social sciences for teaching purposes, it would seem to be an act of wisdom for one interested in the matter to sentence himself to a prolonged contact with the fundamentals of each of the existing ways of organizing the subject-matter of the social sciences for teaching purposes. After emerging from this contact he will probably feel that there is no *the* method of organizing the social sciences for teaching purposes, but only *a* method. To be able to select the method best adapted to the materials to be organized and the pupils to be taught and to apply this method systematically and intelligently are goals to which those whose business it is to organize courses for teaching purposes might profitably aspire.

INDEX

Activity, 524 f.

"Activity units," the term, 512 f.

Adams, Henry, 90

Advertising Club of America, 64

Æneid, The, 51

Alabama, 199, 302

Algebra, 100, 103, 109

Allegheny City, Pennsylvania, 259

American Academy of Political and Social Science, 63, 340

American Bar Association, 4, 58, 59, 61, 63

American Book Company, 189

American citizenship, program on, 60

American Defense Society, 63

American democracy, recommendations in teaching problems of, 17; problems of, 20, 393

American Economic Association, 4, 340

American environment, 48

American Federation of Labor, 64

American Historical Association, 4, 34, 35, 39, 49, 86, 175, 176, 177, 183, 187, 189, 201, 211, 217, 230, 287, 324, 355, 453; founding of, 21

American history, 7, 16, 19, 25, 51

American Legion, 63

American Political Science, 49

American Political Science Association, 4, 47, 297, 317, 323; formation of, 38

American Rights League, 63

American School Citizenship League, 4, 64, 71, 453

American Social Science Association, 408

American Sociological Society, 4, 70, 71

Ancient history, 19, 24, 51

Anderson, George E., quoted, 99 f.

Anderson, J. J., *Manual of General History,* 155, 157; *A School History of the United States,* 155; *Com-mon School History of the United States,* 157; *School History of England,* 158

Andrews, Israel W., *Manual of the Constitution of the United States,* 1874, 275

Anthon, C., *Manual of Greek Antiquities; Manual of Roman Antiquities,* 122–123

Anti-Saloon League, 63

Appleton, D., and Company, 189

Approach to Social Sciences, chronological or logical, 432; psychological or counter-chronological, 438; spiral, cycle, or concentric circles, 447 f.; biographical, 451 f.

Arabian Nights, 51

Arithmetic, 100, 430

Arizona, 199, 383

Arkansas, 302

Arnold, Matthew, quoted, 83

Arrangement of studies, 9

Arthur, King, 51

Ashley, Roscoe L., *Government and the Citizen,* 295; *American Government,* 316

Association of Collegiate Schools of Business, 4, 56

Astronomy, 109

Atchison, Kansas, 270

Atlases, 22

Bagley, William C., 34; quoted, 95

Baltimore, Maryland, 174, 259, 270; meeting at, 5

Bancroft, George, father of American history, 78

Barnard, J. Lynn, quoted, 459 f.

Barnes, *Brief History of the United States,* 157

Bayard, James, *An Exposition of the Constitution of the United States,* 254

Beard, Charles A., quoted, 294, 448 f.

531

* In preparation.

3. Civilization the Social Basis of Education, by Charles A. Beard, formerly Professor of Politics, Columbia University. An Introduction to the History of the Social Sciences in Education, by Henry Johnson, Professor of History, Teachers College, Columbia University.

4. Citizens Organizations and the Civic Training of Youth, by Bessie Louise Pierce, Associate Professor of American History, University of Chicago.

5. Theory and Practice items in the Social Sciences, by Edmund E. Day, Professor of Education, Harvard University, and A. C. Krey, Professor of History, University of Minnesota.

6. The Geography in Relation to the Social Sciences, by Isaiah Bowman, Director, American Geographical Society of New York, with a special essay by Rose B. Clark, Professor of ..., Iowa University.

7. Civic Education in the United States, by Charles E. Merriam, Professor of Political Science, University of Chicago.

8. The Nature of the Social Sciences, by Charles A. Beard, formerly Professor of Politics, Columbia University.

9. Educational Administration as Social Policy, by Jesse H. Newlon, Director, Lincoln School, Teachers College, Columbia University.

10. The Social Foundations of Education, by George S. Counts, Professor of Education, Teachers College, Columbia University, and others.

11. The Social Ideal of American Education, by Merle E. Curti, Professor of History, Smith College.

12. The Social Sciences as school subjects, by Rolla M. Tryon, Professor of the Teaching of History, University of Chicago. Professor of Teaching in the Schools, by Harold K. Beale, formerly Professor of History at Bowdoin College.

13. Methods of Instruction in the Social Sciences, by Ernest Horn, Professor of Education, University of Iowa.

14. A Social Process Approach to Curriculum-making in the Social Sciences, by Leon C. Marshall, Institute for the Study of Law, Johns Hopkins University.

15. The Selection and Training of the Teacher, by William C. Bagley, Professor of Education, Teachers College, Columbia University and others.

16. Conclusions and Recommendations of the Commission.